AF623282

MODERN BAKERY TECHNOLOGY & FERMENTED CEREAL PRODUCTS WITH FORMULAE

LIST OF PUBLICATIONS/BOOKS PUBLISHED BY

ENGINEERS INDIA RESEARCH INSTITUTE 4449, NAI SARAK, MAIN ROAD, DELHI - 6 (INDIA)

CHEMICALS/DYES/PETRO CHEMICALS/LUBRICANT/ ELECTROPLATING

Name of Books	Rs.	US$
* Hand Book of Lubricants, Grease and Petrochemical Technology	750/-	75
* Small Medium & Large Scale Chemical Industries	375/-	40
* Industrial Chemicals Technology Hand Book	1100/-	110
* Project Ideas on All Chemicals & Allied Industries	1300/-	130
* Electroplating, Anodizing & Surface Finishing Technology	750/-	75
* Agro Chemical Industries (Insecticide & Pesticides)	900/-	90
* Technology of Synthetic Dyes, Pigments Intermediates	1100/-	110
* Petrochemicals, Lubricants, Greases & Petroleum Refining	900/-	90
* Modern Technology of Organic & inorganic Chemicals	1400/-	140

GUMS, ADHESIVES & SEALANTS

Name of Books	Rs.	US$
* Technology of Gums, Adhesives & Sealants with Formulations	950/-	95
* Hand Book of Adhesives with their Formulae	650/-	65
* Adhesives Technology & Formulations Hand Book	975/-	100

SMALL SCALE INDUSTRIES/ STATIONERY/PAPER/INKS/ CANDLES & EXPORT BUSINESS

Name of Books	Rs.	US$
* Start Your Own Export Business (How To Export)	350/-	35
* Start Your Own Small Business and Industry	350/-	35
* Candle Making Processes & Formulations Hand-Book	380/-	38
* Stationery, Paper Converting & Packaging Industries	400/-	40
* Modern Inks Formulaes & Manufacturing Industries	325/-	33
* Profitable Businesses to Start for Entrepreneurs	400/-	40
* Modern Small and Cottage Scale Industries	650/-	65
* Profitable Small Cottage Tiny & Home Industries	650/-	65

OFFSET PRINTING, SCREEN PRINTING & PACKAGING

Name of Books	Rs.	US$
* Printing Processes Technologies & Industries	375/-	40
* Hand Book of Printing Technology (Offset, Screen, Flexo, Gravure, Inkjet & Digital)	975/-	100
* Hand Book of Offset Printing Tech.	500/-	50
* Screen Printing with Processes & Technology	350/-	35
* Hand Book of Packaging Industries	1300/-	130
* Hand Book of Packaging Technology	900/-	90
* Modern Packaging Technology for Food Products	600/-	60
* Hand Book of Food Packaging Technology	900/-	90
* Hand Book of Pre Press	800/-	80

PAINT, VARNISH, COATING AND LACQUERS

Name of Books	Rs.	US$
* Paint Pigment Varnish & Lacquer Manufacturing	450/-	45
* Paint Varnish Solvents & Coating Technology	750/-	75
* Technology of Coatings, Resins, Pigments & Inks Industries	975/-	100
* Paint, Pigment, Solvent, Coating, Emulsion, Paint Additives and Formulation	900/-	90
* Mfg. Tech. & Formulations H.B on Thinners, Putty, Wall & Inds. Finishes & Synthetic Resins	900/-	100

PLASTIC/POLYMER PROCESSING, COMPOUNDING, MOULDS, PET RESINS & RUBBER INDUSTRIES

Name of Books	Rs.	US$
* Injection Moulding of Plastics	750/-	75
* Moulds Design & Processing Hand Book	495/-	50
* Plastic Processing & Packaging Industries	450/-	45
* Hand Book of Plastic Projects (Hi-Tech Plastic Projects)	1300/-	130
* Synthetic Resins Technology with Formulations	800/-	80
* PET Preform & Its Products (Bottles/Jar) Mfg.	1300/-	130
* Plastic Compounding, Masterbatches, PET & Other Plastics	750/-	75
* Technology of PVC Compounding and Its Applications	900/-	90
* Hand Book of Polymer and Plastic Technology	950/-	90
* Plastic Water Recycling Technology	750/-	75
* Hand Book Plastic Material & Processing Technology	750/-	75
* Technology of Plastic Films	650/-	65
* Rolalional Moulding Technology	450/-	45
* Hand Book of Fiber Glass Moulding	450/-	50

BAKERY & CONFECTIONERY

Name of Books	Rs.	US$
* Hand Book of Bakery Industries	350/-	35
* Hand Book of Confectionery with Formulations	600/-	60
* Hand Book of Modern Bakery Prod.	750/-	75
* Modern Bakery Tech. & Fermented Cereal Products with Formulae	1250/-	130
* Breakfast, Dietary Food, Pasta, Cereal Product Technology	1150/-	115

AGRO CULTIVATION, ANIMAL FARMING, AGRO PLANTATION & AGRO CHEMICAL/PESTICIDES

Name of Books	Rs.	US$
* Hand Book of Tree Farming	800/-	80
* Hand Book of Poultry Farming and Feed Formulations	450/-	45
* Hand Book of Pig Farming	400/-	40
* Agro Based H.B. of Plantation, Cultivation & Farming	500/-	50
* Agro-Based Plantation Cultivation & Farming	475/-	50

Send Draft in favour of "Engineers India Research Institute, Delhi" (Postage Rs.75/- Extra)

ENGINEERS INDIA RESEARCH INSTITUTE

Regd. Off : 4449, Nai Sarak (B), Main Road, Delhi - 110 006 (India)

* Ph: 9811437895, 91-11-23918117, 23916431, 45626431 * Fax: 91-11- 23916431 * E-Mail : eiribooks@yahoo.com

MODERN BAKERY TECHNOLOGY & FERMENTED CEREAL PRODUCTS WITH FORMULAE

Written By :

EIRI Consultants and Engineers

ENGINEERS INDIA RESEARCH INSTITUTE

4449, Nai Sarak, Main Road, Delhi-110 006 (India)

Ph. : 91-11-23918117, 23916431, 23840361

Fax : 91-11-23916431, 23918117

✶ **E-Mail :** eiribooks@yahoo.com

✶ **Website :** www.eiriindia.org & www.eiri.in

Sole Distributor :

EIRI PROJECT CONSULTANTS & PUBLISHERS

4/54, Roop Nagar, Delhi-110007

Printed and Published by :

ENGINEERS INDIA RESEARCH INSTITUTE

4449, Nai Sarak, Main Road, Delhi-110 006 (India)
Ph. : 91-11-23918117, 23916431, 23840361
Fax : 91-11-23916431, 23918117
★ **E-Mail :** eiribooks@yahoo.com
★ **Website :** www.eiriindia.org & www.eiri.in

Distributed by :

EIRI PROJECT CONSULTANTS & PUBLISHERS
4/54, Roop Nagar, Delhi-110007

ISBN : 978-81-89765-26-2
Printed in New Delhi (India)

Rs. 1250

Printed and Published by Sudhir Gupta for
"Engineers India Research Institute", 4449, Nai Sarak, Main Road,
New Delhi-110 006 and Printed at Swastik Offset, Delhi

Preface

The book **'Modern Bakery Technology & Fermented Cereal Products with Formulae'** covers various methods including Bakery Ingredients, Planning of Bakery Unit, Bakery Premixes, Chapatis and Cookies made from Wheat Flour, Characteristics of Soybean and its utilization of Preparation of bread and biscuits, Health Breads, Ingredients of Production of Bread, Manufacturing Process of Bread, Bread, External and Internal Bread Faults, Fermented Products, Cake Ingredients,Formulations of Cake, Processing of Cake, Cookies, Crackers Manufacture, Manufacturing of Pastry, Manufacturing of Icing and Decoration, Machinery Used in Bakery Unit, Oven, Packaging of Bakery, Formulae of Fermented Products, Production of Puff Pastry, Manufacturing Methods of Cookies, Manufacture of Biscuits (Assorted), Manufacturing of Caks, Fermented Cereal Products, Macaronic Products.

The book has been written for the benefit and to prove an asset and a handy reference guide in the hands of new entrepreneurs and well established industrialists.

Director

ENGINEERS INDIA RESEARCH INSTITUTE

Nai Sarak, Main Road,
Delhi-110 006 (India)
E-mail : eirisidi@bol.net.in

CONTENTS AND SUBJECT INDEX

1

Bakery Ingredients

There are considerations in the production of breads and other bakery products such as ingredients or raw materials and machinery. The baker should have an understanding of the normal use of ingredients in baking. Function of baking is to present cereal flours in an attracting, palatable and digestible form.

Classification of Ingredients

Structure builders: Flour, eggs and milk

Tenderizers: Fat, sugar and baking powder

Moisteners: Milk, eggs

These can be classified depending upon their functions in bakery:

Structure Builders

Provide the structure and texture to the cake e.g. flour, eggs, milk.

Tenderizers

Provide softness and shortness in the product e.g. fat, sugar, baking powder.

Moisteners

Provide moisture and keeping quality e.g. Milk, water, eggs, syrup.

Driers

Absorb and retain moisture and provide the body of the product e.g. Milk solids and starches.

Flavours

Provide natural flavour e.g. Cocoa, chocolate, butter, eggs, and other natural flavour bearing ingredients.

The different ingredients used in baking are:

1. Flour
2. Sugar
3. Shortenings
4. Leavening agents
5. Eggs
6. Water
7. Salt
8. Milk and milk derivatives
9. Minor ingredients

Flour (Atta)

Wheat flour is the basic structural component of most batter and dough products. It is able to perform this textural function because of gluten content, which allows expansion of air cells and provide rigidity after baking. Flour is obtained through the milling process in which bran and germ part of wheat grains are removed as far as possible.

Wheat flour is unique among the cereal flours, when mixed with water in correct proportions, the protein will form an elastic dough which is capable of holding gas and which will set to a spongy structure when heated in oven. Commercially flour is obtained from two types of wheat:

1. Hard wheat
2. Soft wheat

Hard Wheat

Hard wheat is mostly desirable in bread production. They mill well and yield good quantities of flour that is high in good quality protein from which strong elastic dough can be made. Hard wheat dough has high water absorptive capacity, excellent gas-holding properties and will yield bread with good volume, grain and texture.

Soft Wheat

Soft wheat is low in protein and yields flour having low water absorption capacity and poor tolerance to mixing and fermentation. They are undesirable for bread production but are highly desirable in production of cakes, pastries and cookies.

Flour builds the structure of the cake and holds other ingredients together in an evenly distributed condition in the cake. Cakes made from too strong flour will peak in the center and will be tough and dry. Cakes made from too weak flour may flatten or even sink in the center.

It is the wish of every baker to use flour having the following characteristic for the production of quality bread:

Colour

The flour should have a trace of creamish colour, otherwise, the bread will have a dead white crumb.

Strength

Strength is often said that the flour is strong or the flour is weak.

Such statements refer to strength of flour which is capable of producing a bold, large volume, well risen loaf.

Tolerance

The ability of flour to withstand the fermentation process and to produce a satisfactory loaf over a period of time, in excess of what normally is required to bring about the correct degree of ripeness for that practical process, means, tolerance.

Water Absorption

This refers to the ability of flour to take on and hold the maximum amount of moisture without additional mixing for full development of dough. Absorption varies from 54-65 per cent based upon the weight of flour and way the flour is to be used. If the dough is not given the required mixing time because of limited mixing capacity, or for other reasons, the baked product will lack volume and have a dry crumb and inferior eating and keeping quality.

Uniformity

This is also an important aspect which should not be overlooked. Bakery should get uniform flour to obtain good quality end product.

pH

Flour with pH value below 5.0 are generally too acid and give poor result in bread baking; the range for satisfactory flours is usually between pH 5.5 and 6.5.

Composition

Major components of flour are starch (70 per cent), protein (11.5 per cent), water (14 per cent) and minor components are ash (4 per cent), sugar (1 per cent) and fat (1 per cent.). Gluten protein [glutenin and gliadin] is insoluble in water or dilute salts solution. These proteins are responsible for elastic properties of flour dough. Glutenin portion provides strength and firmness to gluten and gliadin adheres to glutenin and holds it together. Carbohydrate is present in the form of starch with small amount of dextrin and sugars, cellulose and gums.

Sugar

It imparts sweet taste. It has tenderizing action on flour proteins and it makes the cake tender. Being hydroscopic, sugar helps to retain moisture in cakes, which improve its shelf life. The golden brown crust and colour of cakes is due to caramelization of sugar. Sugar has lubrication effect on gluten strands and helps in acquiring volume in cakes. Sugar is essential for fermentation activity of yeast to produce CO_2 gas which raises the dough and imparts proper volume to the bread. It enhances flavour and helps in moisture retention due to its hygroscopicity.

Bread flavour depends on the type and quality of ingredients, fermentation and processing of dough and sugar has most pronounced effect on flavour (except salt). Sucrose is superior to the other sweetners in its contribution to flavour. It influences bread flavour by making possible, more rapid baking.

Sugar does not act as softening agent but by developing crust colour quickly it makes possible a reduction in baking time and retention of more moisture in the bread. It also contributes little to anti-firming properties. Browning of crust is due to part of caramelization, as well as to sugar-amine reaction (Mallard reaction). It also act as tenderizing agent.

Amount of sugar used in bread or rolls is entirely within the discretion of the baker and depends on type of bread. Sugar influences the bread yield by adjusting the baking time. and temperature to produce loaves of high original moisture. Sugar has little effect on absorption of the dough but additional mixing is required if percentage of sugar is increased. Sugar also increases the time required to get maximum dough development. Crust colour reflects the type and amount of sugar used. As sugar percentage is increased, the crust becomes darker i.e. sucrose results in more reddish brown crust. High concentration of sugar interferes with gluten formation.

Uses of Sugar

It serves the following purposes:

1. Gives the necessary sweetness in cakes,
2. Serves as a form of food for the yeast in fermentation,
3. Is used in the preparation of a variety of icings for baked products,
4. Assists in the creaming and whipping process of mixing,
5. Provides good grain texture in the product,
6. Aids in the retention of moisture and prolongs freshness,
7. Promotes a good crust colour
8. Adds nutritional values to the product.
9. It increases gas production.

Different Types of Sugars

1. Fermentable sugars which are naturally present in flour e.g. glucose, fructose, sucrose, maltose
2. Non-fermentable sugars which are oligosaccharides.

AVAILABLE SUGARS

Medium Granulated Sugar

It is coarse crystal sugar. Used for sanding cookies, pies and other bakery products in which very coarse grain is desired. Used for decorative purposes also.

Sanding Sugar

Most frequently used for sparkling or sanding purposes for-cookies, pies, bread etc. It has property of reflecting light and give sparkling appearance to the product on which it is used. It is the lightest colour sugar.

Extra Fine Granulated Sugar

Most frequently used product in baking industry. It dissolves readily in water or in other liquefying agents of bakery.

Icing Sugar

As name implies, it is used for high quality icing production. It promotes higher gloss, rapid crusting.

Brown or Soft Sugar

Brown sugar is offered in a wide range of colours from light yellow to dark brown. They are used for flour development to baked products. It is.used in dark breads, many cookies and in devils food, spice and other dark cakes.

SHORTENINGS

Fat lubricates the structure of a baked product. These are essential ingredients of most types of bakery products which shorten pastry, cake i.e. any fat fit for such use e.g. lard, butter and some vegetable oils. It has tenderizing effect on flour proteins and makes the product tender. It is fat part of the mixture which holds large number of air cells incorporated during creaming. Fat used in cake making should be smooth as it can incorporate and holds air cells as granular fats do not fulfill this function. Therefore use of granular fat should be avoided. Vegetable oil is also used for shortening e.g. coconut oil, corn oil, cottonseed oil, peanut oil and soybean oil.

Uses of Shortenings

These

1. Impart shortness, richness and tenderness to the product,
2. Improve the eating qualities of the product
3. Provide aeration
4. Contribute to flavour, particularly special fats such as butter,
5. Promote a desirable grain and texture,
6. Develop flakiness in product
7. Lubricate the gluten for development of yeast-raised dough,
8. Act as emulsifiers for holding of liquids.

Shortenings should be stored at a temperature of 70-80°F. At low temperature it becomes hard and brittle and difficult to work and at high temperature they become excessively soft and show impaired creaming quality. Shortening should not be stored near odourous material because fats are more prone to absorb many foreign odours which are undesirable in shortening. Emulsifier is widely used ingredient in shortening for cakes, icings and bread.

Properties of Shortening

It should have

1. Bland flavour
2. White appearance
3. Good plasticity
4. Flavour and oxidative stability.

Butter

It is considered to be the best of all baking shortenings from a flavour standpoint. It imparts desirable flavour to the finished baked products. It is widely used for specialty breads, sweet goods, cookies and pastries. It has good shortening value. Cake made with butter is generally lower in volume and has coarser grain. But it deteriorates easily by bacterial or mold action. Salt added would act as preservative but not sufficient to avoid deterioration because salt added in separated butter may not be evenly distributed, leaving some water droplets which results in bacterial infection deterioration. Oxidative deterioration results in tallowy flavour.

Lard

Fat rendered from fresh, clean, sound, fatty tissues from hogs in good health at the time of slaughter. Lard has distinctive natural flavour and odour, which is considered desirable in certain baked products primarily bread, crackers and pie crusts. It is most widely used shortenings for bread, pies, soda crackers and find extensive use in pan greasing and in cookie dough.

Leavening Agents

Leavening agents contribute significantly to the textural properties of baked products by expanding the batter or dough, sometimes during mixing and always during baking. Any process by which dough or batter is filled with holes, which are retained upon baking, is a leavening process. Any material which brings this process is called leavening agent.

Generally two types of leavening agents are used:

1. **Biological Agents**: Yeast.
2. **Chemical Agents**: Baking powder, baking soda, ammonium carbonate, etc.

Yeast

Function of yeast in bread making is to lighten the dough and impart to it a characteristic aroma and flavour. Generally four kinds of yeast are available to the bakers-living yeast for leavening, dead dried yeast for nutritional and flavour enhancement, bakers' yeast for white bread and food yeast for rye bread.

Baker yeast is an oval shaped, one celled, and colourless, microscopic plant called Saccharomyces cerevisiae. Yeast is universally distributed, generally growing harmlessly on various plant parts wherever sugar is available. One important process it causes in baking is fermentation.

Characters of Yeast

1. Yeast exists and is active in air as well as in absence of air.
2. In presence of air it grows rapidly and forms little alcohol.
3. In absence of air it grows slowly but alcohol formation increases.

In addition to glucose, baker yeast ferments hexose, fructose and mannose, disaccharides sucrose, maltose, the trisaccharides-raffinose and tetrasacharides stachyose. Lactose (milk sugar) is not attacked by baker yeast. Nitrogen compounds are required in abundance to build protein and nucleic acids. Inorganic ammonium salts, urea and amino acids are metabolized readily. Nitrogenous compounds are present in dough in plenty but ammonium chloride is added to stimulate fermentation. Most favourable temperature for baker yeast growth and fermentation is in the range of 84°F-90°F depending on strain used. Temperature above 95°F decreases yeast activity. Yeast grows and ferment best in acidic environment, tolerating acidities as low as pH 2.

Role of yeast in bread making is to lighten or raise the dough, thereby improving its ultimate palatability, simultaneous production and concentration of alcohol, aldehydes, ketones and acids contributing to aroma and flavour. The principal disadvantage is that it is difficult to control and in some items, fermentation flavour can be undesirable. It is also more expensive than chemical agents.

Baking Soda

It is chemically known as sodium bicarbonate. It will liberate CO_2 gas, a leavening gas, when heated. It also liberates the same gas when mixed with an acid, either hot or cold. When baking soda is heated, the products formed are:

$$2NaHCO_3 \xrightarrow{\text{heat}} CO_2 + H_2O + Na_2CO_3$$

If soda is alone used as a leavening agent a residue of washing soda will remain in the cake. This residue when present in excess, gives the dark colour and taste. The reason is that the washing soda so formed will act upon the shortening which is in the cake batter forming soap. This causes an unpleasant taste brown colour and alkaline odour. Therefore, bicarbonate is not used alone and when used, a suitable quantity of acid is added so that neutral residue is formed.

Baking Powder

Quantity of baking powder should be carefully regulated in the formula in order to achieve good results. If a formula calls for use of more moisture the setting of structure of end product will be delayed. Baking powder will start evolving CO_2 gas as soon as the product is placed in'oven, but the batter being too soft, the gas will not be held by gluten framework and will escape before the structure is set resulting in loss of volume. The quantity of baking powder should be increased in the formula and baking should be done at higher temperature in order to have faster set.

Baking powder is combination of sodium bicarbonate and an arid salt when moistured and heating will evolve gas which leaven the product giving it volume and making light and easy to digest. Baking powder must yield not less than 12 per cent available carbon-dioxide and concept of neutralization value was developed.

Neutralization value = gm of $NaHCO_3$ x 100/100gm of acidic salt

Baking powder is of three different kinds:

Fast Acting

This type of baking powder releases most of its CO_2 gas during bench operation and very little gas is released during baking i.e. mixing operation.

Slow Acting

Such baking powders do not release much of gas during bench operation and all the gas is released when it comes in contact with heat.

Double Acting

This type of baking powder is most widely used by bakers. This baking powder releases part of gas during bench operation, increasing fluidity of cake batter. This action makes the weighing operation easy enabling the baker to apportion the batter in moulds correctly. The remaining of CO_2 gas is released in the oven, which gives volume to the end product.

Baking powder also contains an inert filler which is common corn starch. A baking powder should release its gas in the batter to saturate it with CO_2 gas and liberate the gas uniformly during baking to hold the raised batter until set. This tends to give a uniform crumb and prevent shrinkage and cakes from falling. The starch serves two purposes;

1. It act as a buffer between soda and the acid and prevents reaction when exposed to air by absorbing moisture.

2. It also helps the powder to release standard amount of CO_2,

Sometimes powdered and dried egg albumen is added to baking powder. It dissolves in cold water and increases the viscosity of the dough which helps to hold gas bubbles in the dough, this increase the effectiveness of the baking powder. Baking Powder releases 1-14 per cent available CO_2,

The baking powders are named after the acid ingredient used in the powder i.e. tartrate powder, phosphate powder etc. The time and rate of gas evolution from baking powder can be regulated by the selection of different baking acids that react faster or slower with sodium bicarbonate. Commonly used leavening acids components are:

Tartrates (Mono Potassium Salt of Tartaric Acid)

Tartrates are commonly used as the acid component of baking powder in the form of tartratic acid or potassium hydrogen tartrate. It reacts readily at room temperature and is relatively expensive.

Phosphates

A number of sodium acid pyrophosphate powders are available. They vary in their reaction rates, depending upon how they are made.

Monocalcium Phosphate

Cream of tarter being relatively expensive has been largely replaced by phosphate, reacts readily at room temperature and is widely used as the fast acting component in double acting baking powders. Phosphate powders react somewhat slower than tartrates at room temperature but still lose a high percentage of their gas before baking.

Sulphates

To overcome the above defect, slow acting powders are used. Such powders give very little gas at room temperature but release all the available gas only at the temperature of the oven.

Ammonium Carbonate or Bicarbonate

When ammonium carbonate or bicarbonate are heated, CO_2 and NH_3 are reduced. No solid is left behind in this reaction. However, the ammonia imparts a detectable odour unless it is completely removed. It is used as leavening agent in baking biscuits and crackers as they have large surface to mass ration and ammonia escapes when baked at high temperature. Ammonium bicarbonate can be used in products that are to be baked at low moisture .

Either ammonium carbonate or bicarbonate is used to a small extent as a leavening agent. Its use is primarily limited to a certain types of cookies.

Eggs

Most important function of eggs is to provide structure to the cake. It provides moisture to the cake. It improves the taste and nutritive value of cake. Eggs used in excess amount will give abnormal volume to the cake. Crust will be dark, thick and peeld off as a flake. Texture will be dry and rough due to evaporation of moisture.

Proteins of eggs are of particular importance. Coagulation of protein during baking contributes to the structure of finished product and reduces tenderness.

Function of eggs:

1. Binding action
2. Leavening action
3. Emulsifying action
4. Flavour
5. Colour
6. Nutritive value

Egg White

It is used in candy and baking industry because of its ability to form foams which are stable enough to support large quantities of flour or sugar. These foams must be capable of holding the other ingredients until heat coagulation can occur in the oven and a stable protein matrix develops. Egg white has characteristic property of good foam formation. Globulins are primarily responsible for lowering surface tension and increase viscosity where air gets incorporated. As foam develops bubbles become smaller, surface is greatly enlarged and ovomucin (protein) undergoes surface denaturation to form a solid film, which contributes to the stability of the unheated foam and volume of foam increases. Ovalbumin, which is readily heat coagulable, set up in heat and supports many times its weight of sugar and flour. Albumin having pH 6.5-9.5 has greatest foaming power. The pH of egg white is 7.6.

Egg Yolk

Yolk is not commonly employed as a foaming agent with the exception of a yellow sponge type baked product. It does have characteristic foaming ability. Type of foam is quite different than egg white which is oil-water-air emulsion. It is mostly used in manufacture of mayonnaise and salad dressings. pH of egg yolk is 6.0

Following actions should be kept in mind while using egg as ingredients:

1. Weight of sugar should exceed the weight of flour.
2. Weight of total liquid should equal or slightly exceed the weight of sugar.
3. In pound or layer cake, the weight of egg solids should approximate 1/ 4th of the weight of shortening.
4. In white cake the weight of egg white solids should exceed l/luth of the weight of shortening.

In its pure form, water is a tasteless, odorless and colourless liquid. It is an essential dough ingredient which helps to form gluten, starch-swelling process and to bring dough ingredients into intimate contact with each other so that the complex reaction of bread making can take place. Amount of water added depends on the optimum dough characteristic for proper and easy handling as well as for the best quality bread obtainable. In general water of medium hardness (about 50-100ppm) with a neutral or slightly acidic pH is preferred for baking. Too soft water can result in sticky dough because of absence of gluten tightening minerals. Too hard water may retard fermentation to a certain extent by toughening the gluten. So medium hard water is the best for use in bread production.

Some of the mineral component of water, which does not have any effect on fermentation, is copper salts, iron salts, aluminum salts, tannic acids, silicates and phosphates. Probable effects of following salts are found i.e. calcium oxide, calcium carbonate, calcium sulphate, magnesium chloride, magnesium oxide and sodium carbonate. If the problem in bakery is suspected to be due to water supply, several common tests can be performed which include alkalinity, pH and hardness.

Functions of Water in Baking

Water has several functions in bread making. It makes possible the formation of gluten. Gluten as such does not exist in flour. Only when flour proteins are hydrated, gluten is formed. Water controls the consistency of dough. Water assists in the control of dough temperatures and warning or cooling of dough can be regulated through water. It dissolves salts, suspends and distributes non-flour ingredients uniformly. Water wets and swells starch and renders it digestible. Water also makes possible enzyme activity. Water keeps bread palatable longer if sufficient water is allowed to remain in the finished loaf. It dissolves salts, sugar and suspends other material in dough. It helps the enzymes to carry out their activity and wets and swells the starch to make it digestible.

Salt

Common salt is used for bringing out the flavour of other ingredients, which are used in cakes, and to impart taste to the bread and to other products. Instead of reducing sugar in the cake it can be used as an adjustment of sweetness if the cake is too sweet. Salt also lowers caramelization temperature of cake batters and aids in obtaining crust colour.

In bread, it is used for taste and helps to improve flavour and characteristic of bread. Without salts, dough is wetty. It, therefore, improves grain and texture of loaf by strengthening the dough, thus indirectly helping colour, grain and texture. Salt helps to control the yeast activity, therefore controls fermentation. It also prevents the formation and growth of undesirable bacteria in yeast-raised dough.

Amount of salt to be used depends on several factors but mainly upon the type of flour. Weak flour will take more salt, because salt gives strengthening effect to proteins. The mineral content of water will also affect the amount of salt. When using hard water the amount of salt will need to be reduced. Under normal conditions the amount of salt to use will range between 2-2.25 per cent. Salt is added to develop flavour. It also toughens the gluten and gives less sticky dough. Salt slows down the rate of fermentation. Generally all levels of salt suppress yeast activity.

Functions of Salt

1. It increases gluten stability,
2. Controls fermentation,
3. Develops flavour,
4. Retains water.
5. Contributes to the crust and crumb formation.

Common salt should have the following characteristics for use in the bakery:

1. It should be completely soluble in water.
2. It should give a clear solution. Cloudy solution will indicate presence of certain impurities.
3. It should be free from lumps.
4. It should be pure.
5. It should be free from a bitter or biting taste.

Milk and Milk Derivatives

Milk solids perform the function of structure formation in the cakes. Milk enriches the cake nutritionally and it also provides moisture in cake. Milk is the basic mean of supplying liquid to the dough. It contributes to the crust browning because of its proteins and sugar content and to softening ot crumb texture because of its fat content.

Proper incorporation of milk in dough will result in increased "loaf volume. The grain texture of finished bread is also improved by " using non-fat dry milk. High moisture content of milk bread permits it to remain soft for longer periods than bread made without milk. Milk solids have a binding effect on flour protein, creating a toughening effect. Milk contains lactose which regulates crust colour.

Liberal use of milk in bakery products brings about nutritional improvements i.e. increases mineral content; improves protein quality and supplements carbohydrates to the bread. Wheat is deficient in essential amino acids (lysine, tryptophan and methionine) which can be increased by adding 6 per cent level milk solids i.e. lysine increases to 46 per cent, tryptophan 10 per cent and methionine 23 per cent. Greatest advantage of milk solids in bread is to improvesensory quality.

Milk solids also contribute in cakes:

1. Contribute to greater moisture retention for longer apparent freshness and keeping quality
2. Improved appearance and crust colour and absence of greasiness.
3. Improved flavour, richness and taste appeal.
4. Improved nutritional value.
5. It increases loaf volume, retards staling, increases absorption and dough strengthening.

MINOR INGREDIENTS

Malt Products

These are obtained from cereal grains usually barley. Greatest consumption of malt is in beverage industries but considerable quantities are used in milling and baking. It is classified as malt flour, malt syrups and dried malt syrup. Each of, which is further, classified as non-diastatic malt and diastatic malt.

Non-diastatic Malt

It is used principally to impart flavour and colour to baked products. They also have some effects on texture and supply fermentable carbohydrates and other nutrients to yeast. These are high in sugars.

Diastatic Malt

Have considerable enzyme activity. Malted grain from which these products are derived, is a veritable storehouse of enzymes which convert starch to reducing substances.

Flavourings

It helps the baker to add uniqueness to his product. These are natural-honey, molasses, malt syrup, cocoa, chocolate, lemon oil, vanilla extract, etc.

Classification

1. *Non-alcoholic flavour*: reduces vaporization e.g. glycerin, propylene, glycol, etc
2. *Alcoholic flavour*: used for icing and fillings, very volatile e.g. ethyl alcohol, etc
3. *Emulsifiers*: used in maintaining stability during baking, e.g. gum
4. Powdered flavourings: used in powder form e.g. heavy gum

Cocoa Products

Cocoa is a chocolate from which a substantial proportion of fatty material has been removed. It imparts flavour and colour changes.

Dough Improver

It is usually mixture of several inorganic salts together with starch or flour as an extender. Gluten oxidizing agents such as potassium bromate, potassium iodate or calcium peroxide. Calcium salts usually phosphate or sulphate which corrects any lack of hardness in dough water and provide buffering action to partially offset alkaline condition of water. Ammonium salts supply nitrogen which can be used by yeast for protein building.

Oxidizing Agents

Proper use of oxidizing agents results in larger volume, brighter crumb, better texture and improved appearance of finished loaf, e.g Potassium bromate, calcium oxide and potassium iodate.

Yeast Foods

Use of ammonium salts, phosphates, and sulphate in dough improvers and yeast foods improves the fermentation capacity of yeast in dough.

Spices

These act as aromatic agents, e.g.

1. Cinnamon
2. Nutmeg (produce 7-15 per cent volatile oil)
3. Mace (produce 7-14 per cent volatile oil)
4. Cloves (contain 14-21 per cent non-volatile penetrating oil)
5. Ginger (provide 1-3 per cent volatile oil)
6. Allspice (provide 3-4.5 per cent volatile oil)
7. Cardamom seeds (3.5-8 per cent of oil of the seed weight provide flavour)
8. Caraway seed (used in making rye bread, corn muffins, cheese rolls, compatible with flavour of sugar, apple, peach, apricot and rye.)
9. Anise seed (provide 2-3 per cent essential oil, used in icings and fillings for cakes and sweet rolls.

2

Planning of Bakery Unit

INTRODUCTION

The baking industry has an important role to play in the economic development of the country. This industry holds immediate and perspective future. It has also considerable scope for the additional investment and employment with very little capital requirements per unit compared to the other industries. Many bakery businesses fail and bakery owners see their dreams of success shattered. One important reason why such situtations happen is that bakery-owners do not plan carefully before they start to operate. They assume that they can learn as they go on with their business, but find that problems get accumulated if not solved diligently. If these kinds of results are to be avoided a business plan should be formulated.

Planning and its peformance

Planning is

- A written summery of what you hope to accomplish by being in business and how you intend to organize your resources to meet your goals.
- It is the road map for operating any business and measuring progress along with way.
- It is the blue print for the building a business on solid grounds and making sure that it will withstand the difficult and lean first years.

Planning is important for the following reasons :

- It encourages realism instead of over optimism.
- It helps you to identify your consumer, your market area, your pricing strategy and the competitive conditions under which you most operate

to succeed. This process often leads to the discovery of competitive advantages or new opportunity, as well as deficiency in your plan.

- By putting your plans on paper your overall ability to manage the business will improve. You will also have time to look ahead and avoid problems before they arise. You will be able to make improvements in the plan before conditions become critical.
- The business plan establishes the amount of financing or outside investment required and when it is needed.
- First impressions are important. A well organized plan makes it much easier for the lender or the investor to assess your financing proposal and assess you as a business manager.
- Three of four hours spent each month on updating your plan will save your time and money in the long run and may even save your business.

The major benefits of planning are :

- Helps in reducing an emotional bias.
- Provides SWOT (Strengths, Weaknesses, Opportunities and Threats Analysis.
- Tests one's commitment
- Enables one to justify his/her plans and ideas.
- Tests the ideas on paper.
- Helps one to develop a consistent strategy.
- Helps in convincing others about the ideas.

Now make planning as part of your management style.

Steps in Planning

Planning includes each and every step involved in the business. It is a very long, complicated and endless matter. The major elements for arriving at a decision for setting up any industry involves: size, location and time. The choice with regards to each of these elements is to be based on a comprehensive understanding of the interrelationship between

- Total demand and its growth pattern.
- Spatial distribution of demand both current and incremental, as between different market areas.
- The structure of investment and operating costs including economics of a scale for plants of different size.

To understand this complicated process, try has been made in this paper to categorise, summarise and produce the huge information in a nutshell form in easy language to be understood by a common baker. The step in planning can be divided mainly into three categories :

- Unit location
- Plant Design
- Project profile

Unit Location

Before starting a bakery, it is necessary to decide the location, where it is to be established. Because on the one hand the wrong selection of location adversely affects the business and on the other hand the proper selection of site develops the business to its maximum level. Hence, for selecting site, it is necessary to survey the market for bakery products in the area in order to decide on the size and scope of the project. For a large project, it is advisable to hire the services of marketing agencies that are well equipped to undertake such studies. However the survey must contain the following points :

Hints for site selection

- Selection such place where the raw materials like flour, fat, sugar, yeast etc. (used in bakery products) are easily available. Hence due to non availability of raw material, the production should nto stop. Moreover, if suddenly a big order to placed, the products can be made immediately after purchasing the raw material from the nearby market. In such circumstances if the raw material is not easily available, one has to lose the order and ultimately decreases the profit. In addition to that, due to less distance from bakery unit to raw material supplier, the transportation cost also increaes, which helps to decrease the production cost and ultimately increases to profit.
- As with the easy availability of raw material so should be the market of the product. For the same reason, it is advisable to select a place where the people's mobility is more. Such places are :
  - A place near bus station, railway station, city bus station
  - schools, colleges, hostels, hospitals etc., where numbers of students/people are more
  - Places of high density population like middle part/heart of the city, place where other shops are existing

Table 2.1 : The Detailed requirements of Semi-automatic Plant Layout

Plot Area : 35 x 15 m. Total Constructed area 10 x 15x5 m.

D1 = Door 1 m width W1 = Window 1 m width

D2 = Door 2 m width W2 = Window 1 m width

D3 = Door 4 m width

No.	Particular	Specifications/ Measurement (m)	Note
1.	Store room	3 x 3	construct two racks platform at a height of 1 m an 0.5 on two or three sides of storeroom
2.	Weighing balance	-	-
3.	Water supply	1 x 1	-
4.	Bread dough mixer	1.5 x 2	-
5.	Platform for dough preparation processing	7 x 1.5	Construct and place the marble/cota stone/granite on top and make cupboard below the platform
6.	Moulder	1 x 2	-
7.	Cake mixer	1 x 1.5	-
8.	Biscuit dough mixer	1 x 1.5	-
9.	Oven	3 x 4	-
10.	Emergency door	2 m (width)	Useful to carry out the machinery (shutter installed)
11.	Slicer	1 x 1.5	-
12.	Sealing	1 x 1.5	-
13.	Finished product storeroom	3 x 7	Construct three racks platform at the distance of 0.5 m each.
14.	Office	3 x 3	Fix a glass of 0.5 m height in such a way that the working area can be watched even while sitting in office.
15.	Toilet	1 x 1	-
16.	Bathroom	1 x 1	-
17.	Workers restoom	3 X 3.5	-
18.	Gate Keeper room	2 x 2	-
19	Garden	-	Grow small plants only

Table 2.2 : Estimated Fixed Capital

Particular	Quantity	Cost (Rs. in Lakh)
Land	3000 sq.ft.	04.50
Building (Production & Selling Machineries (Bread Dough Mixer, Cake Mixer, Biscuit Mixer, Bread Slicer, Oven)	2000 sq.ft. 1 no. each	03.50 03.30
Accessories (Bread Tins, Cake, Tins Baking Trays etc.)	As required	00.75
Office equipments (Table, Chairs, Computer, Filling Cabinet, Sell Counter, Show case etc.	1 to 4 No. (as required)	03.25
Preliminary and Preoperative Expenses (Legal, Project, Report Preparation, Technical Know-How, Establishment, Tour and Travels, Stationary, Post, Telephone etc.)	-	01.00
Total Fixed Capital		Rs. 16.00

- Places where more people are accommodated in small area like industrial estate.
- Possibility of getting contract under school feeding program or industrial canteen etc.

• The availability of basic necessary for the development of bakery industry are also necessary. They are :

- Potable water is the most essential commodity for any food processing industry. Particularly for bakery industry water is required to prepare most of the products. It is also required to clean the equipments, working tables, hands etc.
- Electric power is also required for running ovens, machinery, lights etc.
- Transportation facility is required for handling ingredients, products etc. as well as for commuting facility for the workers/employees.
- The communication facilities like post, telephone, telegram, fax etc. are necessary for business relation purpose.

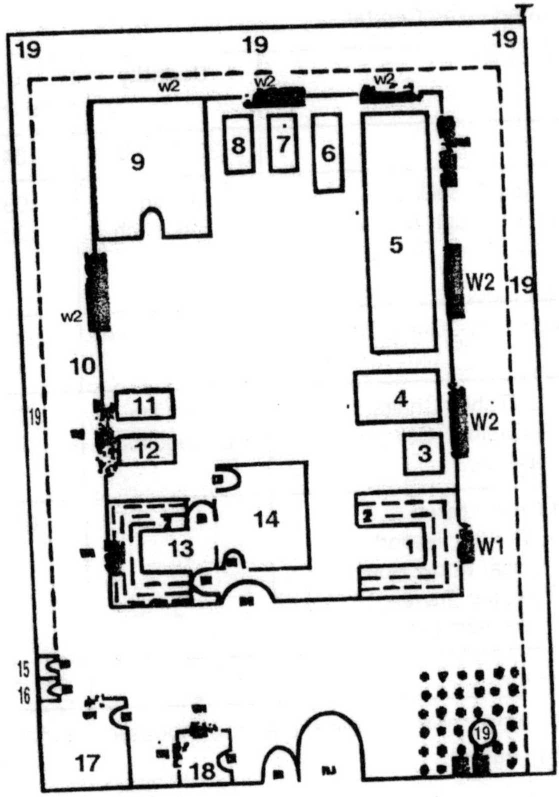

Fig. 2.1 : Lay out for the BakeryUnit

- The facility for water disposal is also required is bakery unit. However, a compared to other industries it is not a big problem in a bakery unit.
- The hospital facilities should be existing nearby which will be useful in case of any accident, injury, sudden sickness, acute diseases etc. of worker/employees.

- Collect the information on economic condition; purchase capacity, choice of food, food habits, choice and habit of bakery products etc. of the people nearby the proposed place of bakery unit. So the bakery may have the exact idea regarding the types of products to be prepared. If the technical information of prepared of such products is not known, that can be obtained from the suitable resources.

- Collect the information regarding volume of sales, production capacity, type and quality of products being produced etc. of the nearby bakeries of proposed place of unit, and analyse and study it carefully. So it can be estimated which type of products are to be produced in what quality at a particular time (e.g. festivals like Diwali, X-mas etc.) at what time.
- In many backward areas, government promotes the establishment of industry by providing benefits like loan/subsidy, free taxes/duties etc. One has to thick over above benefits and establish production unit in such remote places are selling unit at market area.
- If any famous bakery is enjoying large volume of sales in a particular area, it does not mean that a new bakery will also be able to sell equally well. However in a developing economy, it is not difficult to tap the market, because the customer may get attracted towards your bakery gradually.
- The site should be such that, there is enough space for future expansion. If all the space is used then there is no room for necessary extension subsequently on increased business which shows a complete lack of ambition and foresight.
- The site should be so chosen that the finished bakery building becomes a landmark. A fine building dwarfed and hidden by giant factories can never be such; so potential publicity will be lost.

Planning and Lay-Out

It is necessary to have knowledge regarding planning and layout because it can influence the erection cost, operating and maintenance cost, safety and convenience efficiency etc. While planning the plant design, equipment and machinery, electricity supply, financial arrangement etc. are to be studied thoroughly.

Space requirement

One has to plant the layout of the bakery according to the available space and the estimated volume of production. It is desirable to have at least 400 cubic ft. of space for every person employed, not considering the space of more than 14' height from the floor. However, about 1200 sq.ft. production area may be required to produce 3000 bread loaves of 400 gm. each or an assorted production (bread, cakes, pastries, cookes etc.) from bags of flour each of 90 kg.

Table 2.3 : Estimated Income Generated :

Particular (All are essorted types)	Quantity Day	Price (Rs./no. or kg)	Amount (Rs. in Lakh)
Bread (400 gm)	300 No.	8/no.	0.024
Milk Bread (400 gm)	200 no.	12/no.	0.024
Bun (50 gm)	1000 no.	1/no.	0.010
Toast	50 kg.	40/kg	0.020
Cookies /Biscuit	50 kg	60/kg.	0.030
Khari	50 kg.	60/kg.	0.030
Puff	300 no.	3/no.	0.090
Pizza	100 no.	25/no.	0.025
Cake/Pastry	20 kg.	150/kg	0.030
Burger	100 no.	10/no.	0.010
Total Daily Income			**0.212**
Cripple (Unsold material return) @10%			-0.021
Actual Income/Day			0.191
Yearly Income @ 300 day/year			**57.30**

Table 2.4 : Estimated Working Capital

Particular	Cost (Rs. in Lakh)
Raw Material (Flour, Fat, Sugar and other miscellaneous items)	34.00
Wages & Salaries (Manager, Supervisor, Skilled Semiskilled-Unskilled Labour, Clerk, Salesman)	02.80
Utilities & Overheads (Water, Electricity, Transport Communication, Stationary, Consumable Stores, Repair and Maintenance, Sundry Expenses)	03.20
Total Working Capital	Rs. 40.00
Grand Total (Fixed+Working) Capital	**Rs.65.00**

Table 2.5 : Calculation of Interest and Installation on Loan

Particular	Amount (Rs. in Lakh)
Total Investment required for the period (Table 6)	22.67
Loan terms available @ 80% i.e. 18.13 lakh	18.00
Interest on term loans @ 12@ (flat rate bases)	02.16
Installments (yearly)	03.60
Total amount to be paid to financing institute	5.76

Plant Design

- The Building of bakery unit may be single gound floor or multi-storyed. Among them the multi-storyed building is comparatively cheaper to build and has opportunity to take advantages of a gravity flow etc. But on the other hand, it should be constructed strongly. Moreover, labourers deployed in the multistoried factory, would make, supervision are difficult. Thirdly, each production tends to become detached from the whole unit assuming semi-independent production unit.
- The processing stages and flow sheet (indicating the flow the material) should be first prepared and then the plant design should be work in a proper way to get maximum advantages of gravity feed wherever possible. The design should be such that the equipments ramain unhidden and for the same reason pillers should be avoided. A clear flow line will allow for the shortest distance to be travelled by workers for each operation and allow for the maximum working space. This, in turn, will be helpful to maintain the speed of operation.
- While planning the bakery design, carefully thought must be given to the requirements of the factory and other acts. The advice on the same can be easily available from local authorities. Specialists's advice may also be necessary on other matters pertaining to construction equipment and welfare.
- Sufficient distance must be kept between each process equipments and machinery to provide enough space for the movement of men and material and sometimes the machinery/equipments too, as and when required. It is also necessary to comply with the requirements under Factory Act.

Table 2.6 : Commercial Calculations

Particular	Amount (Rs. in Lakh)
Total Investment	
• Fixed Capital	16.00
• Working Capital (2 months)	06.67
Sub total	**22.67**
Cost of Production	
• Total recurring expenditure of the year	40.00
• Depreciation of building @ 10%	00.35
• Depreciation of machinery @ 10%	00.30
• Depreciation of accessories @ 25%	00.19
• Depreciation of office equipment @ 25%	00.81
• Interest on loan @ 12% and installment	05.76
Sub total	**47.41**
Profit	
• Turn over per year	57.30
• Cost of production of year	47.41
Profit per year	**09.89**
Net Profit Ratio	17.26%
Rate of Return	43.63%
Break Even Point*	41.51

* Fixed cost includes Depreciation value. Interest on total investment 40% of salaries. 40% of overheads and insurance.

- The baking oven should be preferably located in one corner of the plant rather than in the middle. Area near the oven should be well ventilated so that the hot atmosphere surrounding the oven is dissipated outside. The installation of exhaust fan is also beneficial to serve the purpose.
- As with the oven-site the water supply should also be located in a corner. Water supply connection in the middle of the unit may spread water throughout the production area.
- Raw material store and finished good store should be situtated in such a way that these could be kept locked without any interference in normal production work.

Table 2.7 : Requirements of Different Levels of Bakery Unit.

Type of Bakery Unit	Production capacity	Requirement (Approximate)					Estimated* Cost of Plant and Machinery, accessories and POP (Rs. in Lakh)	Working+ capital for 2 months (Rs. in lakh)	Estimated Profit (Rs.) in Lakh/ Year)
		Space	Electri-city	Man Power	Equipments & Machinery	Raw material			
Small Scale (Small Unit)	Different bakery products about 1,000 per kg month	400 sq.ft.	Normal house hold	3 person	Baking tray, Bread tin, oven and Miscellaneous equipments	Flour, Ghee, Sugar, Fire wood, Leavening agents etc.	00.50	00.25	00.75
Small Scale (Medium Unit)	Different bakery products about 5,000 kg per month	1,000 sq.ft.	4 KW	8 person	As above plus Bread Slicer and Dough mixer	-do- in large quantity	01.50	01.00	01.20
Semi Automa-tic plant	Different bakery products about 12,000 kg per month	2,000 sq.ft.	10 KW	15 person	As above plus Flour Shifter Biscuit mixer, Cake mixer, Sealing machine etc.	-Do- in large quantity	05.00	07.00	09.00
Fully automatic plant	Different bakery products about 25,000 kg per month	5,000 sq.ft.	16 KG	10 person	As above plus Conveyor belts	-Do- In every large quantity	15.00	15.00	20.00

* Add land and building coast actually prevalent in the area where unit is to be established.
+ Within 2 months your money will be back and flow of rotation will start.

- The design selected should be given maximum benefits of natural scientific principles like gravitional force, lever etc.
- There should be enogh facility for lighting, ventilation temperature-humidity control systems etc. Because, nothing will impair efficiency more than unsatisfactory working conditions. It can be easily maintained by providing enough doors, windows and ventilations.
- The doors (at least one) should be big nough to carry out the machinery/ equipments etc.
- For the benefit of the workers, firms aid accommodation washing and sanitary facilities, preparation of meals etc. should be provided
- Planning for the fighting facilities is essential. For that, a certificate must be obtained from the local authority if required.

A model Layout for a semi automatic bakery unit engaged in production of bread and assorted confectionary products is given in figure 2.1.

Selection of Equipment and Machinery

- It is necessary to calculate the ratio of various tpes of products, the volume, the size and the profitability of the products which are to be produced, each for hand processing and machine processing. Then and then only decide which will be suitable as far as economy is concerned.
- While selecting the equipment, it is necessary to consider the ultimate production goal from the sales point of view, which will also be the deciding factor for the bakery.
- It is a general tendency to select sturdy, long lasting, maintenance free machines, which have minimum power requirement. It is observed that, cheaper equipments may ultimately prove to be more expensive on account of maintenance cost, breakdowns and durability.
- Only essential equipments should be installed in the beginning e.g. for bread production only, bread dough mixes, oven and slicer is essential. If the volume of production becomes more, then moulder can be installed. If the volume is more than 10,000 loaves daily, then only a divider and rounder may be required. Overhead proven and proofing assembly will be necessary only for large size production of more than 10,000 loaves daily.
- If it is desirable to produce cakes, pastries, cookies etc., vertical mixes of suitable size can be added.

- Serious thought should be given to selection of oven. For a small bakery, wood fire oven may appear to be a cheaper proposition, but ever increasing scarcity of firewood, pollution problem, and a general ecological awareness could become a serious hurdle. While considering electric oven, one must ensure the uninterrupted power supply position. Gas, oven although are efficient but availability of proper gas oven, its cost and running expenditure as well as statutory requirements should be ascertained before making a decision. Diesel fired ovens, although are expensive but operational cost may be very favourable and its performance is quite satisfactory.

- There are number of other equipments which could be added as and when necessity arises such as dough sheeter and making puff pastry products, wire cut on despositor cookie machine, freezer, water chiller, cake batter depositor, vegetable cutting machine, mincer, nut grinder etc.

- Once having decided the machinery, collect the addresses of various companies distributors, traders etc. who are selling / manufacturing the machine. Collect the detailed information from each of them. Now compare the prices, durability, working capacity, work efficiency, operating systems. repairing, guarantee etc. very minutely and then decide from whom the machine is to be purchased. Moreover, the cash/credit/hire-purchase scheme and financial position of company are also to be considered in mind.

- It is advisable to make arrangements for working capital for a period of 2 months. Because, bakery products are normally sold against cash, so the turnover will be faster, hence the requirements of working capital could be considerably reduced.

Managing Finances

The financial planning of the project is a very important factor especially under the conditions where the prices of raw material fluctuate vastly. Most projects most core than the estimate, resulting a squeeze on working capital. Most financial institutions are reluctant to finance for the additional cost of the project even when it is justifies the increase in profits.

The main problem that is faced practically by any enterpreneur is getting loans from banks and other financial institutions within a reasonable time frame. The delay in the formalities cause delay in the project resulting in further increase in the cost of the project.

The following precautionary measures must be taken for effectively planning of finances

- The financial reqirements can be estimated by preparing project report.
- A 20% contingency must be added on the firm quotations of all machinery and civil construction work. For more surety 20% contingency must be added on total financial requirements.
- Consider the maximum price of the material in order to prevent high rate problem appearing later on
- Allowances should be made for pre-operational expenses. They include salaries of staff employed during and before erection, installation, transport, insurance, interest, expense incurred on spoiled batches during trial operations etc.
- The implementation of the project must be carefully planned in order to complete it in minimum possible time. For example the construction of building and other civil works can be started as soon as the order for fabrications of machinery is placed. However, possibilities should be explored to take premises on rent or industrial shed offered on installations.
- One should ensure the availability of the total loan from financial institutions such as scheduled banks, State Finance Corporation, small Industries Development Corporation, Khadi Gramodyog Commission etc.

Electricity

It is essential that the local Electricity Board is to be contacted regarding the approximate cost of wiring, cable laying charges and deposits to be paid to the Electricity Board. The cost of power consumption varies from place to place and should be ascertained from the Electricity Board. Depending on the installed equipment, a bakery may require 10-25 KV connected load, considering the future expansion, one should ensure that the wiring is done in such a manner that increaed load can be connected later.

Project Report

Before starting any business, it is necessary to estimate the expenditure and income, requirements of ingredients manpower etc. and finally the profit through project report. The financial institutes (like bank) grants the term loan/subsidy etc. on the basis of project report only. Hence, a model project report regarding medium scale unit is discussed below :

Project Report on Medium Scale Bakery Unit

Introduction

- Potentiality : The poor or middle class families are habituated to have biscuit, bun, khari and toast, along with morning tea, coffee and milk as a breakfast. The school going children also carry bakery products in their lunch box. It is replacing poori, bhakhari and chapatti now a day. Moreover birthday, X-mas day, wedding day etc. is celebrated cake. Hence the bakery products are widely used.

- Marketing ; Readymade bakery products are used at home, hotels as well as bus-station, railway station, garden, public places etc. It can be carried with luggage and consumed immediately during travelling. As out lifestyle changes according to western countries, fast food is being popularized. Hence, there is a potential market for bakery products.

- Management : This business could be run with the help of 10 to 15 skilled-semiskilled-unskilled labourers using simple machinery and equipments.

- Processing : The flour, egg, sugar, fat, essence, leavening agent, yeast etc. ingredients are mixed in a required quantity to a smooth dough. It is shaped into biscuit, khari, puff, bread, bun etc. and baked. Later on after cooling it is packed with appropriate labels.

- Production Estimate : About 1.7 tones assorted bakery products like biscuit, bread, bun, khari, cake, toast, etc, are produced in a year.

- Licence : The licence under Prevention of Food Adulteration Act (PFA) is essential for a bakery unit. And a few licences from local authority.

• Total Capital Requirement : Bakery unit requires various kinds of capital investments. That is mainly divided into two heads i.e. fixed capital and working capital and further sub divided in many other subheads. The estimated cost required is givenin table no. 2.2 & 2.3.

- Means of Finance : The bank loan @ 80% of total requirement can be obtained from nationalised /co-operative/IDBI/SIDBI banks or financial institutions like GSFe. That is to be moratorium period. The rate of interest will be @ 12% per annum. The detail on interest and installments to be paid is given in table 2.4.
- Income : The expected quantity of selling the bakery products and income to be generated through it is given in table 2.5. Normally 5 to 10% bakery products return as unsold therefore cost of the same is cut down from the income. The bakery runs minimum 300 days in a year therefore yearly income is calculated on that bases.
- Commercial Calculations : The final selection of the business is based on the various commercial terms like profit, net profit ratio, rate of return, break-even point etc. The calculation of such term is given in table 2.6 to screen out the project at a glance by entrepreneur.

Conclusion

Thus planning a business layout before setting up a bakery unit a entrepreneur can easily handle his business. Because through planning the owner will be aware well in advance regarding most of all the problems or crises raised in future. Therefore, he can be well prepared for the same and can easily face it. Finally it results in saving of time, money, energy etc. that ultimately helps to achieve our final goal to increase profit. Not only that, it decreases business tension and also provides an enjoyable business atmosphere.

3

Bakery Premixes

Advantages of Using Pre-Mixes

There are a number of reasons why pre-blended mixes and bases are becoming widely popular. Several of these reasons are :

1. Uniformity
2. Simple/Convenient
3. Reduced inventory
4. Cost Control
5. Labour Saving
6. Tolerant to handling
7. Sanitation

The most important reason for use of pre blended mixes and bases is because of the uniformity of products they provide. The baker does not have to worry about differences in ingredients, especially flour, since the mix manufacturer assumes through his quality control checks that the ingredients going to the mix product will be the same every time and confirm to the existing rigid standards particularly in performance.

Mixes are simple and easy to use, many times requiring only the addition of water and single stage mixing to provide quality products which would otherwise require more detailed handling and care. The mix is convenient to use as it eliminates scaling ingredients, simplifies handling and in many cases provides an all around better product to the customer.

When using mixes or bases for producing bakery foods, it is generally not necessary to have an inventory to many inredients. In many cases yeast may be the only ingredients required for the production of several products. This elimination of inventory frees up more space for production, or reduces that amount of floor space required for a particular operation.

Cost control using pre-blended products is easier because the manufacture is not accounting for price fluctuations on a large number of ingredients. Mix companies purchase flour, sugar and many ingredients in bulk, receiving better costs than would normally be attainable by the individual baker. This bulk purchasing by the mix manufacturer keeps the cost of pre-blended products on a more even bases.

PRODUCT CATEGORIES

Formulas have been developed for specific product categories.

1. Complete or fully prepared-Product in this category in ready to eat, requiring little or no preparation. Each ingredients in the formula is combined into a system (batter, dough etc.) which is processed, packed and sold.

2. Semi complete-This category requires additions processing of the formulated product before it is ready to be. consumed. This category consists of frozen unbaked canned, shelf stale and dry mix. The area of dry mix product is one of considerable growth in the food industry today.

    1. Cookie mixes
    2. Cake mixes
    3. Doughnut and other Sweet Yeast Goods mixes
    4. Pancake and Waffle mixes
    5. Biscuit mixes
    6. Pie crust mixes

LIMITATIONS OF USING PRE MIXES

1. Dusty nature of the product. Minor ingredients like leavening aids and flavours are especially susceptible to dusting.

2. Sieving of ingredients in order to ensure uniformity throughout the batch.

3. Order of incorporation of ingredients is another critical area. Usually addition of flours, sugar, dairy, leavenings miscellaneous ingredients and flavouring is followed by fats and oils. In the blendings process, heavier particles will be suspended better throughout the mix prior to fat being added.

4. Incorporation of fat is also be critical phase as the final product should be uniform, free flowing without lumps or greased.

The third market for premixes is in specialty products and contract manufactured products. Specialty products can consist of premixed ingredients for use as baking powders, spice, blends, baking ingredients, additives, icing bases, crumb toppings to name only a few varieties.

The fourth area for premixes is the consumer market or by tradition, made for use by the housewife. These products are made up of pancakes, biscuits, cookie mixes, cakes mixes and more recently bread mixes which are a big seller for use in automated home bread machines.

MAJOR INGREDIENTS USED IN PREMIXES

The major ingredients used in premixes are:

1. Flour
2. Leavening agents
3. Shortening
4. Sugar
5. Emulsifiers
6. Processing aids

Flavourings, spices etc., are also important ingredients in premixes. Many flavouring ingredients such as vanilla, lemon, orange etc. which are added in very small percentage have little effect on baking but flavours such as chocolate, cocoa, caramel, brown sugar, fruits, nuts and other heavy or solid ingredients at times affect the baking results and at times changes in the formula must be made.

1. Flour

The wheat falling into the class "hard" are most suited for the production of bread flour or all purpose family flour, while those wheat which falls into the class "soft" are most desirable for chemically leavened products such as biscuits, cakes, cookies and crackers.

Breakdown of hard wheat flour into 4 different fractions results in the high protein fraction of 20%, an endosperm chunk of 11.5% protein, a cracker flour of 7% protein and a cake flour of 6% protein. The cake fraction made from hard wheat performs excellently in commercial cake baking. Even though hard wheat flours are suitable for bread purposes and not cake production.

The high protein fraction of 20% is so strong that it can be used to strengthen bread flours. It can be blended with mixes to increase the baking strength of such mixes, in fact, it represents a reserve of baking strength which can be added at will to weaker flours.

The breakdown of soft wheat flour into different fractions gives high sugar cake flour having a 7.6% protein that produces outstanding results in cake baking. It is particularly adaptable to angel food cakes where any surface fat is objectionable. This 7.6% protein flour is low in surface fat, whereas the high protein fraction is higher in surface fat.

Characteristics desirable for certain uses

Strong bread flours: These flours are used in hard breads and hard rolls, *have* high protein content, maximum gluten quality (mixing tolerance), great extensibility and resistance to extension.

Bread flours for commercial production: For this we need mid-range protein quantity, medium to strong gluten quality (mixing tolerance) medium to maximum extensibility and resistance to extension, mid range enzymatic activity.

All purpose flours: All purpose flour is needed for family or home use. They have low to medium protein content, weak to medium protein or gluten quality, uniform specific volume (cup weight measurement), this practice size is important having low to moderate enzymatic activity.

Cookie and cracker flours: Cookie and crackers flours *have* low protein content (soft wheat) minimum of starch damage, low alkaline water retention capacity, maximum cookie spread and low enzymatic *activity.*

Cake flour. Cake flour have low protein content (soft wheat), weak gluten quality, medium to large amount of starch damage (for soft wheat), high alkaline water retention (high range for soft wheat), medium to low enzyme activity and uniformly small particle size.

Leavening Agents

Leavening agent is a term used to indicate a source of gas which causes a dough or batter to spring giving a porous, open texture in the finished product. Different leaving agents used in baking are listed in Table-3.1.

TABLE 3.1

Baking Soda	$NaHCO_3$
Monocalcium phosphate (MCP)	Fast Acting
Sodium Acid pyrophosphate (SAPP)	Slow acting
Sodium Aluminium phosphate (SALP)	Slower Acting

Baking soda is used as a leavening agent in bakery premixes. Baking soda contains 52% by weight CO_2 gas which is released by the action of the acid. The commonly used acids differ in the manner in which they release CO_2 from baking soda. Some are moderately rapid and liberate considerable gas during mixing while others show little action during mixing. Certain acids provide a marked action in cold batters while others liberate very little gas until they obtain the heat of the oven. In most cases, it is the gas that is created during mixing of the batter and which is liberated during the mixing that produces the final leavened product.

Another form of chemical leavening is the natural breakdown of Baker's Ammonia (ammonium bicarbonate or ammonium carbonate) by the heat of the oven releasing carbon dioxide, ammonia and water as leavening gases without the formation of residual salts. Ammonium compounds are commonly used in combination with a leavening mixture of acid, salt and soda. The acid, salt and soda supply CO_2 at the lower temperature and the ammonium compounds aid in leavening at elevated temperatures during the later stages of baking.

Ammonium bicarbonate is used in cookies, crackers and similar products where the cellular structure is sufficiently porous to permit the slow escape of the gases formed. If this does not occur completely, the taste and odour of ammonia remains in the baked product. Ammonium bicarbonate performs an additional function in cookies, ammonia helps to increase the cookie spread by altering the protein structure. Strength of different leavening acids are given in Table-3.2.

TABLE 3.2: *Strength of Baking Acids*

Baking Acid	Neutralizing Value Acid strength lbs soda per 100 lbs acid	Comparative Rate of Reaction
Monocalcium Phosphate	80	Immediate
Anydrous Monocalcium Phosphate	83	Delayed
Sodium Acid Pyrophosphate	72-75	Slow
Sodium Aluminium Phosphate	100	Slow
Dicalcium Phosphate Dihydrate	33	Delayed
Sodium Aluminium Sulphate	100	Very slow
Glucono Delta Lactone	45	Delayed
Tartaric Acid	116	Very rapid
Cream of Tartar	45	Rapid
Fumaric Acid	145	Very rapid

Baking powder = Baking Soda + Acid + Starch Plus water and heat = CO_2 + salts

Baking powder has tenderizing and leavening action in bakery products. It controls cake volume, size of grain, smoothness of texture, finished product pH, colour-crust and crumb and *even* taste of the product. Quantity of baking powder used depends on the type of product, mixing and handling operations and character and amount of ingredients. Table-3.3 shows usage *levels* for leavening acid combination.

Table 3.3 : Usage Levels for leavening Acid Combinations

Application	Per cent Baking soda (Flour Basis)	Leavening Acid	Reasons
Cake Donuts	1.1-2.0	SAAP	Little action while mixing holding, extruding. Fast reaction in fryer.
Layer Cakes	1.7-2.3	MCP,SAPP, SALP	Nucleation. Late bake reserve. Al and Ca ions for batter viscosity and crumb resiliency.
Corn Bread and Muffins	1.5-2.0	MCP,Coated MCP,SALP	No advantage for extra delay poor gas retention.
Pancakes and Waffles	2.0-2.5	MCP,Coated MCP,SALP	Much nucleation needed. No reaction needed while holding, fast reaction on griddle.
Refrigerated Biscuits and Refrigerated Dough	2.0-2.3	MCP,Coated MCP,SALP	Little reaction during processing. Some reaction after canning. Most reaction in oven.
Biscuits	1.4-2.0	MCP,Coated MCP,SALP	Some delayed reaction. fast oven action (short bake).

Desired Leavening rates for baking

1. Some CO_2 (gas) released during preparation of the batter **"Nucleation Effect"**
2. Very little after mixing and before baking **"Bench Tolerance"**
3. Uniform release of gas during baking to hold the batter (product) until it is set.

a. Provides uniform crumb

b. Prevents shrinkage

c. Prevents products from falling (collapsing)

3. Shortening

Fats contribute to the tenderness, crispness, softness, volume and to all other aspects connected with the texture of cereal food.

Oxidative rancidity is still a major problem of premixes manufacturers. The widespread use of antioxidants or oxygen interceptors has resulted in a major improvement and has greatly broadened the scope of mix manufacturer in selection of shortenings. Antioxidants commonly used are citric acid, propylgallate, butylated hydroxy anisole, butylated hydroxy toluene.

Sometimes mixes contain natural antioxidants. Unbleached flours used in piecrust mix greatly extend the shelf life of the shortening used in the mix. Ginger and other spices used in spice cake mixes are powerful antioxidants and appreciably increase rancidity resistance. Sugar, acid phosphates, lecithin and several other ingredients used in mixes also possess antioxidant properties.

Creaming or emulsification properties of fats determine to a major degree their usefulness in cake mixes. Included in these properties is the ability of the fat to disperse air throughout an aqueous batter in a finely divided and stable state. The emulsion resulting when fats are mixed in aqueous batters will determine the final character of the baked product. Failure to achieve a uniformly fine emulsion when attempting to distribute the fats in aqueous batters will produce defective baked products of coarse grain, poor volume, poor symmetry and altogether improper palatability.

None of the fat however is sufficient in itself to produce the effect desired by the modern cake mix the industry now leans heavily upon several additives which are known commonly as emulsifying agents.

A good premix shortening should possess the following properties.

1. Quick and easy aeration when subjected to a minimum of mixing.
2. Dry, non-greasy body to prevent undue grease soakage and clumping of the mixture
3. The shortening should be bland in flavour and should remain bland after prolonged storage.
4. The final mix should withstand prolonged storage at temperature as high as 100°F without, serious impairment of volume texture or any other

measurable baking characteristics.

4. Sugars

Sugars are exceedingly important in pre mixes. The functions that sugars play in premixes ae :

1. It improves flavour.
2. Adds to richness
3. It imparts keeping quality
4. It acts as a tenderizing agent
5. It contributes to grain and texture
6. It affects colour of erust.

5. Emulsifiers

Other very important ingredients are emulsifiers like sodium stearoyl lactylate (SSL) and glycerol mono sterate (GMS) which are used in high performance products like bakery premixes.

Table 3.4. : Functions of SSL in Bakery

S.No.	Function	Results
1.	Dough conditioner and softner for bread	Products dough tolerant to production Variation
2.	Excellent flour strengthener	Enhances low gluten quality of Indian wheat
3.	Reduces fat in baking	By ensuring better dispension of fat in baked goods reduces quantity of fat while keeping bread fresh and soft
4.	Increases absorption and dispersion	Ensures more loaves of bread from each batch of water
5.	Improves texture of bread	By ensuring a finer and more uniform crumb structure
6.	Improves whiteness	
7.	Increases shelf life to baked goods	By extended reaction with starch where it stabilizes helical structure of starch
8.	Upto 10% more volume	

The SSL is a technologically advanced and superior emulsifier used by the baked goods industry worldwide. It serves as bread industry where wheat and flour have high Alpha amylase activity, leading to excessive crumb stickness and poor sliceablility, the addition of SSL is the permanent solution function of SSL and results thereof are listed in Table 3.4.

Another important emulsifier of economic use is Glycerol mono sterate (GMS). It contains-40-42% monoester and 50% total monoglycerides. Functions of GMS in bakery are listed in Table-3.5.

Other emulsifier which can be added in premixes are :

Polysorbate-60 (PS-60), glycerol lactyl palmitate (GLP), Propylene glycol monosterate (PGMS), Diacetyl tartaric ester of monoglyceride (DATEM), distilled glycerol monosterate (DGMS) and sorbitan monosterate (SMS).

For Bakery Pre-mixes, Actimix (Baking improver), (Name given by Ganpati Chemisys Ltd.) is a convenient, cost effective ready to use blend that includes all necessary ingredients except flour, yeast and water to produce all types of bakery goods.

Actimix consists of emulsifer, acidulants, special four oxidants, enzymes, salt, sugar and preventives.

Applications of Actimix are given in Table-3.6
Functions of Actimix are lixted in Table -3.7

6. Processing Aids

1. Anti caking agents : They are designed specifically as highly absorptive carriers of liquid ingredients. They are extremely fine inparticle size and hydroscopic in nature. They absorb high velvel of oils and fats found in many powdered ingredients and produce fine, free flowing powder. Because of uniform shape and size, they blend easily and disperse thoroughly. Some common anti caking agents are :

   - Sodium Aluminosilicate
   - Calcium Silicate
   - Tricalcium Silicate

   They are generally used in concentrations upto 2% maximum by weight.

2. Starches : They are used for thickening and water blinding. They produce moistening effect. They help to stabilize the batter system. 2% of a modified starch or galled wheat starch has effect on batter viscosity. It also improves volume.

3. **Gums** : They have similar effect on batter system as with starch. Some

Table 3.5 : Functions of GMS in Bakery

Applications	Functions
Bread and Rolls	• Acts as an anti-staling agent and crumb softener • Increase shelf life by forming complexes with starch
Cakes and Sponges	• Helps in even distribution of fat in the batter of cakes and sponges • Helps in retaining moisture • Reduces use of egg yolk, proving to be cost effective
Biscuits	• Improves the ability of the protein film to entrap air into the batter during creaming or mixing. Giving a porous texture to biscuits, improving palatibility and crispiness. • Facilitates uniform baking and eliminates the raw taste of flour • Allows the uniform dispersion of fat in the dough, preventing crackes or blister burning in biscuits. • Improves colour and appearance of biscuits. • Reduces fat and egg consumption, thereby improving shelf life and saving money. • Improves the release of dough from moulds and cutters to achieve well shaped biscuits.
Noodles	• Provides quick rehydration because of starch complexing • Aids processing and final cooking • Improves texture, creaminess and mouth feel • Reduces stickiness and imparts clean release from the extruder. • Improves shape formation and eating quality • Prevents formation of lumps in noodels, cereals etc.
Pasta Products	• Improves the texture of all pasta products and helps in reducing stickiness
Pudding	• Improves texture consistency

Table 3.6 : Use of Actimix in Baked goods

Standard Bread	Cream Crackers
Sandwich Bread	Wafers
Rusk	Custards
Rolls	Toppings
Hamburger Burns	Icings
Pao Buns	Kulchas
French Bread	Marie Biscuits
Croissants	Naans
Sponge Cakes	Pizza Bases
Danish Pastry	Bread Sticks

gums (Xanthan) provide mouthful or "slippery feed" to eating quality. they are generally used at the rate of 0.1 to 0.5 based on formula weight. Cellulose gums will absorb 40 times their weight in water. They also improve gelling properties during baking which adds strength.

4. **Dextrose**: It caramelizes at lower oven temperature and increases crust colour at 6 to 10% of formula weight or 20 to 25% of sucrose level.
5. **High Fructose Corn Syrups**: They replace body and increases viscosity of batter when fat is removed. They also improve crust colour.
6. **Eggs**: In liquid form they can improve whipping quality and air incorporation of batter. They have natural emulsifierlecithin. Liquid egg whites can provide good air entrapment and increase viscosity and volume.
7. **Dough Conditioners**

a) **Oxidizing Agents**: Azodicarbonamide (ADA), Potassium Bromate, Potassium iodate, Ascorbic acid, Calcium peroxide.

b) **Reducing Agents:** Fumaric acid, sodium bisulfite, Lcysteine, sorbic acid.

i) They weaken dough structure by breaking bands between proteins.

ii) Allows shorter mixing times.

iii) Improves machinability.

c) **Dough Strengtheners/Softners**: SSL, GMS, Mono and diglycerides.

a) They strengthen dough structure by bonding proteins together.

b) Improve dough handling.

c) Increases product volume.

d) Provides tighter grain.

d) Enzymes: Diastatic malt, protease, fungal amylase, bacterial amylase, enzyme active soya flour.

8. Crumb Softners

a) Improves crumb softness by bonding with starches, slowing starch retrogradation.

b) Improves moisture retention.

MAINTENANCE OF PROPER DRY MIX ABSORPTION

1. Reduce total formula fat amount.
2. Use formula fat in beaded or spray dried form.
3. Reduce the amount of coarse ingredients.
4. Reduce fat blending time.
5. Cool dry material before fat incorporation.
6. Reduce fat temperature before adding to dry batch.

FORMATION OF MIXES

Many methods of calculations are used in product development and small batch scale-up. The particular method used will depend somewhat on which segment of the food industry the development is for. For many years bakers have used a system known as "bakers percentage" using flour as a basis by which all others ingredients are calculated. The most widely used system known as "dry ingredient percentage" uses a 100% dry materials system which excludes any moisture from the formula and calculates all ingredients on a dry basis. Many other areas of food product development calculate all ingredients in the formula including water on a 100% basis.

TOTAL DRY INGREDIENT PER CENT

The method of formula development for dry mix products involves totalling all dry ingredients in a standard scratch (wet) recipe (Table-3.8). Percentage of solids for ingredients such as liquid milk and eggs are determined, then added to other dry ingredients in the formula. The total of these dry ingredients

TABLE 3.7: *Functions and Advantages of using Actimix in Bakery Products*

Functions	Results
• Reduction in the use of Fat	Excellent high quality bread can be made using as little as 0.25% fat
• Eliminates the need of Calcium propionate or other preservatives	Cost efficient
• No need to add more emulsifiers	Cost efficient
• Extended shelf life	Cost efficient
• Upto 10% greater volume	Cost efficient
• Greater whiteness without using milk powder	Cost efficient
• Higher yield from yeast	Cost efficient
• No need to add any other ingredients before baking	Improves and standardizes quality
• Better shape	Improves and standardizes quality
• Improved texture and better crust and crumb formation	Improves and standardizes quality
• Better slicing ability	Improves and standadizes quality
• Better fat and water dispersion and retention	Upto 5-7 loaves extra per 90 kg batch

are then divided into the liquid portion of the formula. The result will be dry ingredients totaling 100% and moisture (divided by total dry ingredients) determined as a percentage of these ingredients.

The advantage of using this type of calculation is that regardless of batch size, the total amount of dry ingredients can be multiplied by the per cent water (absorption) to obtain correct amount of water to be used. Since water is generally the only ingredient added, the amount is easy to determine.

TABLE 3.8: ***Conversion of a Scratch Recipe to Pre-mix for Muffin***

Ingredient	Wt of Scratch Ingredi-ents (lb)	Conver-sion to Dry-Form (lb)	Water Remai-ning (lb)	Dry Ingre-dients %	Grams
Sugar	3.25	3.25	None	24.35	243.7
Shortening	2.00	2.00	None	15.00	150.0
Liquid Whole Egg	1.50	0.375'	1.125	2.80	28.1
Salt	0.0625	0.0625	None	0.50	4.7
Liquid Whole Milk	4.00	0.40"	3.60	3.00	30.0
Cake Flour	7.00	7.00	None	52.50	524.8
Baking Powder	0.25	0.25	None	1.85	18.7
Total	18.06	13.34	4.72	100.00	1000

Per cent water required for 100 lbs dry mix: 4.72/13.34 = 35.5%. 'Whole egg solids. "Butter milk solids.

BAKER'S PER CENT

This method of calculation considers flour to be the basis for all formulae (Table-3.9). Any increase in tenderizing ingredients (shortening, sugar etc.) or toughening ingredients (flour, eggs etc.) will have a direct effect on the formula.

TABLE 3.9: ***Calculation of Bakers Per cent***

Ingredient	Weight (lb)	100%	Bakers 100%
Sugar	3.25	18.00	46.43
Shortening	2.00	11.07	28.57
Liquid egg	1.50	8.30	21.43
Salt	0.0625	0.35	0.89
Liquid milk	4.00	22.14	57.14
Cake flour	7.00	38.76	100.00
Baking Powder	0.25	1.38	3.57
Total	18.06	100.00	

Using bakers percentage is more difficult when attempting to develop ingredient quantities based on a specified batch size.

The simplest and oldest formulation is that of the self rising flour. Self rising flour is the grandfather of all pre-mixes. The formula is so common that it is essentially fixed in the Food and Drug Administrations Definitions and Standards or identify for cereal flours and related products.

Self raising flour is a mixture of flour, sodium bicarbonate and the acid reacting substance mono calcium phosphate or sodium acid pyrophosphate or both (Table 10). It is seasoned with salt. Nor less than 0.5% of CO_2 is evolved from this mixture. the acid reacting substance is added in sufficient quantity to neutralize the sodium bicarbonate. The combined weight of such acid reacting substances and sodium bicarbonate is not more than 4.5 parts to each 100 parts of flour used.

Table 3.10 : Formula of self Rising Flour

Ingredients	Percentage
Flour	95.00
Sodium bicarbonate	1.32
Anhydrous calcium phosphate	1.64
Salts	2.04
Total	100.00

The flour used is the one suitable for biscuits and quick breads.

BISCUIT MIX

This mix includes three ingredients which were not found in self rising four, namely shortening, milk and sugar (Table-3.11)

Table 3.11 : Biscuit Mix

Ingredients	Percentage
Flour	80.04
Shortening	12.67
Sugar	0.81
Salt	1.81
Anhydrous calcium phosphate	1.60
Soda	1.27
Nonfat milk solids	0.80
Total	100.00

The non fat dry milk, shortening and sugar are the ingredients responsible for richness and may be increased to change this characteristic.

PANCAKE MIX

Pancake mix (Table-3.12) is .very widely used in the home and in institutions. In this farina middlings are incorporated to make the braked pancake more tender. The sodium acid pyrophosphate is used to slow down the rate of which the CO_2 is liberated. This is desirable for the pancake mix used in institutions where one mixing of pancake better is made during the day and the cakes are continuously baked thereform.

Table 3.12 : Pancake Mix

Ingredients	Percentage
Flour	80.85
Dextrose	4.85
Salt	1.00
Non Fat Milk Solids	4.09
Shortening	3.24
Soda	1.22
Sodium Acid Pyrophosphate	1.01
Anhydrous Monocalcium Phosphate	0.50
Recleaned Fine Middlings (Farina)	3.24
Total	100.00

Before moving ahead, the difference between a mix and base should be clarified. When referring to a yeast raised mix, the product will necessitate the addition of yeast and water to the bag contents in order to produce a finished product which a cake doughnut mix, the product calls for the addition of water only to the bag contents in order to produce a finished product A yeast raised doughnut base is concerned with the addition of flour in varying levels to the bag contents in addition to yeast and water. In relation to cake doughnut bases, it necessitates the addition of sugar to the bag contents in addition to water. Whether the product be cake doughnuts or yeast raised doughnuts, bases are handled in the same manner as a mix, except it is advisable to premix the base and flour together prior to the addition of water and yeast or in the case of cake doughnuts, water.

A mix manufacturer formulates the base by withdrawing one ingredient, all or in part. This ingredient is then added by the baker in the mixing stage.

A concentrate on the other hand is of a paste or shortening type consistency, a material usually packaged in plastic containers or boxes with plastic inserts. One adds flour, yeast and water to the concentrate and in some instances sugar is added. This is due to the high percentage of shortening in a three to one ratio and it makes it practically impossible to keep the material in a flour like form. The concentrates go as far as 8, 9 or 10 to one ratio in some instances. There is also a concentrate that is dry. However in this case, the shortening as well as a large portion of the flour is removed from the mix, resulting in this type of base. The concentrate calls for the addition of flour, shortening, yeast and water and on some occasions, other ingredients. This is however not advisable due to the cake doughnuts strong dependency on a properly blended flour.

USE OF WHEY PROTEIN CONCENTRATE (WPC) IN PREMIXES

Another important development is the development of cake premix using whey protein concentrate as egg substitute. Whey protein concentrate is a bland, odourless, free flowing white/creamish powder available in 15 kg packing.

Three types of WPCs *viz.* WPC 35, WPC 50 and WPC 60 having protein contents of 36.80,51.60 and 62.50% respectively were obtained by ultra filtration technique. Cakes were prepared with WPCs as egg substitutes and the physical and sensory attributes were studied. Highest porosity and specific volume (2.75 cc/g) were observed in cakes containing WPC 60 cake containing WPC 50 had almost similar porosity and specific volume (2.50 cc/g) as that of control cake containing egg whereas WPC 35 cake was found to be inferior when compared with control cake. Incorporation of WPC 60 in lieu of egg in cake formulation produced cake with excellent physical and sensory characteristics.

Recommended Formulations for the production of WPC 60 dry cake mix is

WPC 60	12%
Fat	20-30%
Refined wheat flour	32%
Sugar	32%
Baking powder	2.90%
Flavour	0.80%

Advantage of using WPCs

1. High whipping abilities.
2. Good gelation properties.
3. High protein values.
4. Provides stability to all bakery products.
5. 100% vegetarian.

Similarly whey powder is used as a partial to complete replacer of skimmed milk powder (SMP) in various food systems including bakery pre - mixes for biscuits, breads, confectionery, instant foods, chocolate fillings, soups etc.

Whey powder is 100% milk solids, non-hygroscopic, free flowing powder and is manufactured from fresh milk whey.

For biscuit manufacturing, the product has 'Special applications in various varieties of biscuits and ensures distinctly better quality and taste profile along with reduced costs.

Salient Features/Benefits

1. Improved browning-golden colour.
2. Improved crispness and bite.
3. Better crust promotion.
4. Better development of aroma and taste.
5. Reduced cost.

Extent of replacement of SMP-WMP with whey powder

Salty biscuit	100%
Sweet biscuit	50-100%
Cream Biscuit	50%
Bakery	25-50%
Confectionery	25-50%

EFFICIENT AND ECONOMIC BAKERY MIX PREPARATION

The great variety of bakery mixes available on the market today, such as cake, doughnut and cookie, all require the same basic method of preparation: precise mixing of several dry ingredients followed by the incorporation and dispersion of either a solid (plastic) or liquid shortening into the dry powders.

The bakery industry, however, has been struggling along with an inefficient multi-step process to effectively combine these materials (Fig.1). This usually consists of 1-2 ribbon type blenders to mix the dry powders, each mix requiring at least 10 min. to achieve an acceptable uniformity. Following the dry blending an additional ribbon blender is used to incorporate the shortening, usually requiring an additional 2030 minute mix cycle. However, since the ribbon blenders are low intensity, low shear devices, the end product usually contains undesirable agglomerates of sugar and dry additives and also lumps of undispersed shortening. If it is necessary to remove the agglomerates completely, the bakery mix must be passed through a high intensity, high shear device known as a finisher. Removal of agglomerates or pinheads is usually necessary from the standpoints of uniformity, reproducibility and a more desirable consumer product.

The second process technology and mixer design presents a totally new concept of bakery mix preparation that has been proven to be superior to existing ribbon blender process (Fig.2). The unique action developed by the intermediate intensity mixer assures a rapid and complete mix dispersion of powders and shortening in minimal cycle times. This action is developed by the turning of plow-shaped mixing tools at a speed sufficient to cause the materials of mix to become a pulsating, "mechanically fluidized" bed. The basic plow mix action is supplemented by high speed, high shear, chopping devices that are mounted between adjacent plows and act as a finisher does to deagglomerate powders and disperse shortening. Since the chopping devices can be operated independently of the plows, there is little chance of overworking (greasing) the mix.

Since certain products may require some heating or cooling, the mixing drum can be equipped with a high efficiency heat transfer jacket.

The mechanically fluidized bed of particles is the basis of the mixing efficiency and accuracy on a full range of materials including combinations with diverse specific gravity as well as problems associated with liquid incorporation and heat transfer.

STATUS IN INDIA

A company by the name of Burns Philip India Ltd. (formerly the Indian Yeast Co. Ltd.) situated in Chennai manufactures bakery premixes which are widely popular. These are:

- Bread premixes
- Dough conditioners
- Cheese emulsifiers
- Leaveners

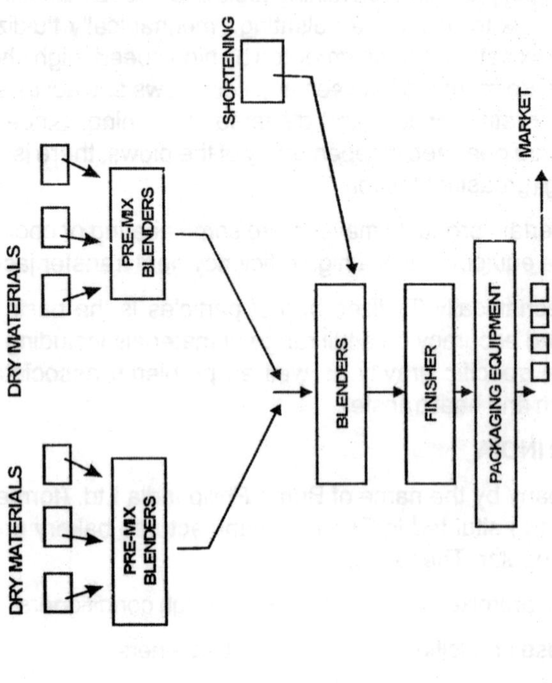

Fig. 3.1 Rubber Blender Process

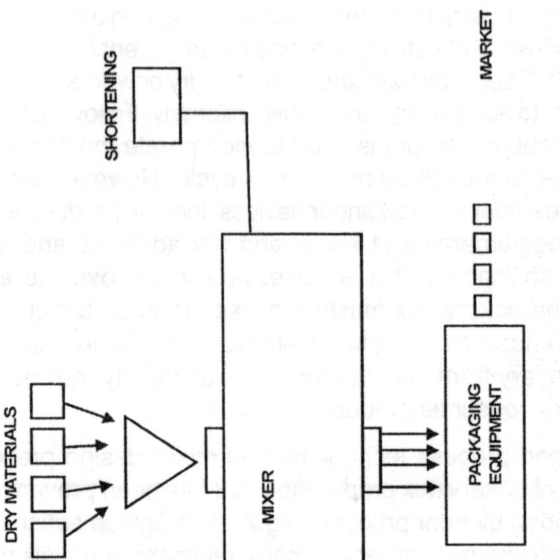

Fig. 3.2 Intensity Mixer Process

- Cheese cake mixes
- Cake mixes
- Cookie mixes
- Croissant mixes
- Doughnut mixes
- Fondants
- Muffin mixes
- Pan release agents
- Pastry glazes
- Sponge mixes

Burn Philp cake mix by the name of Tower *Hilite cake* mix is available in dry powder form and requires the addition of 250g eggs and 300 ml water to 1 Kg of pre mix and baking at 160-180°C for 25 to 30 min.

Tower Egg Free Cake Mix is also available which requires only 320 ml water for 1 Kg mix and baking at the same temperature.

Tower Yeast is also available both as compressed yeast and active dry yeast. They are used at different levels in sponge and dough method- straight dough method and sweet dough method. Dry yeast requires rehydration before mixing with the flour.

Tower GMS is an emulsifier used for making bread and biscuits and is available as powder and flakes. It is added at the rate of 3 g per 1 Kg of flour.

Tower Calcium Propionate is available as powder and in granular form. It retards the growth of moulds and rope in breads. It is added at the rate of 10 gms for 1 kg of flour.

Tower Cake Gel is specially designed for producing superior quality cakes with increased volumes and finer crumb structure. It is used at the rate of 80 g per 1 Kg flour.

Mahaan Proteins Ltd. is a specialty products division situated in New Delhi and manufactures whey powder, a value addition to biscuits, breading confectionery and other dry mixes. It also produces whey protein concentrate which are added in egg less cake and pastries as egg replacers.

Ganapati Chemisys Ltd. situated in Faridabad manufactures emulsifiers for use in bakery products. A special product named Actimix (baking improver) is meant for addition to bakery pre mixes alone. It is a convenient, cost effective, ready to use blend that includes all necessary ingredients except flour, yeast and water to produce all types of baked goods.

Marvel Foods is a Mumbai based company which manufactures additives and improvers, bread improver and puff pastry improver.

Elpe Labs situated in Bangalore manufactures Vit. Premixes for energy food, protein food, weaning and convenience foods.

Fine Organics another Mumbai based company manufactures various food additives like emulsifiers, preservatives, cake gels, bread improvers, ready to use pan greasing emulsions and whipped topping concentrates for softies, cake and pastry fillings, deserts etc.

Pilsbury have introduced eggless cake mix to be prepared in cooker.

Bakels India have introduced egg free cake concentrate to which we have to add flour, sugar, water and bake delicious egg free cakes, which is 100% vegetarian. They have other products like bread improvers monofresh lecimax 1000, universal 500, Dobrim 50, Flour pastes, icing, filling hopping and gels.

Midas Foods India Pvt. Ltd. are preparing dessert mixes, cake, brownies and bread premixes having high quality standards, cost effectively and easy to handle and prepare.

Bakery premixes assume significance when a baker looks at it in the context of turning over high quality fresh and ready to consume products in a short time. Even an ordinary restaurant can invest in an oven and use bakery premixes or frozen batter and dough to produce conistently high quality cakes, muffins, croissants or cookies and add variety to the existing menu. The opportunities are immense. However, we still need to develop the right infrastructure to unleash the potential. Consistency in raw material, development of cold chain stores and product distribution, simplification and updating our food laws will be vital to success. It is hoped that we will be able to pull together as an industry and add value via convenience and quality in the Indian bakery market.

4

Chapatis and Cookies made from Wheat Flour

Wheat has been recognized as the most important crop in the world to sustain self sufficiency in food grains. It is used as staple food in most parts of the world due to its unique bread making quality. Wheat is the second most important cereal crop in India after rice and is being cultivated in an area of 23.50 million hectares with an annual production of 65.20 million tonnes. In India, nearly 90% area is under bread wheat (*T. aestivum*), 9% under macaroni wheat (*T. durum*) which has high commercial value. Wheat is utilized in different forms for preparation of various products like dalia, uppuma, dosa, noodels, macaroni, puri, chapati, biscuits and cookies etc. Extensive work has been carried out on milling and baking quality of different cultivars, but little information is available on the biochemical composition of germinated wheat and the impact of germination on cooking quality of common cultivars. As staple food in India continues to be based on cereals with some portion of legumes and oilseeds, there is a desperate need to enhance the nutrive value of the commonly available food grains to combat malnutrition among children as well as adults. The partial germination of cereals and legumes to enhance their nutritive value has been attempted by many workers. Sharma *et. al.* have reported improvement in milling and baking properties of wheat upon germination Sekhon et. al. have studied the bread, cookie and chapati making characteristics of tritcale. Changes in the functional characteristics of wheat during soaking and subsequent germination were reported by Leelavatti *et. al.* The present study was undertaken to evaluate the chapati and cookie making quality of germinated wheat flour in various combinations with underminated wheat flour with an objective to improve the nutritive and keeping quality of chapatis and cookies.

MATERIALS AND METHODS

The seeds of wheat (T. Aestivum L. Var 'HD3229') were procured from the Department of Plant Breeding, PAU, Ludhiana. Whole wheat meal prepared from both sound and germinated (24 hrs.) wheat grains were blended in the ratio of 0:100, 10:90, 20:80, 30:70 and 100.0 (germinated:sound called 1, 10, 20, 30 and 100 blends.

PREPARATION OF CHAPATI

100 gm meal sample (whole meal/lend was taken and predeterminated amount of water was added to obtain optimal consistency. The contents were mixed in Swanson type mixer and the dough was allowed to rest for 90 minutes after covering with a wet muslin cloth. The dough was moulded and shaped to chapati of 15 cm diameter and baked on hot iron plate on gs stove. Chapati was baked for one minute on each side and puffed for 24 seconds. Chapatis were staked in a pile wrapped in cotton cloth and stored in airtight containers. Physical characteristics were evaluated based on the scoring system as shown in Table -4.1.

Table -4.1: Evaluation of Chapatti making characteristics

Characteristics	Score grade	Score
Dough handling	Non sticky Almost Non sticky Sticky Very sticky	5 4 3 1
Colour of chapatti	Cremish and attractive Slightly creamish Whitish Dark reddish/Black Non-attractive	5 4 3 2 1
Puffing	Full Almost full Partial Slight Nil	5 4 3 2 1
Flavour	Pleasing Good Mild Bland Non-pleasing	5 4 3 2 1

Contd. Table -4.1: Evaluation of Chapatti making characteristics

Characteristics	Score grade	Score
Texture	Very soft and pliable Soft and Pliable Medium soft Leathery Hard	5 4 3 2 1
Taste	Very sweet Sweet Medium sweet Less sweet Non-sweet	5 4 3 2 1
Texture after 2 hrs.	Very soft Soft Medium soft Leathery Hard	5 4 3 2 1

32-35 : Excellent/very good: 28-31: Good 25-27: Fair; 22-24: Poor, 21 or less: Very poor.

Table 4.2 : Effect of Blending Ratios of ungerminated : Germinated (U-G) Wheat Flour on Weight Loss of Chapati during baking

U:G Ratio	Water Absorbed (%)	Water Loss % During		Weight of Chapati (gm)	Weight of Chapati after storage (gm)
		Baking	Storage		
100:0	60	10.30±0.1	5.60±0.1	44.70±0.1	41.90±0.2
90 : 10	64	9.59±0.2	4.14±0.2	45.22±0.2	43.15±0.1
80 : 20	65	10.90±0.1	1.90±0.1	44.55±0.1	43.60±0.0
70:30	66	11.80±0.1	1.70±0.1	44.10±0.1	43.25±0.1
0 : 100	70	12.90±0.2	4.50±0.3	43.55±0.2	41.30±0.1

Table 4.3 : Effect of Blending Ratios of Ungerminated : Germinated (U:G) wheat Flour on organoleptic Evaluation

U : G Ratio	Dough Handling	Colour	Puffing	Flavour	Taste	Texture	Texture at 2 h	Score (35)	Score (100)
100 : 0	4	5	5	4	3	4	4	29	82.8
90 : 10	5	5	5	4	5	4	4	32	91.4
80 : 20	3	4	5	4	4	4	4	28	80.0
70 : 30	4	4	5	3	3	4	4	27	77.0
0 : 100	5	4	5	3	3	4	4	28	80.0

Table 4.4 : Effect of Blending Ratios of Ungerminated : Germinated (U:G) Wheat Flour on Physical Quality of Cookies

U:G Ratio	Width (cm)	Thickness (cm)	Spread Factor (W/T)
100 : 0	5.42±0.2	1.15±0.05	4.71±0.22
90:10	5.53±0.09	1.12±0.02	4.95±0.01
80:20	5.83±0.17	1.14±0.03	4.13±0.26
70:30	5.68±0.04	1.15±0.03	4.94±0.10
0:100	6.25±0.16	1.01±0.01	6.19±0.21

Preparation of Cookies

The following ingredients were used :

Flour	:	225 g
Sugar	:	130 g
Shortening	:	64 g
Salt	:	2.1 g
Sodium bicarbonate	:	2.5 g
Water	:	16 ml
Dextrose (59.3%)	:	33 ml

Sugar, shortening, salt and sodium bicarboante were mixed at low speed for 3 minutes, scraping down after ech minute. Water and dextrose solution were added and mixed for 1 minute at low speed, scrapping down after every 30 seconds. Whole meal/blend was added and mixed for 2 minutes at low speed, scrapping down after every 30 seconds. The dough was rolled after placing on cookies sheet. Cookies were cut suing a dye and baked at once (after removing scrap) at 240°F for 10 minutes in rotating hearth furnace. Physical and sensory characteristics as well as organoleptic quality of cookies were evaluated by a constant panel of eight judges. The parameters studied were spread factor (width:thickness ratio), crust colour surface texture, crumb colour and crispness.

RESULTS AND DISCUSSION

The physical evaluation on chapatis indicated that weight loss as well as water loss was minimum (9.56%) in 100% blends in case of fresh chapatis while it was minimum (1.70%) in 30% blends after 2 hrs of baking (Table - 4.2). Dough handling scored the highest in 10% and 100% blends. There

Table 4.5 : Effect of Blending Ratios of Ungerminated : Germinated (U:G) wheat Flour on organoleptic Evaluation

U : G Ratio	Crust Colour (10)	Surface Smoothness (10)	Crumb Colour (10)	Crispness (25)	Taste (25)	Overall Quality (80)
100 : 0	6.26±0.1	6.96±0.2	7.13±0.1	20.6±0.2	23.1±0.2	64.05
90 : 10	7.86±0.1	7.73±0.2	7.40±0.2	21.7±0.3	22.3±0.1	67.03
80 : 20	8.03±0.3	7.76±0.2	7.56±0.1	21.8±0.1	22.3±0.1	67.53
70 : 30	8.00±0.0	7.94±0.1	7.57±0.2	21.7±0.1	21.4±0.2	66.60
0 : 100	9.40±0.1	8.93±0.1	8.50±0.1	23.3±0.2	23.1±0.2	71.40

was no significant difference in colour of chapati among various blends. Puffing was full in all the blends. Flavour was reported best in 10% and 20% blends while 30% and 100% blends imparts slight malty flavour due to increased proportion of germinated meal. Texture was found to be soft in all the treatments. Taste was best in 10% blend. Organoleptic evaluation concluded that 10% blend was the best for overall quality of chapatis. Based on physical characteristcs, 10% blend is the best if chapatis have to be consumed fresh while 30% blend is the best if they are consumed after 2 hrs. of cooking. Our results are in good agreement with some earlier studies. It has been reported that upto 20% blending ratios of wheat germinated for 48 hrs. produced puffed chapatis of good organoleptic quality. Leelavatti noted that the bread prepared from ungerminated wheat was comparable to that prepared from ungerminated wheat flour. Our results provide the Indian public with immense opportunity to increase the blending ratio upto 30% without deterioration of taste and texture as with the number of working couples on the rise chapatis prepared by servants/cooks are consumed usually after 2-3 hrs. of preparation. Further studies may be carried out to sort out blends between 10% to 30% which satisfy the quality criteria both for fresh and after 2-4 hrs of cooking.

The physical quality of cookies prepared from germinated what at different blending levels indicated that spread factor gradually increased from 4.17 to 6.19 (Table 4.3) with increase in the proportion of germinated wheat from 0 to 100% except at 30% where it showed a slight decrease. The crust colour of 100% blend scored high because of desirable light brown colour as compared to whitish colour of 0% blend. Surface texture and crumb colour also improved with increase in the proportion of germinated wheat meal. However, the teaste of cookies scored highest in case of 0% blend, i.e. ungerminated wheat meal. Based upon overall quality, the cookies prepared from 100% blend, i.e. fully germinated wheat meal scored the highest (Table 4.4). Leelavatti have also reported that germination of wheat for 72 hrs increased the spread and rise factor while improving the flavour and taste of biscuits.

A deep study have indicated (data not given) that the protein and sugar content of wheat increased accompanied with a decrease in starch and free fatty acids content upon germination. This nutritionally improved what can be blended with normal, ungerminated wheat grains to produce food products with improved physical and organoleptic quality. The present studies clearly indicate that germination caused favourable changes in the important characteristics of chapatis and cookies. Based upon our results, 10% and 30% blends for chapatis (for consuming fresh and after 2 hrs respectively) and 100% blend (fully germinated) for cookies are recommended for use.

5

Characteristics of Soybean and its utilization of preparation of bread and biscuits

INTRODUCTION

An amazing diversity in utilization alternatives has earned soybean the title of 'wonder bean' in terms of protein enrichment. Soybean plays a vital role in improving the nutritional quality of the supplemented food products. Considering that protein deficiency is a major dietary problem facing the world today, particularly the underdeveloped and developing countries, there has been a rapidly growing awareness for exploiting high quality, low cost plant proteins (FAO, 1977). Nutritionally soybean protein is an excellent complement to lysine limited cereal protein, hence the basis for the use of soy flour as an economical protein supplement in bread, biscuit and other cereal products. Another bakery related potential use of full fat and defatted soybean flour in combination with cereals is in the production of composite flour. The presence of anti-nutritional factors results in certain physiological disorders but their reduction by mild heat treatment and addition of the treated soybean flour to wheat flour would definitely make soybean a more valuable and acceptable source of plant protein for supplementation. In addition to protein, soybean is good source of fibre and other nutrients. An important application of full fat as well as defatted soy flour in combination with cereals is in production of nutritionally balanced all purpose food blends distributed to the undernourished population or in case of food shortage emergencies (WHO, 1975).

Thus the present study was undertaken to use soybean as high fibre and protein source for incorporation in leavened breads and biscuits.

MATERIAL AND METHODS

The varieties PK-416 and PK-472 were heat treated by soaking in boiling water for 3 min and defatting for oil extraction was done by electrically operated oil mill. The sample of both soybean varieties were used in following combinations:

- Raw
- Heat treated fat
- Untreated defatted
- Heat treated defatted

The preapred samples were stored in airtight containers for further analysis and utilization in preparation of bread and biscuits.

Chemical analysis

Moisture, ash, protein, fat and total dietary fibres were estimated according to the methods described in AOAC (1990). The standard methods as reported in AACC (1976) were used for the determination of free fatty acids, lipase, sugars, alcoholic acidity, starch, pigments, pH, gluten. The methods reported in NIN (1983) were used for determination of crude fiber and carbohydrates. The method of Lie (1973) was used for estimation of free amino acids. The samples for minerals were digested according to method given by Piper (1966) and then minerals were analysed by Atomic Absorption Spectrophotometer. The colorimetric method was used for determining

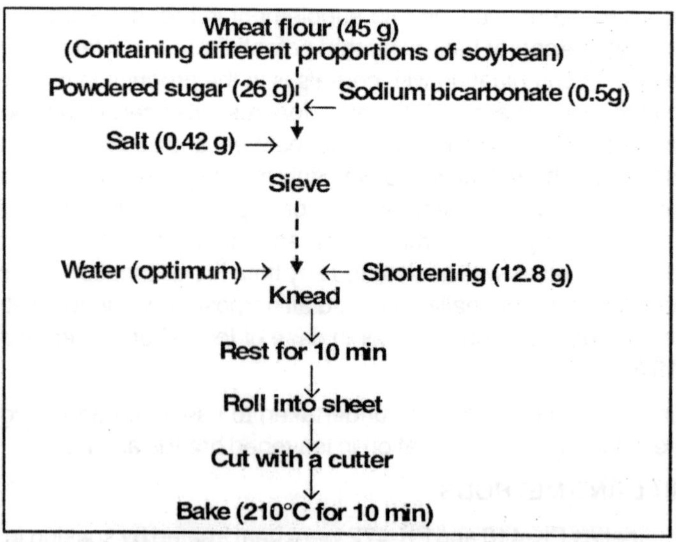

Figure 5.1 : Flow Chart of Steps followed in Preparation of Biscuits (For a set of three biscuits)

Wheat flour (100 g)
(Containing different proportions of soybean)
Sugar (2.5 g) $\rightarrow$ | $\leftarrow$ Salt (1.0 g)
$\downarrow$
Sieve
Shortening (1.0 g) $\rightarrow$ | $\leftarrow$ Yeast (3.0 g)
Water (Optimum) $\rightarrow$ $\downarrow$
Knead
$\downarrow$
Ferment (2 hr 30 min)
$\downarrow$
Remix (25 sec)
$\downarrow$
Recover (25 min)
$\downarrow$
Sheet
$\downarrow$
Mould
$\downarrow$
Proof (55 min.)
$\downarrow$
Bake (230°C for 25 min)

Figure 5.2 : Flow Chart of steps followed in preparation of Bread (For a Loaf)

phosphorus content in the digested samples. Diastase activity was measured according to method of Blish and Sandstedt as given in AACC. Protease activity was determined using Arye and Anderson method as described in AACC.

Product Development and Evaluation

The composite flours contained different levels (0, 5, 10, 15, 20, 25, 30, 35 and 40%) of soybean and were obtained by mixing wheat flour and soybean flour. Before adding soybean, it was finely ground to obtain uniform size particles. The methods used for preparation of bread and biscuits from composite flours were standardized in the laboratory and standardized methods were used for preparation of bread and biscuits. The steps followed in preparation of bread and biscuits are mentioned in Figures 5.1 and 5.2. The products viz. bread and biscuits prepared from different blends of wheat flour and soybean were evaluated for functional, physical and consumer's acceptance.

Table 5.1. Chemical Characteristics of wheat flour used in the Preparation of Bread and Biscuits

Parameters	Values
Protein (%) N x 6.25	10.94
Fat (%)	0.90
Ash (%)	0.65
Crude Fibre (%)	0.45
Dietary Fibre (%)	0.15
Total carbohydrates (%)	73.06
Gluten (% Dry wt. Basis)	7.50
Starch (%)	54.00
Reducing Sugars (% as Glucose)	0.50
Non-reducing Sugars (% as Sucrose)	0.70
Total Sugars (% as Glucose)	1.50
Free Fatty Acids (% as Oliec Acid)	0.038
Free Amino Acids (% as Glycerine)	0.096
pH	6.40
Alcoholic Acidity (% as H_2SO_4)	0.29
Pigment (ppm ß Carotene)	0.25
Calcium (mg/100 g)	20.00
Phosphorous (mg/100 g)	75.00
Iron (mg/100 g)	5.90
Sodium (mg/100 g)	150.00
Magnesium (mg/100 g)	80.00
Manganese (mg/100 g)	2.90

RESULTS AND DISCUSSION

Chemical Characteristics of Wheat Flour and Soybean Flour

The wheat flour used in the preparation of bread and biscuits contained protein (10.94), gluten (7.50), fat (0.9), ash (0.65), crude fiber (0.42) and dietary fiber (0.15) per cent respectively. The reducing, non-reducing and total sugars of the wheat flour used in the study were 0.50% as glucose, 0.70% as sucrose and 1.50% as glucose respectively. The free fatty acid content of wheat flour was 0.038% as oleic acid. The calcium, iron, phosphorus, sodium, magnesium and maganese content of wheat flour were 20.0, 5.9, 75.0, 150.0, 80.0 and 2.90 mg/100 gm of wheat flour respectively (Table 5.1).

Table 5.2. Chemical Characteristics of Soybean used in the Preparation of Bread and Biscuits

Parameters	PK-416	PK-472	Heat treated	Full	Defatted	C.D.
Protein (%) N x 6.25	40.56	41.87	40.48	40.70	41.73	0.02
Fat (%)	12.95	14.00	13.05	21.68	5.31	0.01
Ash (%)	11.25	11.34	11.37	11.51	11.09	0.04
Crude Fibre(%)	4.33	4.16	4.40	3.70	4.78	2.01
Dietary Fibre (%)	1.41	1.45	1.46	1.30	1.56	0.01
Total Carbohydrates (%)	16.88	14.63	16.70	8.41	23.09	0.37
Reducing Sugar (% as Glucose)	1.53	1.62	1.57	1.56	1.59	0.01
Non-reducing sugars (% as sucrose)	0.50	0.28	0.38	0.38	0.40	NS
Total Sugars (% as Glucose)	2.24	2.18	2.17	2.15	2.20	0.002
Free fatty Acids (% as Oliec Acid)	0.188	0.113	0.148	0.211	0.09	0.002
Free Amino Acids (% as Glycerine)	0.186	0.146	0.160	0.160	0.169	0.001
pH	6.48	6.58	6.53	6.65	6.39	0.04
Alcoholic Acidity (% as H_2SO_4)	0.38	0.51	0.43	0.43	0.46	NS
Pigment (ppm ß Carotene)	2.28	3.16	2.71	2.72	2.72	NS
1000 Kernel Weight	122.5	117.5	122.50	-	-	-
Calcium (mg/100g)	82.75	81.63	84.37	81.54	82.83	0.12
Phosphorous (mg/100 g)	540.0	567.75	559.0	549.0	558.75	3.08
Iron (mg/100 g)	15.61	11.13	13.79	13.01	13.73	0.02
Sodium (mg/100 g)	104.75	90.19	89.69	95.00	99.94	0.069
Magnesium (mg/100g)	330.75	323.25	294.0	318.25	335.75	4.33
Maganese (mg/100 g)	2.68	2.30	2.50	2.43	2.25	0.10

Table : 5.3. : Water Absorption (%) and Dough Handling Properties of Composite Flours (Wheat Flour : soybean)

Parameter/ Treatment	Blends (Wheat flour : soybean)									
	100:0	95:5	91:10	85:15	80:20	75:25	70:30	65:35	60:40	Mean
Water Absorption %										
PK-416	43.55	57.11	56.10	56.10	55.44	55.66	55.58	55.08	54.92	54.37
PK-472	43.55	57.56	57.39	57.94	55.22	56.77	56.16	55.88	55.76	55.10
Heat treated	43.55	58.05	57.22	57.05	56.37	56.55	56.33	56.13	56.08	55.26
Full Fat	43.55	56.99	56.55	56.27	55.60	55.61	55.33	54.99	54.94	54.75
Defatted	43.55	57.77	56.94	56.57	56.44	56.44	56.22	55.96	55.74	55.09
Water Absorption %										
PK-416	NS	NS	SS	SS	SS	SS	S	S	S	-
PK-472	NS	NS	SS	SS	SS	SS	SS	S	S	-
Heat treated	NS	NS	NS	NS	SS	SS	SS	S	S	-
Full Fat	NS	NS	NS	NS	SS	SS	SS	S	S	-
Defatted	NS	NS	NS	NS	SS	SS	S	S	S	-

CD ($p< 0.05$)	Varieties	Heat Treatment	Defatting	Blends
Water absorption	0.55	0.55	0.55	1.17

NS : non-sticky, SS : Slightly Sticky, S: Sticky

Table 5.4 : Bakery making Characteristics of Composite Flours (wheat flour : soybean)

Parameter/ Treatment	Blends (wheat flour : soybean)					
	100:0	95:5	90:10	85:15	80:20	Mean
Loaf weight (g)						
PK-416	150.0	112.0	116.6	122.9	127.8	125.0
PK-472	150.0	113.2	118.6	122.5	126.3	126.1
Heat treated	150.0	111.5	117.4	124.1	127.2	126.5
Full Fat	150.0	113.2	118.1	124.0	129.8	127.0
Defatted	150.0	112.0	117.1	121.4	124.2	124.9
CD (p<0.05)	Variety 0.18	Heat treated 0.18		Defatting 0.18	Blends 0.29	
Loaf volume (cc)						
PK-416	350.0	330.0	323.0	304.5	296.3	320.0
PK-472	350.0	320.7	308.8	298.8	291.3	313.9
Heat treated	350.0	323.8	321.8	313.3	307.5	323.2
Full Fat	350.0	325.0	315.0	296.3	288.8	323.0
Defatted	350.0	325.8	316.8	307.0	298.8	319.5
CD (p<0.05)	Variety 0.28	Heat treated 0.28		Defatting 0.28	Blends 0.45	
Loaf Colour /Loaf shape						
PK-416	LB/S	B/S	B/S	B/S	B/AS	-
PK-472	LB/S	B/S	B/S	B/S	B/AS	-
Heat treated	LB/S	LB/S	B/S	B/S	B/AS	-
Full Fat	LB/S	B/S	B/S	B/S	B/AS	-
Defatted	LB/S	LB/S	B/S	B/S	B/AS	-
Crumb Colour /Crumb texture						
PK-416	C/S	CW/S	CW/S	CW/S	SLCB/S	-
PK-472	C/S	CW/S	CW/S	CW/S	SLCB/S	-
Heat treated	C/S	CW/S	CW/S	SLCB/S	SLCB/S	-
Full Fat	C/S	CW/S	CW/S	SLCB/S	SLCB/S	-
Defatted	C/S	CW/S	CW/S	SLCB/S	SLCB/S	-
Grain of Bread						
PK-416	F	F	F	SC	SC	-
PK-472	F	F	F	F	SC	-
Heat treated	F	F	F	F	F	-
Full Fat	F	F	F	SC	SC	-
Defatted	F	F	F	F	SC	-
Crust Colour/Shredding						
PK-416	LB/N	LB/N	B/N	DB/N	DB/N	-
PK-472	LB/N	B/N	DB/N	DB/N	DB/N	-
Heat treated	LB/N	LB/N	B/N	DB/N	DB/N	-
Full Fat	LB/N	B/N	B/N	DB/N	DB/N	-
Defatted	LB/N	LB/N	B/N	DB/N	DB/N	-

Loaf colour : LB: light brown B: brown, Db : dark brown
Loaf shape : S : symmetical, AS : asymmetrical
Crumb colour : C: cream, CB : creamish brown, SLCB : slightly creamish brown, BC : brownish cream
Texture : VS : very soft, S: soft, SH : slightly hard, H : hard
Crumb grains : F : find SC : Slightly coarse, C : coarse
Shredding : N : , Y : yes

Table 5.5 : Effect of Addition of Soybean on the organolpeptic Characteristics of Bread (on the basis of 10)

Parameter/ Treatment	Blends (wheat flour : soybean)					
	100:0	95:5	90:10	85:15	80:20	Mean
Colour						
PK-416	8.03	7.87	7.75	7.65	7.48	7.76
PK-472	8.03	7.98	7.95	7.88	7.55	7.88
Heat treated	8.03	8.33	8.25	8.15	8.12	8.06
Full Fat	8.03	7.88	7.78	7.55	7.25	7.70
Defatted	8.03	7.98	7.93	7.98	7.78	7.94
Texture						
PK-416	8.13	7.68	7.38	6.55	6.45	6.33
PK-472	8.13	7.68	7.35	6.53	6.39	6.32
Heat treated	8.13	7.63	7.05	6.73	6.50	6.41
Full Fat	8.13	7.63	7.23	6.35	5.83	7.03
Defatted	8.13	7.73	7.50	6.73	6.25	7.27
Flavour						
PK-416	8.05	7.95	7.70	7.48	7.20	7.69
PK-472	8.05	7.88	7.65	7.53	7.25	7.67
Heat treated	8.05	8.18	8.05	7.93	7.40	7.99
Full Fat	8.05	7.93	7.70	7.50	7.08	7.66
Defatted	8.05	7.90	7.65	7.50	7.38	7.71
Taste						
PK-416	8.13	8.08	7.73	7.58	7.33	7.75
PK-472	8.13	8.00	7.73	7.53	7.35	7.76
Heat treated	8.13	8.25	8.08	7.95	7.78	8.03
Full Fat	8.13	7.98	7.68	7.55	7.20	7.71
Defatted	8.13	8.10	7.53	7.55	7.48	7.75

CD ($p < 0.05$)	Colour	Texture	Flavour	Taste
Varieties	NS	NS	NS	NS
Heat Treatment	0.13	NS	0.11	0.12
Defatting	0.13	0.11	NS	NS
Between blends	0.20	0.18	0.18	0.20

The chemical characteristics of soybean flour differed with varieties as well as modified by heat treatment and removal of oil (defatting) as evident from the data given in Table 5.2. The heat treatment had significant effect on protein, fat, ash, crude and dietary fibre. The heat treatment enhanced the crude and dietary fibre content as compared to raw soybean flour but the total carbohydrates, non-reducing sugars, free fatty acids, free amino acids, pH along with most of the mineral constituents viz., calcium, phosphorus, sodium and magnesium decreased with heat treatment. The removal of oil or defatting of soybean appreciably increased crude and dietary fibre contents along with the concentration of calcium, phosphorus, sodium, maganese and magnesium. Between the two varieties analyzed, PK-472 had higher concentration of protein, fat and ash. The variety PK-416 had however higher crude fibre content. It also had higher concentration of minerals except phosphorus, which was found to be significantly higher in variety PK-472. The experimental results are in collaboration with the findings of Smith and Circle.

Water Absorption and Dough Handling Property of Composite Flours

The water absorption of wheat flour was 43.55 per cent (Table 3). The addition of soybean flour significantly enhanced the water absorption capacity of various blends. As compared to raw soybean flour, the wheat flour blended with heat-treated soybean flour had still higher water absorption percentage. This may be attributed to the higher water binding capacity of the treated soybean flour. Smith and Circle observed that heat treatment causes agglomeration of soybean in coarser sized particles thus increasing water binding capacity the dough made from wheat flour was non-sticky. Addition of soyabean flour upto 10 per cent also produced non-sticky dough. Addition above this level produced slightly sticky dough. Heat treatment given to soybean produced non-sticky dough upto 15 per cent level of addition of soybean flour into wheat flour.

Bread Making Characteristics of Composite Flour

The data pertaining to loaf weight, loaf volume, crumb and crust characteristics are given in Table 5.4. The addition of soybean flour to wheat floru significantly decreased the weight of the loaf. The bread incorporated with defatted soy flour weighed slightly less than that obtained from addition of raw soybean flour. The mean weight of bread prepared from soy flour incorporated wheat flour eas 126.0 g as compared to 150.0 g weight of loaf prepared from 100 per cent wheat flour. The loaf volume decreased with addition of soybean flour and it was 350 cc in case of wheat flour (100%) bread, which decreased to 293.8 cc with addition of upto 20per cent soybean flour. Varietal difference also affected the volume of the loaf. Bread blended with soybean flour obtained from variety PK-416 had significantly higher volume as compared to those bleneded with PK-472. Incorporation of heat treated full fat soybean flour upto 10 per cent level produced light brown coloured loaf. In all other blends of soybean and wheat flour, the colour deepened to brown hue. However, the shape of the loaf remained symmetrical upto 15 per cent soybean component. Incorporation of soybean flour upto 5 per cent level only produced creamish white crumb, this might have been due to bleaching effect of soybean flour and further increase in proportion of soybean flour slightly affected the crumb colour. The loaves however, remained soft in texture with fine grains of crumb upto 15 per cent level of

Table 5.6 : Effect of Addition of Soybean on the Width. Thickness, Spread Factor and Top Score of Biscuits (a set of three)

Parameter/ Treatment	Blends (wheat flour : soybean)									
	100:0	95:5	90:10	85:15	80:20	75:25	70:30	65:35	60:40	Mean
Width (cm)										
PK-416	17.00	17.2	17.5	17.7	17.8	17.9	18.1	18.2	18.3	17.7
PK-472	17.00	17.2	17.6	17.7	17.8	17.8	18.2	18.3	18.5	17.9
Heat treated	17.00	17.1	17.4	17.5	17.5	17.9	18.1	18.1	18.6	17.7
Full Fat	17.00	17.3	17.6	17.8	18.2	18.2	18.3	18.3	18.5	17.8
Defatted	17.00	17.1	17.6	17.7	17.9	18.1	18.2	18.3	18.4	17.8
Thickness (cm)										
PK-416	3.50	3.40	3.20	3.20	3.10	2.90	2.90	2.90	2.80	3.10
PK-472	3.50	3.20	3.00	3.00	3.00	2.80	2.70	2.70	2.70	2.80
Heat treated	3.50	3.40	3.20	3.10	3.00	3.00	3.00	3.00	2.90	3.10
Full Fat	3.50	3.30	3.10	3.00	3.00	2.80	2.80	2.80	2.90	3.00
Defatted	3.50	3.30	3.20	3.20	3.00	2.90	2.90	2.90	2.90	3.20
Spread factor										
PK-416	4.86	5.06	5.47	5.53	5.74	6.17	6.24	6.28	6.54	5.77
PK-472	4.86	5.38	5.87	5.90	5.93	6.13	6.50	6.78	6.85	6.02
Heat treated	4.86	5.03	8.44	5.65	5.93	5.97	6.03	6.03	6.31	5.69
Full Fat	4.86	5.24	5.68	5.93	6.06	6.28	6.54	6.54	6.61	5.97
Defatted	4.86	5.18	5.50	5.53	5.77	5.54	6.07	6.31	6.34	5.71
Top Score (on basis of 4.0)										
PK-416	3.00	3.50	4.00	4.00	4.00	4.00	3.50	3.50	3.50	3.66
PK-472	3.00	3.50	3.50	4.00	4.00	4.00	4.00	3.50	4.00	3.72
Heat treated	3.00	3.50	4.00	4.00	4.00	4.00	4.00	4.00	3.50	3.78
Full Fat	3.00	3.50	4.00	4.00	4.00	4.00	4.00	4.00	4.00	3.88
Defatted	3.00	3.50	4.00	4.00	4.00	3.50	4.00	4.00	4.00	3.77

CD ($p < 0.05$)	Width	Thickness	Spread factor	Top Score
Varieties	0.01	0.01	0.01	0.14
Heat Treatment	0.01	0.01	0.01	NS
Defatting	0.01	0.01	0.01	0.14
Between blends	0.02	0.02	0.001	0.30

soybean flour. The bread prepared from non-blended sheat flour had loaves with light brown crust. Similar desirable crust colour was also observed in case of addition of raw soybean flour upto 5 per cent level. But the treated and defatted soybean blended breads had light brown coloured crust upto 15 per cent of supplementation. Increase of soybean flour utp 20 per cent deepened the crust colour to dark brown was noticed at 20 per cent level.

Organoleptic Evaluation of Bread

Data pertaining to colour, flavour, texture and taste of bread evaluation on 10 point scale are given in Table 5.5. The addition of soybean flour to wheat flour significantly decreased the colour of bread. Addition of heat-treated and defatted soybean flour improved the colour of bread. Similar results have been obtained for texture of bread. The flavour score of bread decreased with addition of soybean flour, however, addition of heat-treated soybean flour improved the flavour of the bread. The treatments given to soybean had non-significant effect on the taste of bread but heat treatment given to soybean utilized in the preparation of bread improved the taste.

Biscuit Making Characteristics of Composite Flours

Biscuit Making Characteristics of Composite Flours The width, thickness, spread factor and top score of biscuits as affected by addition of wheat flour are given in Table 5.6. The addition of soybean flour to wheat flour significantly increased the width of biscuits. The width of 3 biscuits (a set) prepared from wheat flour (100%) was 17.00 cm which increased to 18.50 cm with addition of upto 40 per cent soybean flour, respectively. However, in case of combined thickness of a set of three biscuits, it decreased significantly with increase in the level of soybean flour. The spread factor of biscuits also improved with addition of soybean flour and as the level of soybean flour into wheat flour increased, the spread factor also increased. Addition of soybean flour also improved the top score of biscuits. Between the varieties of soybean, the biscuits prepared from blends containing soybean flour of variety PK-472 had slightly higher top score.

Organoleptic Evaluation of Biscuits

The colour, flavour, texture and taste scores of biscuits as affected by addition of soybean and evaluated organoleptically are given in Table 5.7. The addition of soybean flour significantly decreased the colour score of biscuits as judged by panelists. The mean colour score of biscuits prepared from wheat flour (100%) was 8.00, which decreased to 7.08 in case of biscuits prepared from wheat flour containing 40 per cent soybean flour. Heat treatment

Table 5.7 : Effect of addition of soybean on the organoleptic Characteristics of biscuits (on the basis of 10)

Parameter/ Treatment	Blends (wheat flour : soybean)									
	100:0	95:5	90:10	85:15	80:20	75:25	70:30	65:35	60:40	Mean
Colour										
PK-416	8.23	8.22	8.28	8.05	7.93	7.73	7.45	7.25	7.10	7.78
PK-472	8.23	8.35	8.15	8.03	7.85	7.55	7.50	7.25	7.05	7.78
Heat treated	8.23	8.30	8.08	8.08	7.83	7.68	7.73	7.53	7.38	7.87
Full Fat	8.23	8.45	8.13	8.10	8.00	7.98	7.78	7.50	7.48	7.97
Defatted	8.23	8.00	8.05	7.98	7.78	7.40	7.18	7.00	6.68	7.59
Texture										
PK-416	8.00	8.50	8.20	8.73	7.83	7.65	7.53	7.15	6.98	7.84
PK-472	8.00	8.63	8.15	7.90	7.70	7.48	7.25	7.03	6.85	7.67
Heat treated	8.00	8.50	8.33	8.13	8.08	7.85	7.80	7.73	7.55	8.00
Full Fat	8.00	8.55	8.23	7.98	7.80	7.55	7.48	7.15	7.05	7.75
Defatted	8.00	7.43	8.20	7.87	7.73	7.58	7.30	7.03	6.78	7.55
Flavour										
PK-416	8.00	8.33	8.13	7.98	7.73	7.53	7.28	7.13	6.98	7.68
PK-472	8.00	8.35	8.08	7.88	7.68	7.58	7.33	7.23	6.93	7.67
Heat treated	8.00	8.45	8.23	8.10	8.03	7.95	7.88	7.73	7.50	7.99
Full Fat	8.00	8.40	8.15	7.80	7.75	7.65	7.55	7.85	7.25	7.83
Defatted	8.00	8.28	8.05	7.88	7.65	7.45	7.05	7.00	6.65	7.56
Taste										
PK-4'i6	8.00	8.15	8.15	7.83	7.53	7.32	7.28	6.80	7.48	7.62
PK-472	8.00	8.35	8.13	7.98	7.75	7.55	7.40	7.05	6.88	7.68
Heat treated	8.00	8.43	8.35	8.20	7.98	7.88	7.88	7.75	7.40	7.96
Full Fat	8.00	8.25	8.15	7.95	7.78	7.62	7.62	7.38	7.29	7.79
Defatted	8.00	8.50	8.13	7.85	7.50	7.25	7.25	6.73	6.58	7.50

CD ($p < 0.05$)	Colour	Texture	Flavour	Taste
Varieties	NS	0.05	NS	0.05
Heat Treatment	0.05	0.05	0.05	0.05
Defatting	0.05	0.05	0.05	0.05
Between blends	0.11	0.11	0.11	0.11

given to soybean flour had improving effect on the colour of biscuits. The texture and flavour of biscuits also varied significantly with addition of soybean flour. Addition of heat treated soybean flour improved the flavour of biscuits. Similar results were obtained for taste of biscuits.

6

Health Breads

Around the world, bread is the principal food and provides more nutrients than any other single food source. Among flour and its main baked products, bread is the least expensive of our staple foods. Health baking refers to the production of bakery products that meet special consumer dietary needs. For e.g. some consumers must be on sugar free or limited sugar intake diets. Others must be on a salt free or limited salt intake diet. Since a large number of consumers are thus effected, the dietetic aspect of baking has grown considerably in order to meet these needs. Manufacturers of bakery supplies have developed a number of prepared mixes to meet the baker's demand to produce dietetic baked goods. Some retail and wholesale bakers have developed their own recipes or formulas for dietetic products. The fact that these "dietetic formulas" contain no sugar (only sugar substitutes) may make them acceptable for use by diabetics but does not necessarily qualify the products as "low calorie" as the formulas contain fairly normal quantities of shortening or butter, milk, eggs and so on.

Also replacing salt (NaCl) with a salt substitute does lower the sodium contents somewhat, but in most cases not significantly enough to qualify the baked products as "low-sodium". Sodium is naturally present in relatively high quantities in milk, dough conditioners, egg and even in flour. A truly hypertensive person (with high blood pressure) may require low-sodium products rather than just salt free products. Normal white bread is prepared with flour, fat, sugar, salt, yeast, milk-solids etc. and the nutrient components of normal bread are given in Table 6.1.

Table : 6.1. NUTRIENTS COMPOSITION OF BREAD (per 100 gm of bread)

Nutrient	White Bread	Whole meal bread
Water,g	39.0	40.0
Protein,g	7.8	8.8
Fat,g	1.7	2.7
Sugar,g	1.8	2.1
Starch & Dextrin,g	47.9	39.7
Dietery fiber,g	2.7	8.5
Energy, KJ	975.0	904.0
Thiamine, mg	0.18	0.26
Riboflaving, mg	0.03	0.06
Nicotinic acid,mg	1.4	3.09
Potential nicotinic acid,mg	1.6	1.7
Pyridoxin,mg	0.04	0.14
Folic acid,mg	27.0	39
Pantothenic acid,mg	0.3	0.6
Biotin,ug	1.0	6.0
Vit.E,mg	trace	0.2
Sodium,mg	540	540
Potassium,mg	100	220
Calcium,mg	100	23
Magnesium,mg	26	93
Phosphorus, mg	97	2.30
Iron,mg	1.7	2.05

Potential nicotinic acid is calculated as 1mg per 60 mg tryptophan

Various types of health bread suggested to meet the dietetic needs of a particular segment of population are :

a) Gluten Free Bread
b) Reduced Fat Bread
c) No Cholesterol Bread
d) No Sugar Bread
e) Low sodium Bread
f) Reduced Calorie Bread

g) High Fiber Bread
h) High Protein Bread
A) Gluten Free Bread

(A) Gluten Free Bread

Here an old proverb " One persons's food is another person's poison: is most appropriate. Bread has wheat protein called gluten. It is an important nutrient then, why gluten free bread? Because some people especially children have allergy from gluten. They suffer from a diseases called celiac or coeliac disease. It is also known as celiacsprue, non tropical sprue or Gluten sensitive enteropathy (GSE)- a most appropriate term use for this disease. Celiac disease is condition of gluten intolerance in children, sometimes persisting into childhood. Symptoms of celiac disease are listed in Table 6.2.

Table 6.2. Symptoms of Celiac disease

1. Passage of abnormal stools
2. Abdominal distension
3. Loss of weight
4. Anemia
5. Anorexia
6. Stunted growth

Patients recover on a strict free diet. Wheat, rye, barley oats are deleterious to celiac patients. Maize and rice are tolerated satisfactorily. Suggested explanation of the disease mechanisms are deficiency of a specific enzyme in the intestinal mucosa or reduced efficiency of the mucosa as a barrier that normally prevents absorption of the deleterious agents. It has been alleged that gluten may be concerned in the etiology of multiple sclerosis. Consumption of gluten free diet brings benefits to sufferers of this disease. Inhalation of cereal flour causes asthma in some occupationally exposed individuals such as millers and bakers. Also wheat is the most allergenic of all the cereals.

It is useless to try to make a normal appearing loaf of bread that contains no gluten. Gluten provides typical form, structure and texture of bread. No other edible substance functions in the same way as gluten. But some efforts are made to develop gluten free bread. Gluten free breads can be prepared from maize starch and some non-cereal ingredients as rice bread. The best can be done to make gluten free bread is to use eggs as the structure forming ingredients and rice or corn flour as the cereal or bulking component. Corn starch can also be used to eliminate any cereal protein. Chances of success are more if piece or loaf size is kept small. Normal fermentation and proofing steps are out of question for such products. Although the addition of fermented liquid at the final mixing might be helpful, degassed beer addition enhances the bread flavour also. Gluten free breads require polymeric substances that mimic the isoplastic properties of gluten in bread doughs. Gluten free breads can be successfully formulated by incorporating gums, soy protein and egg white into non-wheat flours. Gluten free pocket type flat breads compatible with regular wheat bread in key textural attributes can be formulated from a bake mix based on pregelatinized rice flour and corn starch that incorporated methyl cellulose, gum arabic and egg albumin as a gluten replacement. Inclusion of 3g of gum arabic (with methyl cellulose levels 3.10-4.12g, egg albumin levels of 2.18-4.10g) in the bake mix yielded gluten free breads that were compatible with regular wheat bread in the frequency of cracks, separation of layers, rollability, tearing quality, first bite harness, masticatory hardness, adhesiveness and cohesiveness. Higher levels of gum arabic c results in more cohesive products. Lower levels of (1.37g) gum arabic resulted in loaves that were less cohesive and inferior to wheat bread in rollability. All breads possessed a perceptible corn flavour, a light yellow crumb with apparent waxy patches and a faster rate of staling than that of regular bread.

(B) Reduced Fat Bread

Since it is quite obvious that fats and oils with their nine calories per gram. creates major problems in the designing of diets for persons desiring to reduce weight. Excess of fat causes various health disorders such as cardiovascular ailments and obesity.

Fat has become the food formulating challenge of the decade. Consumers want fat taken out of food without the taste and texture of the food being adversely effected. The reality is that fat contributes texture and pleasing mouth feel and positively impacts flavour, intensity and perception. So the food manufacturers continually strive to meet the demands of consumers to reduce fat. They must identify systems that mimic fat's attributes (Table 6.3) without its disadvantages.

Table 6.3. Attributes of Fat contributed in baked goods

1. Flavour
2. Viscosity/Body
3. Richness
4. Texture/grain
5. Aeration
6. Tenderness
7. Shortness
8. Leavening
9. Lubricity
10. Dough handling

11. Batter stability

Fat Replacers: Fat replacers are the ingredients used to replace fat in food system. Fat replacer should be non-toxic, cost effective and able to mimic fat without increasing calorie intake. Various fat mimetic are listed in Table 6.4.

Table 6.4. Fate mimetic

1. Carbohydrate based :- Microcrystalline cellulose, maltodextran modified starches, oatrim, Z-trim, polydextrose, inulin, pectin, hemicellulose.
2. Protein based: Soy protein hydrolysate, casein-concentrates (simplesse), whey protein concentrates, egg white powder, gelatin.
3. Gums: Guar, xantahn, gellan curdlan.
4. Synthetic Fat substitutes: Sucrose polyesters such as olestra, esterified propoxylated glycerol and polysiloxane, Trialakoxycitrate (T AC).

When fat is to be removed and replaced with water and other ingredients, a total formulation approach must be used to build in all the desired properties. The fat mimatic impart sensory characters such as creaminess and smoothiness. -Body cling and firmness are developed with addition of maltrodextrin, corn syrups and grains. Emulsifiers are incorporated to interact with carbonhydrates and proteins and to modify tenderness, reduce set back and provide lubrication. Flavours are added to replace the flavour profiles that had been provided by fats and oils. Plant derived carbohydrate formulations for fat replacement has some benefits over protein based substitutes, gum formulations, sucrose polyesters, synthetic substitutes. They are often more effective in reducing the water activity in a low or reduced fat formula. These carbohydrates are hydrophilic due to a large number of hydroxyl bonds available to blind with water molecules creating a carbohydrates water network that can mimic the texture of fat. Physical side effects some times associated with synthetic replacements are not apparent.

Plant Carbohydrates are completely digestible as part of the normal metabolic process. The ideal carbohydrates fat mimetic will possess a structure to bind and orient water in such a way to provide mouthfeel like fat. Then clear the palate in same length of time as fat does. Several ways to use carbohydrate fat replacers in food are:-

1. Mimetic is simply dry blended with other ingredients. These blends are then mixed with water and used.
2. Mimetic is slurried and sheered to prepare a cream which has fat like

characters. Then cream is incorporated with other ingredients to prepare a finished food.

Recommended Fate intake 30% of total calorie need per day e.g, adult require 1800 kcal/day needs 60 gm fat (540 kcal from fat).

(C) No Cholesterol Bread

Cholesterol is the chief sterol in the body fund in all tissues especially liver, nerves, brain and adernal cortex. It is synthesized in liver (endogenous cholesterol) and found in animal products (exogenous cholesterol) as egg yolk, liver and other granular organs, milk fat, butter and meats. More than 200 mg/dl of cholesterol causes atherosclerotic diseases. Atherosclerotic is due to patchy deposites of various materials in the inner side of arteries. Materials are fatty substances such as cholesterol, triglycerides, phospholipids, complex carbohydrates and lipoprotiens.

This leads to narrowing of lumen and decreased blood carrying capacity. Sufferer should take low cholesterol and saturated fats diet. Cholesterol content of selected foods is given in Table 6.5.

Table 6.5 : Cholesterol content of selected foods, (10g edible portion)

Food Item	Cholesterol (mg)
Barley bran	0
Corn germ	0
Oats germ	0
Rice bran	0
Wheat bran	0
Wheat germ	0
Whole egg	548
Egg yolk	1602
Egg white	0
Whole milk	14
Butter	219
Lard	766

No cholesterol bread can be made simply by eliminating any animal fat or ingredients made from animal fats. Formulation changes required are minimal. Any Baker can easily make them with little or no effect on the finished product. Vegetable shortening can be used as substitute. They should have similar physical characters as animal shortening being replaced.

Following points should be checked before making "no cholesterol" claim :

- Emulsifiers are made from animal fats
- Pan greases may contain animal fat
- Washes to impart glossiness to the crust may contain material with cholesterol content.

(D) Sugar Free Bread

We want sugar free bread mainly for 2 purposes.

(1) To reduce the calorie content for obese persons.

(2) To maintain blood glucose level in blood for diabetic patients

Sugars are carbohydrates giving 4kcal/ g of food. For sugar free bread alternative sweeteners are available with no nutritive value.

Alternative Sweeteners :Sweetening agents other than table sugar or sucrose syrups, honey and molasses. They are grouped as nutritive and non-nutritive sweeteners.

Nutritive: Fructose, glucose, glycine, mannitol, sorbitol, xylitol.

Non-nutritive : Low calorie sugar substitutes used for diabetics and obese persons are aspartame, saccharin, cyclamate, dulcin etc. These sweeteners are several times sweeter than sucrose. To reduce their sweetness, polydextrose as bulking agent is used. It reduces their sweetness. Relative sweetness of various substances are given in Table 6.6.

'Table 6.6. Relative sweetness of various substances. (Sweetness compared to sucrose as 100)

Saccharin	300
Aspartame	150
Cyclamate	30

In white bread formulation, sugar is present in very small amounts (1.8g) so it do not have much influence on the health of diabetics. Most of the carbohydrates in bread is in the form of' starch. Some glucose and maltose is formed in the dough after water is added, provided amylases ;Ire present, but only a small quantity of sugar remains at the end of a normal fermentation.

E) Low Sodium Bread

High concentration of sodium in body fluids causes various diseases as hypertension or high- blood pressure and edema. High blood pressure is due to persistent elevation of blood pressure above normal. Normal blood pressure is 120/ 80mmHg. Hypertensive person suffers from dizziness. frequent headaches, impaired vision, shortness of breadth, chest pain, failing memory. In edema there is swelling of the tissues because of presence of abnormally large amount of fluids in tissue spaces. This is due to disturbance in the mechanisms involved in fluid exchange. In these disturbed states intake of sodium should be reduced.

The sodium content of wheat flour is very low. So, in bread, sodium is contributed try added salt, leavening acids and sodium bicarbonate. Three slices of bread contribute 1 g salt, which is equivalent to 12% of the recommended intake of 3.2 g sodium/day. Daily consumption of [3 slices of bread with the NaCL/KCl blend could reduce consumption of NaCl by 0.58% of the recommended daily intake of 3.2g sodium/ day. So 50:50 KCl/NaCl mixture can be successfully used in bread making. But yeast does not respond to KCl in same way as it responds to NaCl. So baker will have to establish new times for fermentation and proofing. Lite salt (1: 1 NaCl/KCl: alongwith additional sucrose, milk replacers, soy oils and dough conditioner in bread formula has been used successfully.

Salt in dough effects a number of processing responses but the main reason for which bakers use this ingredient is for enhancement of the flavour of the finished product-. It also inhibits fermentation. It also improves crumb colour and grain in bread.

(F) Reduced Calorie Bread

Fats give 9 Kcal/gm of food. Carbohydrates give 4kcal/g of food and proteins gives 4 Kcal/g of food. So to make reduced calorie bread, we have to replace above components with non-caloric ingredients.

A low calorie food must not have more than 0.4K calories/g. A food may be called as "Reduced Calorie" if the calories are reduced by at least one third that of the traditional product. Because of the complex nature of bread and its sensitivity to formula modification the usual approaches to calorie reduction are seldom practical. Use of non- digestible substances such a purified cellulose (with no calorie addition) can be done to replace flour. Corn bran or rice bran can also be used. Calorie reduction can also be done by replacing sugar with non-caloric sweeteners such as aspartame. Bulking agents which do not supply energy are used as filler ingredients· Non caloric fat substitutes such as gums, pectins, sucrose polyesters can be used. Polydextrose is also used. It is a polymer of dextrose, providing only one calorie per gram.

Another approach has been tried to reduce not the calories per unit weight but the calories per serving. A serving being defined as a certain number of slices, usually two. Calorie: reduction is accomplished by reducing the weight of a slice generally by making it thinner but sometimes by modifying the height or width. There is some logic to this approach because generally two slices per sandwich would be consumed whether the slice weighed one ounce or three quarters of an ounce. Some manufacturers have tried to puff up the bread so that it has same dimensions as regular bread.

C) HIGH FIBER BREAD

Fiber is the portion of plant material in diet which are resist ant to digestion by enzymes produced by man". Simply dietary fiber is called unabsorbed and undigested portion of the food. The components of fiber that can be chemically characterized include:

Insoluble fibers - Cellulose, hemicellulose, lignin, insoluble gums and pentosans.

Soluble fibers - Soluble germs, soluble pectin and polysaccharides.

Recommendation of total fiber consumption is 25-30g/day of which about one-fourth should be soluble. Lack of dietary fiber in the diet causes diverticular diseases, coronory heart disease, cancer of colon or diabetes, constipation· Diverticular disease is characterised by outpouchings of the mucous membrane through gaps or weak spots in the circular muscles of colon .This results in abdominal tenderness, distention, pain in intestinal spasm Major sources ill dietary fiber supplementation of bakery foods are listed in Table 6.7.

Table 6.7 . Sources of fiber suggested for bakery foods

Source	% TDC (True digestible cellulose)
Cereals	
Wheat genn	16.9
Wheat bran	47.1
Oat bran	17.2
Barley	19.1
Rice	3.1
Millet	8.5
Corn bran	89.02
Purified cellulose	Close to 100% fiber on dry weight basis

Raisins	4.43
Legumes	
Cow pea	30.7
Lime bran	21.2

1. Some bakers use powdered cellulose, a FDA approved purified substance derived from- wood, to provide the fiber without adding calories.
2. Some opt for increased amounts of bran, the fiber source in whole wheat bread.
3. Enrichment of foods by addition of high fiber cereal grain components is another way to increase fiber in take.
4. Combination of cellulose, grain and legume fiber can also be used to increase amount of fiber in bread.

Several adjustments have to be made for benefit of quality of high fiber bread as given in Table 6.8.

Table 6.8.

Effect of high fiber in bread	Compensation
1. Fibrous material dilutes the gluten protein, volume is decreased.	Addition of vital wheat gluten. Use of strong flour.
2. Fiber tends to cut gluten strands.	Addition of SSL (Sodium steroyl-2-lactylate) is helpful.
3. Fiber has high absorption and it interferes with hydration ration of gluten protein.	A high amont of H_2O is added.
4. High amount of added water makes the product especially susceptible to mold growth.	Adequate amount of propionate is added
5. Care must be taken to avoid, because the point of full dough development is hard to judge in the presence of added fiber.	

(H) High Protein Bread

Some people suffer from deficiency of proteins. They are recommended eat high protein breads. To make high protein breads, the addition of say flour to a bread flour so far has been the most satisfactory method of increasing the protein concentration in bread. Soy flour also increases the quality of the bread-protein because lysine is the limiting amino acid in wheat flour but not in soy flour. Addition of synthetic glycolipids increases the levels of supplementation that are possible.

Gluten powder produced commercially is also used to increase the protein contents. Deficiency of protein causes a disease called Marasmus. Supplementation of protein can also be done by addition of whey extract, casein and yeast. High protein breads and protein must contain not less than 22% protein, while bread must contain not less than 16%. Formulation for health breads are given in Table 6.9.

Table 6.9. Formula for health breads (on percent basis)

Ingredient	No salt added	No Fat added	Gluten Free	Cholesterol Free	High Fibre
Flour	56.7	57.9	0.0	53.6	50.3
Water	35.0	34.7	35.8	34.9	35.2
Yeast	1.1	1.2	2.5	2.7	1.2
Salt	0.0	1.0	0.8	1.3	1.0
Shortening	2.5	0.0	2.5	0.0	3.0
Dried sltim milk	1.7	1.7	0.0	2.6	2.0
Sugar	3.0	2.9	0.0	2.0	2.0
Liquid whole eggs	0.0	0.0	3.3	0.0	0.0
Diastatic malt syrup	0.0	0.6	1.2	1.3	0.5
See Notes	0.0	0.0	(1)	(2)	(3)

7

Ingredients of Bread

Introduction

Basic ingredients used for the bread preparation are divided into two parts, i.e. essential and optional. Without *essential raw material* bread cannot be made. Even though, if the bread is made without essential raw material, it will have major qualitative deterioration. The *optional ingredients* are added to formula to improve the quality of the flour

Raw Material

Essential	**Optional**
• Flour	• Fat
• Yeast	• Sugar
• Salt	• Milk
• Water	• Water

Flour

A baker prefers the flour having the following characteristics :

Colour : The flour colour directly affects the crumb colour and bloom. Baker prefers white colour flour having a creamy tinge. Normally, high grade flour is whiter in colour as compared to low grade flour, because while preparing high grade flour much of the testa (the part of bran having colouring pigment) is removed. Flour colour is also affected by the wheat colour, hence it should be chosen carefully while preparing flour. Only the endosperm portion of the wheat is used for the milling purpose. The flour should be bleached adequately after milling as bleaching makes the flour whiter.

Strength : Strength in a flour means the ability of the flour for gaining large volumed well risen loaves, provided any deficiency in the rate of gas production in the dough is adjusted in a suitable manner. The conditions required for large volume are :

- Sufficient quantity and quantity of protein to retain gas produced during fermentation or other process of bread preparation.
- Sufficient sugars and sufficient diastetic activity to produce enough and uniform gas.
- Sufficient alpha amylase to properly condition starch.

Generally, strong flour, having extensible gluten, possesses all the above chracteristics, hence it is desirable for break production. However, strong flour having hard and tough gluten requires longer fermentation time to mellow properly.

Tolerance : If the better quality bread is made even in the over fermentation condition then the flour is said to have tolerance. It is directly related to gluten i.e. tolerance of flour is its ability to withstand the fermentation process in excess of what is normally required to mature its gluten property.

Water Absorption Power : Water Absorption Power (WAP) means the quantity of water required to prepare a dough having similar consistency of the bread dough. Generally, the WAP is around 60%. However, if a good quality bread is prepared even if flour has absorption more water, the flour is said to have high WAP.

Uniformity : To maintain uniform quality of bread, it is necessary to obtain uniform quality flour from one flour mill throughout the year. if the quality of flour varies the baker will need to adjust the formula, processing schedule etc. If such adjustments are necessary off and on then it is very difficult for baker to produce uniform quality products.

Diastetic Activity : Diastetic activity means the effect of diastase enzyme (for activity of alpha and beta amylase) present in the flour. The enzyme beta-amylase acts on damaged starch cells present in the flour and covnerts into maltose sugars, which further breaks down to carbon dioxide and alcohol. The alpha amylase partly breaks down the sound stach cells to form dextrins, which in limited amount gives sheen to the bread and improves its eye appeal.

(i) Effect of Low and High Diastetic Activity on Bread :

- If the diastatic activity is less :

The less starch converted into sugar

⇓ hence

there will be no sufficient sugar present during the final proof

⇓ hence

sufficient carbon dioxide cannot be produced

⇓ hence

- the volume of the resultant bread will be low
- simultaneously, insufficient sugars results in less caramalization and less bloom of the bread.

- High activity of beta-amylase (generally, taking place in the case of presence of excessive damaged starch cells) will cause undesirable amout of maltose sugar, only a part of which wll be needed by yeast. In such cases doughs become slask, sticky and difficult to handle. The bread produced from such dough will have dark crust and crumb colour and will be poor in volume and texture.
- High activity of alpha-amylase (generally in case of doughs made from flours obtained from sprouted wheat or wet wheat or use of excessive diastetic malt in the formula) converts more starch into dextrin, which is sticky in nature hence the bread crumb. too. will be sticky. Such bread will be difficult to slice and slices will stick together and will break when separated.

(ii) ***Preventive Measures*** : When flour lacks in diastetic action, it can be supplemented by using diastetic malt in the formula.

If the flour has excessive diastetic activity, it is useful to take the following precautions :

- Use plenty of yeast for vigorous fermentation of dough as overall reduction in production time will give less opportunity to enzymes to remain active.
- Use emulsifiers liberally to prevent stickiness in the crumb. Use of soya flour could also be helpful in this regard.
- Keep the doughs cool, as high temperature will promote the amylase activity.
- Keep strict control on over fermentation and prevent the doughs from becoming acidic. Enzymes are more active in acidic medium.
- Bake the bread thoroughly so that it has even golden brown colour all around.

- Slice the bread only when it is thoroughly cooled.
- Potassium aluminium sulphate has retarding effect on diastetic action. A small lump of potassium aluminium sulphate rotated three to four time in doughing water will give enough of this chemical to control the diastetic action at least to some extent. After turning the lump of potassium aluminium sulphate the water should be used the next day. As this chemical is banned in some countries, it will be appropriate to ascertain the legal position in this matter.

To decide the quality of the flour having above mentioned properties, gluten quality and quantity, pelshunk value, quantity of moisture, ash quantity, experimental baking etc. practicals can be carried out.

8

Production of Bread

Introduction

Bread processing method is too long and continuous which involves following successive steps :

Selection of ingredients and balancing the formula

- Mixing
- Bulk fermentation
- Knock back
- Dough make-up
  - Dividing
  - Rounding
  - Intermediate proofing
  - Moulding
  - Panning
- Proofing
- Baking
- Depanning
- Cooling
- Slicing
- Packing

SELECTION OF INGREDIENTS

The first and the most important step of obtain uniform products is the selection of proper quality raw material and its adjustment according to a formula.The raw material should be weighed accurately after deciding its quantity. May factors affect the selection of raw material. The important ones are :

- **Bread Processing Method** : Sponge and dough method of bread preparation requires less yeast as compared to straight dough method.

- **Types of bread :** White bread requries 100% flour, brown bread requires 50% flour and 50% wheat flour while whole mill bread requires 100% wheat flour. Milk bread requires milk powder, more fat and sugar.
- **Type of flour :** Strong flour requires more water and yeast than weak flour.
- **Fermentation time** : Less fermentation time requires more yeast.
- **Atmosphere :** Cold atmosphere requires more yeast and hot water.
- **Consumer choice :** Rich people prefer high quality bread while the poor prefer cheap bread.

MIXING / KNEADING : Mixing is an important step involved in bread preparation for the production of better quality bread, provided that, the raw material selected are of proper quality and weighed in specified quantity.

Purpose : Mixing has two purposes :

- Each raw material gets dispersed evenly in the dough, which results in uniform dough.

Dissolve little sugar in luke warm water [37°C (100°F)]	⇒	The water should atleast 4 times to the weight of the yeast
⇓		
Add all the yeast after crumbling and mix properly		
⇓		
Keep the suspension aside till the yeast start to float on the water	⇒	which requires about 5 to 10 minutes Be sure that no lump is settled at the bottom
⇓		
Add little flour, beat at and prepare a thick paste	⇒	beating ensures air incorporation inside the paste, which is useful for vigorous yeast function
⇓		
Keep it in a warm atmosphere [32 to 38°C (90° to 110°F] till the paste in rise	⇒	it will take about 10 to 15 minutes
⇓		
The paste is termed as *flying ferment*		

- It develops the gluten and thereby produces dough with uniform characteristics like smoothness, extensibility, viscous flow etc.

Flying Ferment : Preparation of flying ferment is the first step involved in mixing process of straight dough method. It can be prepared by :

(i) Process :

(ii) Importance :

- If the paste is not rise, the yeast is not capable to carry out the fermentation. Hence, it should not be used for the bread preparation. Which saves bakers from economical loss due to preparation of inferior quality bread.
- The rate of rising in the paste also indicates the rough idea about the quality of the yeast.
- Flying ferment is thinner compare to dough, hence yeast activity is faster, which helps in vigorous fermentation.

Other Preparation : Which flying ferment preparation is going on, the following preparation are carried out :

- Flour is sieved to remove the impurities
- Salt and remaining sugar are dissolved in the remaining water and strained, hence sugar and last can be evenly dispersed in the dough and any impurities present in water can be removed.
- Calculate the desired water temperature (DWT). Obtain the DWT either by heating the water or adding the ice and thereby maintain the desired dough temperature (DDT) It is necessary because the yeast activity is at its best at 25.5° to 28°C (78° to 82°F) temperature and water is the best media to change the dough temperature.

Dough Temperature : It is necessary to maintain the dough temperature to obtain good quality bread. Low dough temperature requries much time for fermentation, intermediate proofing and other processing. However the bread made from such dough will be of the best quality. On the other hand, high dough temperature decreases water absorption and water retention power of the bread, hence less bread will be produced and it would state quickly. Due to high dough temperature, the crust formation will be faster hence more proofing time is required. Bread produced from such dough will have less oven spring, which results into less volume, cave-in side from bottom and side. Other yeast present in the atmosphere may grow in the dough temperature should be adequate. Bakers should calculate the dough temperature by using the following formula :

- **For straight dough method :**

DWT=(DDT x 3) - (FT + RT + FF)

- **For sponge and dough method :**

DWT = (DDT x 4) - (FT + RT+FF+SPT)

Where . DWT : Desired water temperature
FT : Floor temperature
FT : Room temperature
FF : Friction factor
SPT : Sponge temperature

Example :

If desired dough temperature is 27°C (80.6°F)
∴ let us assume that FT is 30°C (86°F)
RT is 29°C (84.2°F)
FF is 4°C (39.2°F)

Hence, as per one formula :

DWT = (DDT x 3) - (FT + RT + FF)
= (27 x 3) - (30 + 29 + 4)
= 81 - 63
= 18°C (64.4°F)

If the desired water temperature is more than the tap water temperature, than heat the water. But if desired water temperature is less then required, it can be obtained by keeping water in a freeze. as it consumes a lot of time, ice can be added to shorten the process. The quantity of ice to be added can be calculated by the following formula :

$$\text{Wt. of ice} = \frac{\text{Wt. of the water} \times (\text{TWT - DWT})}{\text{TWT+80}}$$

Note : If the temperatures are in °F instead of °C, replace 80 by 112

If we refer to the aove example, the temperature of water required is 18°C. But, the actual water temperature (i.e. tap water temperature-TWT) would be near to RT (i.e. around 29°C) hence ice is to be added to bring down the water temperature. So the quantity of ice required can be obtained by the following method ;

∴ Assume the weight of the water required is 60 kg and

Tap water temperautre is 28°C

Hence, as per the formula :

$$= \frac{60 \text{ kg } \times (28°C - 18°C)}{28°C + 80}$$

$$= \frac{60 \times 10}{108}$$

$$= 5.5 \text{ kg ice}$$

Hence, Total 60 kg of water requires - 5.5 kg ice calculated

= 54.5 kg water required

∴ 54.5 kg water + 5.5 kg ice is to be used.

However, in case of sponge and dough method of bread preparation the next formula can be used and find out the results as per the method given above.

Friction factor can also be calculated using the above mentioned formula. In that case, actually running trial dough where temperature of water used for dough making and the temperature of the finished dough is recorded

Hence, the formula DWT=(DDT x3)-(FT+RT+FF) is changed to FF = (DDTx3)-(FT+RT+TWT)

For example :

Spouse

Spouse	TWT	is 70°F
	FT	is 69°F
	RT	is 71°F
	DDT	is 82°F

As per our formula : FF=(DDTx3) -(FT+RT+TWT)
FF=(82x3)-69+71+70)
=246-210=36°F

Mixing Process : Dough can be mixed either with hand or machines, which is termed as hand mixing and machine mixing respectively.

Hand Mixing : Dough can be mixed properly by hand. In this method dough sticks with table and hand at the initial stage. which has to be stuck-off with dough cutter and mix properly.

At the initial stage mix the dough with gentle pressing

⇓

As mixing proceeds, the dough become non-sticky and cohesive mass but its surface remains rough

⇓

Now, mix the dough with pressure so its surface become smooth

Machine Mixing : Mixer machine is used to mix large quantity of dough in a short time with better quality

The machine are available with :

- high and low speed
- horizontal and vertical arrangement
- Single and double arm
- steady and moving bowl
- different capaicty

Baker has to choose the machine according to his situation.

The machine can be divided into three parts:

Slow speed, high speed and spiral mixing

- **SLOW SPEED MIXING**

Dilute the salt, sugar and bread improvers (if added) into water ⇒ Add in to bowl (save little water)

It prevent sticking of the dough with bowl

Mix for few minutes

so yeast cell can be mixed thoroughly ⇐ Add flying ferment

⇓

Add flour ⇒ Mix for about 7 to 8 min.

Rest for 10 min. ⇐ Add the saved water

⇓

Remix for 7 to 8 min ⇒ add fat after completion of half mixing. It helps to reduce mixing time and early addition of fat may reduces the water absorption powder of the flour. Salt may also be added along with fat, which reduces the mixing time.

- **HIGH SPEED MIXING :** Mixing is finished within 2 to 5 minutes (normally 2½ to 3 minutes)

Mix all the dry ingredients

⇓

Add flying ferment

⇓

Mixing is continued with gradual addition of water

⇓

Add shortening/fat when mixing reaches half the way

⇓

Add salt at the last stage of mixing (it saves time)

• **SPIRAL MIXING** : It is a combination of high speed and slow speed mixing. In this process spiral shaped mixing arm is used which provides much better mixing, ensures even crumb structure resulting into whiter crumb colour. In this process :

Add all the ingredients in a bowl

⇓

Mix at slow speed for 2½ to 3 min.

⇓

**Mix at high speed for 3 to 10 min.
(The speed is slower compare to high speed mixer)**

Mixing Stages : Dough passes through different stages while mixing that are :

Stage	Dough Characteristics
Initial	All the beginning • All the ingredients are evenly distributed roughly • Machine does not labour much • Dough is slack, wet and sticky
Pick-up	As the mixing proceeds • Dough becomes dry (as gluten absorb te water) elastic and much cohesive mass. • Dough is still sticky and adheres to the sides of the bowl as well as the mixing arms
Developments	As the mixing procceds • Dough cleans the sides of the bowl and pulls away from the mixing arm • Dough also becomes much dry, elastic and become smooth and glossy from dry and rough
Final	The last stage of proper mixing. • Dough is completely dry, elastic, smooth, velvety • It can be stretched in the form of even semitransparent membrane without breakage. • Stop the mixing
Let Down	If mixing still continues • Dough losses etc elasicity and becomes excessively soft, smooth, velvety and rubbery by stretching action of the mixing arm.
Destruction	If mixing still continues • Dough becomes slack, thin, sticky, excessively soft and loose its elasticity completely.

Mixing Time : The dough is considered as properly mixed when it reaches the development stage. Hence, many factors affect the mixing time :

(i) Flour Quality :

- The quality as well as quality of the gluten effects the mixing time i.e. the strong flour requires much time compare to soft flour.
- Mature flour requires more time as compared to green flour.
- When flour requires less mixing time, the quantity of yeast and salt should be increaed and v/s.

(ii) Bread making Method :

- In sponge and dough method of bread making, sponge requires less mixing (i.e. not even upto the cleanup stage).

(iii) Dough Temperature and Consistency :

- If the actual dough temperature is more or less than desired dough temperature, it requires less or mor time, respectively.
- It is noticed that changes of even 2°F temperature may cause considerable changes in the mixing time.
- Tight dough requires more while slack dough requires less mixing time.

(iv) Fat and Salt Quality and Stage of its addition :

- Excessive salt and fat increases mixing time.
- Addition of both (salt and fat) at the begining of mixing also increases the mixing time.

Over or Under Mixed Dough : The dough that have undergone more mixing and less mixing are known as over mixed and under mixing dough, respectively. The chracteristics of such dough are :

(i) Over Mixed Diough :

- Its gluten structure will result in less elasticity and gas

holding capcity
⇓ hence
the dough will stretch easily and will slow
down the fermentation speed.

- The dough will be too soft, slack and sticky

⇓ hence
It will be difficult to handle and may flatten
out during intermediate or final proofing
⇓ which
would result in lack of volume and
crumb structure in the resultant bread

(ii) Under Mixed Dough :

It will be sticky and lumpy

Its gluten is not sufficiently developed

⇓ hence

it will be less elastic

⇓ hence

it would not extend with the expanding gases

produced during proofing or baking

⇓ hence

bread will collapse at any stage of preparation

⇓ leading to

• low volume • rough surface • walls cave inside • streaks

• lumps • poor texture in the finished bread.

Changes During Mixing :

(i) Physical Changes :

- All the ingredients spread evenly throughout the dough
- The temperature of the ingredients used gets equal
- Heat produced during mixing rises the dough temperature
- Decreases the moisture content due to water evaporation
- Water-soluble ingredients dissolve in water
- Water insoluble ingredients get dispersed in the dough

ii) Chemical Changes

- Water insoluble protein hydrate and form the gluten
- Damaged starch cells absorb more water and swell much
- Oxygen of the air gets incorporated in the dough. So yeast cells, start reproduction which help in fermentation
- Yeast starts producing cabon dioxide by utilizing sugar and water soluble protein i.e. beginning of fermentation

- Air provides center for cell, which produces cellular structure of the bread.

Bulk Fermentation : Dough is allowed to rest for the predecided time limit (after mixing to the beginning of dividing). which is termed as bulk fermentation.

Dough mixed in the mixture is transferred into big vessel. which are known as dough troughs where yeast ferments the dough. if baker has extra mixing bowls, the dough can be allowed to ferment in the bowl itself. The best condition for fermentation is 26.6°C (80°C) temperature and 75% rh.

Physico-chemical Reactions :

- Dough gets ripened.
- As the fermentation proceeds, the dough volume increases steadily till it acquires three times that of the original volume.
- The heat generated during the fermentation increases the dough temperature. No doubt this rise is concentrated at the bottom.
- Starch present in the flour gets converted into maltose and dextrin by distase enzyme with water hydrolysis. The produced maltose is again converted into glucose by maltose enzyme present in the yeast. This glucose and other simple sugars like fructose get converted finally into alcohol and carbon dioxide by the zymase enzyme present in the yeast.

Starch+Water=Diastase⇒Dextrin+Maltose
Maltose+Water=Maltose⇒Glucose+Glucose
Glucose/Fructose+Water=Zymase⇒Carbon Dixode
(Simple sugar) +Alcohol

- Out of the total alcohol produced :
  - Some part gets evaporated
  - Some part is converted into acetic acid.
  - Teh remaining part contributes flavour to the bread and also influences the colloidal nature of the protein.
- Out of the total carbon dioxide produced :
  - Some part gets combined with water and forms carbonic acid.
  - The rest raises the dough volume by aerating action.
- Thus, there are three sources of sugar in the fermenting dough :

- Natural sugar present in the dough.
- Formula sugar added in the mixer
- Sugar produced by the enzymatic action.

$$\text{Protein} \xrightarrow[\text{enzymes}]{\text{Proteolytic}} \text{Peptones+ Polypeptides} \xrightarrow[\text{enzymes}]{\text{Proteolytic}} \text{Peptides+ Amino Acic}$$

- Proteolytic enzymes act on soluble protein and convert them into peptones and polypeptides, which further breakdown to peptides and amino acids. These simple products are assimilated by yeast for its growth and development.
- Proteolytic enzymes also assist in the mellowing of the gluten and softening of the dough.
- As the fermentation proceeds the dough pH is successively decreases as the result of the following processes :
  - Part of the carbon dioxide generated by yeast combines with water and forms carbonic acid which being weak, unstable and slightly ionizable contributes only little in lowering the dough pH.

$$\underset{\text{(Carbon dioxide)}}{CO_2} + \underset{\text{(Water)}}{H_2O} \longrightarrow \underset{\text{(Carbonic acid)}}{H_2Co_3}$$

  - Lactic acid bacteria present in the flour ferment dextrose into lactic acid which being fairly strong acid and produced in sufficiently large quantity, exerts measurable reduction in the dough pH.

$$\underset{\text{(Dextrose)}}{C_6H_{12}O_6} \xrightarrow[\text{acid bacteria}]{\text{Lactic}} \underset{\text{(Lactic acid)}}{2HC_3H_5O_3}$$

  - Acetic acid bateria present in the flour converts alcohol into acetic acid. It exerts in a small quantity and being weak and slightly ionizable its effect on pH is less pronounced.

$$\underset{\text{(Ethyl alcohol)}}{C_2H_5OH} + \underset{\text{(Oxygen)}}{O_2} \xrightarrow[\text{bacteria}]{\text{Acetic acid}} \underset{\text{(Acetic acid)}}{CH_3COOH} + \underset{\text{(Water)}}{H_2O}$$

- Yeast food contains ammonium last, which produces completely ionisable strong acids during yeast assimilation, hence their lowering effect in the dough pH is quiet pronounced, even though these acids are present in very small quantity.

$$(NH_4)_2SO_4 \xrightarrow[\text{assimilation}]{\text{Yeast}} H_2SO_4 + 2NH_3$$

amonium sulphate (Sulphuric acid) (Ammonia)

$$NH_4Cl \xrightarrow[\text{assimilation}]{\text{Yeast}} HCl + NH_3$$

Ammonium chloride (Hydrochloric acid) (Ammonia)

- The gluten is subjected to following changes :
  - Proteolytic enzymes gradually mellow.
  - The last strengthens the gluten and increaes its stability.
  - The gas produced within the dough stretches gluten.
  - By manipulation and enzymatic action, gluten finally acquires web like structure.

The balance between elasticity and extensibility of gluten in a properly conditioned dough should be such that the gluten should remain strong enough (elastic nature) to hold the gases and still mellow enough (extensibility) to expand with the expanding gases.

As fermentation proceed, the dough assumes somewhat drier feeling, which results in sheen surface. Such dough is less extensible and breaks cleanly when stretched.

⇓

Later on, when the dough ripens completely it is known as *mature dough*. It assumes a very smooth as well as spongy apprearance and acquires maximum volume. It breaks quickly with short clean fractures when pulled. bread made from this dough exerts better characteristics.

⇓

If the dough is allowed to ferment beyond this point, its volume starts decreasing, which is known as drop or brack. it turns dough wet and sticky with bucky characteristics. The exact time when dough starts dropping in known as break point.

Under or Over ferment Dough :

(i) **Under Ferment Dough** : If the dough receives less fermentation time (than the required time), it is termed as *under ferment doug.* It is also sometimes referred to as *young* or *bucky dough.* The under fermented dough will produce bread with :

- Less volume
- harsh and reddish brown crust colour
- dull and dark crumb
- close and compact texture having big round cells with thick cell walls
- tendency to be crumbel due to insufficient conditioning of the gluten
- tendency to dry out faster
- flat taste and aroma

(ii) Over Ferment Dough : If the dough receives more fermentation time (than the required time) it is known as over *ferment dough.*

- Such dough becomes soft, wet and sticky due to over action of proteolytic enzyme and low pH.
- Structure forming capacity of gluten weakens and depending on the degree of over fermentation, the bread may have an excessive volume with very open texture or it may collapse during proofing or braking.
- In any case, the water binding capacity of the bread gets reduced resulting in crumblylness quick staling of bread
- The resultant bread will have :

- irregular appearance with rough top and/or caved inside the bottom.
- open, irregular, thick and crumby texture
- light crust and crumb colour due to more utilization of sugar during fermentation
- Sour taste and aroma

Knock Back : In the straight dough methd of bread processing dough is usually knocked back after 2/3 of its estimated fermentation time. In case of long fermentation time, the dough may be knocked back twice or thrice. This device may be useful when oven is not ready to bake and dough is already fermented. The process of knocking back usually done by hand. In this process.

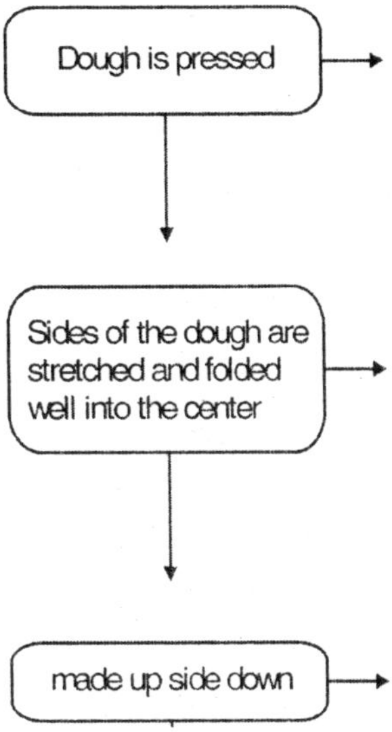

hence gas surrounded by the yeast cell (which is produced during fermentation) is expelled out, hence the yeast cell is again in the position to carry out its function efficiently. Because when yeast cell is surrounded by the gas its activity is slow down, as it is drawn away from its food.

During this step the maximum dough surface is exposed to atmospheric oxygen, which helps in yeast growth. Simultaneously the stretching and folding process aids in the development of the gluten and thereby improves the characteristics of the resultant bread.

It equalizes the dough temperature and thereby equalizes the fermentation speed through out the dough, otherwise the temperature of the upper surface increases at lower speed than the lower surface hence there will be uneven dough temperature which might make variations in the fermentation speed.

The knocking back process may be done by machine, which is known as *punching machine*. After knocking back, the dough is allowed to ferment for the remaining 1/3 time during which, the dough is filled with gases and gluten becomes pliable and ready for further processing.

DOUGH MAKE-UP : The basic function of dough make-up is to transfer fermented bulk dough into properly scaled and moulded or formed dough pieces, which after proofing and baking, yield the desired finished products. It involves five short processes, namely, scaling, rouding, intermediate proofing, moulding and panning.

Scaling : Scaling is also termed as *dividing* or *cutting*. During this process, the bulk of fermented dough is divided into individual pieces of predetermined uniform weight and size. The weight of dough-piece depends on the desired weight of the finished bread. normally 12% additional dough is taken than the desired weight of the finished bread so that the accurate weight of the bread could be obtained after baking and cooling lose. The accuracy in weight should be strictly followed because of Government laws.

In small and medium scale bakery units, the scaling normally carried out by hand. It is desired to cut the dough with a regular dough cutter. Pulling and breaking the dough with hand should be avoided as it disturbs the trend of the gluten strands, which adversely affects the final texture.

Dividing can also be carried out with machine, which is termed as divider. It divides the dough by volume nd not by weight. Therefore it is very necessary that the dough is correctly fermented, otherwise in case of over ferment dough a particular volume of dough will weigh less due to excessive gas in it and the same volume of under fermented dough would weigh more due to lack of gas in it.

The divider available in the market is single pocket divider, double pocket divider, multiple pocket divider etc.In which, the dough is transferred to the hopper of the machine that feeds dough in to the divider's compression chamber. A horizontal plate or dough knife at the bottom of the hopper cuts the dough that fills the chamber from the rest of the bulk dough. The dough pieces are then forced out by the piston.

Rounding : When the dough is cut (during scaling) some of the gas escapes from the cut surface partly through compression and partly as a result of shaving and cutting action. This process of gas escaping is technically known as bleeding. while cutting, the dough pieces become uneven and the cut surface may become sturdy. If such pieces are moulded in this stage, the texture of bread will be uneven. Therefore the dough pieces are rounded in such a way that its cut surfaces become uniform by pressing the dough towards bottom. That is known as rounding or handling up.

During rounding the dough pieces acquire a sufficient thick and continuous skin that retains the freshly produced gas, which aid in the expansion of the dough.

This process may be carried out by machine known as rounder. Normally conical or cylindrical type rounder is used for this process. The dough pieces conveyed from the dividers enter in the rounder generally at the bottom from where it is forced upward along a stationery spiral shaped dough trackup a revolving drum or cone shaped surface. In its upward travel, the dough pieces are continuously rolled and turned in such a manner that it emerges from the rounder as a uniform ball completely employed a continuous skin.

An excessive use of dusting flour at this stage will results in streaks in the bread loaves. In order to prevent this, use of starch for dusting purpose has been found more advantageous. The starch is pneumatically dusted on the dough pieces.

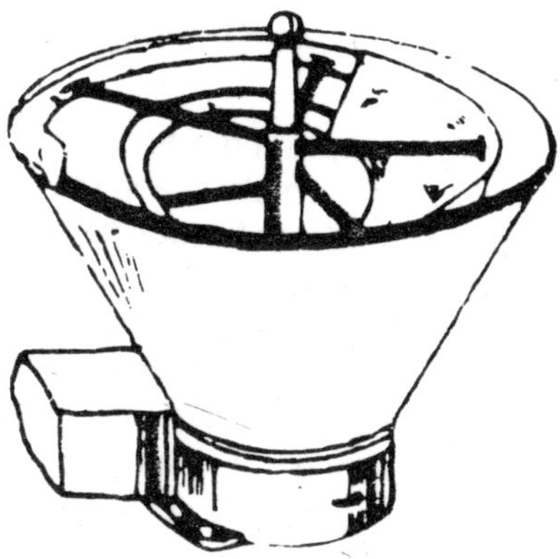

Intermediate Proofing : During dividing and roundig operation, the dough pieces lose a little of their gas & majority of their pliability, gluten strands collapse and become difficult to mould. In order to enable them to withstand the further stresses of moulding without having their skin turn and their cell structure disrupted, the dough given relaxation period, during which the dough pieces get (again) filled with gas and regain pliability. The dough is relaxed for 2 to 20 minutes (normally 10 minutes) at 27°C to 29°C (80° to 85°F) temperature and 75% rh, which are known as *intermediate proofing.*

Moulding : The dough is soft and pliable after intermediate proof, is moulded into cylindrical shape before keeping in bread pan for baking, is known as *moulding*. Moulding is carried out in such a way that it improves the grain the texture of the finished bread. it is an important step in the dough make up process hence it should be carried out properly, otherwise the finished bread may have faults like streaks, core, thick grain, holes etc. Moulding could be carried out by hand or machine.

Hand Moulding :

Press the dough
(to expel out the gas produced
during fermentation)

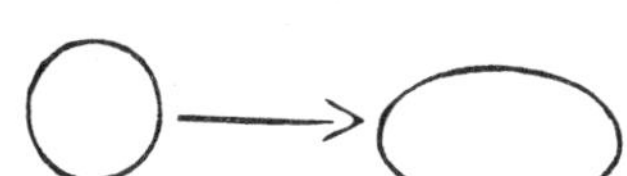

⇓

The upper and lower
ends fix together

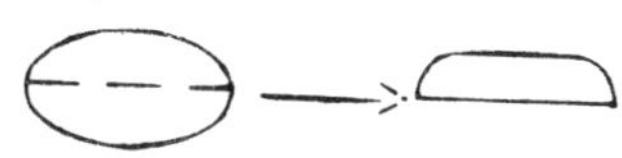

⇓

Stretch both the end turn
in the center
(to make a rectangular shape)

⇓

Start making turn round
from one end
(to make a cylindrical shape)

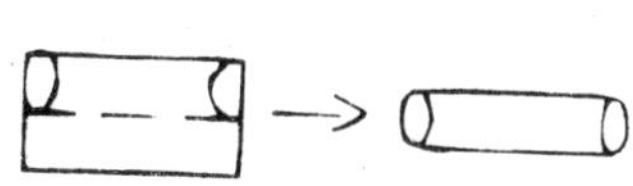

Machine Moulding : The moulding machine is known as moulder. The moulding operation involves three steps :

- *Sheeting* : The round dough ball is rolled through three sets of rollers. The firtst pair of the rolls called head rolls are normally spaced about 0.64 cm (¼") apart and serve the primary purpose of degrassing the dough and flatten the dough. The dough is then passed through second and third roller sets. The distance between two rollers is adjusted to 0.32 cm (1/8") and 0.16 cm (1/16") respectively, where the dough sheet becomes thinner and oblong in shape. This helps to obtain optimum grain and texture development in the finished loaf. The rolls are made of steel and are generally covered with Teflon to reduce sticking of the dough.
- *Curling* : Sheeted dough is carried by a conveyor belt under a flexible woven mesh chain,which rolls the sheeted dough into a cylindrical form. This rolling operation should produce a relatively tight curl that will avoid arid entrapment within the loaf.
- *Sealing* : The curled dough pieces finally pass under a pressure board, which eliminates gas pockets within the dough and also seals the seams of the loaves. The pressure exerted by this board should be adequate to accomplish this purpose.

While moulding we should remember :

- The moulding pressure is even throughout the dough piece. Uneven pressure will leave gas pockets of uneven size in the dough piece. which will eventually results in uneven texture of the resultant bread.
- The dough pieces should not be moulded too tight or too loose. Too tight moulding may tear off the surface, which should remain smooth and may also increase the proofing time. Too loose moulding will open up the texture to an undesirable extent and the shape of the bread may get disturbed.

Panning: The moulded dough pieces are immediately placed into clean and well greased baking pan of appropriate size is known as *panning.* It should be carried out in such a way that, the seams of the dough must be situated at the bottom of the pan. This will prevent subsequent opening of the seam during proofing and baking otherwise it results in rough and irregular crust surface.

Before panning the loaf, the pan must be brought down to appropriate conditions that are:

Tempering the Pan: The pan must be at 32°C (90°F) while panning. However, some bakeries have standardized on higher pan temperature, up to 49°C (120°F), in the interest of somewhat shorter final proof times. This may require pre-warming the pans at the start of day's operation or cooling down the pans by forced air circulation in next successive operation.

Greasing / Glazing the Pan: For easy removal of the bread, the interior surface of the bread pan is either applied with greasy material like ghee/oil/special oils at each panning or with silicon resin layer for several hundred panning operations, which is known as *greasing and glazing*, respectively .

- PAN GREASING: Now-a-days, the ghee/fat is replaced by pan release oil/agent or depanning oil. The pan release agent is the mixture of food grade oils (like cottonseed oil, so bean oil or other food oil which have high smoking point, white mineral oils, surfactants and antioxidants. *Smoke point* represents the temperature at which oil decomposes rapidly enough to produce visible smoke. Hence, the high smoke point prevents early production of smoke from fat and that way diminishes the formation of undesirable off-odours that may be absorbed by the bread. The use of correct quantity of appropriate oil plays a significant role in the ultimate quality of the bread as the pan oil is absorbed by the baked product. Depending on its physical quality, the oil contributes either favourably or unfavourably flavour and crust characteristics of the baked product. Rancid pan oils tend to impart unpleasant off flavours to bakery foods. The excessive amounts of pan oils may result in :

- economic waste
- darkening lower side crusts
- thickening of the bottom crust
- weakening of the side walls which may collapse while slicing
- the crust produced has fried rather than baked character.

The generally accepted quantity of pan oil is 0.1 to 0.2% of the dough (i.e. maximum I gm for 440 gm dough) .

- PAN GLAZING: Application of special silicon resin layer at the interior surface of the bread-tin is known as *Glazing*. Silicon is a synthetic material and has :

- excellent heat stability

- inertness
- electric resistance
- waterproofness
- water repellency and easy handling of bread tin.
- ***Manufacturing :-***

Spraying or deeping the pan → in silicon solution made with appropriate solvent

⇩

Air drying → until coating lost its tacking

⇩

Curing → in an oven at temperature ranging from 205° to 220°C (400° to 425°F) for about 4 to 6 hours.

Note : The care must be taken that the curing temperature of the tinned pans should not exceed 220°C (425°F) as the melting point of the tin is 231.7°C (449°F)

BENEFITS:

- The walls and slicing ability of the bread made in glazed bread tin is better.
- No chance of off-flavour, which are caused in the case of rancid fat or burning of fat when pans are greased.
- The floor, equipments, racks etc. remain clean as there is no scope of fat deposition, as in the case of greasing the pan with fat.
- It is also economical because properly glazed pan can be expected to give effective service up to 400 bakes.

One should be careful that vapour condensation in the pan is limited during proofing or baking as it makes silicon soft.

Bread Pan: Bread pan can be made from, tin plate, black iron, aluminium or aluminium steel. There is no doubt that the tin plate is the best metal for the purpose. The thickness of the metal should be 0.05 em (0.02). Bread quality is markedly influenced by the relationship between pan size and the amount of dough deposited in the pan. Pans which are either too large or too small for the amount of dough used will produce bread with various defects such as coarse uneven grain, small volume, unsatisfactory break and shred etc.

The following pan sizes are suggested for different types of bread :

Bread Type	**Pan Size**
Round top bread (Bread with round crust)	330 to 350 cc/100 gm dough (5.8 to 6.0c in oz dough)
Sandwich bread with close grain texture (Bread with flat crust)	350 cc/100 gm dough (6.0c in /oz dough)
Sandwich bread with open grain texture	400 cc/100 gm dough (7.0 c in /oz dough)

The total volume of a bread pan is obtained by multiplying the width of the pan bottom by its length and depth as measured vertically at the center of the pan. As the bread pans have outward flares of 0.63 to 0.95 cm. (0.25 to 0.375"). the actual pan volume is more than the volume obtained by the above calculation because we have measured the bottom width and length, which is lesser as compared to the top portion. This is corrected by dividing the calculated volume by the factor 0.87. Hence the exact formula is :

$$\text{Bread pan volume (cc)} = \frac{\text{Length of the bottom of the bread pan} \times \text{Width of the bottom of the bread pan} \times \text{Pan's depth at the center}}{0.87}$$

Note : In case of non-flare-pans. no need to divide by factor 0.87.

The flare of pan is useful:

- For minimizing cave-ins of the side walls of the bread loaf as it shrinks during cooling
- Ease in depanning the bread
- To facilitate the nesting of pans in one another.

In addition to that the height of bread-tin should not be more than its top width.

Sometimes:

- for the easy removal of bread from pan
- easy placing of bread tin into oven
- better baking of the bread

3 or 4 pans are joined together which are known as *three-step* or *four-step pan.* In between such bread pans. 2.0 cm (0.75") and 2.5 cm (I") space should be provided in case of open top and sandwich type bread respectively for easy

circulation of the heat which helps in proper heating of the bread pan.

The new bread pans are whipped off with the cloth and heat at 227°C (440°F) temperature for 8 to 12 hrs. before using first time.

PROOFING: After panning. the bread loaf is relaxed under suitable conditions [35° to 36°C (95° to 98°F) temperature and 80 to 85 % rh]. This is known as *proofing.* It is carried out in pan itself hence also known as *pan proof and* being last proof it is also termed as *final proof:*

While proofing:

- Dough relaxes from the physical punishment received during moulding
- Acquires gas that is lost during moulding. as it aerated again
- Gluten is matured to such extent that it expands with the expanding gas and still retains sufficient strength to hold the gas.

Factor Affecting the Final Proof: The normal proofing time is 55 to 65 minutes. But the more common practice is to proof the dough up to the predetermined height [normally I cm (0.5") less than the height of the bread pan)] rather than for a fixed time. Hence the final proof time will vary somewhat with the following factors. However, the actual proof time can be determined only through practical experimentation.

(i) *Temperature:* If the panned dough temperature is lower than the proofing temperature, fermentation will proceed at a higher rate in the warmer outer zone of the dough than in its interiors, giving rise in the finished loaf to a fine texture at the outer rim and dense at the center. On the other hand, if the proof box temperature is maintained too low, proof time is extended which results in coarse texture.

(ii) *Relative Humidity:* Low humidity tends to promote the formation of a dry crust. which interferes with loaf expansion in the oven and results in low volume & adverse effect on the crust colour. Excessive humidity causes moisture condensation on the loaf which gives rise to tough crust and/or the formation of blisters in the finished product.

(iii) *Diastetic Activity of the Flour:* During critical stage of proofing operation, the yeast should have sufficient food (in the form of fermentable sugar) to carry out its function (fermentation) efficiently, which may be the result of optimum diastetic activity of the flour. If the flour has insufficient diastetic capacity, the proofing period is unduly prolonged affecting the texture adversely. Excessive diastetic action will also adversely affect the texture as there will be excessive gas production and gluten will also be excessively mellowed causing collapse of the dough.

(iv) *Fermentation:* If the dough is under fermented, the gluten will have less stretcheability and more resistance. which may results in excessively long proofing time.

Under or Over Proofing:

(i) *Over Proofing:* The dough acquires more proofing is known as *over proofdough.* Over proofing results in loaves with pale crust colour, coarse grain, poor texture, low volume, irregular shape, impaired keeping quality and a flavour with acid over stones due to over fermentation.

(ii) *Under Proofing:* The dough. which acquires less proof. is known as *under proof dough.* It produces bread similar to less fermentation, like small loaf volume, shell top, foxy red crust colour and occasional bursting at the sides.

BAKING: Baking is the final and most important step in bread processing. During baking process the raw dough pieces. under the influence of heat are transferred into a light, porous. readily digestible and flavoured product due to many physiochemical changes.

Time and Temperature : Normally, the breads are baked in between 220° to 245°C (430° to 470°F) temperature for about 20 to 30 minutes. However the good average temperature is 232°C (450°F) and time is 25 minutes. The main factors influence on time and temperature are:

- If a formulation contains more than 6 % sugar or any amount of milk solids (i.e. milk bread. french loaf) the product should be baked at lesser temperature for longer time as the higher temperature may cause more caramelization and may result into dark crust colour.
- The sandwich bread should be baked at low temperature for a longer time as compared to open top bread.
- Large size products are baked at low temperature for a longer time than small size products.
- When the oven is over loaded, the baking time should be increased and the temperature should decreased and *vis.*

Physico-chemical Changes :

(i) *Oven Rise and Oven Spring:* When the bread pan is kept inside the oven, for the first few minutes, the dough pieces may increase volume gradually, known as *oven rise.* But after sometime the sudden expansion in bread loaf by about *1/5* of its original volume is take place due to following reactions. which is known as *oven spring:*

- Dough contains millions of minute air cells, which expand due to heat that increase the bread volume.
- Carbon dioxide produced during fermentation is dissolved in the aqueous phase of dough, which is released from the dough when temperature reaches 49°C (120°F) and migrates into existing cells, thereby adding to their internal pressure and ultimately to their size.
- Alcohol and many other organic acids. esters. aldehydes and ketons (produced during fermentation) are in liquid state changed into gaseous state at 80°C (175°F). The production of vapour contributes to the gas pressure within the cells and their expansion.
- Water also converts into vapour just like alcohol and similarly expands the volume.
- In the first few minutes of baking stage, the fermentation speed increases. which produces more carbon dioxide suddenly and expands the volume.
- In addition to these. one physical law also contributes to expand the volume, i.e. small gas cells require considerably greater pressures to expand than large gas cells. Hence, once the pressure in the minute gas cells of the dough exceeds due to the above mentioned processes up to a certain limit the restrictive fortes of the cell walls suddenly give way and the cells undergo an abrupt expansion.

(ii) *Yeast Activity:* Yeast starts functioning vigorously due to increase in temperature but it gets inactivated at 60°C (140°F) temperature during the last stage.

(iii) *Enzyme Activity:* The enzymes still remain active up to 76°C (170°F) producing sugar from starch. This activity is enhanced due to the fact that the starch is partially gelatinized making it more susceptible to enzymatic action. As the yeast which had been consuming sugar is already inactivated, this sugar remains in bread and performs its usual functions of retaining moisture, imparting colour to the crust and improving flavour & taste.

(iv) *Starch Gelatinization:* During baking, the starch granules begin to absorb water and swell at about 40°C (104°F) temperature.

This is known as *galatinization.* It protects the oven spring. Gelatinization would not complete due to lack of water. time and temperature.

(v) *Protein Denaturation:* The water absorbed by starch during gelatinization generally comes out from gluten due to its denaturation. During this process. the gluten film surrounding the individual gas vacuoles. gets transferred into a semi-rigid structure by interaction with the swollen starch. As the gas cells expand. the flexible starch granules within the cell wall are elongated. enabling the gluten film to become thinner and ultimately to rupture. During this time. starch swelling has advanced sufficiently to prevent a collapse of the dough structure.

(vi) *Protein Coagulation:* As baking proceeds further. the proteins are coagulated at 74°C (165°F). setting the structure of the product, afterward there will no further rise in the bread volume. Once the structure of protein is set, it starts to gain temperature. so that the weight is lost due to the evaporation of the moisture from the product and the crust starts acquiring golden brown colour. The protein coagulation continues till the end of baking.

(vii) *Browning Reaction:* Browning reaction in oven is caused due to caramelization and maillard reaction. It makes the crust brown .

- **CARAMELIZATION** : At about 170°C (340°F) temperature. sugar is hydrolyzed initially into monosaccharides followed by polymerization which makes the product brown. This reaction is taken place into the crust only. because the internal temperature of the bread never exceeds 100°C (212°F). hence the crust is always darker than crumb .
- **MAILLARD REACTION:** It starts at 160°C (320°F). This involves the reaction between free reducing sugar and free amino groups of amino acids / peptides / protein and produces successively melanoid in which provides brown colour as well as specific smell and taste to crust.

(i) *Insufficient Oven Heat:* If the oven is too cold, the dough temperature rises steadily. which leads to delayed protein coagulation resulting in late setting of crust and crumb. Simultaneously. yeast remains active for longer period will increase the fermentation, ultimately results in the excessive volume and light crust colour. Due to the lack of sufficient temperature, bread requires longer baking time resulting in more evaporation of moisture. Hence, the resultant bread is shortweighed, dry, crumbly and stales faster. This condition is useful when the bread is to be made from green flour. weak flour or young dough.

(ii) *Excessive Oven Heat:* This may be due to excessive heating or inadequate loading of the oven. If the oven is very hot, the coagulation of protein on the outer surface (i.e. forming of crust) will take place very soon. That will block the easy transmission of heat inside. As a result when gas expands in the inner portion and crust being non-stretchable, there will be exaggerated break. low volume, poor shape and uneven grain with large flat holes (due to collection of air cell). The crust will be too dark and bread will not be baked properly from the inside. The excessive oven heat is useful when the bread is to be made from old tlour or lean formula (having low sugar).

(iii) *Excess Steam:* When the dough piece emerges from the final proofer, its surface temperature is generally within a range of about 35° to 40°C (95° to 105°F). If such dough is placed in a steam-saturated oven. moisture will condense on its cool surface. This would results in tough & leathery crust and surface blisters. The adequate amount of moisture may not be baked off from the bread may make the crumb over moist and vulnerable to mould infection. This situation may favour good oven spring and volume.

(iv) *Insufficient Steam:* Lack of humidity in the oven will cause faster evaporation of moisture from the external surface of the bread. As a result, there will be premature formation of crust.

Hence, the gas produced in the crumb after crust formation will exert pressure and finally erupt through crumb just below the crust causing separation of crust from crumb in the form of a shell. It is referred to as a *shell top.* It can be markedly detected in case of open top bread. The same situation may arise in case of insufficient humidity during proofing, young dough or dough made from strong flour. If the shell top is not formed the hard crust may prevent the expansion of the loaf resulting in low volume and poor shape.

(v) *Improper Heat Distribution:* For the most part, faulty heat distribution in oven manifests itself in insufficient bottom heat. i.e. the heat conducted through the hearth. Such maldistribution of heat produces loaves possessing a well-baked top crust but an under baked bottom crust and side walls. Hence, the sides of the resultant bread cave-in during cooling and collapse on slicing & stacking on retail shelves.

(vi) *Incorrect Pan Spacing:* Bread moulds having 400 gm dough, should always be placed in oven at a distance of about 1 cm (1/2") and· parallel to each other which will ensure proper circulation of heat results into evenly baked products. If moulds are loaded too close to each other. the sides of the bread, which are in close contact, will be insufficiently baked. Hence, the possibility of causing rope/mould disease is increased. So, it is beneficial to use three step or four step pans to keep proper distance between pans.

DEPANNING : Bread should be released from the mould immediately after baking otherwise the moisture trapped between the bread and the interior surface of the mould will make the product soggy, technically known as *sweating*. In such cases the possibility of fungal infection increases.

COOLING: The bread should be allowed to cool after releasing from the bread pan. There are no fixed criteria for cooling the bread but the general concept is that the interior (middle part) crumb temperature should be reduced within a range of 35° to 40°C (95° to 105°F). The cooling operation should be accomplished within the shortest possible time and without excessive evaporative moisture lose. While cooling the bread, its surfaces should be kept open as much as possible and the bread should not be in contact with each other otherwise there might be moisture condensation.

SLICING: When the bread is hot. starch granules are in a swollen state and are held unstably in gluten framework. If the bread is sliced in this condition. the unstable starch granules will lump-up together giving a poor appearance to the slice. In addition to that, if such hot bread is sliced in a slicer. the crumb pieces may stick with slicing knives that may affect by fungal infection. If the fresh bread is sliced in this condition. the microorganisms stuck with the slicing knives will stick into the crumb of the fresh bread and infect it. Hence. it is very essential that the slicing knives should be properly cleaned before use. After the bread is brought down to room temperature, the starch granules will shrink and stabilize In gluten framework. Hence. bread could be sliced neatly.

PACKAGING OR WRAPPING OF BREADS : Bread is packed in order to preserve freshness and protect from the hazards of external contamination. Airtight packing is not advisable in tropical countries like India. Hence. use the packing material. which permit the bread to breath and not expose the bread unduly. The airtight packing material may condense the moisture while the highly porous material may increase the drying rate. Previously, wax coated papers were used to pack the bread for this reason but now indented polypropylene (plastic bags) is widely used. For attracting the consumer and to catch the eyes of the people the packing material is always printed.

When the bread is withdrawn from the oven after baking. the process of moisture evaporation continues as long as it is warm. If the bread is wrapped during this stage. then some of the water vapour will absorbed by the bread (specially crust) while some part will remain as free moisture. The free moisture part will be conducive to fungus infection. Therefore. bread should be packed only when it is thoroughly cooled.

9

Manufacturing Process of Bread

BRIEF : Various methods of bread preparation have been introduced during the past several decades. Each baker has to select his own method after careful consideration of a prevailing situation. The different bread making methods are divided basically in two groups. i.e. conventional and mechanical.

TRADITIONAL : This group includes straight dough method, sponge & dough method. salt delayed method and ferment & dough method.

Straight Dough Method: In this method. all the ingredients are mixed in one stage of mixing and the dough is allowed to ferment for a predetermined time. Fermentation period may range between 30 minutes and 16 hours depending on the quantity and quality of yeast water, salt, flour, temperature etc. If the fermentation time is upto 5 hours. the method is termed as *short process* while if the fermentation is more than 5 hours it is termed as *long process.* During long process, it is difficult to' control the rise in dough temperature. which invariably increases the fermentation speed. causing more production of acid, which makes the taste and flavour of the bread acidic and also makes the gluten soft and sticky. Hence. it is advisable to use short process instead of long process. In the short process. it is advisable to adopt the process having 3 to 4 hours fermentation period. While using long process the temperature, yeast quantity should be decreased whereas the sugar and salt quantity should be increased (which make the gluten stronger and control over fermentation). The dough should be knock back after 2/3 times of total bulk fermentation period.

(i) *Merits and Demerits*:

- All the ingredients are mixed together at once in this method. hence it requires: • less time • equipments • place • labours • electricity as compared to sponge and dough process which requires twice the mixing and weighing etc.
- All the ingredients are added together hence sugar. salt etc. increase he osmotic pressure, which results in decreased yeast activity. In order to compensate with that more yeast is required that results in poor control over fermentation.
- There is no chance to improve any mistakes in this method.

Sponge and Dough Method: The ingredients are mixed in two stages i.e. sponge and dough. The sponge usually contains 50 to 75 % (1/2 to 3/4) of the total flour. all the yeast & yeast food and malt together with enough water to make slack dough. Addition of all or part of shortening may also be made at this stage (although it is more common to add it later). 50 to 75 % of total salt may also be added to control the fermentation. All these ingredients are mixed just sufficiently to incorporate them evenly. Yeast starts its function immediately after mixing. as it is capable to ferment the dough speedily at the sponge stage due to slack dough. Simultaneously, the gas produced during fermentation increases the volume of the dough. but the quantity of yeast is proportionately more as compared with flour. Hence, the resultant dough is not capable to retain the produced gas hence after sometimes gas breaks the dough and comes out so the dough begins to decline in volume. is called the *drop or break*. And the point at which the dough starts to collapse is known as *drop stage*. The time required for drop to occur depends on many factors like temperature, type of the flour, amount of yeast, type of malt etc. Mostly, the dough temperature is maintained between 24° to 29°C (72° to 78° F) and all other variables are adjusted in such a way that, the dough drops or breaks within 3 to 5 hours.

The second stage in sponge and dough method is dough stage. In this stage. the sponge is return to the mixer and mixed with all the remaining ingredients. It is advisable to test the sponge physically for its readiness before mixing the dough. The dough can be tested by :

- Take a small piece of sponge and try to break it with both the hands. If the piece breaks with a clean fracture. the sponge is ready for mixing. If the sponge is not ready. the piece will stretch to some extent and will break in unevenly stretched shreds. In such a case the sponge should be allowed more fermentation time.

- Tear the sponge apart from the center with both hands and examine the web structure. If the web structure is very fine the sponge is ready.
- An adequately fermented sponge feels dry to touch without any stickiness present.

When the sponge is ready, it should be break down properly in the water so that its even mixing in the dough is ensured. Broken down sponge is mixed with remaining flour. sugar. salt, fat, milk powder etc. ingredients remaining for a complete formula. The dough after proper mixing is returned to the fermentation room, where it is relaxed for 15 to 60 minutes. that is known as *flour time.*

Out of the total flour required. the part of it is added at sponge stage and the remaining part is added at dough stage. i.e. if 60% of the total flour is added in sponge stage then 40% is added in dough stage. This method is known as *60:40 sponge and dough* method. If the sponge time is less then 2 hours. it is termed as *flying sponge.* However, in such cases the quantity of yeast and water should be increased.

(i) ***Merits and Demerits :***

- The fermentation is to be carried out in two stages. Hence, it may be useful to adjust the total fermentation time by adjusting at any stage of fermentation.
- The quantity of yeast required is less due to long fermentation time. It is estimated that about 20% of the yeast could be saved as compared to straight dough method.
- All the formula yeast works only on a part (usually 1/2 to 3/4 of total requirements) of the flour, effecting better maturing of gluten. Therefore. the resultant bread will have greater volume. more desirable texture & grain. better water retention capacity (which prevents quick drying of the bread) and a pleasant flavour.
- Weak flour could be used in this method, which is not possible to use in the case of straight dough method. However. the weak flour should be used at dough stage only, because in sponge stage much fermentation is carried out leading to more gas production which would not be retain by the weak flour. while in dough stage less fermentation is carried out which produces less gas, that could be retain by the weak flour.

- Baker can ward off a number of minor irritants like temperature variations due to weather conditions, lack of diastetic capacity in flour, too high gluten in the flour. low dough rising capacity of the yeast etc. by using this method.
- In this method, each batch is to be mixed twice, ingredients are weighed in two lots and dough is to be handled several times. Hence. labour. equipments, floor space. time. electricity etc. are required more than straight dough method.
- The mixing and fermentation loss of the dough (due to twice mixing and fermentation) leads to less production.

However those small disadvantages are far outweighed by better quality of products, hence it is advisable to use this method for big plant.

Salt Delayed Method: This method is similar to straight dough method except the salt is added at a later stage of fermentation. As the salt has a controlling effect on enzymatic action of yeast, the speed of fermentation of salt less dough will be faster that leads to reduction in total fermentation time. The salt is added at the knock back stage (i.e. after 2/3 part of the total bulk fermentation time). The method of salt addition is applied as per the convenience of individual baker, like:

- It may be shifted (dry) on the dough. It is made into salt solution by diluting in water and the solution is mixed along with flour. Both water and flour are saved previously from the total quantity required. Flour is added to prevent slipperiness caused by addition of salt solution.
- Some baker creams the salt with fat and mixed with the total dough.

The dough is then remixed for 1/4 part of the total mixing time because initially it was mixed only for 3/4 part of total mixing time.

(i) *Advantages and Disadvantages*: Due to absence of salt the fermentation speed is enhanced and gluten does not became hard (as salt provides hardness to the gluten) hence. gluten is matured in a reasonably shortertime. So, this method is specially suitable for hard flour and method with shorter fermentation time.

No Dough Time Method: Dough is not fermented in this method but. it is just allowed to rest for a brief period (about 30 minutes). So. it recovers from the strain of mixing. Since dough is not fermented. the twin function of fermentation (i .e. production of gas and conditioning of gluten) is achieved to some extent by increasing the quantity of yeast (2 to 3 times of original quantity) and by making the dough little slacker and warmer. Now-a days. the small scale bakers widely use this method due to high speed.

(i) *Advantages and Disadvantages:* The bread made by this method has· lack of aroma • poor keeping quality • low moisture retention power • strong yeast flavour

To improve the quality of such bread· acetic acid • calcium propionate • potassium bromate • potassium iodate etc. chemicals /bread improvers are to be used. even though only fairly good bread could be made.

Ferment and Dough Process: This method is similar to sponge and dough method except a few variations. Very often a bread formula contains milk powder, egg, substantial quantity of fat and sugar (i.e. milk bread, special toast, sweet dough. danish pastry etc.). All these formula ingredients will have retarding effect on yeast activity. If all the formula yeast, part of flour. yeast food and sufficient water are mixed together just like flying ferment. the yeast gets initially an environment which is conductive to vigorous activity and at the end of fermentation time (of ferment) it is in a fit condition to take the extra load of fermentation. Ability of ferment for fermentation depends on the product desired, that is decided by the individual baker differently:

- Some bakers consider the ferment ready for mixing when it drop by itself.
- While others may considerjust prior to its dropping.
- Some bakers may consider sometime after dropping off the dough.

Once the ferment is ready. it is mixed into dough, along with the remaining ingredients and allowed to ferment for the second stage. Then it is processed similar to other methods.

MECHANICAL DOUGH METHOD :

During the past many years various methods of bread making have been developed to accelerate the speed and improve quality. The mechanical method is one of them. In this method dough development process is carried out by mechanical energy instead of bulk fermentation. Due to absence of fermentation, its main function of gas and alcohol production cannot take place. which leads to absence of pleasant characteristics (i.e. sour taste and smell) in the bread. Such bread losses its palatability hence it is not accepted by people. Hence. liquid brew (or broth) is added to provide taste and smell. Liquid brew is prepared by mixing of water, yeast, milk powder, MYF. salt, liquid sugar and part of flour in a steel tank and by stirring it for about 6 hours at 30° to 38°C (86° to 100°F).

Mechanical method is divided in two parts: batch process and continuous process. The batch process includes Chorleywood process and Sheeting process whereas continuous process includes Do-Maker process, Amflow method, Strahmann method, Ivarsson method, Konpetua method, Buss method, Rabinovich method etc. All these methods are more or less basically similar except minor differences particularly with type of mixer machine. Moreover these methods are not popular in India hence a general flow sheet is explained here in short.

Liquid Brew	
⇓ **pumped into** ⇒	other ingredients like flour, shortening etc. high speed mixer roughly incorporated together
Incorporator (Premixer)	
⇓ **gradually pumped into**	
Dough developer ⇒	fast rotating spindles mellows the dough and liquid air incorporated at high pressure is converted into vapour that increases the dough volume (in conventional method it is achieved by fermentation)
Dividing and Moulding ⇒	dough extruded through divider in a measured quantity and in the shape of moulded bread.
⇓	
Panning ⇒	moulded dough falls in a bread tin which travel at a constant speed on a conveyor belt.
⇓	
Proofing ⇒	belt passes through overhead proover
⇓	
Baking ⇒	fully proofed dough enters in tunnel oven and baked completely when reach to other end.
⇓	
De-panning ⇒	by vacuum or jets of air
⇓	
Cooling ⇒	through cooling chamber (including refrigerator)
⇓	
Slicing and Wrapping	

10

Bread

Baking bread is one of mankind's more important discoveries, possibly ranking alongside the discovery of fire and the invention of the wheel. Bread has played a key role in the development of mankind and is one of our principal sources of nutrition. Historically, it has contributed to language, social structuring, and spiritual imagery. Today it contributes convenience, variety, and a healthy dietary component to modem lifestyles and £2 billion per annum to the UK economy.

Although wheat grains have been found in Neolithic burial sites dating back 30,000 years, it took man many thousands of years to learn to make bread out of the grains he had roasted or eaten as porridge. The precise origins of bread-making remain obscure, but it is known that our ancient ancestors were familiar with baking. Remains of bread have been found in ancient Egyptian tombs and settlements throughout the Pharaonic period (approximately 3100-330 B_e), (Figure 10-1), and for a time bread formed the basis of their entire administrative system, being both a unit of measure and currency. For example, priests and temple officials received 900 fine wheat breads, 36,000 flat breads annually, whereas the average peasant received just 3 breads and 2 jugs of beer a day.

Baking bread is a sophisticated cooking operation and a relative newcomer to cooking methods. The first and simplest form of cooking is roasting over an open fire. Boiling foods is more complex, requiring the facility for retaining both food and water in a heat- and water-proof container. Baking is more sophisticated still, requiring a container able to generate and retain dry heat. Baking ovens are more permanent structures than open fires and more suited to permanent settlements such as villages and cities. This permanence allowed for longer preparation times and more complex cooking operations; hence the major product of baking, bread, is arguably mankind's most complex staple food. Having settled in villages and cities, the luxury of lengthier times in which to prepare food allowed our ancestors to perfect raised bread, which requires lengthy proving times to develop the aerated structure. This is why, for example, the Jewish Passover is celebrated with unleavened bread; the Hebrews fled Egypt hur-riedly, not having time to prepare raised bread. So when the God of the Israelites established a memorial feast for the Exodus, it sacrificed the eating of raised bread, as a reminder of the haste with which the children of Israel left Egypt: "Celebrate the Feast of Unleavened Bread ... as a lasting ordinance for the generations to come ... And when your children ask you 'What does this ceremony mean to you?' then tell them 'It is the Passover sacrifice to the LORD, who passed over the houses of the Israelites ... when he struck down the Egyptians.' " (Exodus 12: 17,26-27, Holy Bible).

Fig. 10.1 Ancient Egyptian Breadmaking

The aeration of bread is central to its appeal; hence the focus on the exclusion of leavened bread in the Passover as a reminder of the luxuries of time and settlement that raised bread demands. Therefore, in this chapter we also focus on breadmaking from the point of view of aera-tion. Understanding how bubbles are entrained during mixing, grow during proving, and are set during baking is the key to understanding the effects of ingredients and processing on bread-making and to improving breadmaking processes. The technology of bread making is a vast subject, beyond the scope of this single chapter, and has been recently reviewed extensively by Cauvain and Young. Here we confine ourselves largely to this aeration perspective, believing this to be a neglected aspect of bread-making and one that gives a sound basis from which to understand the uniqueness of bread, its production processes, and technology.

In this chapter we first outline the breadmaking process in terms of its major unit operations and typical processes. We then present the background understanding of dough rheology required to understand the development of bread structure and its origin in dough protein chemistry. We then move on to consider the three major breadmaking operations in detail, mixing, proving, and baking, focusing at each stage on the effect of each operation on the bubbles. Finally, we bring this understanding together to identify the characteristics of good breadmaking wheat varieties and indicate how viewing breadmaking from an aeration perspective offers commercial opportunities for improving the breadmaking process.

BREADMAKING

Breadmaking is about aeration. Why do we eat bread? For food-for its nutritional value in terms of energy and body-building proteins. But the irony is that in making bread, we actually lose some of the original nutritional content of the flour, because the yeast turns it into carbon dioxide gas to make the bread rise. So turning flour into bread means that about 3% of the flour is turned into gas and wasted, in terms of nutrition. We feed the yeast rather than feeding ourselves. Also, all the trouble we go to make raised bread is enormous, allowing it to rise for hours under carefully controlled conditions of temperature and humidity, when it would be much more efficient, both in terms of time and nutrition, just to boil up the flour to gelatinize the starch, and then eat it as a paste. In many countries, the staple local cereal is eaten in just this way. So why do we go to all the trouble of making bread from wheat flour when it wastes some of the flour and takes so much time and effort? The reason is that we like raised bread. We like the texture and appearance of aerated baked loaves. Not all bread is aerated; many breads are flat. But the unique thing about wheat flour is that it will allow this aerated structure, much more than other cereals will. The unique gluten proteins in wheat, when mixed with water, form a viscoelastic network that is able to retain gas during rising without premature rupturing. For this reason, for its ability to produce raised bread, wheat is the world's number one cereal.

So we make bread because we like the aerated structure, and wheat is the only cereal to give us such a good aerated structure. But if you ask the average baker what the ingredients in bread are, he or she will most likely say "Flour, water, yeast, salt, improver, fat," and possibly a few others. What he or she is unlikely to mention as an ingredient of bread is gas. Chamberlain described gases as "the neglected bread ingredients," and it has very much been the case over the past 100 years of bread research that aeration aspects have tended to be neglected. In recent years this is primarily because aeration is difficult to study directly, and because the chemistry of breadmaking has tended to dominate over the physics. But aeration is an essential element of every stage of the breadmaking process, and understanding bread aeration has commercial and technical benefits. Breadmaking is about aeration, controlling the gas phase throughout the process. The essential stages of a breadmaking process are mixing, proving, and baking. Each of these stages involves aeration. During mixing, small bubbles are incorporated into the dough; these bubbles are inflated with carbon dioxide gas during proving; and the aerated structure is modified and set by baking.

Manufacturing Process

There are many breadmaking processes around the world, and a great variety of types of bread. In this section, we will concentrate on just two contrasting breadmaking processes, traditional bulk fermentation processes and a newer mechanical dough development (MDD) process, the Chorleywood bread process (CBP). We will highlight the fact that although aeration is key in both, in the newer process an understanding of bubble behaviour throughout the process is even more important.

Bulk Fermentation Processes

The major traditional breadmaking process is the bulk fermentation process, in which the dough mass is allowed to ferment over a lengthy period of time. Cauvain lists the three essential features of bulk fermentation as:

- Mixing of the ingredients, usually at slow speed, to form a homogeneous dough
- Resting of the dough in bulk for a prescribed period of time (typically 1-3 hours), during which the yeast ferments to inflate the dough mass
- Remixing of the dough part way through the bulk fermentation to remove most of the gas produced and increase the number of gas cells (known as "punching" or "knock-back")

The purpose of this bulk fermentation period is partly for flavour development, but primarily for developing the dough protein structure so that it is better able to retain gas and retard co-alescence of gas cells during subsequent proving. The slow inflation during bulk fermentation stretches the dough proteins biaxially, so that they align into a co-operative network that imparts superior elasticity and extensibility to the dough. Historical experience taught bakers that this structure development produced a larger loaf volume and finer crumb structure, and bulk fermentation has thus been a feature of bread-making for centuries.

Baker and Mize showed that gas cells must be incorporated into the dough during mixing to act as nucleation sites for the carbon dioxide produced during proving; yeast is unable to generate bubbles from nothing. Without these sites, the CO_2 has nowhere within the dough to diffuse and is largely lost from the dough, resulting in a loaf of low volume and a coarse, unattractive structure. The operations of punching and molding (in which the dough is sheeted between rollers, then rolled up into a "Swiss roll" to orient subsequent bubble growth and give a firmer crumb structure) serve to redistribute the gas bubbles, so that the relationship between aeration during mixing and final baked loaf structure is weak.

The Chorleywood Bread Process

The biaxial extension during bulk fermentation is not the only way to develop dough protein structure and rheology. Swanson and Working reported that, for small doughs, development could be achieved by mixing at high speeds. This eliminated the need for the lengthy bulk fermentation period and reduced flour losses caused by yeast metabolism, thus promising a huge economical benefit. The development process is now called MDD. Major sources for the following description of the subsequent exploitation of this finding are Williams, Campbell, and Cauvain. The problem of scaling up MDD to plant scale remained until Baker introduced the Do-Maker process in the United States (US Patent 2953460). Baker and Mize had found earlier that the use of chemical oxidants, such as potassium iodate or sodium chlorite, reduced the amount of mixing required to develop the dough mechanically, thus facilitating scale-up of the MDD process. The Do-Maker process was continuous, producing bread with a large volume and soft, fine texture suited to the American market.

A number of other continuous MDD plants followed the Do-Maker process, including the Amflow process in the United States and the Brimec process in Australia. Those in Britain (such as the Baker Perkins' continuous sponge and dough plant and the Oakes continuous mixer/modifier) attempted to produce a coarser loaf than that produced by the Do-Maker process; however, the expense of continuous processing technology and the poor economic and practical performance, compared with traditional bulk fermentation methods, prevented significant acceptance of these new processes.

The British Baking Industries Research Association at Chorleywood was among those investigating MDD and its potential for application to breadmaking in Britain. Beginning their studies with continuous systems, they soon discovered that bread quality was greatly improved if the dough from a small continuous mixer was mixed further in a high-speed batch mixer before proving. They then measured the work input to the dough and decided that the critical factors for optimum dough development were the amount and rate of energy imparted to the dough, irrespective of whether this energy was applied in a continuous or batch mixer. A work input of 40 kJ/kg, imparted in less than 5 minutes, was found to be suitable for a wide range of flour types and for several mixer designs, although subsequent industrial practice has reduced the mixing time to around 3 minutes. The significance of batch MDD was that such a process could have a sufficiently low capital cost to be affordable by many small bakers; it has since become the predominant breadmaking process in Britain and other countries including New Zealand, Australia, and South Africa.

A large part of the subsequent development of the CBP centered on the design of a batch mixer powerful enough to impart this energy at plant scale. The mixer was designed and built by the Tweedy Co. of Burnley and is known as the Tweedy mixer. On scale-up of the original prototype mixer to plant scale, it was found that the bread texture was no longer acceptable, having developed large holes and a coarse texture. This was apparently due to excess air being entrained into the dough on scale-up and was rectified by applying a partial vacuum during mixing; this has been a characteristic of the CBP ever since. The requirement for oxidants to facilitate dough

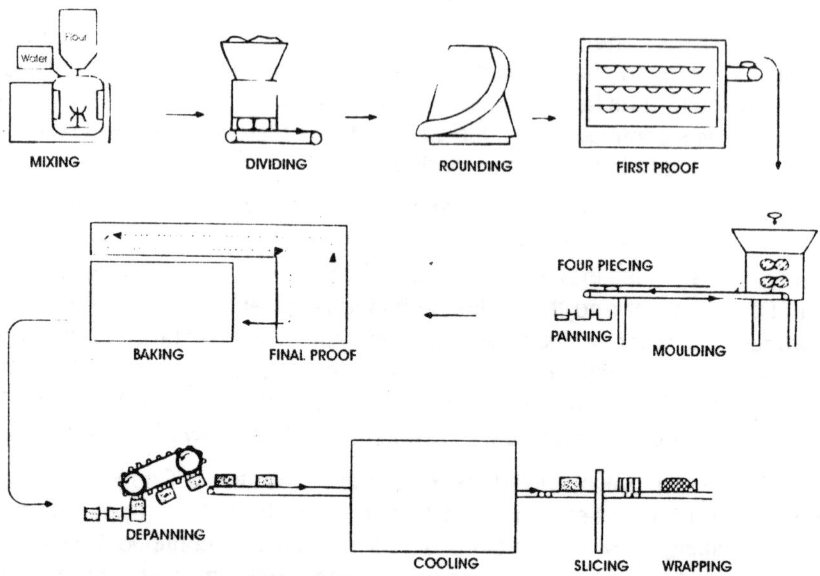

Figure 10.2 Steps in the Chorleywood Bread Process

development remained. Potassium bromate has now been banned for use as an oxidant in bread- making in the United Kingdom and elsewhere, leaving ascorbic acid (vitamin C) as the only permitted oxidant in the United Kingdom. Ascorbic acid requires atmospheric oxygen, which is limited by mixing under partial vacuum. This has led to the development of pressure-vacuum mixing, in which doughs are initially mixed under positive pressure to increase oxygen availability, then vacuum applied toward the end of mixing to reduce the air content.

The CBP was the first batch MDD process and has become the predominant breadmaking process in Britain and elsewhere today. Figure 10-2 describes the major operations in the CBP, and Table 10-1 contrasts these with bulk fermentation processes. Increased yeast levels are required in the CBP to ensure adequate CO_2 production, because the yeast has less time to multiply. The yeast metabolizes less of the flour; therefore extra water is required in the dough, thereby increasing yield. The CBP can also use flour with a lower protein content than that required for bulk fermentation. High-melting-point fats are required in the dough formulation for CBP bread to aid bubble stabilization during baking. Because the CBP eliminates punching and performs molding before much yeast activity has occurred,

Table 10.1 Major Operations in the Chorleywood Bread Process Compared and Contrasted with the bulk Fermentation Processs

	Bulk fermentation		Chroleywood Bread Process	
Operation	Function	Typical details	Function	Typical Details
Ingredients weighing	Inclusion of minor ingredients	Weighed manually and added to mixer, Yeast level -1%	As for BF.	Yeast level-2.5% Lower protein content and more water relative to BF. Oxidants requried for dough development High melting point fat required.
Mixing	To hydrate and blend ingredients	Slow mixing possibly by hand	To hydrate and blend ingredients develop dough, and incorporates air bubbles.	Intense batch mix, 40 kj/kg in < 3 min, under partial vacuum of pressure-vacuum.
Bulk fermentation	Flavour development Dough development	1-3 hours. Final dough temperature 21-27°C		
Punching	to expel gas and subdivide gas cells, even out temperature variation and incorporate air into dough mass.			
Delayed ingredient addition	To modify progress of fermentation			
Dividing	To divide dough mass into approx 1-kg portions	A volume of dough is sucked into a chamber and ejected onto a conveyor	As for BF	As for BF
Rounding	To set the shape of the dough piece.	A rotating cone carries the dough in a spiral fashion along a curved channel.	As for BF.	As for BF.

Table 10.1 Contd.

Operation	Bulk fermentation		Chroleywood Bread Process	
	Function	Typical details	Function	Typical Details
First Proof			To allow stresses in dough to relax, improving handling properties	Dough pieces travel through cabinet in individual pockets, residnece time 10-15 min.
Molding Four-piecing and panning	To convert dough piece into cylindrical shape with appropriate internal structure and deposit into pans.	Dough piece sheeted between rollers, rolled into Swiss roll, divided into four pieces, rotated through 90°, deposited into pan,	As for BF.	As for BF.
Proving	To allow dough to rise through the action of yeast producing, CO_2	38°C, 80% relative humidity, 45-50 min.	As for BF.	As for BF.
Bakign	To set loaf strucuture and develop baked flavor and color.	Continuous oven, 200°C, 20-25 min.	As for BF.	As for BF.
Depanning	To remove baked loaves from tins	Loaves are sucked out of tins by vacuum.	As for BF.	As for BF.
Cooling	To cool loaf sufficiently to allow slicing and prevent moisture migration on wrapping.	Cooled to a center temperautre ot <27°C in cold air, residence time-2	As for BF.	As for BF.
Slicing and wrapping	Hygeinic, aesthetic and convenient presentation to consumer	Reciprocating frame of blades, followed by automatic wrapping.	As for BF.	As for BF.

the bubble size distribution at the end of mixing has a much greater influence on baked loaf structure than for traditional bulk fermentation processes. This has renewed interest in the aeration processes occurring during high-speed dough mixing and in how the bubble size distribution incorporated during mixing grows and changes during proving.

Having contrasted bulk fermentation processes and the CBP, it remains that the three major operations in both processes are mixing, proving, and baking. Understanding breadmaking from the point of view of aeration means understanding bubble behaviour during each of these three stages. We will use this breakdown into the unit operations of mixing, proving, and baking to understand the physical and chemical phenomena involved in transforming flour to bread. But first, we need to review the background understanding of dough chemistry and rheology required to understand bread aeration.

DOUGH RHEOLOGY AND DOUGH DEVELOPMENT

Within the cereal science community, there is a widespread conviction that baking quality is in some way related to the rheological properties of dough, mainly because of subjective manual assessments of dough rheology before baking. Here we will review those rheological properties that are thought to be relevant to breadmaking performance.

Dough is a nonlinear viscoelastic fluid that is shear thinning, work hardening, and possibly exhibits a small yield stress. Dough rheology changes during mixing, and in MDD processes it is the mixing action that develops the required dough rheology for good bread volume and structure. The rheology of breadmaking is a vast and complicated subject; see Bloksma (1990a,b) for a good review. Dough may not be the most rheologically complex system on the planet, but it is close, and is often quoted as an example of a complex rheology. Because of its complexity and the fact that the rheology changes during mixing, dough rheology has mostly been assessed using empirical instruments developed for quality control in the bakery but, in the absence of more fundamental rheometers, applied to baking research. The interpretation of the results of these instruments in engineering terms is difficult. An irony is that it is dough rheology that confers bread-making potential on wheat flour by allowing bubble growth, but that in measuring dough rheology, the contribution of the bubbles is neglected. Bubbles in dough influence dough rheology; at the least, whenever measurements of dough rheology are reported, the air content of the dough should be reported as well, alongside the usual information of protein content and water absorption.

In this section, we will first define the science of rheology and fundamental rheological parameters. We will then consider empirical and fundamental methods for characterizing dough rheology, and ultimately identify the important rheological parameters for good bread quality. Finally, we will consider how the complex rheology of dough arises from the chemistry of gluten proteins and how this relates to dough development during mixing.

Rheology is the study of the flow and deformation of materials. Deformation or strain is applied to a material, and the resultant forces or stresses are measured to give an indication of the stiffness, modulus, or viscosity of the material. The general aims of rheological measurements are:

- To obtain a quantitative description of the material's mechanical properties
- To obtain information on the molecular structure and composition of the material
- To characterize and simulate the material's performance during processing

Rheology can tell us how a material will behave under a given set of conditions and can be used to characterize and predict the material's performance during deformation, for example, during mixing, proving, and baking of dough. Sometimes it is not possible to make precise measurements during the actual deformation process: for example, it is difficult to access the dough during mixing or baking. We therefore have to calculate the range of conditions the dough experiences during a given process and then extrapolate from rheological measurements made under much more controlled laboratory conditions. What is necessary is to have a good idea of the range of physical conditions that are experienced during the deformation process being studied, for example, strain state, strain rate, pressure or force, temperature, humidity, etc., and then to perform rheological experiments under that range of conditions.

Rheological Test Methods

Many test methods are used to measure rheological properties. It is not possible to describe all the available testing geometries here, and the reader is referred to reviews by Whorlow, Ferry, Barnes, Hutton, and Walters, Dobraszczyk and Vincent, and van Vliet. The ones chosen here have been applied particularly to doughs. It is common to categorize rheological techniques according to the type of strain imposed: e.g., compression, extension, shear, torsion, and the relative magnitude of the imposed deformation; e.g., small or large deformation. The main techniques used for measuring dough properties related to breadmaking quality have traditionally been divided into descriptive empirical techniques and fundamental measurements.

Descriptive Rheological Measurements

There has been a long history of predicting baking quality using descriptive measurements of the physical properties of dough, such as the Farinograph, Mixograph, Extensograph, and Al-veograph. This probably originates from the common practice among bakers of assessing the quality of a dough by stretching the dough by hand. Although this is a subjective method of measuring rheology, it has proved remarkably successful and should indicate the type of rheological measurements necessary to predict baking performance. These measurements are not strictly "rheological" tests because:

- The sample geometry is variable and not well defined.
- The stress and strain states are complex and nonuniform.
- It is therefore impossible to define any rheological parameters such as modulus or viscosity.

Therefore, these instruments are purely descriptive and depend on the type of instrument, size, and geometry of the test sample and the conditions under which the test was performed. Empirical instrumental tests have been developed to characterize processing variables such as "handling ability" or "mixing tolerance" while processing dough in a mechanized plant. For example, empirical tests have been used to characterize the behavior of bread doughs during processing, such as the Farinograph and Mixo-graph. Many of these are used as "single point" tests, in which a single parameter is used to correlate with performance, which is appropriate only to the set of conditions under which that test was performed and is generally not applicable to any other conditions. Because dough experiences a wide range of conditions of stress states and strain rates during processing and baking and the rheological properties of dough depend both on time and strain, there is often a discrepancy between such single point type tests and actual performance on the plant, where conditions of strain and strain rate may be poorly defined and different from those in the laboratory test.

Most food materials are viscoelastic, and therefore their properties depend on how quickly the test is performed (the strain rate or frequency) and also how quickly the measuring instrument responds to that change. This is important in many aspects of dough processing: if the dough is deformed quickly, such as in mixing or sheeting, then the rheological properties of the dough will be very different if measured at the typically slower rates of deformation found in conventional testing machines. Alternatively, the dough may experience strains very different in magnitude and nature from those generally available in a rheological test. Thus, a test under only one particular set of conditions of rate, temperature, and strain will almost certainly not be applicable to another set of conditions. What is necessary is to define the set of conditions under which the dough operates in practice and perform tests under similar conditions. However, such descriptive instrumental measurements have provided cereals scientists with useful information on product performance and evaluation of quality during processing.

Farinograph and Mixograph

The Brabender Farinograph and associated in-struments measure force or torque during mixing of doughs. This instrument is possibly the most widely used physical dough-testing machine found in cereals laboratories throughout the world, and its main use is as a quality control tool to predict the amount of water to add to a flour to achieve a fixed consistency of dough during mixing. The Mixograph, another recording dough mixer, is used to classify wheat according to its mixing characteristics and to predict product performance, such as baking. At first sight, it is difficult to see why measuring forces developed during mixing should have any relationship with baking performance. Typical strain rates in the Farinograph (10 S-1) are different from those experienced by the dough during baking expansion (10-4 -10-3 S-1), and the nature of deformation during mixing (mainly shear) is entirely different from that in baking (biaxial extension). Nevertheless, Farinograph and Mixograph measurements have been correlated with baking quality. Traditionally, higher Farinograph consistencies are related to better baking quality.

Measurements during mixing give some indication of gluten quality in the flour, and differences in gluten composition are considered to lead to differences in the development of structure during mixing. It is known that higher molecular weight (MW) gluten protein fractions are related to improved breadmaking performance. The larger molecules present in high MW glutenin fractions require more time for alignment during mixing than shorter molecules, and the larger molecules will produce a higher elastic response during mixing. The combined effect of the presence of the higher MW protein fractions is to give a longer mix time and more water required to produce a fixed consistency. This indirect effect of protein structure on mixing development has led to the strong empirical association between baking quality and mixing measurements.

Extensional Instruments

The Brabender Extensograph and Simon Research Extensometer are two empirical instruments widely used to obtain descriptive measurements of the uniaxial extensional properties of dough. In the Extensograph a ball of dough is shaped into a cylinder, clamped in a cradle, and stretched by a hook passing through the center of the sample. Force and time are recorded, and the main parameters derived are maximum resistance to extension (RM), the maximum extensibility (E), and the area under the curve. Desirable dough properties combine high resistance to extension with good extensibility. In the Extensometer, a ball of dough is impaled on the two halves of a split pin. One of the pins is driven upward at constant speed, stretching the dough into an extended ring shape. Force and time are the recorded parameters. A recently developed instrument for the measurement of extensibility of doughs and glutens is the SMS/Kieffer attachment for the TA-XT2 Texture Analyser.

Alveograph

Chopin attempted to develop a test that would simulate as closely as possible the conditions that dough experiences during baking. A circular sheet of dough is clamped at its circumference and inflated by air passing through a central hole in the base plate, resulting in an expanding bubble of dough until rupture. Pressure and time are recorded, giving a typical trace. The commonly measured Alveograph parameters are the maximum pressure (PMAX), maximum length or extensibility (L), and the area under the curve (W). Alveo-graph parameters are widely used to assess the breadmaking quality of French wheats. Highly significant correlations between W values and loaf volume have been found for flours of different quality. Bloksma (1 957b) found correlations between Alveograph parameters and baked loaf volume were poor ($r^2 = 0.48$) when a number of different varieties of varying quality were compared, but that the correlations improved ($r^2 = 0.78$) if samples of the same variety were compared. Weipert compared loaf volumes from four types of German flours and reported the strongest correlations with Alveo-graph parameters ($r^2 = 0.80$) within individual flour types. Launay found a good correlation ($r^2 = 0.90$) between relaxation times determined from a modification to the Alveo-graph (Relaxo-calculator) and loaf volumes for 30 samples of French wheat flours.

Fundamental Rheological Tests

Rheological tests attempt to measure the forces required to produce given controlled deformations, such as squashing (compression), bending, or pulling apart (tension), and to present them in such a way as to be independent of sample size, geometry, and mode of testing. They measure a well-defined property, such as stress, strain, stiffness, or viscosity. A small test piece of the material is usually deformed in a controlled way, normally on a motor-driven machine, and the force is measured, as well as the distance moved or displacement of the object. The force is then usually plotted against the displacement to give a force-displacement curve. Normally, we would divide the force and displacement by the original sample dimensions to obtain stress (force/area) and strain (displacement/original dimension); this allows us to remove the sample size as a variable. In materials that undergo large deformations such as dough it is necessary to normalize by actual dimensions during deformation, because the geometry often changes in a nonuniform and unpredictable manner (for example, a sample of dough under large extensional deformation will become thinner in the middle, see "Strain Hard-ening and the Stability of Bubble Expansion").

Material properties should be independent of size, shape, and how they are measured; in other words, they are universal, rather like the speed of light or density of water, which do not depend on how much light or water is being measured or how it is being measured. It would be comforting to know that the modulus of bread measured in a laboratory in Reading will be the same modulus as that measured in a colleague's laboratory in Hong Kong, even if they are measured using different tests, sample sizes, or shapes. The whole point of the rheological approach is that the properties that are measured are reproducible and can be compared between different samples, test sizes and shapes, and test methods. Empirical measurements frequently measure a single point number under a particular set of test conditions for one particular material. Although this may give the illusion of a "scientific" test by being performed on a machine (frequently with a computer attached) and may give satisfactory correlations with a textural or processing parameter, it is impossible to compare results from different testing machines, and once you start to apply that test under different conditions or to other materials, the correlations break down or become irrelevant.

Problems encountered with such fundamental tests are complex instrumentation, which is expensive, time-consuming, difficult to maintain in an industrial environment, and requires high levels of technical skill; often inappropriate deformation conditions; difficulty in interpretation of results; and slip and edge effects during testing. Furthermore, these tests often show no clear relationships between the parameters measured and the baking performance of doughs.

In dough testing, there are three main types of fundamental rheological tests used: (I) dynamic oscillation, (2) creep and stress relaxation, and (3) extensional measurements.

Dynamic Oscillation Measurements

Adapted from techniques developed for measuring viscoelastic properties of polymer melts and solutions (Ferry, 1980), this is one of the most popular and widely used fundamental rheological techniques for measuring doughs. It has the advantage of a well-developed theoretical background, readily available instrumentation, and simultaneous measurement of elastic and viscous moduli, whereas the nondestructive nature of the test enables multiple measurements to be performed while temperature, strain, or frequency are varied.

Disadvantages of the dynamic oscillation method are that the deformation conditions are often inappropriate to baking, because they are carried out at rates and conditions very different from those experienced by the dough during processing or baking expansion. For example, rates of expansion during proof and oven rise are between 5 x 10^{-3} s^{-1} to 5 X 10^{-4} s^{-1}, compared with measuring rates in rheological tests several orders of magnitude greater, as shown in Table 10-2. Dynamic oscillation measurements can be made only over a relatively narrow window of frequencies, which are not relevant to the strain rates observed during fermentation and baking. It is possible to extrapolate dynamic oscillation measurements over a much wider range of frequencies using the time-temperature superposition principle. This states that time or frequency and temperature are interdependent. The time over which a material is deformed is important, especially if it is a polymeric material such as gluten. If the time is short (high frequency), the polymer

Table 10.2 Comparison of Deformation Conditions during Proof and Baking and Those in Dynamic Oscillation Rheological Testing

Deformation Conditions	*Conventional Rheology*	*Proof and Baking*
Strain rates (s^{-1})	10^{-2}-10^{2}	10^{-4}-10^{-2}
Strain (%)	Low : 0.01-1	High : >>100%
Type of deformation	Dynamic shear	Biaxial extension

molecules have little time to adjust to the imposed deformation, and the material registers a high stiffness and an apparently gel-like or elastic behaviour. If the imposed deformation occurs over a long time (low frequency), the polymer molecules have time to flow, and the material registers a lower stiffness and a fluid-like or viscous behaviour. Temperature has an equivalent effect to time by changing the speed at which the polymer molecules respond: low temperature decreases the molecular mobility and is equivalent to increasing frequency or decreasing time, so that the elastic zone is extended into the lower frequency region. For example, ice behaves as a viscous liquid in glaciers over long periods of time, but if deformed rapidly by a hammer, it will behave like a brittle elastic solid. By conducting rheological measurements over a fixed range of frequencies at a series of temperatures, it is possible to extend the frequency range by several orders of magnitude to the much lower frequencies relevant to baking expansion.

Conventional oscillatory shear rheological tests usually operate in the linear region at small strains in the order of up to 1%, whereas strain in gas cell expansion during proof is expected to be in the region of several hundred per cent. Furthermore, most rheological tests are carried out in shear, whereas most large-strain deformations in dough (i.e., sheeting, proof, and baking) are extensional in nature. It is not widely recognized within the cereals science community that measurements in one deformation field such as shear are not always directly applicable to a different deformation such as extension. Polymer melt fluid dynamics show that very different results are possible in shear than in extension because of the different physical effects these deformations can have on networks of molecules. From extensional studies on long-chain high MW polymer melts, it is known that entirely different rheological properties are obtained in shear than in tension, especially if the polymer chains are branched. For example, the elongational viscosity of low-density (branched-chain) polyethylene melts increases with both strain and strain rate (strain hardening), whereas the shear viscosity decreases with strain and strain rate (shear-thinning), see Figure 10-3. At short times (high frequencies) or low strains, shear and extensional viscosities are identical and follow the theoretical steady state relationship. At higher strains or longer times, extensional viscosities start to deviate considerably from shear viscosities in a nonlinear manner. This indicates the difficulty in extrapolating large-deformation behaviour from small-deformation rheology and also the danger in assuming that shear and extensional viscosities are connected by a simple theoretical relationship. In molecular terms extensional flows can be visualized as uncoiling, stretching, orientation, and entanglement of long-chain molecules during extensional flow, whereas in simple shear they remain coiled and can slip past each other. The molecular stretching and entanglement in extensional flow causes viscosity to increase with strain and strain rate, a phenomenon known as strain hardening.

Relationship of Dynamic Oscillation Tests to Baking Performance. Most dynamic rheological measurements have investigated the effects of water, temperature, mixing conditions, and added ingredients on the dynamic moduli of dough. Figure 10-4 shows the viscous (0") and elastic (0') moduli for dough over a range of frequencies. Elastic properties predominate over viscous properties, and the moduli are slightly frequency dependent. This is typical of a cross-linked polymer gel.

No convincing relationship has been established between the dynamic rheological properties of doughs and their baking performance compared two flours of different baking quality and measured lower values of elastic (storage) modulus (0') for the higher baking quality flour. Similarly, Weipert and Amemiya and Menjivar found lower values of 0' corresponded with better baking quality. Others, however, have found that a higher value of 0' for glutens and doughs relates to better baking performance. Small deformation dynamic rheological measurements have provided useful information about the properties of isolated glutens and their subfractions in relation to baking quality, but similar measurements on whole dough systems have not shown any significant differences. It is postulated that these conflicting results are

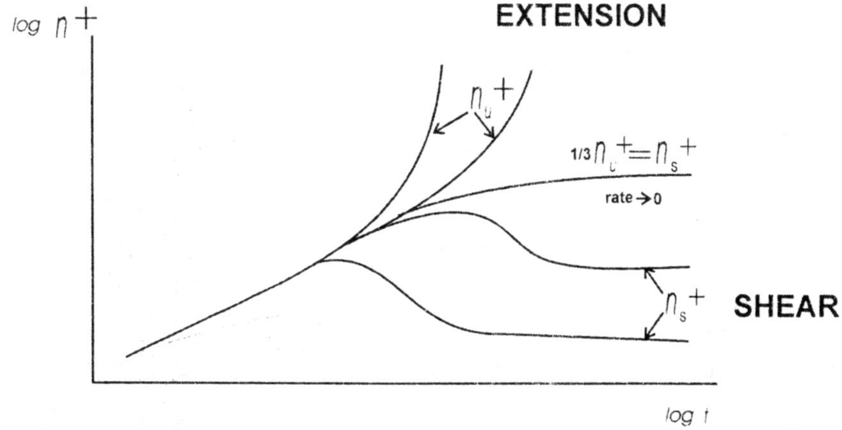

Fig. 10-3 Schematic Comparison of the Defferences between Transient Shear (ns^+) and Transient Uniaxial Extensional (nu^+) Viscosities Compared with the Theoretical Steady-State Relationshop ($nu^+ = 3ns^+$)

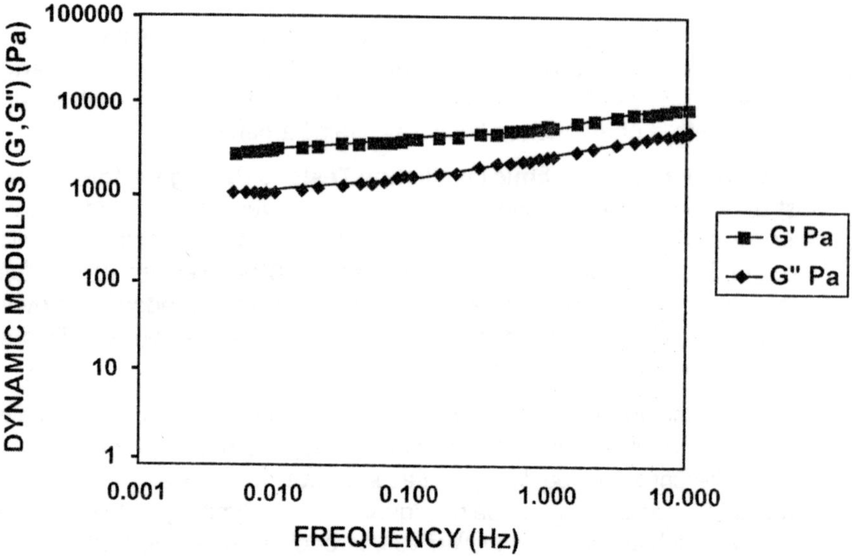

Fig. 10-4 Elastic (G') and Viscous (G") Dynamic Moduli for Bread Dough over a Range of Frequencies

obtained because most of these tests are carried out at rates and conditions very different from those experienced by the dough during baking expansion.

Creep and Stress Relaxation

In stress relaxation measurements, deformation is held constant, and the force response is measured; whereas in creep the stress is held constant, and the deformation is measured. Schofield and Scott Blair first measured the creep response of dough and obtained values for elastic moduli and viscosity that are still relevant today. Gluklich and Shelef and Bloksma applied constant stress and measured elastic and viscous creep moduli for doughs. Bloksma and Bushuk surveyed the experimental results from the literature for stress relaxation measurements for a number of doughs. None of the curves showed the ex-ponential decay typical of a single relaxation time, but corresponded to a decay typical of a spectrum of relaxation times. This suggests that no one molecular mechanism is responsible for the relaxation process within dough.

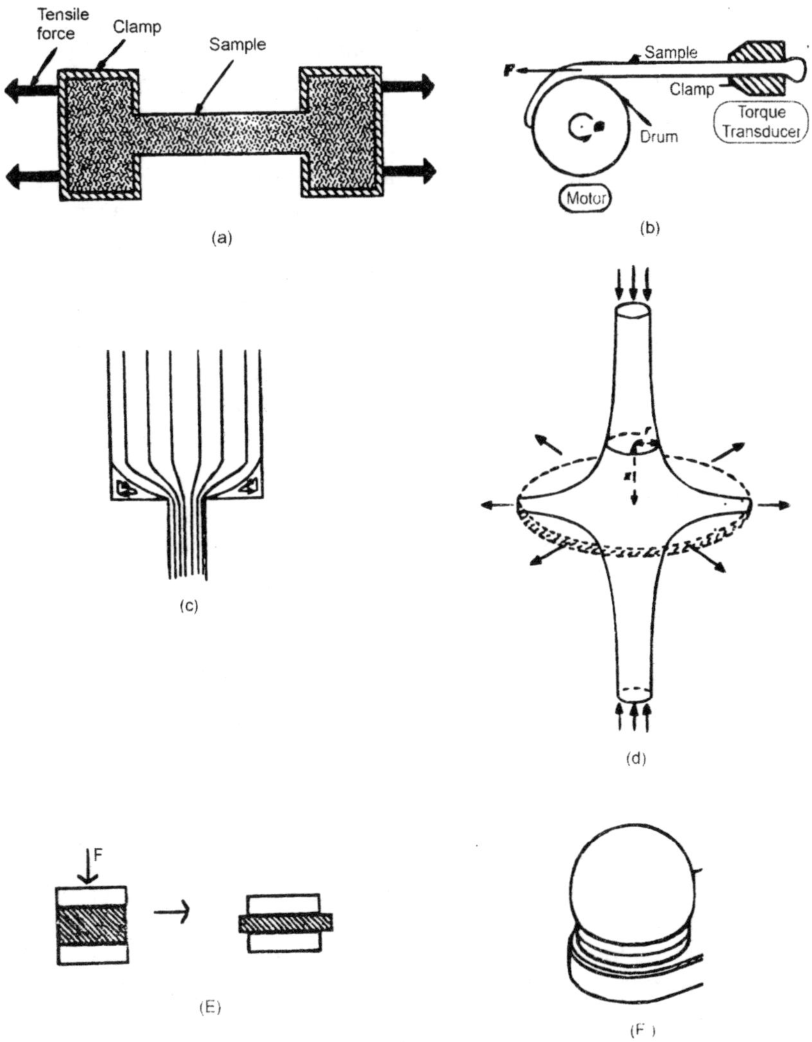

Fig. 10.5 Various Types of Extension Flow Measurements : (a) Uniaxial Extension (b) Fiber Windup; (c) Converging Flow ; (d) Opposed Jets; (e) Lubricated Compression; (F) Bubble Inflation

Launay and Bure and Launay indicated that a slower relaxation time is associated with good baking quality, and Launay found relaxation modulus is relatively independent of water, mixing time, or temperature. Bohlin and Carlson performed stress relaxation measurements on dough and gluten in shear and showed that the relaxation behavior of dough could be described by two relaxation processes: a rapid relaxation over 0.1 to 10 seconds and a slower process occurring over 10 to 10,000 seconds. Frazier, Fitchett, and Russell Eggitt measured stress relaxation properties of dough after compression. They found relaxation times passed through a maximum that was considered to indicate optimum dough development for baking. Dobraszczyk measured relaxation properties of good and poor breadmaking flour doughs in rapid compression and found stress relaxation gradients greater for the poor flour, indicating a more viscous response in the poor breadmaking flour and a more elastic response for the good breadmaking flour. Measurements of large-deformation shear stress relaxation properties have been found to be useful in discriminating between different wheat varieties of varying quality, and relaxation parameters were found to be closely associated with baking volume.

Extensional Techniques

Types of extensional flow measurements include simple uniaxial tension, fiber wind-up or spinning, converging flow, capillary extrusion, opposed jets, lubricated compression, and bubble inflation (Figure 10-5). Several methods have been used to measure the rheological properties of dough in extension: simple uniaxial extension, where dough is stretched in one direction; and biaxial extension, where the dough is stretched in two opposing directions, which can be achieved either by compression between lubricated surfaces or by bubble inflation.

Uniaxial Extension. One of the oldest and most popular test methods to measure materials properties is the uniaxial tensile test. A strip of material is clamped at both ends and pulled apart at a fixed rate in a suitable testing machine, and the force measured at the same time as the displacement of the object. The force is generally plotted against the displacement (extension) to give a force-extension curve. Tensile tests may produce an approximately uniform extension of a sample provided necking and flow does not occur. Normally the force and extension are divided by the original sample dimensions to obtain stress and strain and allow removal of the sample geometry as a variable, although in the case of dough actual sample dimensions during deformation should be used, because the sample geometry changes considerably and non-uniformly. The slope of the stress-strain curve then gives the elastic modulus or stiffness.

The earliest attempts to characterize the fun-damental rheological properties of dough were in a series of uniaxial extensional measurements by Schofield and Scott Blair, who stretched a cylinder of dough floated on a mercury bath and measured the elongation and force. Plastic and elastic components of defor-mation were resolved and viscosity and elastic modulus were calculated. Schofield and Scott Blair showed that the rheological behavior of dough is nonlinear with strain and strain rate (i.e., elastic modulus and viscosity varies with both rate and strain) and therefore showed it is impossible to predict the behavior of dough from measurements made under conditions different from those it experiences in practice. Rinde, Tschoegl, and Smith measured the large extension properties of doughs by extending a ring of dough suspended in a liquid of density equivalent to that of the dough between two hooks at constant deformation rates until rupture. Strain and stress at rupture were considerably less for poor quality flours than good quality flours.

Biaxial Extension and Bubble Inflation. In biaxial extension, a sample is stretched at equal rates in two perpendicular directions (x and y) in one plane, as in an expanding spherical balloon (Figure 10-6). The inflation technique has been one of the most widely used methods for measuring biaxial extension properties of biological materials, polymer melts, and rubbers. The major advantage of this test is that the deformation closely resembles practical conditions experienced by the cell walls around the expanding gas cells within the dough during proof and oven rise (i.e., large deformation biaxial extension). Extensional rheological properties can be measured at large strains up to failure, and the gripping problems normally as-sociated with uniaxial tests can be minimized. Treloar showed a good approxi mation to equal biaxial extension near the pole of an expanding bubble of rubber. In this technique, a sheet of the material is clamped between two flat plates, one of which has a circular aperture and the other a hole through which a controlled volume of air or liquid is pumped to inflate the sheet. Denson and Gallo, Denson and Crady, Joye, Poehlein, and Denson, and Rhi-Sausi and Dealy used inflation to study the biaxial extensional proper-ties of molten polymers. Shadwick reviewed the use of biaxial testing on arteries of invertebrates, worms, guts, and cow teats. Infiation was first used as an empirical technique to measure wheat gluten and bread dough exten-sibility in the 1920s by Hankoczy and Chopin. This method was later developed for use as a rheological tool by Launay, Bure, and Praden, based on equations derived by Bloksma. Dobraszczyk and Roberts used an inflation

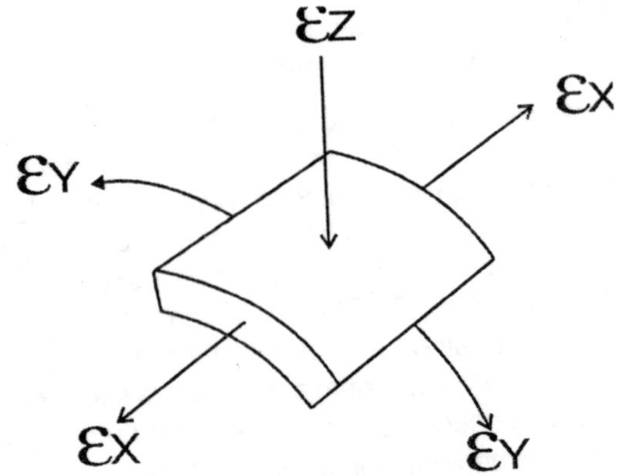

Fig. 10.6 Biaxial Extension of a Sample Stretched at Equal Rates in Two Perpendicular Directions (ε_x and ε_y)

method to mea-sure the fracture and biaxial extensional rhe-ological properties of wheat doughs, further developed by Stable Micro Systems as a commercial test system for wheat flour doughs, called the D/R dough inflation system.

Stress, strain, and apparent viscosity can be derived directly from a knowledge of the pres-sure and height of the bubble during inflation. Bloksma derived equations from which bubble inflation data derived from the Alveograph could be converted directly into rheological units of stress, strain, and strain rate from a precise knowledge of the bubble height, pressure, and inflation rate with time. These equations were verified by Launay et al., who found calculated values to be in good agreement with experimental values.

Other methods of biaxial extension measure-ment include compression between flat plates using lubricated surfaces, which produces purely extensional flow provided no friction occurs. Bagley and Christianson, Huang and Kokini, and van Vliet, Janssen, Bloksma, and Walstra measured the extensional rheological properties of wheat doughs using lubricated compression. Wikstrom and Bohlin and Kokelaar et a1. found differences in extensional strain hardening among varieties of different baking quality, with good breadmaking varieties showing greater strain hardening. Meissner developed a rotating clamp technique for measuring both uniaxial and biaxial elongational properties of molten polymers, and a more recent modification using conveyor belts has been used to measure the extensional properties of bread doughs. Wikstrom and Bohlin used converging flow through a parabolic contraction nozzle to measure the extensional properties of wheat flour doughs.

Biaxial Extension Rheology and Baking Performance

During proof and baking, the growth of gas bubbles determines the expansion of the dough and therefore the ultimate volume and texture of the baked product. It is postulated that the limit of expansion is related directly to the rupture of the bubble walls caused by the loss in gas retention. Therefore, the stability of the cell wall around the expanding gas bubble is considered to be an important factor in determining baking quality. The relevant rheological conditions around an expanding gas cell during proof and baking are biaxial extension, large strain, and low strain rate. The rheological behavior of dough is known to be non-linear with both strain and strain rate, and because the dough experiences very large strains in gas cell expansion and sheeting, the prediction of extensional properties from small deforma-tion shear measurements is not possible (see section "Dynamic Oscillation Measurements" and Figure 10-3). Any rheological tests that seek to relate to baking performance should therefore be performed under conditions similar to those of baking expansion, such as large strain biaxial extension. Bubble inflation therefore potentially offers the most appropriate method for measuring rheological properties of doughs and has the advantage that, through the equations of Bloksma, fundamental rheological parameters can be derived.

Strain Hardening and the Stability of Bubble Expansion

Strain hardening is shown as an increase in the slope of the true stress-Hencky strain curve with increasing extension, giving rise to the typi-cal J-shaped stress-strain curve observed for highly extensible materials (Figure 10-7b). Strain hardening (sometimes called work hardening) gives an increase in stiffness with increasing strain or an increase in transient extensional viscosity with strain rate (Figure 10-3). Assuming the rheological behavior of dough is approximated by a power law relationship:

$$\sigma=k\varepsilon^{n}$$

the strain hardening index is obtained from the slope of log stress versus log strain plot (Figure 10-7c).

$$n=d\ln\sigma/d\ln\varepsilon$$

Recent work has shown that bread doughs exhibit strain hardening in large deformation biaxial extension and that these extensional rheological properties are related to baking performance. The occurrence of strain hardening is known to be essential to maintain stability against premature failure in materials that need to stretch to large deformations, such as polymers drawn into fibers or inflated into thin films, metal drawing and forming, and biological materials. When stretching occurs, there are bound to be local inhomogeneities and some areas that are thinner than others. At low strains these inhomogeneities are relatively unimportant, but as the material becomes thinner on stretching, the stress in the thinner areas increases relative to the surrounding material. This would eventually cause failure in a nonstrain-hardening material as the increased stress in the thinner areas leads to a greater rate of thinning, eventually leading to catastrophic failure. Strain hardening acts to compensate against this increased rate of thinning by increasing stiffness locally, stabilizing any regions of localized thinning, and allowing greater total deformations before failure.

During stretching of materials beyond their yield stress, the plastic strain is uniform throughout the sample up to the point of maximum force dF = 0 (Figure 10-7a). Beyond this point, force begins to decrease, and it is at this point that localized and nonuniform plastic deformation begins to occur. The cross-sectional area begins to change in a nonuniform way, and a neck or localized constriction forms, which can either stabilize or propagate in an unstable manner to failure. If the cross section at any point is slightly less than elsewhere or there are any irregularities in the sample when the force is increasing in plastic flow, the stress will increase locally. While the force is increasing, the deformation will be stable (i.e., any local constructions are self-arresting). In contrast, under a decreasing force the deformation is no longer stable, leading to the formation and cumulative increase of necking and eventual failure. Hence the force maximum (dF = 0) defines a point of instability in tension, beyond which fracture is inevitable. The occurrence of strain hardening in a material stabilizes any regions of incipient localized thinning that could lead to unstable necking and eventual fracture during high extensions and can allow much larger extensions before rupture than would otherwise be possible.

Dobraszczyk showed that the critical strain at which instability (e_{crit}) occurs under large extensions is directly related to the strain hardening index (n):

$$n = e_{crit}$$

This is an important relationship: it shows that the strain at instability and subsequent failure of the expanding bubble walls are defined only by the rheological strain-hardening properties of the material. The higher the value

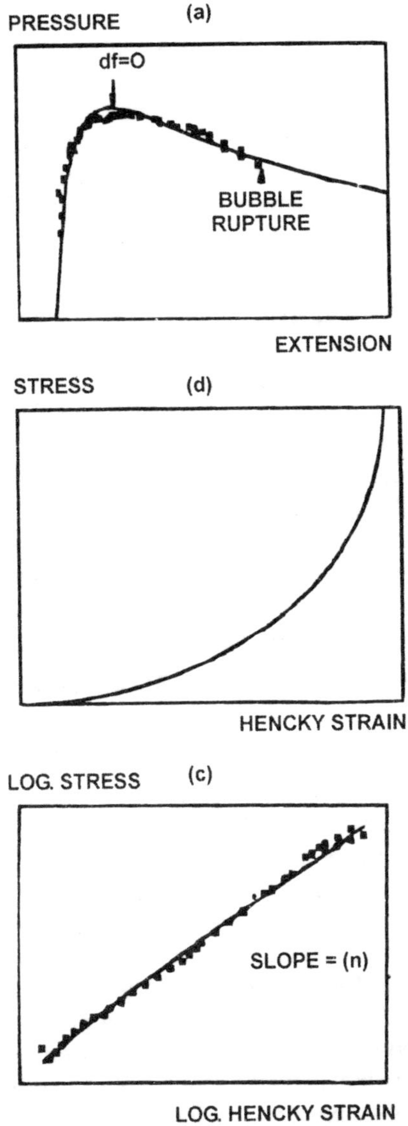

Fig. 10.7 (a) Pressure-Extension Plot for the Polar Region of an inflation Dough Bubble Showing Point of Tensile Instability at df=0;(b) Stress vs. Hencky Strain Plot of an Inflating Dough Bubble Showing Strain Hardening (c) Power-Low Fit to Stress Strain Data Giving Slope ($d\ln\sigma/d\ln\varepsilon$)=Strain-Hardening Index (n)

of n, the greater the strain hardening and the greater the strain at which instability occurs. In terms of dough bubble stability, this means that bubbles will inflate to a larger volume before failure occurs. This has been confirmed by Dobraszc-zyk, who showed that final inflation volumes (failure strain) of single bubbles of dough were highly correlated with the dough strain-hardening index (Figure 10-8). Thus, the strain-hardening properties of the dough will be critical in determining the limit of expansion of gas cells within the dough during baking, and hence the final bread volume and texture.

For those who consider breadmaking to be about understanding the bubbles, there is a satisfying appropriateness that perhaps the best approach for measuring the rheological properties of dough is one based on blowing bubbles in the dough. This work has shown that, although wheat proteins are unique in their ability to produce a viscoelastic network able to retain gas during proving, it is perhaps the strain-hardening characteristic of wheat dough rheology that is critical in stabilizing these growing bubbles. Whatever the relative importance of these effects, the ability of wheat to produce an aerated baked loaf depends on dough rheology, which arises from the dough proteins. Viscoelasticity and strain hardening are critical characteristics contributed by wheat proteins. The next section considers the wheat proteins and how they impart these unique qualities of viscoelasticity and strain hardening.

Wheat Proteins and the Origin of Dough Rheology and Dough Development

Dough rheology is complex and difficult to characterize and arises from the nature of the unique gluten proteins found in wheat. As noted earlier, dough rheology is developed in MDD processes by high-speed mixing to give a viscoelastic network that is sufficiently elastic to retain gas during rising but sufficiently viscous to flow rather than rupture. It is for this reason that rheological measurements on doughs being mixed are indicative of proving and baking performance; the proteins conferring viscoelastic and strain-hardening properties during proving are the same proteins being rearranged during mixing. The origin of dough rheology is the wheat gluten proteins. This section describes these proteins and presents a model of gluten protein structure that explains why doughs are viscoelastic and strain hardening, why they de-velop during mixing, and why oxidants aid mechanical dough development.

Wheat Gluten: A Unique Protein

Wheat flour is unique among the cereal flours in its ability to retain gas during proof and baking and therefore to form the typical aerated foam

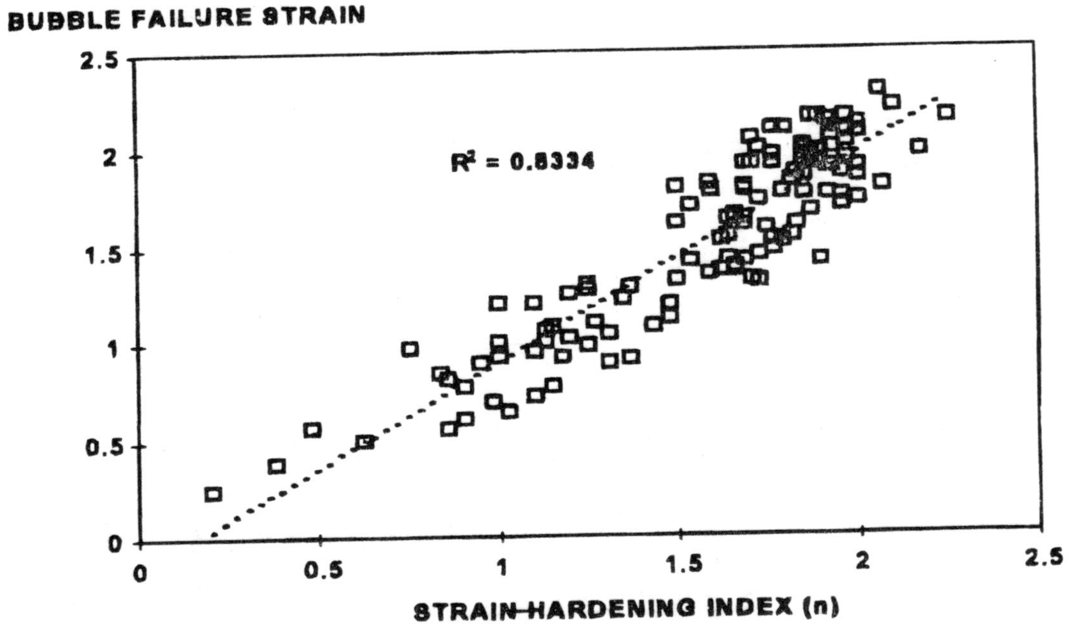

Fig. 10.8 Relationship between Extension Strain-Hardening Index (n) and Bubble Failure Strain for a Number of Wheat Flour Doughs Inflated on the D/R Inflation System

structure that we know as bread. It is widely believed that this is largely due to the gluten proteins within wheat. Although other cereals contain very similar protein groups to gluten, their gas-holding capacity is limited. Johnson and Bailey found that although the gas production capacity of rye doughs was equal to or greater than that of wheat flour doughs, its ability to retain gas was limited. Other cereals such as barley, oats, and rice contain large amounts of glutelin proteins but cannot retain gas during proof and baking. He and Ho-seney measured differences in gas retention of wheat, rye, rice, and maize flour doughs during proof and found that although all cereal doughs produced gas (CO_2), wheat flour doughs retain gas for much longer and up to higher tem-peratures than the other cereals (Figure 10-9). Wheat flour retained gas up to noc, whereas other cereal doughs released gas much earlier during proof.

So what is it about wheat gluten that makes it so different from the other cereals? It is thought that the gas-retention capability of wheat flour doughs is due to their viscoelastic properties. Viscoelasticity is the ability of materials to exhibit both viscous (flow) and solidlike elastic behaviour, depending on the conditions of temperature, time, and deformation experienced. A viscoelastic material can flow if deformed over a long period of time or at elevated temperatures but can behave as a rigid, brittle material if deformed very quickly or at low temperatures. This property is important in retaining gas bubbles within the dough. Wheat gluten is made up of a mixture of two groups of proteins: glutenins and gliadins, which make different contributions to the viscoelasticity of gluten. The gliadins are viscous and extensible, and doughs made from gliadin alone behave like a highly viscous liquid but have little resistance to deformation (elasticity). The consequence is that any gas bubbles in such a dough should expand very quickly and would not be retained for long during proof. Doughs made from glutenins alone lack the extensibility of gliadin doughs but exhibit substantial strength and elasticity (Figure 10-10) rather like a rubber ball. Gas bubbles would be retained in such a material, but they would not grow. Thus it appears that it is the combination of gliadin and glutenin that imparts the unique viscoelastic properties responsible for gas retention in wheat flour doughs. However, the mechanisms that control gas retention in doughs are still poorly understood and are discussed in further detail in Section 10.5, "Molecular Mechanisms of Bubble Stabilization in Doughs."

Gluten consists primarily of two types of protein, gliadins and gluten ins, present in roughly equal proportions and together making up 80% to 85% of the total protein content of wheat. Gliadins and glutenins are distinguished

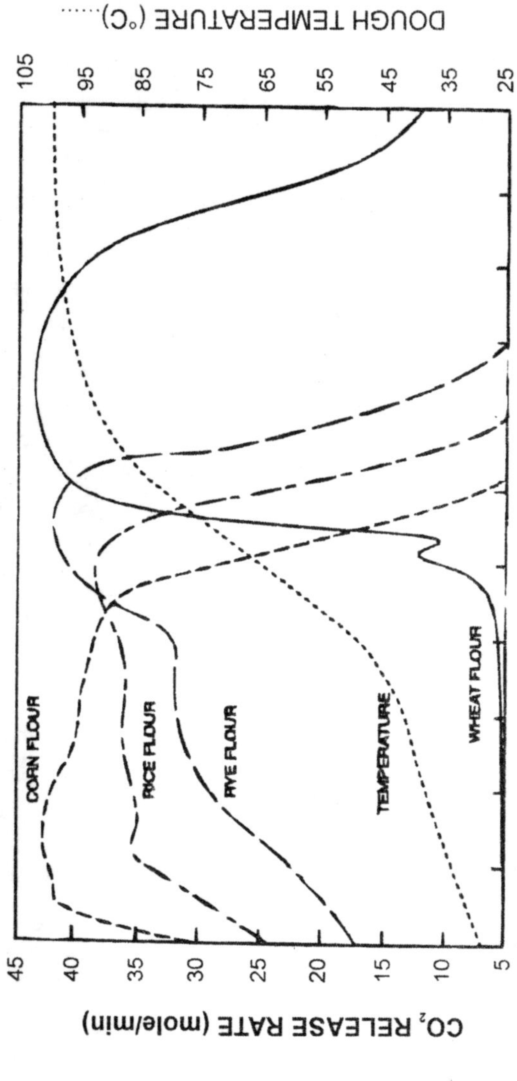

Fig. 10.9 Rates of CO_2 Loss from Doughs Made from Corn, Rice, Rye, and Wheat Flours during Baking

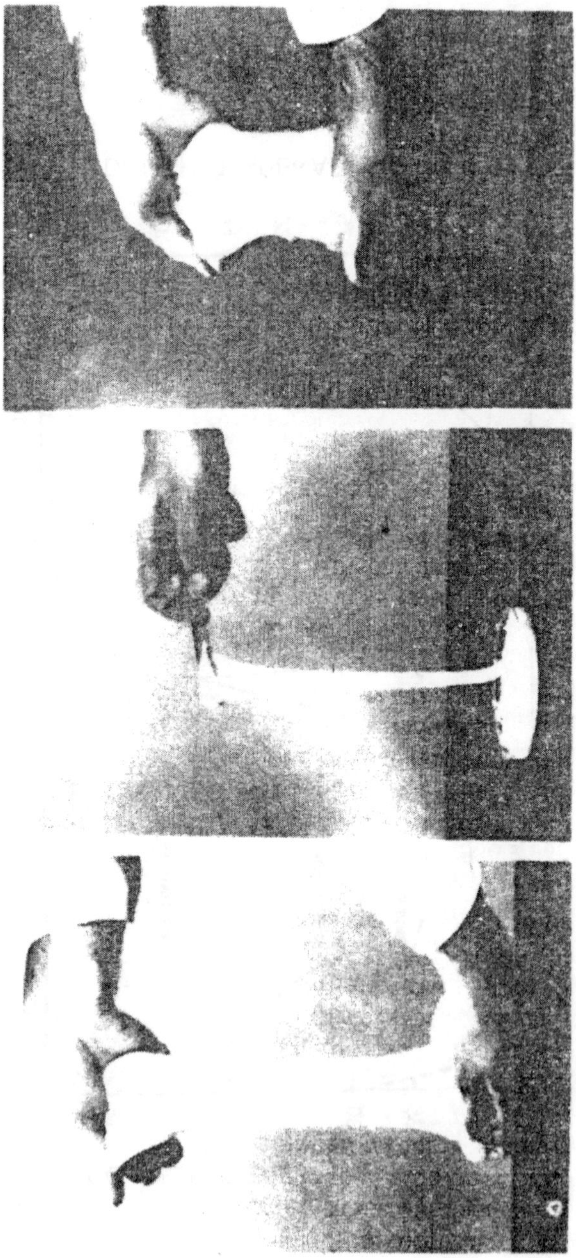

Fig. 10-10 Extensibility of Gluten (Left), Gladian (Center) and Glutenin (Right)

from the albumins and globulins by being insoluble in both water and salt solutions. Glutenins are distinguished from gliadins by being insoluble in 70% aqueous ethanol. All these distinctions are somewhat arbitrary. Gliadins are larger than albumins and globulins and are predominantly monomeric polypeptides (i.e., proteins with a single polypeptide chain of molecular weights mostly in the range 30,000--40,000). Gliadins are prolamins, characterized by high levels of proline (15%-30%) and glutamine (35%--45%) and low levels oflysine (0.2%-0.9%), hence the lysine deficiency of wheat and some other cereals. Glutenins are polymeric polypeptides (i.e., have several chains joined together by disulfide bonds). Their molecular weights are therefore very high, ranging from 104 up to 109. The content of ionic amino acid residues in the gluten proteins is very low, whereas the content of hydrophobic residues is high, resulting in a low water solubility; gluten proteins are among the lowest charged proteins existing. Gliadins and glutenins are storage proteins, pro-viding protein for the growing seedling. They are intended therefore to be digested rather than having a functional purpose. They are mainly stored in the endosperm, along with the starch (also a storage molecule).

The total number of gliadins is high, 20 to 25 within a single variety, but many more exist among different varieties. Gliadins can therefore be used for wheat variety identification, because the pattern of gliadin bands is genotypic (i.e., characteristic of the variety). It does not change over the years or as a result of growth condi-tions, total protein content, or sprouting. Glu-tenins have very high molecular weights, and this is one of the reasons for their insolubility (the other reason is the predominance of hydrophobic amino acids). It is not clear whether the glutenin molecules are polymerized during synthesis in the kernel or whether exposure to air during milling and subsequent dough mixing is the cause of the polymerization. Glutenins can be reduced to break them down into their individual subunits. These are usually divided into two groups: high molecular weight (HMW) subunits (90,000-150,000), and low molecular weight (LMW) subunits (30,000-51,000). Some researchers also add a group of middle molecular weight (MMW) subunits. Reversed-phase high-performance liquid chromatography shows LMW to be most hydrophobic, then HMW, with MMW the least hydrophobic group. Cysteine residues are located in the terminals of each subunit, allowing for disulfide bonding between the subunits. Interchanging gliadin fractions between wheat flours of different baking performance do not have much effect compared with interchanging glutenins. Also, the correlation between loaf volume and glutenin content is better than between loaf volume and gliadin content. Glutenin composition is more important than gliadin composition for baking quality. Glutenins are therefore considered the major contributors to the baking performance of wheat flours.

Glutenins affect baking performance through:

- The gliadin/glutenin ratio; a higher proportion of glutenin seems to be beneficial for baking performance
- The molecular weight distribution of glute-nms
- The presence of certain HMW glutenin sub-units

A good breadrnaking wheat (strong) with good Farinograph characteristics (medium-long mixing time, good tolerance to overmixing) contains more HMW protein. Adding HMW-rich fractions increases loaf volume. The total number of different HMW subunits is around 20 (depending on the number and type of varieties studied and the separation method used). Each subunit has been assigned a number, and the presence of certain combinations seems to relate to different quality aspects (i.e., certain combinations appear to be present in varieties of good breadmaking performance, whereas other combinations are present in varieties of poor breadmaking performance). On the basis of these results, quality scores were assigned for each of the HMW subunits, so that by adding the scores for those subunits present in a particular variety, a quality score could be calculated: the Glu-l score. The Glu-l score is positively correlated with baking performance, explaining 47% to 60% of the variation in breadmaking quality of a range of British wheats. The Glu-l score is negatively correlated with cookie making performance, as would be expected. Although the HMW subunits are correlated with baking performance, this does not mean they are the reason for good performance. It may just be that their presence coincides with other properties that are the direct cause (e.g., the total amount of glutenin).

Glutenin Structure and Bread Dough Rheology

Bread dough from wheat flour is a nonlinear viscoelastic fluid that is shear thinning, strain hardening, and possibly exhibits a small yield stress. The viscoelastic behaviour of dough is generally described in terms of glutenin viscoelasticity. Glutenins are the wheat proteins that exhibit viscoelasticity, whereas suspensions of gliadins form viscous liquids. Understanding dough viscoelasticity and development therefore starts with understanding glutenin structure.

The following model of glutenin structure, called the "linear concatenation model," was promoted and modified over several years by Ewart, and was reviewed favourably by Eliasson and Larsson and more recently by Stauffer. It gives a descriptive understanding of glutenin visco-elasticity, explaining the observed rheological phenomena of elasticity, viscous flow, dough development and breakdown, strain hardening, and the action of oxidants. It does not explain every observed chemical and rheological phenomenon of bread dough or gluten, but it provides a useful practical basis for understanding dough rheology. The model needs to explain glutenin elasticity, viscous flow, strain hardening, and dough development. An earlier model, based on the theory of rubber elasticity, suggested that glu-tenin molecules form a cross-linked network, linked by disulfide bonds throughout the dough, to give a single "giant protein molecule." This explains elasticity but not dough development, relaxation, or viscous flow. Ewart suggested that instead of a three-dimensional cross-linked structure, glutenin subunits are joined by disul-fide bonds into linear concatenations of up to 50 molecules. Under shear or extensional flow, these concatenations align; the closeness of the alignment and the bulky nature of the concatenations allow for numerous noncovalent interactions between adjacent molecules because of hydrogen bonding, hydrophobic interactions, and van der Waals forces. The aligned glutenin concatenations are therefore held strongly in relation to one another under deformation. This increased resistance to deformation on alignment is the cause of dough development. The glutenin is also elastic, because deformation causes the partial unfolding of individual molecules; on removal of the defonnation the chains tend to revert to their most favorable compact confonnations. Figure 10-11 illustrates the linear concatenations of the Ewart model and their interactions.

The Ewart model explains viscous flow of glutenin partly by slippage of one concatenation past another and additionally by means of a mechanism called "thiol-disulfide interchange." A thiol is an organic molecule offonnula R-SH, where R mayor may not be a polypeptide chain. A disulfide bond has the formula R'-S-S-R", where R' and R" are polypeptide chains. The following reaction takes place readily:

R'-S-S-R" + R-SH→R'-S-S-R + R"-SH

Therefore, if a thiol is present, it can split a disulfide bond. If the disulfide bond is within a glutenin concatenation under stress, this mechanism relieves the stress by splitting the concatenation, allowing viscous flow or relaxation to occur. If too many thiols are present, the stress will be relieved too rapidly, and the concatenations will never align effectively. As described previously (in "Creep and Stress Relaxation"), the relaxation behavior of dough shows

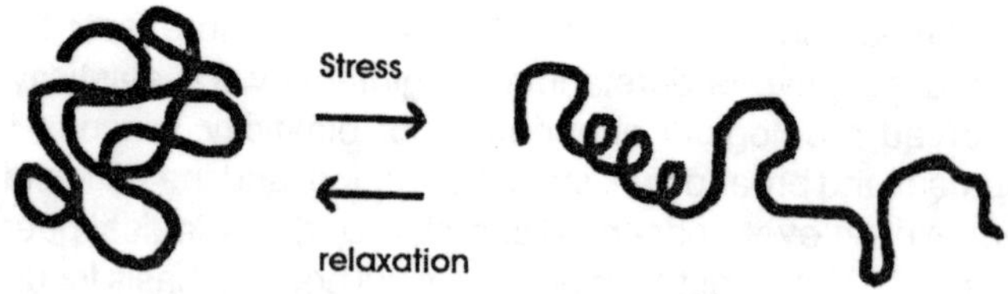

(a) Unfolding of a glutenin polypeptide under stress, and relaxation on release of the stress

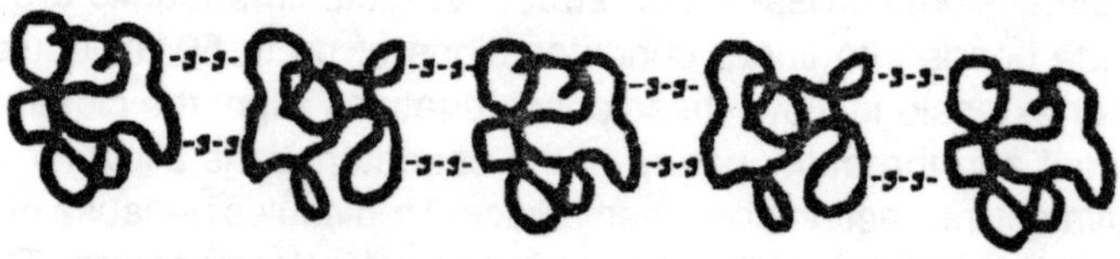

(b) Concentration of glutenin subunits viadisulfide bonds

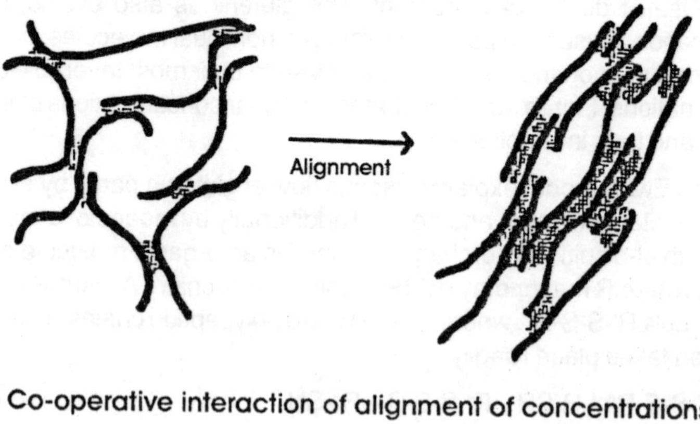

(c) Co-operative interaction of alignment of concentrations

Figure 10.11 The Viscoelasticity of Gluten, Illustrated by the Linear Concentrations of the Ewart Model and their Interactions.

two distinct relaxation processes: a rapid relaxation between 0.1 to 10 seconds and a slower process occurring at approximately 1000 seconds. This can be shown to be related directly to the molecular weight distribution of gluten, with the low MW gliadins (average MW= 10^4) mainly controlling the rapid relaxation process, and the higher glutenins (average MW=106) associated with the long relaxation process (Rao, Mul-vaney, & Dexter, 2000). The purpose of oxidants in dough mixing is to oxidize thiols to prevent excessive thiol-disulfide interchange, and so to allow alignment and therefore dough development. Dough development during high-speed mixing (mechanical dough development) arises because shear and extensional forces during mixing cause the glutenin concatenations to align and interact in the co-operative way described earlier. The breakdown in the dough development curve on a Farinogram occurs be-cause thioldisulfide interchange reactions and molecular slippage do not occur sufficiently rapidly to relieve the stress. The glutenin concatenations therefore break into smaller concatenations under the mechanical stress of mixing. Smaller concatenations do not interact so effectively, so resistance to mixing decreases.

The Ewart model explains strain hardening by noting that the glutenin network gains its viscoelastic structure through noncovalent interactions. If the structure arose from covalent interactions, on the application of stress sufficient to cause these to break, the resulting network would be weaker. However, because the network arises from noncovalent interactions, alignment of the linear glutenin concatenations on stretching increases the co-operation of these interactions, resulting in a stronger network after the application of strain. A dough based solely on this model would be very stiff. The role of gliadins in gluten structure appears to be as plasticizers, imparting extensibility to the gluten structure by hindering interactions between concatenations. An optimal balance between glutenins (for viscoelasticity) and gliadins (for extensibility) seems to be crucial for good breadmaking performance.

The Ewart model, although undoubtedly a simplification, provides a basis for understand-ing:

- Elasticity
- Viscous flow and relaxation
- Dough development
- Dough breakdown on overmixing
- Strain hardening
- Action of oxidants

The effectiveness of the dough rheology in bringing about good baked loaf structure is modified by the action of surface active molecules, as considered in detail later. However, it is the dough rheology that makes wheat unique; an understanding of the origin of bread dough rheology is therefore essential to understanding bread aeration.

As noted earlier, the action of oxidants is to prevent thiols from splitting glutenin concatenations. In recent years, the use of the oxidant potassium bromate has been banned in the United Kingdom and elsewhere. This has left ascorbic acid (vitamin C) as the only oxidizing improver allowed to be added to doughs during mixing. Ascorbic acid is, in fact, an antioxidant, and imparts its oxidizing action in doughs through conversion to dehydroascorbic acid by reaction with elemental oxygen. This means that adequate oxygen must be available during mixing. As noted earlier, a feature of the CBP is mixing under a partial vacuum, which limits oxygen availability. With the banning of potassium bromate, this became an issue that led to a refocus on aeration during dough mixing. The next section considers the purposes of dough mixing, the effect of mixing under a partial vacuum on the dough, and how oxygen availability has been increased through a better understanding of aeration processes during dough mixing.

Dough Mixing

Most foods are multi-ingredient; therefore most food processes involve mixing at an early stage. Mixing is required simply to bring the ingredients together. But mixing often serves to develop texture also by controlling the nature of alignments and interactions between biopolymers such as starch molecules and proteins. The mixer design and operation interacts with the food; different mixing operations may produce the same degree of homogenization but exert a different controlling influence over structure development. This is evidenced by the great variety of mixers used in the food industry and the fact that certain mixer designs are unable to produce the desired texture, although they achieve homogeneity perfectly adequately.

Nowhere is this more true than for dough mixing. Forty per cent of the food-mixing literature is concerned with dough mixing, and most of these articles are concerned with the interaction between dough properties and mixer design and operation. Either different doughs require different mixing operations (e.g., different energy inputs), or different mixing conditions produce different dough properties (e.g., rheology, density). Either way, there is a close interaction between mixer design and dough properties, and much of the research literature is concerned with this interaction.

Bread dough mixing serves three functions:

- To blend and hydrate the dough ingredients
- To develop the dough, i.e., to produce a viscoelastic structure that is able to retain gas without rupturing
- To aerate the dough

Aeration has two purposes:

- To provide nucleation sites for CO_2 diffusion and bubble growth during proving
- To provide atmospheric oxygen to assist dough development

Blending and hydration occur somewhat incidentally; by the time the dough is developed, the ingredients are well hydrated and well blended. Dough mixer design is therefore concerned more with development than homogeneity. However, mixer design and operation need to achieve homogeneity before development can begin, and some mixers (e.g., the Biplex) are operated at slow speed initially to achieve homogeneity, then at a higher speed to develop the dough. A single-speed mixer such as the Tweedy needs to ensure both homogeneity and development; it is difficult to design a mixer that achieves both efficiently. In MDD processes such as the CBP, dough mixing is mostly about developing the dough structure or rheology and about aerating the dough. Dough development requires an intense energy input, which varies with mixer design and flour type, as described in the next section.

Dough Development and Energy Input

Dough Development and Energy Input Mechanical dough development requires a substantial energy input; in the CBP this is 40 kJ/kg imparted in less than 3 minutes, corresponding to a power of several hundred watts. This makes dough mixing one of the most energy-intensive mixing operations in the food or other process industries. The price of this energy intense operation is two fold: in the actual price of electricity to operate mixers, and in the temperature rise in the dough caused by mixing. In the United Kingdom, the baking industry spends around £5 million annually on electricity just to run its mixers. A 20% reduction in mixing time therefore has potential to save millions of pounds. Regarding dough development, high-speed mixing is only about 15% efficient, so there is scope to develop more energy-efficient mixer designs.

The temperature rise during mixing is important in that yeast activity depends critically on the final dough temperature. Typically a temperature of 30°C ± 1°C is aimed for. This is controlled by adjusting the water temperature for a given flour temperature and work input. Some strong flours have such great mixing requirements that it is difficult to maintain the dough temperature below 30°e. Again, this is an incentive to develop more energy efficient mlxers.

Energy Requirement of Different Mixer Designs

During the development of the CBP, a work input of 40 kJ/kg was found to be suitable for a wide range of flour types and for several mixing machines. (This is the work input to the dough and does not include energy losses within the mixer motor, which are accounted for by sub-tracting the no-load energy input.) This is surprising, given that flours differ in their water absorption and protein quality and quantity and that different mixer designs shear the dough in different ways. Kilborn and Tipples in their series of articles from 1972-1977 investigated factors affecting MDD. They found:

- The total energy input required for peak development differs between flour types .
- For a given flour, there is a minimum mixing speed (the critical mixing speed) below which development could not be achieved, resulting in a loaf of poor volume, color, and texture.
- Both the total energy required and the critical mixing speed for a given flour differed among mixers with different mixing actions.

They concluded that a constant total energy input and constant mixing speed were unlikely to achieve peak development for all flour types and all mixers. This contradicts the claim made for the CBP; however, in practice the range of flour types received by a bakery is narrow, so a constant work input and mixing speed is an acceptable and practical practice.

Critical Mixing Speed and "Unmixing"

Tipples and Kilborn also found that if a dough that had already reached peak development was mixed further at a slow speed (below the critical mixing speed), the dough re-verted from being optimally developed to having an appearance of being underdeveloped. They termed this phenomenon "unmixing." Unmixed doughs produce loaves of similar appearance to underdeveloped doughs (rather than overmixed doughs). In terms of the linear concatenation model of dough development, it seems that slow mixing facilitates the misalignment of concatenations, through random molecular motion and thioldisulfide interchange, whereas rapid mixing facilitates alignment. This explains why a critical mixing speed is required for dough development; below this speed, alignment occurs less rapidly than misalignment, so development does not occur. It also explains the different mixing efficiencies of different mixers; some mixing actions expend more of their energy in stretching deformations that aid alignment of glutenin concatenations.

Kilborn and Tipples also studied the development of dough using repeated sheeting between rollers, achieving development using only about 15% of the energy required for a MDD mixing process. This is because sheeting expends all its energy in aligning glutenin concatenations, causing strain hardening in the dough and allowing greater increases in elastic stiffness than possible in shear. This further confirms that the type of mixing action, and in particular the proportion of energy that acts to stretch the dough, determines the mixing efficiency ofa mixer. Dough development by sheeting is difficult to automate so it has not been applied to bread production on a commercial basis but is used for the labor-intensive production of pastry.

In summary, dough development occurs through the alignment of glutenin concatenations. In bulk fermentation processes, this alignment occurs slowly because of biaxial extension as the dough rises. In sheeting, all the energy input goes into aligning the glutenin. In the high-speed mixers used for MDD processes, there is a balance between alignment and misalignment; below the critical mixing speed alignment is not favoured, and development does not occur. Mixer designs should therefore aim to promote extensional deformation of the dough to maximize energy efficiency and minimize the temperature rise during mixing. In doing so, energy-efficient mixer designs must also consider the aeration of the dough.

Aeration during Mixing

Aeration during mixing provides small bubbles that act as the nucleation sites for CO_2 diffusion and bubble growth during proving. Without these nucleation sites, the CO_2 would have nowhere to go and would be largely lost from the bread. Mixing doughs under a very high vacuum to exclude bubbles results in bread with very few gas cells, a coarse, open and unat-tractive structure, and low volume.

Aeration aspects of breadmaking have been somewhat neglected, in part owing to the lack of experimental methods for measuring aeration. Two aspects of dough aeration are important:

- The total void fraction of air incorporated into the dough
- The bubble size distribution

In recent years techniques have been developed for measuring both of these fundamental parameters of dough aeration.

Measurement of the Void Fraction of Air in Dough

The void fraction of air in dough can be found by measuring dough density; less dense doughs contain more air. Dough density has been measured by oil displacement, by placing dough samples into a series of test tubes containing calcium chloride solutions of known density, by measuring the density of a solution in which the dough sample is neutrally buoyant, and by measuring the weight of dough in air and immersed in water.

To calculate the void fraction of air in the dough, the gas-free dough density must also be known. The void fraction of air is then calculated by:

$$\alpha = 1 - \frac{P}{P_{gf}}$$

Where α = Void fraction of gas
P = Dough density
P_{gf} = Gas Free dough density

The gas-free dough density has been estimated by mixing doughs under a very high vacuum or by considering the individual densities of the dough con-stituents; both of these methods give inaccurate estimates that underestimate the void fraction of air in the dough. A better approach is to measure the density of doughs mixed at different pressures and extrapolate back to zero absolute pressure, as shown in Figure 10-12. The relationship between density and mixing pressure is linear, indicating that the void fraction of air in a dough is proportional to the mixing pressure. Gas-free dough density varies with fiour type and mixing conditions and should be measured for each experimental investigation. Figure 10-13 shows the void fractions of doughs mixed at different pressures, for doughs mixed from flours of different strength and at different speeds. Strong flours occlude less air during dough mixing, and the air content varies with mixing speed.

Measurement of Bubble Size Distributions in Doughs

The bubble size distribution can be measured by slicing frozen dough and measuring the holes appearing on the slices. If bubbles in dough are sliced, on average they will be sliced off-center; also, larger bubbles have a

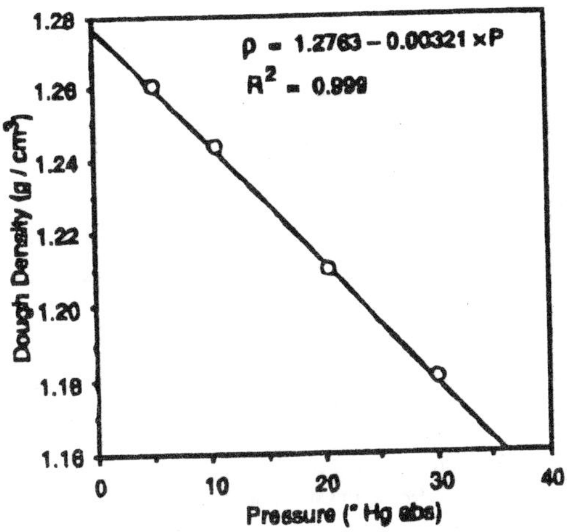

Figure 10.12. Change in Dough Density with Mixing Pressure and Extrapolation Back to Zero Absolute Pressure To Find the Gas Free Dough Density

greater probability of being sliced than smaller bubbles. The size distribution of holes measured on slices will therefore be different from the true bubble size distribution (Figure 10-14). It is necessary to reconstruct the true bubble size distribution using stereo logical techniques. Figure 10-15 shows the bubble size dis-tribution reconstructed from slices for a dough mixed in a Tweedy 10 mixer.

Carlson and Bohlin measured bubble size distributions from photomicrographs of 30-µm thick slices of dough, down to a resolution of 90-llm diameter. They estimated the average bubble size to be around 110 µm. Campbell et al. measured bubbles size distributions directly from 30-µm thick slices, with a resolution of 39-µm diameter after stereological reconstruction and reported a number mean diameter of 90µm and a number density of around 33,000 bubbles cm-3 for doughs mixed in a Tweedy 1 0 mixer under a partial vacuum of 15" Hg. Whitworth and Alava, using a similar technique, measured bubble size distributions in doughs mixed in a Tweedy 35 mixer after mixing, first mold, intermediate proof, and final mold.

Aeration Processes during Mixing, the Air Content of Doughs, and Why Mixing under Partial Vacuum Gives a Finer Baked Loaf

As noted earlier, during development of the CBP, it was found that too much air was entrained into the dough on scale-up of the prototype mixer.

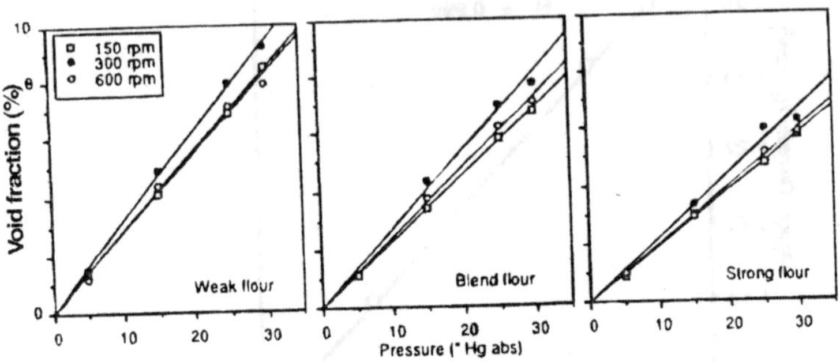

Figure 10-13 Change in Void Fraction with Mixing Pressure for Flours of Different Strength. Mixed at Different Blade Speeds

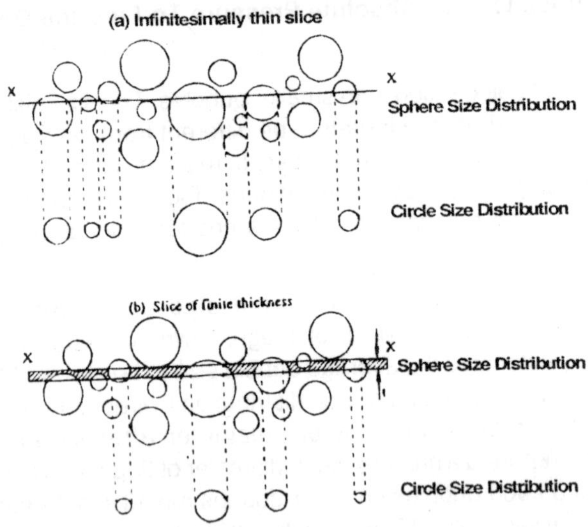

Figure 10-14 Schematic Showing How When bubbles in Dough are Sliced, the Circle Appearing on the Slices Are smaller in Diameter Then the Bubbles from Which They Came. When the Slice is Thick. Relative to theBubbles Sizes the Circle Distribution Is Distorted even further.

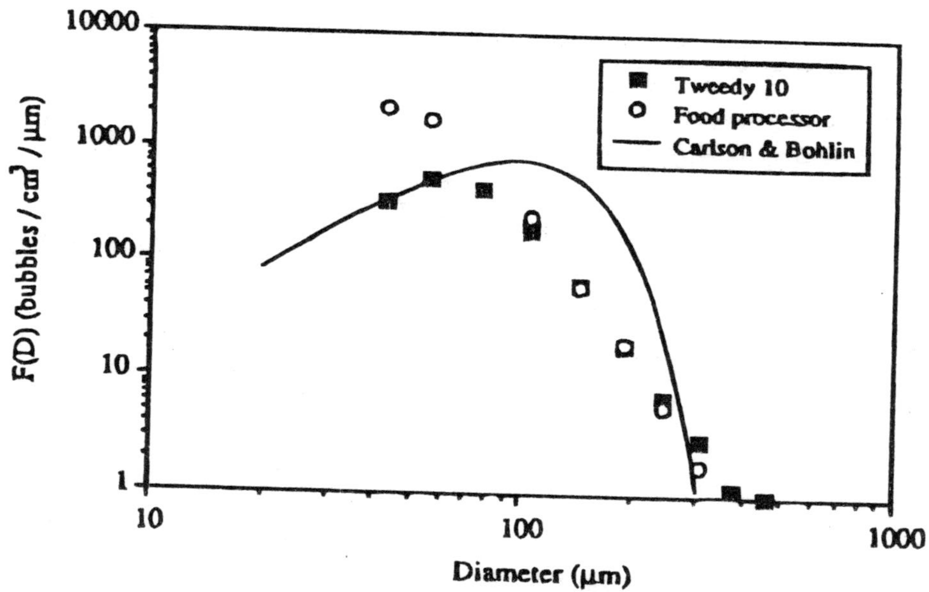

Figure 10.15 Bubble Size Distributions Measured for Dough Mixed in a Tweedy 10 Mixer (20,000 Bubbles Measured) and a Food Processor (8000 Bubbles Measured) The solid Line Shows a Fitted Distribution Function of Carlson and Bohlin.

This gave bread with large holes and a coarse texture and was rectified by mixing under a partial vacuum of 0.5 bar (15" Hg) to control the amount of air incorporated. Thus mixing under partial vacuum became a feature of the CBP. However, why there should have been increased aeration on scaleup is not known, and until recently the mechanism by which mixing under vacuum affects dough aeration and bread texture has not been understood. Mixing under partial vacuum has the undesirable effect of reducing oxygen availability during mixing, and therefore the effectiveness of ascorbic acid. It was recognized recently that there is a turnover of air during dough mixing, which means that it is not necessary to apply a partial vacuum throughout the mixing operation. Doughs can be mixed at atmospheric pressure to maintain oxygen availability; then a vacuum is applied near the end of mixing to reduce the air content. This is called delayed pressure reduction. A further development of this is the Flour Milling and Baking Research Association pressure-vacuum mixer, which mixes initially under a positive pressure, increasing oxygen availability even further. In addition to the improving effect of oxygen, it also bleaches colored components in the dough, giving a whiter crumb in the baked loaf.

What aeration processes occur during dough mixing? As alluded to earlier, it has been found that there is a turnover of air during mixing, implying that air is entrained and disentrained simultaneously. This is demonstrated by mixing doughs initially under vacuum or at atmospheric pressure, changing the pressure midway through mixing, and measuring the change in density as air is entrained or disentrained. Campbell and Shah describe a mathematical model of the turnover of air that defines entrainment and disentrainment coefficients, showing that the air content of dough depends on the mixing pressure and the balance between entrainment and disentrainment. Flour strength also affects the air content of doughs, with stronger flours giving doughs with a lower air content. The fact that air disentrains allows for delayed pressure reduction and pressure-vacuum mixing. It is also probable that there is bubble breakup during mixing, although this has not been demonstrated experimentally. These are three fairly obvious aeration processes. Some workers, e.g., Junge et a!', propose that surfactants aid bubble breakup during mixing, hence giving a finer baked loaf structure; however, it is much more likely that surfactants exert their effect during proving and baking by retarding coalescence. Nevertheless, there is a generally shared assumption in the literature that bubble breakup occurs during mixing.

From the broader field of rheology, it is known that bubbles in a viscoelastic fluid under stress experience an extra compressive stress because of the normal stresses generated in the liquid. Dough is a viscoelastic fluid under stress during mixing; it is likely that the bubbles in dough experience this compression during mixing. This means that bubble size distributions should only be measured in doughs that have been allowed to relax for several minutes after the end of mixing. Bubble compression also allows the explanation as to how mixing under vacuum improves bread quality. Mixing under a partial vacuum reduces the air content of dough by reducing the number of bubbles per unit volume; these bubbles tend to remain discrete (i.e., do not coalesce) for longer during proving and baking, so that ultimately more gas cells are produced in the baked loaf, improving the structure and quality. The likely reason that these bubbles resist coalescence is that, with fewer bubbles, there is more protein and other surfactant available to stabilize each bubble against coalescence. The explanation as to why mixing under vacuum produces fewer bubbles in the dough depends on this process of bubble compression during mixing.

Mixing under vacuum also gives slightly smaller loaf volumes (Figure 10-16); here the explanation is that there is a smaller surface area for mass transfer of CO_2 during proving, so less gas is transferred into bubbles and more lost to atmosphere. This is allowed for by proving for slightly longer.

PROVING

Mixing creates the initial bubble structure and develops the viscoelastic dough structure necessary for successful proving. But although mixing is the most critical operation in the CBP and other MDD processes, proving is still the heart of all breadmaking processes. Without proving, there would be no need to aerate the dough during mixing or to develop dough rheology, and no aerated baked loaf structure, which makes bread so popular.

Qualitative Description of Proving

Proving expands the original bubble structure to give a dough mass that is predominantly gas, the structure of which is modified and set by baking. The aim of dough development during mixing is to create a dough that will prove optimally (i.e., which will expand to give a loaf of good volume while retaining a fine bubble structure). The relationship between the bubble size distribution created by mixing and that at the end of proving is complicated by differing rates of bubble growth (diffusive mass transfer rate depends on bubble size) and by bubble coalescence, as well as external factors such as the shape of the container and ambient temperature changes.

Four factors are important during proving:

- The rate of gas production by the yeast
- The extent of gas retention
- The change in the bubble size distribution due to CO_2 diffusion
- The rate of bubble coalescence

The first two of these factors are concerned with the gross, macroscopic gas behaviour, and the latter two with the behaviour of individual bubbles. An important characteristic of yeast is how rapidly it produces CO_2 under various conditions. Typically the rate is around 2.5×10^{-5} kmole gas per m^3 liquid dough phase per second. The saturation level of CO_2 in dough is estimated to be 0.04 kmol/m^3. At this rate of CO_2 production, it takes 1600 seconds, or around 27 minutes, for the dough to become saturated. So for the first half of proving the dough is not saturated with CO_2. This possibly accounts for the observation in the literature that the rate of bubble growth increases after about 20 minutes of proving, although even below saturation bubble growth occurs. Once the gas is produced, the extent of gas retention largely determines the baked loaf volume, and many dough ingredients, such as surfactants, probably exert at least part of their influence on gas retention during proving.

Wheat bread dough is a multiphase and multicomponent system composed of proteins, polysaccharides, lipids, water, gas, and other minor nutrients and additives. On a macro scale, it has a foam structure with continuously growing gas bubbles dispersed in an apparently homogeneous semisolid aqueous dough phase. As the volume fraction of the gas increases during fermentation and the early stages of baking, high surface energy generated by rapidly increased interfacial area, together with substantial density differences between the phases, render the system thermodynamically unstable. Thus, a crucial aspect of the breadmaking process is to promote foam or bubble stability, which affects directly the end-product texture (the number, size, and distribution of the bubbles) and volume (how long gas bubbles survive). The following sections describe the continuous and dispersed phases of proving doughs and the structural transformation taking place during proving. This is followed by a discussion of the key factors involved in the stabilization of gas bubbles in wheat bread dough.

The gas phase of a proving dough exists as a dispersion of discrete gas

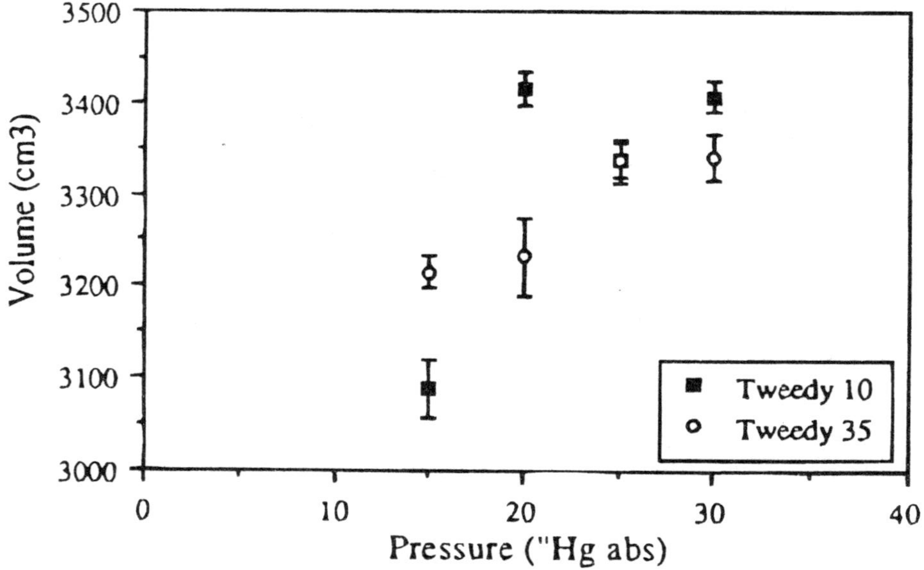

Fig. 10.16 Loaf volume Measured for Loaves Baked from Dough Mixed at Different Pressures, in Tweedy 10 and Tweedy 35 Mixers and Proved for the same Proving Time.

bubbles in a semisolid dough phase. The nuclei of the bubbles are incorporated by the occlusion of air during mixing with considerably high level of energy inputs. The technological significance of the gas cells immediately after mixing is that a sufficiently large number, estimated to be between 10^{11} and 10_{13} m^{-3}, is required. The bubbles expand as CO_2 produced by yeast fermentation in the aqueous phase diffuses to the bubbles and generates within them an excess pressure.

The Aqueous Phase

Irrespective of the process involved, the primary event in breadmaking is the addition of water to a dry flour at the onset of mixing, forming a cohesive, viscoelastic dough. Approximately half the water added (typically 0.6-0.8 g water/g of dry flour) is "free" or freezable. The free water forms a second aqueous phase that can be obtained by ultracentrifugation. The aqueous phase contains most of the wheat flour water-soluble components, including water-soluble proteins, nonstarch polar lipids, and nonstarch polysaccharides, which may play critical parts in bubble stabilization in bread dough. It also provides a medium for extremely complicated chemical and physical reactions to take place.

The Model Process of Structure Transformation

Bread dough undergoes a structural transformation from a foam into an open sponge during baking as indicated by previous studies and confirmed by recent scanning electron microscopy observations (Figure 10-17).

Hypothetically, the transformation occurs in two closely related, consecutive stages during expansion (Figure 10-18). During the first stage, the expanding gas cells are embedded in a continuous dough phase made up of highly hydrated starch-protein matrix. The dough phase develops into thin, continuous membranes between adjacent cells until there is simply not enough material to maintain the continuity of the matrix, leaving areas containing only thin liquid films. The second stage involves primarily an increase in the surface area of the lamella films as discontinuities in the starch-protein matrix become increasingly frequent during expansion. Surface active materials, such as endogenous flour polar lipids, proteins, and pentosans dissolved in the dough aqueous phase may have a significant role to play in stabilizing the surface films so that they can expand to a larger surface area without rupturing.

Soon after mixing, the dough consists of discrete gas bubbles embedded in a continuous semisolid aqueous dough phase (hydrated starchprotein

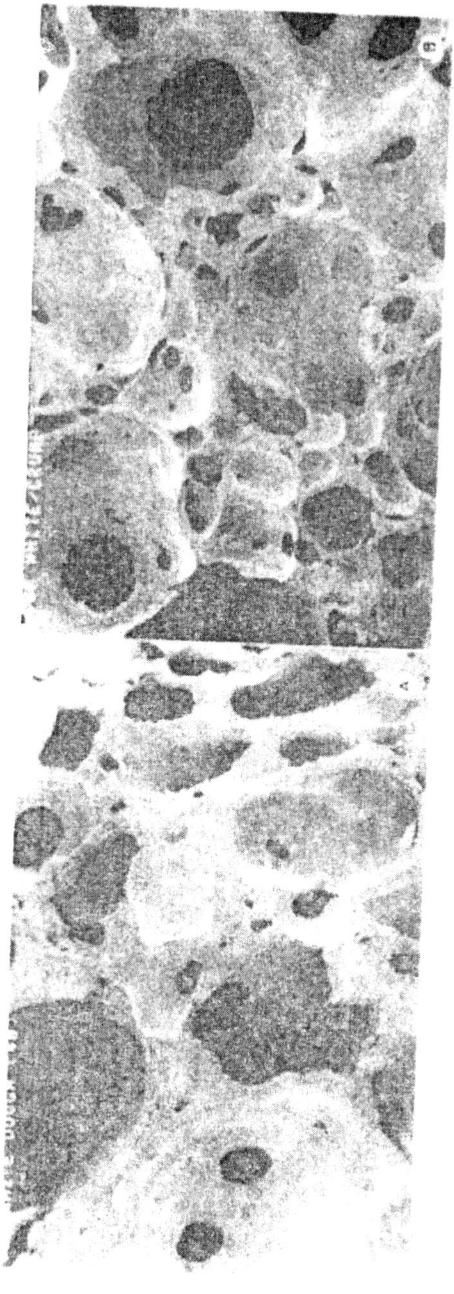

Fig. 10-17 Scanning Electron Micrographs of Wheat Bread Dough and Bread Prepared by the Chorleywood Breadmaking Process (CBP), Showing (a) the Apparent Interconnections in Bread Doghs at Advanced Stages of Proving, and (b) the open sponge Structure of Bread Crumb at the End of Baking.

matrix). The matrix fails to enclose the bubbles completely at advanced stages of fermentation, leaving areas that contain only a thin liquid lamella. Baking increases the rate of expansion until the lamella films are incapable of meeting the demand for new surface area generation, thus converting the foam structure into an open sponge, leading to the loss of gas retention.

Molecular Mechanisms of Bubble Stabilization in Doughs

Bubble/Foam Stabilization Fundamentals

Key Definitions and Concepts. A foam is a coarse dispersion of gas bubbles in a continuous liquid, semisolid, or solid phase. Foams are usually created by highly energetic and dynamic processes facilitated by a lowering of the interfacial tension in the presence of surface active materials. But facilitating foam formation is not the main role of surface-active materials. What these materials also do is to stabilize the gas bubbles. For freshly prepared foams containing thick lamella films (> 100 nm), the mechanical and dynamic properties of the surface-adsorbed layers are critical for retaining foam stability. For well-drained quasistatic foam containing thin films <100 nm), stability is determined primarily by interfacial interactions influenced by intermolecular forces.

Important parameters in foam stabilization include surface dilational elasticity; viscosity (bulk and surface); gravity drainage; capillary suction; and hydrophobic, electrostatic, and steric forces (Table 10-3).

The stability of a foam varies widely, from an unstable or transient foam with a lifetime of seconds to a metastable or permanent foam with a lifetime of hours, days, or even months and years. Unstable foams break down or collapse mainly through three mechanisms: coalescence, disproportionation, and buoyancy. The buoyancy-driven instability mechanism, however, does not have a significant role to play in bread doughs because of the high viscoelasticity of the bulk phase and the relatively short time scale involved. The mechanism of coalescence is most relevant in bread dough processing; disproportionation is also discussed by some workers. These will be discussed in detail in the following sections.

Coalescence. Coalescence involves the fusion of gas bubbles through the rupture of the thin film between them. The rupture can be induced by several mechanisms such as thermal and mechanical disturbances, causing thickness fluctuations and local thinning. The presence of hydrophobic particles (e.g., fine bran materials) or particles containing spreadable material such as emulsion droplets may also lead to film rupture and coalescence. A

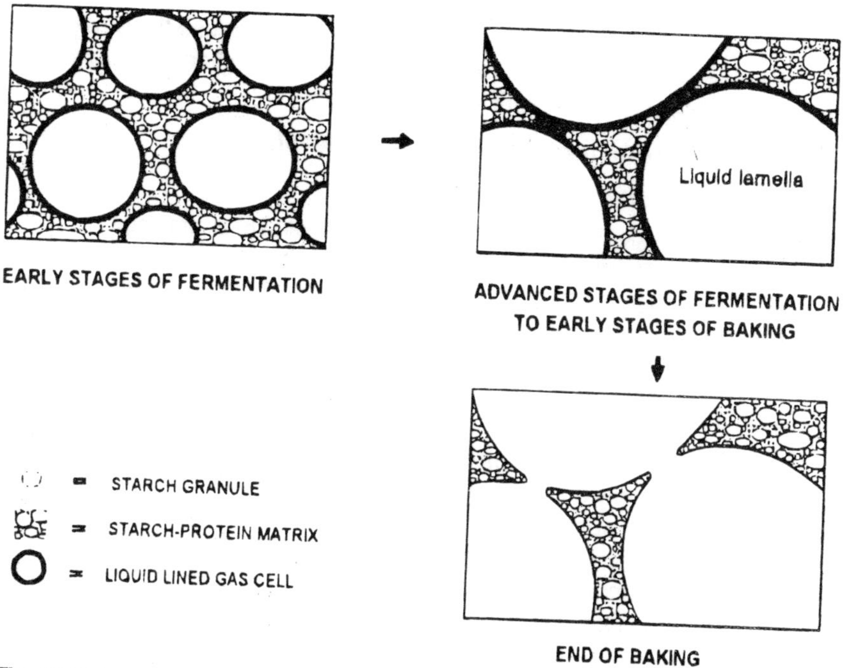

Fig. 10-18 A Model of Dough Expansion

hydrophobic particle may force hydrophilic aqueous film surfaces into a convex shape when the particle is in contact with both surfaces, leading to higher Laplace pressure in the region and rupture as a result of the liquid in the film flowing away from the particle. On the other hand, the spreading of an emulsion droplet over a film surface causes film liquid to flow with it. If the penetration depth of the spreading motion is of the same order as film thickness, mpture occurs.

Disproportionation. Foam instability can also be caused by a diffusion mechanism, in which gas is forced across thin films from smaller bubbles to larger ones. This is known as disproportionation and the driving force for this behaviour is the Laplace pressure over a curved surface. Because the pressure inside a small bubble is greater than inside a large bubble and the gas solubility increases with pressure, more gas dissolves near the small bubble than near the large one. This causes the diffusion of gas to occur across the concentration gradient, resulting in the growth of large bubbles at the expense of the small ones. The process is selfaccelerating because the smaller the gas bubbles become, the higher the Laplace pressure inside them, assuming that the bubbles have constant surface tension.

Table 10.3 Some factors affecting Foam stability

Enhanced Stability	***Reduced Stability***
• Surface dilational elasticity	• Gravitational drainage
• Viscosity (bulk and surface)	• Thermal and mechanical shock
• Gibbs-Marangoni effect	• Local thinning, rupture
• Film net surface charge (electrostatic)	• Hydrophobic particle, emulsion droplets
• Intermolecular interaction	• Gas solubility, diffusion
• Film thickness	• Permeable film

Disproportionation is especially important in cases in which the gas concerned is readily soluble in the bulk phase. Carbon dioxide (CO_2)based foams are highly susceptible to disproportionation because of their high solubility in aqueous media. The diffusion of gas cannot occur significantly in polyhedral foams (e.g., doughs at advanced stages of fermentation), because the lamellae are planar and there is no greater pressure difference across the interface. Disproportionation does not necessarily result in a breakdown of the foam. The latter can only be achieved by film rupture or coalescence. In bread doughs during proving, there is a higher CO_2 concentration in the dough phase than in the bubbles, so mass transfer is from the dough to the bubbles. It seems therefore highly unlikely that disproportionation could occur during dough proving; for CO_2 to travel from smaller to larger bubbles, it would first have to travel "uphill" into the aqueous dough phase, which is not possible. Also, initially the bubbles in dough contain nitrogen, which is only about 1/50 as soluble as CO_2 and is unlikely to migrate from small to large bubbles significantly during proving. In fact, calculations on the time for a 100-μm diameter nitrogen bubble to shrink to nothing, based on the de Vries equation reported by van Vliet, suggest times of around 50 minutes. Another consideration is that dough at the end of mixing is likely to be saturated with nitrogen anyway, and even if it were not, simple calculations show that, for a dough with a typical air content of 5%, dissolution of nitrogen from bubbles into the dough would achieve saturation with very little decrease in size of the bubbles.

Some workers report that they have observed shrinkage of bubbles, which they credit to disproportionation. This may reflect the system used to observe these bubbles under a microscope, and, in the light of the preceding discussion, appears unlikely to represent accurately the actual physics of bubbles in proving doughs.

The Function of Surface-Active Materials in Bread Doughs

Nonstarch Polar Lipid. The non starch polar lipid (PoL), derived from various membranes and organelles, made up of numerous glycolipids and phospholipids, is associated closely with the liquid phase of dough (about 0.3%). PoL in the lamella, liquid-crystalline form (which can transform spontaneously in an aqueous environment on mixing into lamella dispersions, comprising small and bilayer aggregates [liposomes]) provides lipid depots for adsorption at gas/liquid interfaces in dough processing. Indeed, PoLs are generally found to have a positive effect in breadmaking. However, because doughs prepared from defatted flours can expand, it must be assumed that PoLs are not essential for gas retention and that other surfaceactive components such as non gluten proteins dissolved in the dough aqueous phase are also involved in the stabilization of gas bubbles in bread doughs.

Nongluten Proteins. Although low molecular mass surfactants are more effective than proteins in reducing surface or interfacial tension, foams formed by such surfactants are mostly unstable. Stable foams are usually formed by proteins that have the ability to form cohesive, viscoelastic films around gas bubbles by means of noncovalent intermolecular interactions and covalent disulfide cross-linking. Not all proteins, however, are equally surface active. For a protein to be a good foaming agent, it should possess the following attributes:

- Capable of rapid adsorption at interface
- Capable of undergoing rapid conformational change and rearrangement and of rapid reduction in surface tension
- Capable offorming a cohesive, viscoelastic film by means of intermolecular interactions

The rate of adsorption or at which the protein reduces interfacial tension is essential for better foamability, whereas the ability to form viscoelastic film is important for foam stability. These attributes depend on intrinsic factors of the protein molecules (Table 10–4), which in turn depend on environmental factors such as pH, ionic strength, and temperature.

The wheat gluten proteins, therefore, may have a very limited role to play in surface film stabilization because of their well-known insolubility in the aqueous phase of dough. On the other hand, the nongluten proteins of the wheat flour are readily soluble in salt solutions and represent about 2% to 3% by weight of the aqueous phase of dough. It is these proteins that seem likely to fulfill the role of interfacial film stabilization. Gan and Schofield have recently isolated a group of very surface-active proteins from the aqueous phase of dough using a simple foaming technique. These proteins are extremely effective in foam stabilization, and are thought to have an important role to play in bread dough processing.

Also of interest in relation to the role of protein in stabilizing interfacial films in bread doughs is the recent discovery of a group of lipid-binding and amphiphilic proteins in wheat flour. These proteins, designated puroindolines, have intrinsically good foaming properties and their lipid-binding properties confer to puroindolines the unique capacity of preventing lipidinduced destabilization. The most important functional properties of puroindolines in bread dough processing are therefore related to their ability to stabilize, along with polar lipids, interfaces in expanding doughs.

Nonstarch Polysaccharides. Pentosans are the major nonstarch polysaccharides of wheat flour. They originate from the endosperm cell walls of wheat grains and are mainly made up of arabinoxylans and arabinogalactans, which are partly extractable with water. Aqueous solutions

Table 10.4 Molecular Properties of Proteins Affecting Foaming

Molecular Properties	*Foaming Properties*
Solubility	Rapid diffusion to the interface
Amphipathicity	Distribution of charged, polar, and non polar residues for enhanced interfacial interactions.
Segment flexibility	Facilitate unfolding at the interface
Interactive segments	The disposition of different functional segments facilitates secondary interactions in the gas, aqueous, and interfacial phases.
Disposition of charge groups	Charge repulsion between contiguous bubbles.
Disposition of polar groups	Prevents close approach of bubbles; hydration, osmotic, and steric effects.

of water-extractable pentosans are highly viscous, and the arabinoxylan fraction has been identified as the major component responsible for the high viscosity. The arabinoxylans of high intrinsic viscosity were found to be more effective in stabilizing aqueous protein foams during thermal expansion. The addition of arabinoxylan was also shown to produce a substantial reduction in the surface tension of water. Thus, apart from playing a positive role in bulk dough rheology, water-extractable pentosans may contribute to the stabilization of gas bubbles by improving the mechanical strength of the liquid films in the dough. Firm conclusions about the functional role(s) of pentosans in breadmaking will only be possible when the structure and properties of wheat flour arabinoxylans and their variation, especially those of the water-extractable fraction, are more fully understood.

Surfactants or Emulsifiers. It has been known for some time that the addition of a small amount of surfactants or emulsifiers such as SSL (sodium steroy 1-2-lactylate) and DATEM (diacetyl tartaric acid esters of monoglycerides) to bread dough leads to improved volume and finer, more uniform crumb structure with thin gas bubble walls. Surfactants that are most effective in breadmaking include SSL, DATEM, and ethoxylated monoglycerides, which are able to form lamella mesophases or gel structures in water. Both SSL and DATEM suspensions were found to have very high values of surface dilational modulus after mechanical treatment. Dynamic measurements showed that SSL and DATEM surfaces have considerable viscous components. Considering the high surface dilationa l modulus, the low surface tension caused by the addition of SSL or DATEM can retard coalescence to a greater extent.

Foam Stabilization by a Combination of Surface-Active Components (Mixed Films)

Food foams such as bread doughs are not stabilized by single pure proteins or surfactants but by multicomponent mixtures of macromolecular proteins together with various lipids and non starch polysaccharides. In systems containing both low molecular and macromolecular surface-active materials, stability primarily depends on protein films adsorbed at the interfaces despite the fact that low molecular mass surfactants have superior foamability. For most of the protein stabilized foams, the presence of completing low molecular mass surfactants may act to compromise stability. Problems of stability can be particularly acute if the adsorbed protein layer is susceptible to disruption by the competitive adsorption oflow molecular mass molecules such as polar lipids. This may be precisely the case when polar lipids are added incrementally to defatted flour (MacRitchie, 1987); the protein-stabilized bubbles in bread dough are first destabilized, reaching minimum stability probably by formation of a mixed film, with reduced intermolecular interactions of proteins at the interface. As more polar lipids are added, proteins may be displaced from the interface and stability returns as the concentration of the competing surfactant increases.

In some cases, however, the addition of low molecular mass lipids may actually increase foam stability. In puroindoline-stabilized foams, for example, polar lipids can act co-operatively with proteins in interfacial films, resulting in increased foam stability. Nonstarch polysaccharides on the other hand may improve the stability of foam by increasing viscosity (of both the bulk and the surface) ofthe system. Complexing of proteins with polysaccharides by covalent or electrostatic interactions may also produce large improvements in foam stability.

Surface Properties Versus Bulk Rheological Properties

Gluten proteins undoubtedly play a major role in determining the baking performance of wheat flours through their effects on dough rheological properties. However, the important role of the surface properties in bubble stabilization and gas retention should not be overlooked. The change in free surface energy has been calculated to account for about 80% of the elastic energy involved in the deformation (expansion) of dough. Although this calculation has been disputed, the conclusion remains that a greater pressure in gas cells is needed to overcome surface tension than viscous resistance of the dough.

Surface and bulk rheological properties affect bubble behaviour at different stages of bread dough processing in different ways. The size of the bubbles immediately after mixing is determined by wheat polar lipids, other low molecular mass surfactants, and commercial improvers such as SSL and DATEM, which are capable of rapidly reducing surface tension, resulting in decreased bubble radius and increased bubble numbers. At the advanced stages offermentation and the early stages of baking, stability against coalescence of gas bubbles as a result of lamella film rupture becomes critically important. At elevated temperatures and increased expansion rate during baking, bulk properties (e.g., strain hardening, extensibility, and rupture strain) continue to play an important part in dough expansion. But the increased rate of new surface area generation makes the stabilization of the thin lamella film essential for good gas retention and oven spring.

Clearly, the significance in bubble stabilization of the liquid film relative to that of the bulk dough phase during breadmaking may vary among flours. A stable liquid film could compensate for a bulk phase of relatively poor extensibility and strain-hardening properties, as may occur when surfactants are added to improve gas retention, or vice versa, as may occur when gluten is added to improve baking performance. If both the surface and the bulk rheological properties are unsatisfactory, a dough with poor bubble stability and poor gas retention will result.

Bubble Stabilization Strategies

The expansion of bread dough is a dynamic and multifactorial process controlled by both the surface and the bulk rheological properties of the system. Thus, from the previous discussion, three strategic options are available in bubble stabilization:

- Optimizing bulk rheological properties (e.g., optimal resistance to extension, high extensibility, and high strain-hardening properties)
- Optimizing surface properties (e.g., low surface tension, high surface dilational modulus, and high viscosity)
- Achieving synergy between surface and bulk rheological properties

The first option is determined primarily by the structure and function of gluten proteins, glutenin polymers in particular. The second option is determined primarily by surface-active materials, such as endogenous flour polar lipids, proteins, and pentosans, dissolved in the dough aqueous phase. The third option offers true economic potential if the effects of the surface and bulk rheological properties are balanced effectively.

Modeling Bubble Growth during Proving

Measuring bubble growth during proving is a difficult challenge that has not yet been fully achieved. Whitworth and Alava measured the bubble size distribution ex-mixer and after intermediate proof, and also produced computed tomographic images of proving doughs, but resolution limits precluded the measurement of the bubble size distribution and its change with time. In the absence of ready measurement techniques, modeling offers a useful tool that can complement such measurement techniques as are available. Bubble growth during proving is a classical chemical engineering mass transfer problem that can be modeled using diffusive mass transfer theory. Some models consider also the dough rheology; however, proving is a slow process and, as noted previously, surface tension dominates over viscous effects in resisting growth and generating excess pressure in the bubbles. Shah et al.

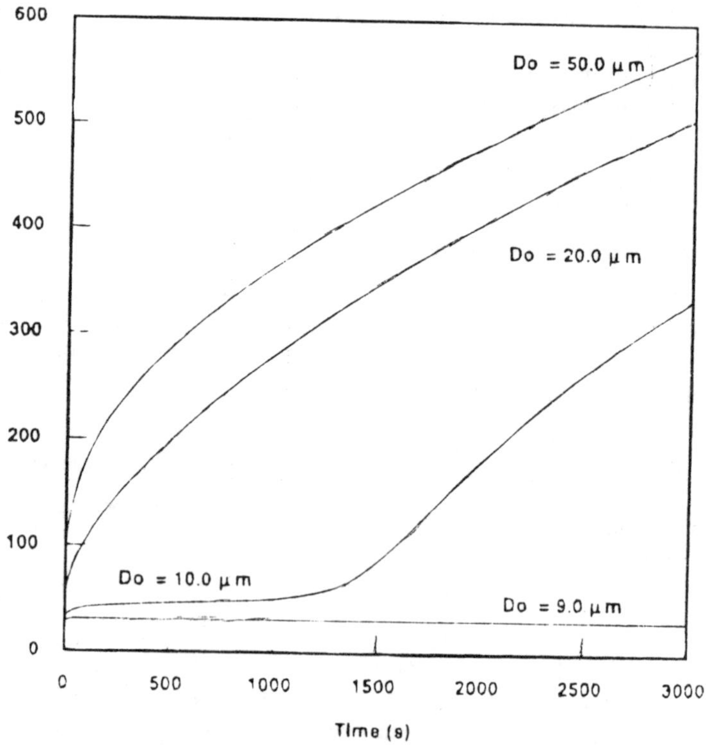

Fig. 10.19 Influence of the Initial Diameter (*Do*) on Subsequent Bubbles Growth under slightly Supersaturated Conditions, Showing How a small Change in Bubble Size from 9 to 0 µm Affects Long-Term Growth.

modeled single bubble growth, showing that when the carbon dioxide concentration in the dough is below saturation, all bubbles eventually reach an upper size limit, beyond which they will not grow. Above saturation, bubbles larger than a critical diameter will grow indefinitely. Figure 10-19 shows the predicted growth for bubbles of different initial diameters, for a dough with a CO_2 concentration slightly exceeding saturation.

Validation of such models of bubble growth during proving is difficult. Ideally the bubble size distribution during proving would be measured and compared with predictions. During the early stages of proving this would be possible by measuring the size distribution on slices, but during the later stages of proving there is too little dough to be able to take intact slices.

Shah et al. modeled instead CO_2 production and bubble growth in the one-dimensional system of the Chopin Rheofermentometer, which measures gas production and gas retention during proving. Gas production and retention were measured for doughs mixed at different vacuum levels and compared with model predictions; the greater CO_2 loss from doughs mixed under vacuum, and the rate of growth of the dough piece, were qualitatively in agreement with model predictions, giving some validation to the diffusion-based model developed.

BAKING OF BREAD

Qualitative Description of Baking

From a food processing point of view, baking of bread finally renders the processed wheat in a state that is shelf-stable, nutritious, and palatable. From a nutritional point of view, baking gelatinizes the starch, making it available for digestion. From a rheological point of view, baking converts the viscoelastic continuous dough phase into a solid, set structure. From an aeration point of view, baking transforms the proved dough from a foam, containing discrete gas cells, into a sponge, made up of a porous network of interconnected gas chambers. This change is perhaps the most well understood of the three bread aeration stages, albeit mainly qualitatively. As a cooking method, baking is a relative newcomer-roasting over an open fire was probably the first cooking method, followed by boiling. Baking is somewhat more sophisticated, as is the major product of baking, bread.

Baking is a dry heat cooking method that relies on a combination of radiation from the oven walls and air convection to heat the food. Typical baking temperatures for bread are around 200°C to 230°C, with the oven walls no hotter than about 260°C. At these temperatures, both radiation and air convection are slow heat transfer processes, so baking is a slow, gentle cooking method suitable for food items of large volume. Baking easily dehydrates the surface of foods being cooked, allowing temperatures to exceed 100°C, and therefore allowing browning reactions to occur at the surface. Hence the crust of bread is dry and colored, whereas the center (crumb) is moist and white. At its simplest, baking involves heat transfer from the surface of the loaf to the center such that the starch at the center reaches complete gelatinization at the same time that the crumb attains an attractive colour and sufficiently rigid structure without burning or becoming over tough. The end of baking is achieved when the center temperature reaches about 90°C to 92°C. The baking temperature is controlled such that this center temperature is achieved without overcooking the surface.

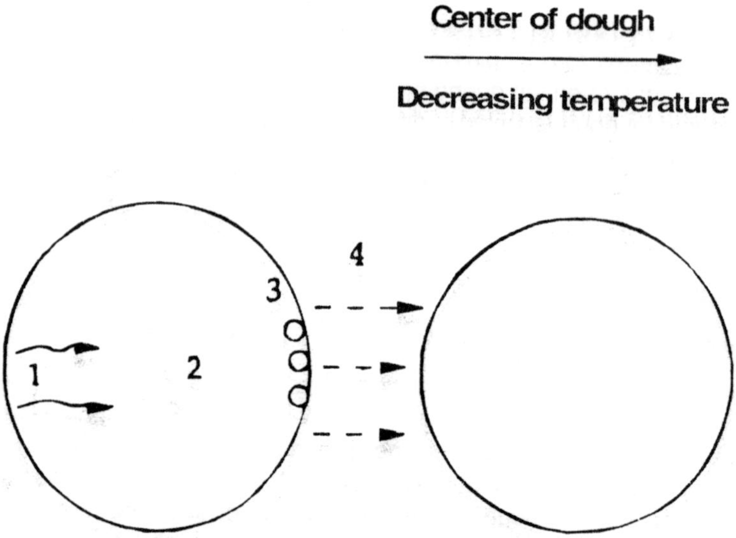

Fig 10-20 Heat and Moisture Transfer by Evaporation / Condensation during baking of Bread

Heat transfer within the loaf is by conduction (as for most foods), in combination with evaporation/condensation (which is unique to porous foods), as shown in Figure 10-20. (Once again, bubbles in bread are the factor that make bread unique) If a bubble has a temperature gradient across it, water will evaporate at the warmer side, absorbing the latent heat of vaporization (1). The steam migrates across the gas cell (2). Hitting the cooling side of the bubble, the steam condenses, releasing the latent heat of condensation (3). Heat and water are then transported by conduction and diffusion through the gluten/starch matrix to the next gas cell (4), and the process starts again. This heat transfer process of evaporation/condensation also means that water is transported toward the center of the loaf; there is therefore a moisture gradient and a temperature gradient throughout the loaf, affecting the rate of physical and chemical changes at different points in the loaf.

Evaporation also occurs at the surface of the loaf, drying the surface and allowing the formation of a firm, coloured crust. This evaporation means that there is a weight loss during baking, so that the dough piece entering the oven must be greater than the target loaf weight. For an 800-g loaf, this may require a scaling weight of 900 g. (This includes a safety factor because loaves in different parts of the oven may lose more or less weight by evaporation.) Minimizing weight loss by evaporation allows lower scaling weights to be used, thus increasing baked loaf yields and saving money. Some bakers reduce surface evaporation by adding steam to the oven; steam addition reduces weight loss by about 10 g per loaf. Steam initially condenses on the cool proved doughs, increasing the weight initially, and reducing the overall weight loss by the end of baking. The initial moistening of the surface alters the surface chemistry and crust formation, maintaining an elastic dough surface and resulting in a slightly leathery crust, which bakers of top-quality bread consider unacceptable; these bakers do not add steam to their ovens.

Physical and Chemical Changes Caused by the Temperature Increase during Baking

The baking process requires that heat transfer cause certain events to occur at the right time: gas expansion and evaporation, yeast deactivation, starch gelatinization, melting off at, protein denaturation, and flavour formation. The temperature gradients during baking mean that these chemical and physical changes within the loaf are occurring to different extents at different times.

With regard to aeration, five processes occur during baking:

1. Increased gas production caused by increased yeast activity at higher temperatures, until the yeast is killed at about 50°C to 60°C. The resulting increase in loaf volume is termed oven rise and may be considered a high-temperature extension of proving.
2. Gas expansion caused by the temperature increase.
3. Evaporation of water, carbon dioxide, and ethanol. Combined with gas expansion, this causes an increase in loaf volume that is termed oven spring. Oven rise and oven spring are often used interchangeably, but for the sake of precision should be used as defined here, to maintain the distinctions between the different factors affecting the increase in loaf volume during baking.
4. Gas cell coalescence (in which the fluid membrane between bubbles bursts at *low* temperatures) and gas cell rupture (in which the membrane between gas cells or separating a gas cell from the outside atmosphere bursts because of the increase in tensile strength on heat setting of the dough structure at *high* temperatures).

5. Setting of the sponge structure.

In proving, much of the aim is to retard bubble coalescence to maintain a fine crumb structure and achieve a large loaf volume. In baking, the aim is largely to delay gas cell coalescence and rupture to maximize oven rise and oven spring by maintaining the pressure in the gas cells and preventing loss of gas until the structure is set. As with proving, many dough ingredients probably exert their influence here. If gas cell rupture (caused by heat setting) occurs too early, gas will be lost and will no longer contribute to volume expansion of the loaf. If gas cell rupture occurred, but the starch gluten matrix did not set immediately, the loaf would deflate like a burst balloon. Baking must therefore ensure that rupture and setting occur simultaneously and at the optimum time to maximize volume expansion. Fortunately, the mechanism for membrane rupture is the increase in tensile strength that occurs on heat setting (starch gelatinization and protein denaturation), so rupture and setting do occur simultaneously. Setting is required to maintain the baked loaf structure that is no longer maintained by the pressure in the gas cells. Starch gelatinization, and therefore setting and rupture, occur above *60°C;* additives such as emulsifiers that delay starch gelatinization (by increasing the gelatinization temperature) generally serve to increase loaf volumes.

If gas cell rupture does not occur throughout the loaf such that some bubbles are still intact and discrete separated from the outside atmosphere, then when the loaf is cooled, these bubbles will shrink again, causing the loaf to collapse. (This is true in cakes also, especially sponge cakes, which are notorious for collapsing. The reason for sponge cake collapse is that there are still intact bubbles in the cake that shrink when the cake cools.) If a porous network has been achieved, when the loaf cools, air from the atmosphere can enter to fill all the pores on cooling. Bloksma modeled oven spring (which he called oven rise) by considering the contributions of thermal expansion of gases and evaporation of water, carbon dioxide, and ethanol, concluding that water evaporation is the major contributor to oven rise. Eliasson and Larsson consider this probably to be an overestimate. Experimentally the volume increase contributed by oven rise is around 1.5 to 2.5 volumes/volume liquid dough phase. This changes the relative volume (volume relative to dough volume ex-mixer) from between 4 and 5 at the end of proving to between 5 and 7 after baking.

Bakery Fat

Fat is an optional ingredient for "traditional" long or bulk fermentation breadmaking processes. For "no time" mechanical dough development processes, such as the CBP, however, it is an obligatory ingredient for production of bread of acceptable quality. Furthermore, not only must fat be included, but a proportion (5%) of that fat must be solid (i.e., in crystalline fonn) at proof temperature. The association off at crystals with the surfaces of gas bubbles in bread dough has been recently described by Brooker. Fat crystals can act as vehicles for the transfer of additional interfacial material to gas bubble surfaces during proving and baking and thereby prevent coalescence. It is thought that during the mixing process, fat crystals emerge from droplets of liquid fat in large numbers and become "adsorbed" at the gas/liquid interfaces of bubbles, the expansion of which during proving leads to increased adsorption. In general, small fat crystals of the ß-polymorph are more likely to be brought into direct contact with bubble surfaces than the much larger ß-crystals. As the temperature of the dough increases during baking, the fat crystals melt and provide a source of extra interfacial material for the bubble surface, which allows expansion without rupturing. A further advantage of the p-fat crystals over the p-polymorph in this respect may be that the former has a lower melting temperature and thus may be more readily available for contributing to gas cell surface integrity during baking than the latter. The consequence is that a large number of small bubbles may survive baking and thereby contribute to crumb quality.

From a consideration of the preceding observations, Brooker developed ways for reducing the fat content required for CBP-type breads, while maintaining acceptable loaf quality. If fat crystals act as mediators for the transport of stabilizing surfactant material to bubble walls during expansion, more crystals should do so more effectively. Using rapid liquid nitrogen cooling, Brooker produced fat with many more smaller crystals. Less of this fat was required to stabilize gas cells during bread baking. Going one step further, Brooker then removed the liquid oil, which does not contribute to gas cell stabilization, adding only the fat crystals to the dough formulation. Again, acceptable baked loaf quality was maintained, with a fat content only J 5% of the usual fat content of bread. Reducing fat content in food is the primary goal of food research around the world; here it was achieved for bread by a careful study of the bubbles and their stabilization during baking.

PHYSICAL AND CHEMICAL REQUIREMENTS FOR BREADMAKING PERFORMANCE

Having established the factors affecting bread aeration at the mixing, proving, and baking stages, it is useful to consider in the light of these the requirements for a good breadmaking wheat flour. We have established that bread dough rheology underpins the creation of aerated bread. The viscoelastic character of dough is created during mixing through the alignment of the unique glutenin proteins found in wheat, giving sufficient elasticity to retain gas during proving but sufficient extensibility to avoid premature rupturing. The strain-hardening feature of dough rheology plays a major factor in maximizing bubble inflation and baked loaf volume. Dough rheology is underpinned by dough protein chemistry, and it is here that we should look, at least initially, to identify good breadmaking potential. The bulk rheology conferred by the wheat proteins is then complemented by the surface activity of endogenous or added emulsifiers.

It is known that certain wheat varieties consistently produce good breadmaking performance, whereas others do not. For example, the UK wheat varieties, Hereward, Mercia, and Charger, produce the highest baking volumes in the CBP process, whereas Soissons and Magellan give lower baking volumes.. It is widely believed that this is due to the presence or absence of certain biochemical components within the protein fraction of the wheat endosperm, although it is by no means clear how these components affect the physical processes that occur in breadmaking. It is well known that baking quality is determined to a large extent by the quantity and quality of gluten proteins. Quantitative and compositional differences in those proteins are the main determinants of quality variation among different wheat cultivars. The rheological properties of gluten are thought to arise mainly from the properties of its two main subfractions, gliadin and glutenin, as discussed earlier in the section "Wheat Proteins and the Origin of Dough Rheology and Dough Development." Variation in the composition and properties of the glutenin fraction plays a major role in variations in breadmaking quality among different varieties. Payne et al. classified glutenin subunits using gel electrophoresis and ranked their effects on breadmaking quality. They found that higher MW glutenin subunits have the strongest relationship with baking volume.

During proof and baking it is the growth of gas bubbles within the dough (caused by an increase in gas pressure) that determines the expansion of the dough, and therefore the ultimate volume and texture of the bread. It is thought that the limit of expansion is related directly to the expansion, stability, and rupture of the bubble walls caused by the eventual loss in gas retention on bubble rupture. The stability of the cell walls around the expanding gas bubbles is considered to be an important factor in determining baking quality.

Toward the end of proof and during baking the cell walls between expanding gas cells have thicknesses less than the diameters of starch granules, and therefore these films cannot be considered as homogeneous dough films. They are likely to behave as a highly extensible protein phase interspersed by aqueous components of surface-active materials and starch particles. Therefore, both the rheological properties of the protein phase and the surface properties of the spreading aqueous components will be important in maintaining bubble stability. Interactions between proteins, surfaceactive components, and starch will become important at this point. There are many hypotheses for the physical criteria that control baking quality. The unique rheology of wheat flour doughs is a prerequisite for producing raised bread, but the nature of the dough-bubble interface also contributes to the growth and coalescence of bubbles. A flour with good gluten quality can therefore be enhanced or compromised by the effects of minor components such as lipids and surfactants.

COMMERCIAL BENEFITS OF UNDERSTANDING BUBBLE BEHAVIOUR IN BREADMAKING

It has been the argument of this chapter that breadmaking is about aeration and that understanding aeration can lead to improved product quality and process effectiveness. Examples have been mentioned throughout the text; this final section aims to summarize and highlight these. The essence of effective bread aeration is first dough rheology and second the control of the dough-bubble interface. These two factors are balanced and optimized through the interaction between bread ingredients and processing.

A key aspect of dough rheology is strain hardening. This discovery, combined with the development of a method for determining fundamental rheological properties of doughs, based on blowing bubbles in dough, is aiding the identification of genetic, ingredient, and processing factors contributing to bubble stability during proving. Dough rheology arises from dough protein chemistry. The identification of HMW glutenin subunits associated with good breadmaking quality is aiding the development of better breadmaking varieties. Understanding that there is a turnover of air during dough mixing has led to the development of processes based on delayed pressure reduction and pressure-vacuum mixing. An understanding of the contribution of fat to bubble stabilization during baking has led to a reformulation of bakery fat, which allows an 85% reduction in the fat content of bread.

The preceding examples illustrate the benefits of understanding aeration aspects of breadmaking. We believe there are many more, such as even better breadmaking varieties; more energy efficient mixing; vacuum less mixing; reduced use of expensive minor ingredients; reduced proving and baking times; greater versatility in the range of breads that can be produced from a given process; greater ability to respond to technological, ingredient, and legislative changes; better product quality; increased process throughout and productivity; and a more effective baking industry. Baking has underpinned civilization for 5000 years, yet there is much still to understand. The bubbles in bread make bread unique–it is time they were no longer "the neglected bread ingredients."

11

External & Internal Bread Faults

INTRODUCTION

Deviations from normal bread quality standards, whether perceived subjectively or determined by objective measurements, are designated by the collective term *bread faults*. They arise from two principal sources : inferior ingredients and improper processing. In many instances, bread faults result from a combination of various factors so that it is more conveninet to classify them into broad categories and indicate the possible causes that may be involved in each.

It is said that, every bakery encounters as many bread faults as it deserves. This implies that bread faults can be held to a minimum by paying close attention to the quality of the ingredients and by accurate control on the production process. For that

- A thorough knowledge about raw material and its functions.
- Adequate understanding of bread making procedures.
- Necessary information on time, temperature and humidity at different stages of bread making.
- Above all person skills and experience of the baker

Go a long way in avoiding faults in bread and also in finding out remedies, if any fault occurs.

A skilled baker should examine the bread carefully, and by reasoning, deductions, elimination and if necessary by experimentation should be able to detect the cause(s) of fault and subsequently find the solution.

Bread faults are divided into two parts

External Faults	Internal Faults
• Faults in volume • Lack of volume • Excessive volume	• Holes and tunnels in bread • Cores, seams, streaks & condensation marks
• Faults in crust • Lack of crust colour	• Damp, clammy & closed crumb Dryness and rapid staling
• Dark crust colour	• Crumbliness of the crumb
• Cracking of crust • Leathery crust • Hard crust • Thick crust • Blisters • Lack of bloom • Shell tops • Irregulatory of shape • Lack of cleanliness	• Defects in taste and aroma

The main causes of above faults are discussed below in detail white the other the other causes are summarized in table at the end of the chapter.

EXTERNAL FAULTS : The bread faults, which can be seen outer side, are divided into five major parts :

Faults in Volume : Proper volume of bread is the outcome of adequate conditioning of the gluten and sufficient gassing power of the dough at the time of baking. The imbalance in the same may results in less or excessive volume.

(i) **Lack of volume** : This fault may be caused due to many factors beginning from improper selection of raw material to cooling process. Among them fermentation is the principal cause. In addition to that, lack of sugar at proofing stage is also important cause because insufficient sugar would not produce carbon dioxide in sufficient quantity hence the product may not rise adequately. Moreover factors affecting gluten quality is also one of the major cause of lack of volume, as the carbon dioxide gas produced during fermentation is retained in the gluten cell framework.

(ii) **Excessive Volume :** Generally the opposite causes to lack of volume produce excessive volume. Excessive quanity of yeast, strong flour, low salt, loose moulding are the chief causes of the fault. It is advisale to keep in mind that too much quantity of the above mentioned raw material would produce bread with lack of volume.

Faults in Crust :

(i) **Lack of Crust Colour :** Crust colour largely depends on quantity of the residual sugar, although the baking temperature also should be adequate (at the same time). Under any circumstances, when the yeast activity is vigorous, the utilization of sugar is much, resulting in light crust colour.

(ii) **Dark Crust Colour :** More quantity of residual sugar results in foxy red dark crust colour, which is the result of opposite conditions to light crust colour.

(iii) **Cracking of Crust :** This fault is principally caused by the excessive oven heat. Because in such a condition gluten stretches much, which shrinks speedily when bread comes out of oven, as a result crust get cracked. Sometimes, the speedy cooling of bread may cause cracking of the crust.

(iv) **Leathery Crust :** The bread crust should be crispy and should break easily when it is stretched. But sometimes crust feels leathery when it is stretched. This fault may be caused due to improper ripening of dough (particularly in case of strong flour) results is insufficient gluten ripening which make it leathery. Secondly, when crust absorb the water during baking or processing followed after baking the crust becomes leathery.

(v) **Hard Crust :** Sometimes, bread crust feels hard and breaks just like egg-shell is known as hard or flinty crust. Strong flour with insufficient conditioning is the chief cause of hard crust. But the Indian wheat is not so hard, hence there are less chances of such a fault.

(vi) **Thick Crust :** When expansion of the bread in the oven (oven spring) is insufficient or bread is left in oven for too long time, there will be more concentration of heat on the outer surface of the bread rather than heat penetrating in the bread. This condition results in bread having thick crust.

(vii) **Blisters** : If the bread is prooved or baking or baked under highly humid atmosphere, the moisture may accumulate or droplets. Hence, the water content of that particular part results into more extensibility of gluten (just like slack dough), when that part absorbs heat during baking, it increases in volume and finally come up a blisters. Secondly, in case of machine moulding, if the pressure board are kept tight, it will result in to hard moulding and some air may erupt between gluten-layer & will rise during proofing and baking results in blisters. Thirdly, in case of sandwich bread, if less proofing time is allowed, there will be a gap between lid & dough, where the steam is accumulated (particularly in corners) which results into blisters.

(viii) **Lack of Bloom** : This fault is generally caused when low maltose figure flour is used for the bread production. Sometimes, over ripened dough may results in such fault.

Shell Top : This fault of bread can easily be determined (particularly in case of open top bread), as the crust is separated from crumb in the form of shell. Its main cause is early setting of crust.

Irregularity of Shape : Irregular shape of bread is the result of many factors. But the loose moulding is the chief cause. Secondly, the seal of moulding dough does not arranged at the bottom while panning.

Lack of Cleanliness : If the bread seems dirty (without any external fault) the consumer will not prefer to purchase it. In such a situation time, raw material, labour etc. will be wasted. Except one or two causes lack of cleanliness is caused due to carelessness of bakers. then it can be said that the baker is not perfect.

INTERNAL FAULTS : Internal faults are divided into six parts :

Hole sand tunnels : Some gluten strands break (due to any reason), either during proofing orinitial stage of baking, it has a chain reaction and the neighbouring gluten strands also continue to bread (results into hole and sometimes into tunnel) until the protein are coagulated under the acton of heat and the structure of bread is set.

Core, Seams, Streaks & Condensation Mark :

(i) **Core** : When the cut surface of crumb is gently pressed into finger tips, it feels that entire surface may not be evenly soft and presence of occasional hard spots may be left. These hard spots are known as cores . The main cause of core is addition of dough scrap (produced on hand, surfaces of mixing bowl, working table, dough cutters etc.)

after mixing operation is over. This dough scrap being hard as compared to dough, produces cores.

(ii) **Seams** : Very often, sandwich bread may show dense layers on the outer periphery of the crumb specially near the top crust. If the cut surface of such bread is observed, it could be clearly seen that the central part has open soft structure while the outer periphery has very close and compact structure. These dense layers are known as seems. The main cause for the same is restriction of dough expansion (during baking) by sidewall or cover of the bread tin.

(iii) **Streaks** : Sometimes, while layers of flour are observed inside the cut surface of bread is known as streaks. It is the result of (unweated) flour, which remains in the dough at any stage of bread processing.

(iv) **Condensation Mark :** If the bread is not allowed to cool properly before packing, some of the water vapour will deposit in the crumb structure causing dark colour patches known as condensation mark.

Damp, Clamy & Closed Crumb : Flour having more diastetic activity produces dextrin, it being gummy, imparts stickness to the crumb. Hence the normal quanitty of moisture will not be baked off leaving crumb over moist. However, over moist crumb with pineapple smell is indication of rope disease.

Dryness and Rapid Staling : Tne main cause of dryness of rapid staling is the improper development of gluten, because such gluten could not retain the moisture for longer time, hence bread becomes dry speedily.

Crumbliness of the Crumb : Adequately ripened gluten has proper elasticity, hence the crumb will also have similar properties. The improper elasticity of the crumb may break it while slicing of buttering. It is known as crumbliness. The main factor responsible for proper elasticity is adequate fermentation, which makes the proper development of the gluten.

Defects in Taste and Aroma : Pleasant taste and aroma in the bread is the result of proper fermentation, because it produces sufficient quantity of acid & alcohol and these two components are mainly responsible for flavour in the bread. Over fermentation may produce sour taste and aroma. If the dough temperature or temperature of fermentation room is high or the period of fermentation is too long, the yeast itself stops functioning after sometimes, but the acid producing bacteria (particularly lactic acid) will still remain active, which produces the typical sour taste and aroma in the bread. However, sometimes rope may produce sourness in bread but it has a fruity acidic aroma.

Causes	Remarks
5.2.1 (i) Lack of Volume	

• Wrong types of flour
  • Green Flour
  • Too strong or soft flour
  • Low maltose figure in the flour
  • Over bleached flour
  • Flour containing more chemical improvers
  • Excessive diastetic capacity
	• In all these conditions gluten could not ripen adequately or got over ripened, which cannot retain the produced gas properly

• Wrong types of yeast
  • Too much or too less yeast
  • Poor quality or old or miss handled yeast
  • Disintegrated yeast in too cold or too warm water
	• In all these conditions there will be less fermentation resulting into poor volume.

• Gluten affecting factors • Excessive salt	• Makes gluten harder
• Excessive fat	• Fat surrounded to gluten strands, hence, gluten, structure could not be framed.
• Excessive use of milk powder of milk	• Makes gluten stronger
• Under or over mixing	
• Excessive bran quantity in flour	• Breaks of gluten cell framework

• Adequacy of fermentation
  • Too slack o stiff dough
  • Too warm or chilled dough
• Dough chilling
	• In all these conditions either fermentation will be less, resulting in less gas production ultimately less volume or fermentation will be more resulting into

• Insufficient dough weight for pan size	break down of gas-cell and less volume

• Improper proofing
  • Stiff batter not allowed to ferment properly
  • More or less temperature or humidity in proof box
  • Excessive pan greasing
	• It results in over or under proofing.

• Skinning during any bread processing operation	• It makes the crust harder which does not allow the crumb to rise

• Improper baking
  • Excessive heat during baking
  • Improper distance between bread pan	

(ii) Excessive Volume	
• All the opposite causes those are mentioned above result in excessive volume	
(i) Lack of Crust colour or Pate Crust Colour	

• Low maltose figure of the flour
• Old flour
• Low sugar in formula
• Over fermentation or proofing may result of
  • Excessive water, yeast, MYF, pH. temperature
  • Less salt sugar, diastase enzyme	

<table>
<tr><td>• Soft water.
• Excessive dusting flour
• Insufficient humidity (skinning or dough)
• Under baking
• Cold oven
• Low top heat in oven</td><td></td></tr>
<tr><td colspan="2">(ii) Dark Crust Colour</td></tr>
<tr><td>• Opposite conditions of the above mentioned causes result in dark crust colour
• Excessive milk powder
• Lack of humidity in oven
• Flash heat</td><td></td></tr>
<tr><td colspan="2">(iii) Cracking of Crust</td></tr>
<tr><td>• Dough skinning before baking
• Short process of bread preparation
• Over proofed dough</td><td></td></tr>
<tr><td colspan="2">(iv) Leathery Crust</td></tr>
<tr><td>• Excessive humidity during proofing or baking
• Insufficient cooling before packing
• Too slack dough</td><td>• In such conditions absorbs the water and results in leathery crust
• Excess water could not evaporate while baking results in soggy crumb, which in turn is absorbed by crust during storage period hence crust becomes leathery</td></tr>
</table>

(v) Hard Crust	
• Excessive use of bread improvers or bleaching agent	
(vi) Thick Crust	
• Too strong or weak flour • Less diastetic activity in the flour • Less sugar and fat in formula • Over ferment dough • Low humidity in oven	• All these conditions result in lack of oven spring ultimately causing thick crust
(vii) Blisters	
• Improper mixing • Young dough • Improper distribution of baking pan in the oven • Rough handling in the oven • Excessive vacuum in the depanner	
(viii) Lack of Bloom	
• Inferior quality of raw material • Inbalanced formula • Improper fermentation • Improper proofing or baking conditions	
Shell Tops	

• Under ripened dough
  • Green flour
  • Low diastetic activity of the flour
  • Stiff dough	

• Inadequate oxidation • Young dough • Under proofing • Insufficient humidity while proofing • High baking temperature in case of insufficient oven steam	
Irregularity of Shape	
• Too strong or weak flour • Less bread improvers • High maltose figure in the flour • Improper mixing • Too slack or stiff dough • Over ripened dough • Excess dough as compared to bread pan size • Dough skinning due to insufficient humidity or over proofing • Rough handling of bread • Over loading in oven	
Lack of Cleanliness	
• No sieving or cleaning of flour as well as other raw material	• Threads, jute threads of bag, chunks of wood of other impurities present in raw material may get mixed with dough and find a thread
• Carelessness while working	• Impurities present on table or nearby working place may mixed into dough
• Excessive fat used for, greasing	• Some fat may get deposited in bread tin corner resulting into dark spots

• Use of uncleaned working table (particularly after cake decoration). machinery and equipments, bread tins or cooling racks etc. • Handling or bread (after baking) with dirty hands • Falling of soot from chimney (in case of wirewood oven) • Presence of sugar crystal of lumps of milk powder produces dark spots • Use of colour for writing brand name of logo etc. on jute bag	• This may be caused to improper dilution of sugar or milk powder • In this condition, dye is absorbed by flour but cannot detected with naked eyes, but when such flour is made into dough, the water develops the colour spots.
Holes and Tunnels in Bread	

• Weak gluten
  • Green Flour
  • Old flour
  • Soggy flour
• Excessive use of yeast for strong flavour
• Improper distribution (in case of improper mixing) of yeast, fat, milk powder, salt, sugar etc.
	• Weak gluten cannot retain the expanding gas results in breaking of strands
	• It results into inadequate gluten developing and excessive production of CO_2. The combined effect of both results into gluten strands breaking.
	• Wherever, the excess or less quality of such ingredients is present, it breakdown the gluten strands. The excess salt holes are sticky and smell salty

<table>
<tr><td>

- Over fermentation
  - Excessive yeast, MYF
  - Less salt
  - Soft water
  - High diastetic activity
  - Sack dough

</td><td>

- It produces more gas which breaks the gluten

- Excess water produces water holes which are sticky and shiney.

</td></tr>
<tr><td>

- Over mixing and ripening

</td><td>

- It produces the gas holes which are dull

</td></tr>
<tr><td>

- Excessive fat, improper mixing of fat, addition of fat in machine during dividing, moulding or handling up

</td><td>

- In all those cases, fat covers up the flour particles, which does not allow the gluten structure formation

</td></tr>
<tr><td>

- No knock back

</td><td>

- Gas produced during fermentation will not escape hence breaks the gluten strands.

</td></tr>
<tr><td>

- Too hot oven (particularly) hearth)

</td><td>

- The hot surface may destroy the extensibility of gluten resulting in break down of gluten strands

</td></tr>
<tr><td colspan="2">Core</td></tr>
<tr><td>

- Under mixing of dough
- Raw materias do not mix thoroughly

</td><td>

- This may caused in case of hand mixing

</td></tr>
<tr><td>

- Skinning during fermentation, intermediate proofing, moulding

</td><td>

- The hard skin of dough pieces mixed while nock-back, rounding or moulding and may cause core

</td></tr>
<tr><td>

- Improper stretching of dough while moulding

</td><td>

- Some part may stretch less will made dense core

</td></tr>
<tr><td colspan="2">Seams</td></tr>
<tr><td>

- Excess dough in bread tin
- Placing cool dough in hot tin or hot dough in cool tin

</td><td>

- In this condition fermentation on the dough surface which come in contact with bread tin is arrested, hence that part become dense

</td></tr>
</table>

• Improper handling of bread tin after completion of proofing.	
Streaks	
• Improper mixing • Excessive dusting flour • Insufficient water	
(iv) Condensation Mark	
• High maltose flour • High sugar content in the formula • Insufficient dilution of sugar or milk powder	
Damp, Clammy and Closed Crumb	
• Excessive humidity while proofing or baking	
• Insufficient baking	• Less moisture evaporation results in over moist crumb
• Insufficient fat compared to milk powder	• The milk protein makes the gluten harder, which do not allow to leaven the dough properly resulting in damp crumb.
• Excessive fat in plain white bread	• Excess fat do not allow to gluten formation resulting in damp crumb.
• Excessive use of bread improvers (particularly potassium bromate)	
Dryness and Rapid Staling	
• Insufficient salt and sugar	• They are hygroscopic, so less salt and sugar could not retain moisture for longer time

<table>
<tr><td>• Excessive mineral improver
• Insufficient fermentation incase of stiff dough
• Imbalanced formula in case of excess milk powder

• High fermentation temperature

• Over fermentation

• Long baking time</td><td>• Gluten could not get ripened properly
• Make gluten harder and water retention power is less hence bread becomes dry quickly
• Evaporate more moisture during fermentation as well as it also makes fermentation speedy hence the time required less, so the gluten development wil not proper
• Results in open grain structure through which moisture escapes speedily that makes faster drying of the bread
• Much moisture evaporation in oven will results in dryness.</td></tr>
<tr><td colspan="2">Crumbliness of the Crumb</td></tr>
<tr><td>• Under fermentation

• Over fermentation

• Slack dough
• Excess or less salt
• Excess fat
• Slicing of hot bread
• Excess mineral improvers</td><td>• Insufficient glutent development
• Dough become weak and losses elasticity</td></tr>
<tr><td colspan="2">Defects in Taste and Aroma</td></tr>
<tr><td>• Poor or inferior quality wheat used for flour production

• Placing flour or other raw material near strongly flavoured ingredient</td><td>• Such wheat contains off odour which transfer to flour and finally into the product
• The strong flavour is transfer to flour and finally to bread.</td></tr>
</table>

12

Fermented Products

INTRODUCTION: There is a whole range of fermented products other than breads like bun goods,doghnut, danish pestry, pitza base etc. Many bakers consider it as confectionery goods, because these products are usually consumed as a breakfast or snacks along with biscuits, cakes etc.

BUN GOODS: It includes all kinds of buns, fruit breads, tea cake etc. The raw material, process etc. for the same are discussed below in short :

Raw Material: All fermented buns contain a considerable percentage of enriching agents such as fat, sugar, egg etc. in addition to common raw materials for bread preparation like flour, yeast, water etc.

(i) ***Flour:*** To obtain a bold bun, high-class flour suitable for bread making is required for all types of buns.·

(ii) ***Yeast:*** Bun doughs contain high amount of enriching agents, which tends to retard fermentation hence quantity of yeast must be greater than bread making. Similarly, strong or fast working types of yeast are best since these are capable of bringing about a thorough maturing of the dough followed by rapid gas production during final proof.

(iii) ***Egg:*** The use of eggs was formerly limited to the richer types of fermented goods but research has shown that the use of eggs in all types of fermented small goods should be widely practiced. Because it imparts silkiness on the texture of the finished products and also enables to increase the volume that helps in decreasing scaling weights.

(iv) ***Shortening:*** For bun dough. vegetable oil is undoubtedly the best, since it is more evenly distributed in the dough and so it brings about a greater modification of the gluten which helps in production of bulky buns. It also keeps bun moist and fresh for longer time with silky crumb appearance. In case of richer varieties of *continental buns,* extra fat is incorporated after the dough has fermented. so as to produce an effect similar to the layer formation in puff paste. As with the puff paste, a good flavour is required, therefore butter should be used. Although, for cheaper varieties, a high grade margarine, in conjunction with demerara sugar will prove quite satisfactory.

(v) ***Fruit:*** The sugar present in the fruit may retard the yeast activity and thereby delay the fermentation. Hence, it is better to add the fruits in the dough after fermentation .

Processing: With these types of products, the ferment, is generally used as preparatory to dough making (although a straight dough is sometimes employed) especially where overnight dough are favoured. Such dough gives very satisfactory results when properly manipulated. The following are the main steps:

(i) ***Ferment Preparation:*** 28.37 gm (loz) milk powder & 28.37 gm (1 oz) sugar dissolve in 12.7 kg (1 quarter) water by whisking → add 28.3 gm (1 oz) yeast → mix 28.37 gm (1 oz) flour to produce clear batter > whisk thoroughly to aerate which stimulate yeast activity → allow to rest till drop (not more than 30 minutes) at 32.2°C (90° F) temperatures.

(ii) ***Mixing:*** Mix (at the same temperature) with rest of the ingredients.

(iii) ***Fermentation:*** All bun dough should be kept at 25.5° to 27.7°C (78° to 82°F) and should not be worked wanner. otherwise product will become dry & stale very quickly and will be lacking in bloom. Cool dough containing more yeast is always preferred to warm dough because it produces better buns.

(iv) ***Knock Back:*** In short process dough fermentation becomes very vigorous hence knock back should be carried out in early stage and for the same reason it should knock back frequently (every 20 minutes interval) which produce bun with large volume and silk like texture.

(v) ***Proofing:*** Proofing should be done at 25.5° to 27.7°C (78° to 82"F) and be careful that temperature does not rise. otherwise the dough will work too fast and become exhausted, which produce bun with poor volume bloom & appearance and also dry to eat. The humidity should be controlled strictly. Excess steam makes more condensation on surface results into rapid working of yeast and skin may be broken.

(vi) ***Baking:*** Most of buns are baked at 238°C (460" F) hence a substantial oven (which can bake fast) is required, that will produce buns with good volume and pleasing bloom. In such oven the loss of moisture will be just sufficient to bring about the correct baking without any excessive drying.

(vii) ***Glazing:*** Wash the buns when they slightly cool down after baking for pleasing appearance. which js the most important characteristics of all buns. There are many mixtures used for glazing- purpose known as *bun washes.* That is :

- PREPARED MIXTURES: Many preparations are marketed now in such a way that: it requires only the addition of warm water to produce a liquid as a glaze.
  - An egg and water glaze. consisting of 2 parts egg to 1 part of water thoroughly whisked. Fresh eggs will give better glaze than frozen eggs.
  - 1 egg, 150 ml water and 28.37 gm (1 oz) sugar. are thoroughly whisked. This will produce a good gloss. but will be slightly sticky.
  - Stock syrup, in which 28.37 gm (1 oz) of gelatine has been dissolved, will produce a good glaze. Stock syrup alone produces an extremely sticky glaze. Hence il should be used according to consumer choice.

PITZA BASE / CRUST: Pitza may be defined as *flat bread products that are topped by a sauce based chiefly on tomato paste.* But commercially it finds to contain various vegetables, meats, cheeses, spices, flavours and many other garnishes on top to provide variety. The quantity of topping may vary from 25 to 45% of finished pitza weight. Pitza base may be differentiated into two categories:

- **Thin, crisp, crackers like crust**: Produced by pressing.
- **Thick, so called dip dish crust**: Produced by sheeting.

Raw Material: The crusts are quite different in their properties hence their raw material. procedure, formula etc. vary accordingly.

(i) ***Flour:*** relatively strong flour with a protein content of 12 to 14% is recommended. However, for thin pitza crust higher protein flour is preferred to minimize soakage of sauce into the crust and to preserve its desirable crispness. However, for thick pitza crust, flours of lower protein content will be found more suitable as these will minimize dough shrinkage and impart a more desirable chewiness to the finished crust.

(ii) ***Leavening Agent:*** Pitza crust is usually leavened with yeasl but sometimes it may be leavened with baking powder. However yeast leavened pitza are better in most of all the characteristics. The quantity of yeast or baking powder required depends on many factors hence it may vary from 1 to 5% (on f.b.) usually 3 to 4%.

(iii) ***Water:*** The water absorption will range from 55 to 70%. Thin crusts generally take less water- 55 to 60% - whereas absorption of 60 to 70% is normally used for thick crusts. A correct absorption of each type of crust is essential to avoid sticky dough with poor machining properties that results from excessive absorption. However, in case of under absorption fragile dough produces rather leathery crusts.

(iv) ***Shortening:*** Shortening levels are relatively high, particularly in thin crusts where fat creates a more tender texture and a greater resistance to soakage of the sauce. Liquid or plastic shortenings are equally suitable for this application.

Processing :

(i) ***Mixing:*** By hand or conventional horizontal mixers upto cleanup stage.

(ii) ***Floor Time Fermentation*** : Either fermented for 30 to 40 minutes or given just 10 to 15 minutes floor time to relax in case of yeast leavened dough but chemically leavened dough are directly taken for make-up.

(iii) ***Sheeting or Pressing:*** It is sheeted into desired thickness by machines in the series of sheeting rolls while by hand with rolling pin. Then cut into selected circular shape either by cutting wheel or by hand with simple pitza cutter. The scrap dough may be remixed, rested for 5 to 10 minutes and resheeted or may be used for other products. In case of *pressing* or *stamping.* dough is scaled. rounded into appropriate size circles. allow to rest for 2 to 3 minutes & press again in order to minimize subsequent shrinkage, which are then proofed for a short time (15 to 20 minutes).

(iv) ***Baking:*** Bake at 205°C (400°F) for 15 to 20 minutes. Allow cooling at ambient temperature and then toping is applied.

(v) ***Serving:*** Pitza should be served hot. So one may apply toping vegetable, meat etc. before baking & afterwards retopping with cheese & sauce etc. and serve, It has a typical taste, which liked very much but the appearance may be somewhat poor compare to non-topped pitza before baking. However, in commercial market generally baked pitza crust is topped and

DOUGHNUT: Doughnuts are served quite extensively in hotels, restaurants and snack bars in many countries of the world. It has plenty of varieties. The doughnuts are different from bakery products, as it is cooked by deep-frying in heated edible fat instead of baking. It can be devided into two parts based on leavening agent used for preparation:

- **Cake doughnut**: Leavened with baking powder and batter will be similar to layer cake.
- **Yeast raised doughnut**: Leavened by yeast similar to sponge & dough or straight dough method.

(i) ***Flour:*** A mixture of soft and hard wheat flours having 10 to 10.5% protein, 0.38 to 0.42% ash and 13% moisture is suitable for doughnut production.

(ii) ***Leavening Agent:*** In case of cake doughnut 2 to 5% (on f.b.) fast acting baking powder (depending an type of formula, size and weight of doughnuts) is used for preparation. Too much leavening will always result in poor texture and flavour as well as excessive fat absorption. In case of yeast raised doughnut 4 to 6% yeast is used similar to straight dough or sponge & dough method.

(iii) ***Egg:*** The egg yolk. is preferred because it has ability to emulsify and disperse the shortening present in the batter. Moreover, yolk protein coagulates during heating helps to strengthen the structure of doughnut. It also improves volume as well as eating and keeping quality. The albumen, has a toughening effect hence it is not generally used.

(iv) ***Shortening:*** Any shortening can be used for dough preparation. However, the frying fat should be carefully chosen because it transmit the heat for cooking and also ellter into doughnut and become a part of the products. Hence, the quality of frying medium also affects the characteristics of the doughnut. Therefore; hydrogenated shortening having high smoaking point [i.e. more than 193°C (380°F)] is preferred to avoid any objectionable odour during frying.

(v) ***Sugar***: Sugar is used for dough preparation as well as for outer application hence it should be pure, clean, white in colour and free from any impurities.

Processing: When doughnut is correctly formulated and properly fried. it is characterized by :

- Rich golden brown exterior colour that has eye appeal and also conveys an image of quality product.
- Crisp crust, that is formed by the dehydration of the outer portion of the doughnut.
- Inner core which comprises the major quantitative portion and resembles a baked product more than a fried product.

Doughnut can be prepared either directly from ready made mixture with addition of water or weighing each ingredient individually as per formula. But ready made mixtures are mostly preferred due to consistence quality production.

The detail of process is :

(i) ***Mixing:*** Similar to straight dough or sponge & dough method of bread preparation.

(ii) ***Fermentation*** : Dough is fermented for about 2 hours.

(iii) ***Sheeting & Cutting:*** The dough is sheeted and cut on makeup table either in round or haxagonal shape having 6 to 8 cm (2.5" to 3") diameter.

(iv) ***Proofing:*** Proof the individual pieces at 35° to 46°C (95° to 115°F) and 35 to 45 rh for 20 to 35 minutes. The low humidity helps to skin formation on top which finally give crispiness while eating.

(v) ***Frying:*** The temperature of frying medium should be maintain 204° to 213°C (400° to 425°F). The doughnut pieces should be fried for 45 to 60 seconds per side.

(vi) ***Granishing:*** Granish with sugar powder when the doughnut cooled down to room temperature.

13

Cake Ingredients

BRIEF DETAILS : The major ingredients used for the cake preparation are same as that of bread production. except for the quality and functional properties (rather than basic properties). No doubt the chemical leavening agent (replaced by yeast) and certain flavour. spices and colouring material are more or less restricted to cake production. A lot has been discussed regarding ingredients hence only some important information on cake ingredients are discussed here.

Ingredients used for cake production are very important because the quality cake can only be produced with the help of quality ingredients. Hence, cake made by small bakers (who do not pay attention on ingredients) are not so good as compared to the cakes made by specialised bakers (who are paying full attention on ingredients quality). If small bakers pay proper attention they can also produce quality cake.

CLASSIFICATION: Cake ingredients can be classified mainly in two parts. followed by various sub-parts:

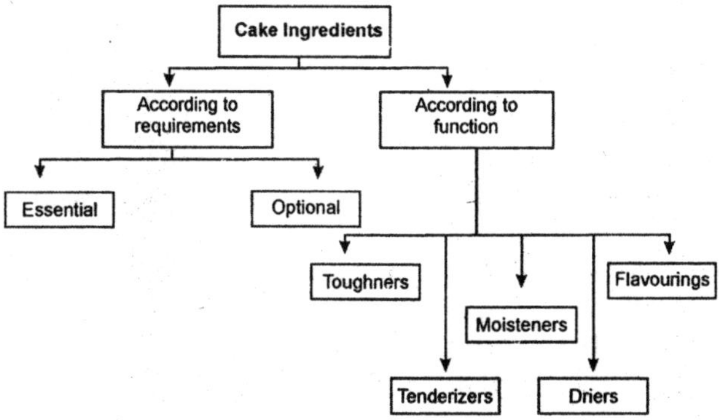

According to Requirement: It can be classified into two parts:

(i) *Essential Ingredients:* The ingredients without which cake cannot be made or if at all made it has drastic qualitative changes. they are known as *essential ingredients.* It includes flour. sugar. fat and egg.

(ii) *Optional Ingredients:* The ingredients. when added into cake preparation improves the cake quality, are known as *optional ingredients.* It includes baking powder. milk or milk powder. fruits etc. (in short ingredients added other than essential ingredients).

According to Function: Cake ingredients can also be divided into five groups, in this category:

(i) *Toughners or Structure Builders :* Flour, egg, milk

(ii) *Tenderizers:* Sugar. shortening, baking powder

(iii) *Moistners:* Milk. water. egg. sugar. fat

(iv) *Driers:* Flour, milk powder

Many of the ingredients that are common ly used in cake making perform more than one of these roles. A detail on ingredients is discussed below :

FLOUR: It is preeminently a toughner involved in establishing the crumb structure of the cake. Cake made from too strong flour will peak in the center, be tough and dry in eating. Sometimes such peak may develop at the bottom also. To overcome that one may add cornflour, which makes flour soft. In case of too weak flour. the cakes may flatten out or sink. However. the table (next page) may be used as a guideline while selecting flour for making specific type of cake:

Special Cake Flour: Flour builds structure of cake and holds other ingredients together in an evenly distributed condition in the cake. The cake flours are normally milled from soft red winter wheat or soft white winter wheat varieties. The different properties required for cake flour is given below:

(i) ***Protein:*** Soft wheat flour having lowest protein and ash content should be used for high-sugar layer cakes. Normally, flour having 45 to 65% extraction rate based on total flour possess such qualities. Gluten produced during cake batter mixing by cake flour should be mellow and totally devoid of the tough properties that are associated with bread dough. However. it should possess sufficient strength and be quantitatively adequate to assure the formation of a fine foam cake structure. In general cake made from fancy or short patent flours milled from soft wheat possess superior crumb tenderness and softness of the texture than lower grade flour. Different types of cakes require somewhat different flour specifications as :

Cake Variety	Flour used
Small chamically aerated cake like maideria, queen cakes	*Medium strong flour.* Strong flour yields products having a drawn and tough nature.
Light Slab and Pound cake	*Soft flour* is the best. Strong flour yield product with dry, tough harsh ckae, hence more eggs are required to moisten batter which results in more expenses.
Cherry and Heavy Fruit cake	*Medium strong flour.* It prevents fruits from sinking and also helps to avoid crumbliness in the cakes
Cheaper cake	*Medium strong flour.* This flour absorb more liquid and can be aerated by baking powder instead of eggs, which helps to bring down the prices.
Rich cakes like Weeding, Special Birthday cakes	*Combination of medium and soft flour.* Strong flour results in dome shape cake while soft flour has tendency to produce crumbliness.

Product (Cake)	**Protein (%)**	**Ash (%)**
Angle food	4.70	0.23
Chiffon white and yellow layer cakes	7.35	0.29
Sponge, chocolate, pound and other heavier cakes	8.30	0.32
Lower grade cakes	9.10	0.42

(ii) ***Ash Content:*** The quantity of ash should be low. since this indicates a short extraction flour which is vital important. Ash content is positively correlated with extraction rate.

(iii) ***Acidity:*** The acidity of the flour must be higher than bread flour. That can be accomplished by more bleaching. It also makes flour whiter.

(iv) ***Granular Size and Uniformity*:** The smaller and uniformed particle size will make better cakes than bigger and un-uniformed particles. Hence usually the patent flour obtained by milling is normally further reduced in average particle size by passage through pin mill or by other means.

(v) ***Chlorination:*** Chlorination treatment increases the hydratio capacity of the cake-flour by hydrolytic de-polymerization of the starch molecule. which improves baking performance.

(vi) **Typical Specifications :**

Particular	Specification
Protein	8.5±0.5%
Ash Content	0.25±0.04%
pH	5.0±0.2
Particle size	10±0.5μm

SUGAR: Sugars are used as sweetners. The following points are to be kept in mind while using sugar:

Sugar used for all types of cakes should be of fine granulation to ensure an even grain and soft texture in.the cakes because, this type of sugar dissolves very readily and will produce a smooth creamy mass. Large sugar crystals produce a coarse texture.

- When creaming the sugar and shortening the best results are obtained by using twi.ce as much sugar as shortening. The excess sugar called for in the formula should be dissolved in milk or water.
- Eggs and sugar are best beaten when equal amounts of each are used.
- Sugar has a mellowing or tenderizing effect upon the cell ·structure hence when too high sugar is used the cakes may sag in the center or fall. Shortening also has similar effect.
- Sugars like invert sugar, honey, molasses and glucose are hygroscopic. These sugars not only help to retain moisture but also impart a characteristic flavour to the product.
- Sugar lowers the caramelization point of the batter allowing the cake crust to colour at a lower temperature.

SHORTENING: Shortening helps to retain moisture and also provides tenderness to the finished cake. Shortening for cakes should have:

- Good creaming properties (i.e. granuler fat should be avoided because that have very poor creaming quality).
- A neutral flavour and odour.
- Excellent emulsifying properties.
- White in colour,
- Plastic in nature while used. Very hard shortening will not cream up well, while too soft shortenings will not be able to retain aeration. If cold and hard fat is creamed with soft fats, the hard fat will break into small pieces which will be scattered in the whole mix. These hard lumps will be difficult to break and will adversely affect the process of aeration:
- Shortenings used for cake making should not melt by the heat produced due to friction during creaming process when use.
- It should at temperatures between 21° to 24°(70° to 75°F). Butter is considered to be the best of all baking shortenings from a flavour stand point. The creaming quality of butter is rather poor. Cakes made with butter are generally lower in volume and have a coarser grain. than those made with a high quality shortening (which has good creaming characteristics). For this reason, some bakers use part of butter or margarine and part of shortening which improve flavour and volume as well as finer grain respectively (Generally at a ratio of 1:4::Butter :Margarine) and that way acquire specific characteristics in the cake. However, for the same reason some companies started marketing specilized fats which are quite better than conventional fats.

EGG: Egg and flour form a skeleton. which acts as support to the framework of a cake. It also contributes moisture. flavour and colour. Keep following points in mind while using egg:

- Beating of the eggs is very important. They should be beaten up to such extent that they will hold a fairly good crease, This crease is made by running a pallet knife through the baten mass.
- Poor quality or excess use of egg results in poor quality cake.
- When egg is used in cake preparation. the quantity of baking powder from the formula should be reduced.

- Egg can moisten the same quantity of flour by its weight. hence additional milk or water is required when the quantity of egg used is less.

MILK: Milk when used as dry milk solids adds richness and structure to the cake. The milk sugar lactose regulates the crust colour. Milk solids are good moisture retaining and tlavour improving agents.

WATER: Water adds moisture to the cake and in that way regulates the eating qualities of the finished cake. It regulates the consistency of the banner. develops the protein in the flour (which acts to retain the gas produced from the baking powder) acts as leavening agent and creating vapour pressure (when the internal batter temperature reaches 99°C (208°F) during baking).

Looking to many functions. the quantity of water in formula should be calculated exactly on the bases of quantity of water present in other ingredients used for cake making.

SALT: Salt is one of the cheapest ingredients. It has the property of bringing out flavour. It has an important place in the palatability of baked products and therefore pinch of salt should always be added in batter even though it is not mentioned in the formula. It also lowers caramelization temperature of cake batter and aids in obtaining crust colour.

FLAVOUR: Due to the variations in strength of flavour. it is not possible to set any given amount to be used. It is much better to use a small amount of good flavour than to load up the cake with a poor flavour.

LEAVENING: Cakes are leavened in three ways:

- by incorporation of air during mixing
- by use of chemical leavening agents
- by vapour pressure created in the oven.

The manner of leavening depends upon the type of cake being made, with. regards to richness of formula. consistency of batter and baking temperature. Generally cake made by lean formula and more water, requires more leavening agent as compared to cake made by rich formula and less water.

14

Formulations of Cake

PRODUCT DETAILS : Each ingredients has certain definite function in cake making e.g. :

- Flour and egg give structure
- Sugar, fat and baking powder act as tenderizing agent
- Egg and milk impart liquid to cake

If haphazard quantities of these ingredients are used in a cake, the resultant product vary from day to day. Therefore, in order to have consistently good quality of product, it is very necessary that all ingredients are used in definite proportion and in a definite manner. Such proportion of raw material which can produce a desirable cake as termed as *cake formula*. In such formula, if the quantity of one ingredient is changed then the quantity of other effected ingredients must be changed accordingly. How are they changed is necessary to understand.

Types : Cake can be devided on the bases of quantity of fat as well as sugar.

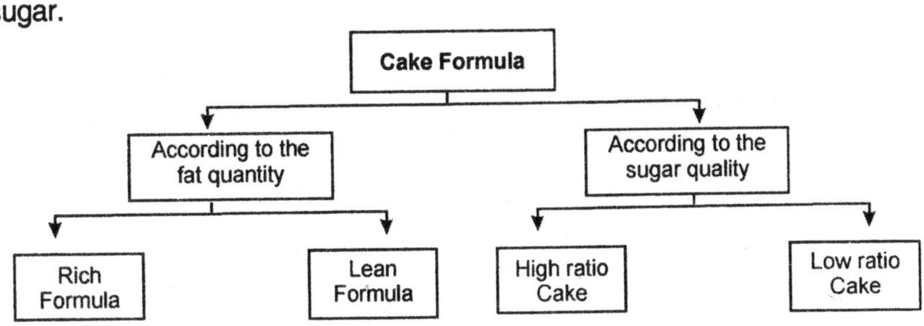

According to Fat quantity : According to qantity of fat, the cake formula can be devided into rich and lean types. The differences between them are :

Rich Formula	Lean Formula
• Formula containing more fat is known as rich formula.	• Formula containing less fat is known as lean formula.
• More fat requires much creaming and will incorporate more air, hence less quantity of leavening agent (baking powder) is required.	• Less fat requires less creaming and will incorporate less air hence more leavening agents are required to compensate the air by means of production of more carbon dioxide gas.
• More fat prevents the gluten formation and also make the batter more tender, hence the quantity of liquid required is less.	• Due to less fat there is a possibility of gluten development during mixing operation, to avoid that the quantity of liquid should be increased
• Due to less liquid, the cake setting in oven will be faster which prohibits expansion of cake hence baking temperature should be reduced.	• Due to more liquid, cake setting in oven will be slow hence the carbon dioxide gas released from leaavening agent will escape leaving the cake flat appearing hence the oven temperature should be higher in order to have a faste setting.
• The cake thus produced has much aeration which results into more volume and ultimately less density / specific gravity.	• The cake thus produced has less aeration that results into less volume more density / specific gravity.

According to Sugar Quantity : On the bases of quantity of sugar, the cake formula can be devided into high ratio and low ratio grups. The differences between them are :

High Ratio Cake	Low Ratio Cake
• Formula contain more sugar than flour is known as high ratio cake.	• Formula containing either equal proportion of sugar and flour or less sugar than flour is known as low ratio cake.
• Higher sugar helps in retaining moisture for longer period and thus increases the shelf life of cakes	• The shelf life of cake produced will be less than high ratio cake due to less sugar. Which is a moisture retentioner.
• The total liquid (quantity of egg +milk) should be more than quantity of sugar (i.e. Total liquid = Liquid Egg+Liquid milk = Sugar + 25%) Generally, 25% more sugar gives better results.	• The total liquid (the quantity of egg+milk) should be equal to the sugar. TL=LE+LM=Sugar
• The quantity of egg should be more (about 10%) than fat.	• The quantity of egg should not be more than fat.

BALANCING : The following important points should be kept in mind while balancing the cake formula :

- Salt content will vary between 0.8 to 2.0% (on f.b.) depending on the quantity of sugar in formula and the amount of the flavour desired in the product.
- The quantity of sugar is changed according to types alongwith factors i.e. different high ratio cakes have different quantities of sugar.

Types of cake	Sugar (% on f.b.)
• Yellow layer cake (made from whole egg)	110 to 140
• White layer cake (made from egg white only)	110 to 160
• Devils food cake (made with cocoa as one ingredient)	110 to 180

However majority of cake formulations call for the average of 125% (on f.b.) sugar

- As the percentage of sugar is increased, the quantity of egg should also be inceased by approximately the same percentage. Because sugar is tendeizer which make better tender, to compensate that eggs are added asa toughner. But this additional egg produces dry eating, to prevent that, the quantity of fat should be increased.
- When the ingredients having more liquids (such as invert syrup, honey etc.) are replaced the sugar is the formula, quantity of liquid in the formula should be decreaed indirect proportion to the moisture present in ingredients, so that the total moisture content of formula does not change.
- When cocoa is used in the formula, it is necessary to increase the moisture content as per the following equation, because cocoa acts as a drier. The quantity of fat should be decreased from the formula that is similar to the quantity of fat present in cocoa.

Total Liquid=Liquid Egg+Liquid Milk= Sugar + (1.5 x Cocoa)

- When using cocoa, sodium bicarbonate should be used to react with natural acidity present in the cocoa, thereby imparting leavening action and also darken the crumb colour. However, it should be remembered that alkalinity of soda will be conducive to microbial spoilage of cake and calcium propionate as athe preservative will be less effective in alkaline medium.
- When only egg whites are used, slightly acidic, mateial (like cream of tarter, citric acid, mono acid calcium, acetic acid or lime) may be used at desired levels (0.1 to 0.5%). It improves the air entrapping capacity and makes cake crumb whiter due to bleaching action.
- When only egg whites are used, its quantity should be increased upto 1.25 to 1.30 times more than the whole egg. And looking to the formula. (Total liquid = Total Egg+Total Milk), the quantity of milk should automatically be reduced.
- When only egg yolk is to be used, additional moisture will be necessary, as the moisture content of egg yolk is less then whole egg.
- Too much solids will give undesirable results in cakes unless compensated with necessary amount of water.
- When using sugar with low caramelization point, it may be necessary to use same amount of acid salt in order to prevent too dark colour in the crust.

15

Processing of Cake

BRIEF DETAILS : There are many methods for cake preparation. which differ from one another mainly by mixing procedure. as well as by quantity & type of ingredients and baking temperature & time. Much of the discussion on ingredients is given earlier. hence mixing and baking are discussed here.

MIXING: The primary purpose of cake mixing is to bring about a complete & unifonn dispersion and homogeneous mutual emulsification of the various ingredients. usually with the entrapment and size reduction of air cells and a minimum development of the gluten in flour. Depending on the nature of cake being produced. the mixing procedure will differ in such aspects like the order of ingredient incorporation. the duration & rate of mixing action during the different stages in multistage methods. the temperature of ingredients etc. Here. more common and traditional mixing procedures encountered in practice are discussed below.

Sugar Batter Method: It is also termed as *creaming method.* It is mostly applied to high class cake and gives good result as the good quality ingredients are used and better care taken during manipulation.

In practice. all the fats should be first creamed together (either by machine or by hand) in order to blend them thoroughly. Then sugar is added gradually continuing the creaming process. All the sugar should not be added to fat at a time as this will adversely affect the aeration process and it may take extra time to achieve the desired results and also requires much force. When adequate aeration is achieved. the mixture becomes very light and brighter in appearance. About 15 to 20 minutes creaming of the fats and sugar is generally sufficient.

When adequate aeration is achieved in the fat - sugar mixture eggs are added gradually. Eggs should be at room temperature 21° to 24°C (70° to 75°F) at the time of adding to the cream. It is good practice to whip the eggs to a stiff consistency before adding to the creamed mixture for small batches mixed by hand. while using a mixer, it is not necessary. If any emulsifier is to be used. it can be added along with eggs rather than with fat. Essence is also added before beating the eggs. Egg should be added not more than 4 at a time to each kg of fat. Once eggs are added to the creamed mixture (little at a time) that are mixed just sufficiently. so the air cells of whipped eggs either diffuse into the air cells already present or increase the number of air cells in the cream and the liquid part of egg is evenly distributed in the mixture giving it a smooth. velvety appearance.

If the eggs are stale. or too much egg is added at a time or after each addition of egg. it is not mixed properly. the perfect blending does not take place and the fat is broken into small fragments separated by liquid component of egg. If too cold eggs are used. the fat will solidify soon as it comes in contact with eggs and perfect amalgamation of fat and egg will not take place. In this case also, the fat will break down into small lumps which will be coated with egg. The breakdown of fat into small fragments separated by egg is known as *curdling* of batter. Whenever and for whatever reason the batter is curdled. there is loss of aeration which results in low volume and poor texture of cakes. Ifthe batter is curdled due to first reason an adequate quantity of flour should be added and mixed gently. This flour will absorb the excessive moisture hence mixture will aga,in become smooth. When batter is curdled due to low temperature of eggs, the mixture should be slightly warmed over a pot of hot water. Direct heating of mixture is not advisable as the fat will melt or egg may coagulate. In both the cases there will be loss of aeration.

A part (1/2 to 2/3) of liquids such as liquid sugars. water. milk, fruit juices, fruit pulp etc. along with essences, colour and salt can be added at this stage. This is done in order to have sufficient moisture in the mix to prevent toughening of gluten while mixing flour.

Next stage is to incorporate flour in the mixture. However, before mixing flour should be sifted with other dry ingredients such as baking powder, corn flour, calcium propionate etc. That ensures through dispersion of dry ingredients into flour. sifting also aerate the flour and removes any impurities present.

Incorporation of flour in the cream is an important stage in cake making and even slight mishandling of the mixture will spoil the cake hence it is advisable to mix flour by hand even though the mixing operations are carried out by machine. If it is desired to use machine. each portion of flour should be added alternately with water at low speed. If any fruits are to be mixed, these should be added alternately with flour. Flour should not be added all at once, but it should be divided into two or three portions and each portion should be added at a time and mixed with straight open fingers with just necessary movements of hand, because excessive mixing may form the gluten, its toughness spoil the cake quality.

When all the flour is mixed, the remaining liquid is added. Generally, milk or water is added as liquid. This liquid brings the batter to a definite level of fluidity which is necessary for even and gradual rise of cake during baking operation. This liquid also serves an important function of easing the strains on gluten which are affected during mixing operation and which. otherwise, may cause toughening of cake. Precisely. for this reason, even during earlier stages when the flour is being mixed. if the mixture appears to be tough. little water should be added to avoid toughening of gluten. The mixing of water results fluffy. smooth and velvety batter. The batter is now ready for panning and baking.

Flour Batter Method: In this method. fat and a quantity of flour not exceeding the weight of fat is creamed together. Fat should be in smooth and plastic state and the flour should be added gradually. The whole mass is whipped till it becomes light and fluffy.

Sometimes butter. margarine and shortening all together are used as a fat. Hence. it is first essential to have all the fats in a similar condition. It is useless to place soft shortening and hard butter into machine and expect to obtain a smooth cream from them. The butter will simply breakdown into small pieces and it is most difficult to beat out the lumps afterward. The proper method is to soften the butter. warming it a little (if necessary) and beating it alone at first. Then add margarine (in a creamy condition) and shortening together with desired quantity of sieved flour. All these ingred ients will now cream up nicely together, provided the temperature is maintained at about 22.2°C (72°F). If the materials are too cold, a light batter cannot be obtained. In such condition. the batter can be warmed up by hot water bath system (never place batter on direct fire for warming up). On the other hand, the batter should not be too warm otherwise butter will get oily and creaminess will not be obtained until the temperature has again been reduced. During the creaming operation. it is advisable to scrap down the bowl once or twice because there is a space between the outer edge of the cake beater and the inner surface of the bowl. Any material in this space remaining unmoved by the revolving beater, and unless scraped off once or twice does not become sufficiently aerated.

When the flour batter is well on the way, egg and equal quantity of sugar is placed together in the other machine and steadily whisked to a semi stiff sponge. Here, again, temperature is more important as desired earlier. If the cold sponge is amalgamated with the flour batter, the cold sponge immediately reduces the temperature of the fats, causing them to harden. That prevents the easy and perfect amalgamation, which is essential for making good cakes. On the other hand. too warm sponge may coagulate the egg before they are sufficiently aerated and secondly. if warm sponge is amalgamated with the flour batter, the fat may become oily that results in the loss of aeration and toughening of the cakes. When the sponge and batters are maintained at approximately the same temperature, they amalgamate perfectly and the best results may then be expected.

Having prepared the batter and the sponge. the latter is poured into fonner. Although there is less risk of curdling of batter. still sponge should be added in small portion (about 1/ 5) at a time. After each addition. it should be mixed thoroughly, then beating sponge well and add the next position again. Follow this process until all of it has been amalgamated. Scrap out the sponge bowl so that nothing may be lost. and add it to the batter.

At this stage, the remaining sugar is dissolved in milk or water and added to the mixture. Any colour or flavour is also added along with this liquid.

Lastly. the remaining flour sifted with baking powder. is mixed. During last stage of mixing. if the formula is rich, the mixing operation should be carried out gently. because in case of rich cakes. most of the aeration is achieved during creaming operation of fat and flour. Hence, a vigorous mixing will knock out the air cells and the cake will have poor volume. On the other hand, lean cakes acquire most of the aeration due to baking powder hence there is no risk of losing aeration. A thorough treatment of batter ensures smoothness of the batter which is desirable for obtaining good texture in cakes. As, all the liquid is already present in the batter, it is possible to give it

In case of very lean cakes specially. where there is less quantity of fat and eggs and more of flour and sugar, some difficulty may be experienced in mixing large quantity of flour and sugar. In such case, milk (or water). part of sugar and part of flour equal to that of milk is mixed into a smooth paste and added. The remaining flour should be sifted with baking powder and added at the last stage of mixing.

Fruit. which must be well cleaned. is added last with proper care for evenly distributing in the batter. However. care must be taken so it want break while mixing.

(i) ***Merits and Demerits***: There are several advantages in using this method and also a few drawbacks:

- MERITS : The chief advantages are:
  - As the major portion of flour is coated with fat before any liquid is added. the development of gluten is avoided. This fact makes it possible to use slightly strong flours which, otherwise, are unsuitable for cake making. Again very small quantity of flour remains to be added at the last stage of mixing. which avoids possibility of much gluten development.
  - Egg & sugar is whisked to a stiff consistency and fat & flour is creamed to a light and fluffy consistency. Chances of curdling of such a mixture are minimum. Because, curdling takes place when eggs are added to fat, however in this method eggs are already mixed with sugar before being added to fat. Moreover. curdling may prevented by addition of flour into mixer, it is already present with fat in this method.
  - Initial creaming of fat and flour, thorough whisking of egg and sugar. presence of enough moisture during last stage of mixing are some of the factors due to which toughening of gluten is avoided and cake acquires a good texture. Hence, this method is specially suited for making lean cakes which do not contain much fat or egg and most of aeration is achieved through baking powder.
- DEMERITS
  - Most of all the ingredients are divided into two parts hence require more time to weigh.
  - More utensils and equipments are needed to keep the divided (more) ingredients separately.
  - While mixing large quantity of batter into machine. two machines/two bowls are required. one for fat & flour mixture and another for sugar & egg mixture.

Blending Method: This method is suitable for making high ratio cakes. Where emulsified shortening. flour. baking powder and salt are whipped together to a very light and fluffy consistency. Sugar. milk or any other liquid. colour and flavour are mixed together and added to the previous mixture. Eggs are added next and the whole mass is mixed to a smooth batter.

Boiled Method: This method is used for making good quality madeira cakes and genoese sponge. It is not suitable for fruit cake because batter is so soft and liquid. that the fruit may sink at the bottom.

Butter or margarine is placed in a bowl and heated till it melts and water in them actually starts to boil. Remove the bowl from heat and add about 2/3, (or less) flour and mix thoroughly, with the wooden spoon. On the other hand. egg & sugar is whisked to a stiff sponge. Colour and flavour may be added while whisking the sponge. This sponge is added to the fat & flour mixture in about 4 to 5 equal parts. After each addition of sponge, it should be mixed thoroughly. Remaining flour can be added at this stage. When the mixture becomes smooth. it is scaled-off into paper-lined baking sheets to about 2.5 cm (1") thickness for making genoese. For making madeira cakes, mixture is based in moulds lined with grease-proof paper.

Sugar Water Method: There has been increasing use of liquid sugar by the large scale cake bakers because it produces better quality products. In this method, all the sugar and approximately half the quantity of water (then sugar) is agitated in a bowl till all the sugar is dissolved. Then the remaining ingredients except egg are added and the mixture is well agitated to acquire aeration. Lastly, egg is added and the mixture is cleared.

Due to more aeration and better emulsification obtained in this method, the cakes so produced have better texture and longer shelf life. The better aeration helps to reduce the quantity of baking powder (generally about 10%).

All In One Process / Single Stage Method: For making cakes by this method, it is necessary to use emulsified type of shortening and special cake flours (having soft gluten. fine granulation and low pH). Non-emulsified type of shortening will not be able to hold excessive moisture present in the formula. Similarly. special cake flours will tolerate the amount of mixing given to the batter without toughening the gluten. Both these would help to aerate batter much.

In this process. all the ingredients are put into the mixing bowl together and the mixing is carried out successively as per following steps. Aeration of the mixture is achieved by controlling the speed of the mixer as well as the mixing time. Hence, a three speed mixture of good quality should be used. Moreover. it is better to use wire-whip for this operation which ensures a faster breakdown of ingredients and helps to achieve good aeration.

Time	Speed	Function
½ minute	Slow	All the dry ingredients are moistened without flying off from the bowl.
2 minutes	Fast	All the ingredients break up and are incorporated evenly throughout the mass. The batter is also well aerated.
2 minutes	Medium	The larger air-cells break up into smaller cells and the aeration of the mixture becomes even.
1 minutes	Slow	Eliminate any possible larger air pockets and still finer breaking down of air cells.

Continuous Process: In this method, the cakes are prepared continuously in machines. Hence, naturally be useful for large cake factories in which standardized lines are produced mainly for sale through large stores / super markets. But this process is merely suitable for smaiL high-class confectioners because they need greater flexibility which cannot acquire in mechanical process.

To a large extent, in this method, first liquid sugar, eggs. milk, flour etc. are amalgamated into slurry and emulsified with pumpable shortenings. Then the mixer is passed through convoluted channels of a continuous cake mixer. where all the ingredients are blended thoroughly with the complete emulsification and produce a constant stream of cake batter. This batter is then continuously deposited into tins, pans. frames, paper cases etc. then conveyed automatically through the travelling oven. Eventually the cakes emerge, pass through a cooler to the wrapper and so to the stores. ready for dispatch.

If fruit cakes are required, the fruit has to be blended into the stream of batter as it leaves the continuous mixer and this is done by the aid of a machine that can be adjusted tc deliver and blend into the batter.

PANNING OF CAKE BATTER: When the batter is ready by anyone method, it is weighed in the moulds. Moulds should be lined with grease-proof paper or should be greased and dusted with flour. Excessive greasing of moulds is undesirable because it will have a frying effect on the bottom part of the cake and the cake will have a greasy feel. After dusting the mould with flour, the mould should be turned upside down and tapped gently in order to remove excessive flour which, otherwise, will adversely affect the appearance of the cake.

The mixture should be put in the moulds in as large portions as possible. Putting the mixture in small portions at a time may cause entrapping of air pockets between one portion and the ·other. These air pockets will create holes in the cakes. Moulds should be filled upto 2/3 of its height leaving sufficient space for cakes to rise during baking. If hard flour is used a pit in the center is to be made so that cake does not attain dome shape.

After the batter is weighed in the moulds. it should be leveled properly in order to have an even expansion of cakes. Back of hand moistened with milk may be used for leveling the batter. Slight moisture on the upper surface prevents early crust formation, allows the cakes to expand evenly and crust acquires a desirable golden brown colour (due to caramelization of milk and sugar).

BAKING: The panned batter is conveyed to the oven with the minimum loss of time. otherwise leavening agents. having entered into solution during mixing and have begun to interact & are evolving carbon dioxide gas. will escape & results into coarsening of the cell structure. In the more fluid batters. this gas tends to rise upwards. with the small bubbles coalescing in the process into large cells that have greater buoyancy.

The optimum baking conditions are determined by many factors like sweetener level. amount of milk. fluidity of the batter, pan size etc. Hence. different cakes are baked at different temperature. The oven temperature is adjusted according to :

- **Richer the formula, lower the temperature** because reach formula contain more fat and egg hence acquire all its aeration during creaming of fat and sugar or by way of whipped eggs. These cakes contain very little baking powder. The batter does not contain much moisture and is comparatively less fluid. Such cakes should have a .very slow and gradual rise in the oven in order to have thorough baking and this is precisely the reason for baking them at low temperature. If rich cakes are baked at high temperature, there will be faster crust formation on cakes. Such crust will prevention of hit penetration inside the cake. resulting in an under baked product. There will be much concentration of heat on the crust giving it too dark colour. When, ultimately heat does reach inside the cake. the internal part will expand bursting the crust and spoiling the appearance of the cake.

- **Leaner the formula higher the temperature** because lean formula contains less amount of fat and eggs hence most of all the aeration in such cakes is achieved by baking powder. Moreover. lean cake batter is more fluid in comparison with rich cake batter. such cakes are baked at high temperature so that evolution of gas from baking powder, acquiring of volume by cake and setting of structure of cake takes place simultaneously. If such cakes are baked at low temperature. there will be evolution of gas from baking powder which will expand the cake, but due to low temperatl re the structure of cake wi ll not set and the cakes will collapse.
- **Cakes baked as large units** should have a slow and gradual expansion in the oven which is possible only when the baking temperature is low. Whereas smaller units require less baking time. that required faster setting of structure. which can be achieved by baking at higher temperature.
- **When oven is not filled to the capacity**, it is necessary to reduce the oven temperature. Which can be achieved by :
  - Placing a pot of water in the firewood oven. because water will absorb some of the excessive heat and at the same time the water vapours wi ll delay the process of crust formation on cakes thus allowing the cake to rise evenly and acquire proper volume.
  - Lining the moulds with paper.
  - **Covering the cakes in the oven with moist brown paper**.
  - Placing the moulds on baking sheets while baking are some of the means to cut down absorption of heat by cakes and these measures should be adopted while baking such cakes which require too long baking time or while baking a small batch of cakes in large oven.

When baking at high altitude the following changes are required due to atmospheric low pressure:

- Decrease / increase the quantity of ingredient as shown in the following table :.

Height	Ingredients		
	Flour (increase)	Egg (Increase)	Baking Powder (reduce)
610m (2000')	-	-	15%
762m (2500')	-	2.5%	-
1067m (3500')	2.5%	-	-
2438m(8000')	10%	15%	60%

- The cake pan must receive a heavier coating. The use of silicon-coated pans will be found useful.
- Replace whole egg or yolk to white.
- Increase baking temperature about 14°C (25°F).

Temperature: Most cakes are baked between 160° to 190°C (320° to 375°F). If cakes are baked at too low temperature. the gas evolved from baking powder will escape before the structure has a chance to set resulting in small volume. flat appearing cakes. On the other hand. if the cakes are baked at too high temperature. the cake will peak and burst in the centre, will be tough and ma) also not be baked adequately. As a thumb rule. large cakes and rich cakes should be baked at low temperature while lean cakes and smaller cakes should be baked at higher temperature. The cakes are baked best in large quantity in a closed oven.

Cake Type	Baking Temperature
Pound cake: (450 gm)	190°C (380°F)
: (bigger than 450gm)	175°C (350°F)
Cheap cake: (450 gm)	215°C (420°F)
: (bigger than 450gm)	190°C (380°F)
Slab & wedding cake: (more fruit)	165°C (330°F)
: (less fruit)	175°C (350°F)
Madira and Seed slab cake: (simple)	190°C (380°F)
: (more nour and liquid)	205°C (400°F)

While baking slab cake. the oven temperature should be successively decreased.

Baking and Cooling Loss: Normally there is about 12% baking and cooling loss in cakes. Excessive baking and cooling loss will result in dry eating cakes. If there is lack of temperature in the oven. the cakes will take longer time in baking and consequently there will be excessive evaporation of moisture resulting in dry eating cake. But most important factor in determining baking and cooling loss in cakes is the amount of batter filled in a given size mould and the depth of the mould. A mould should be filled with sufficient amount of batter so that when due expansion has taken place during baking. the mould. remains filled with the cake. If a small amount of batter is baked in a large pan. there will be excessive baking and cooling loss which will result in not only a dry eating cake but also will mean economic loss to the baker. Normally. cake-pan having 13 to 18 cm (5 to 7") diameter and 2.5 to 5 cm (1 to 2") depth is sufficient for the batter made from 100 to 120gm flour. However as the cake pan is smaller and depth is more. the cake psychologically feels much leavened, which preferred by end user.

16

Cookies

BRIEF DETAILS : Cookies may be defined as *small cakes made from dough thai is sufficiently viscous to permit the dough pieces to be baked on flat surface.* In Asian countries like India it is also called *biscuits* which are widely popular and produced throughout the country with almost infinite diversity in shape, size, composition, texture. tenderness. colour. flavour and taste as their definition is broad enough to encompass each and any of them.

CLASSIFICATION : Despite the apparently seamless transaction on one cookies type into the next, there are certain fundamental distinctions that permit them to be classified into several basic categories. However the two popular ways of classification are according to mixing method & recipe adopted and according to the basic forming machine employed in their production.

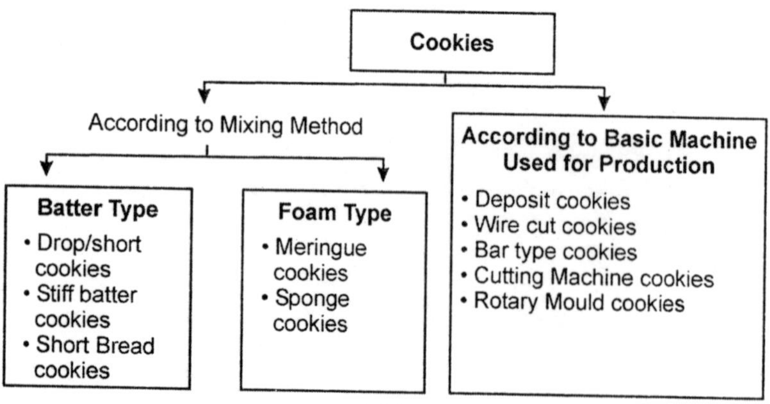

According to Mixing Method: Under this head, cookies can be divided into two types: batter type & foam type.

(i) ***Batter Type:*** They are akin to cake in recipe except they have less liquid (i.e. egg, milk, water etc.). This helps to mix the dough to a desired consistency to retain the required shape when deposited on baking sheets. In case of more liquid (i.e. batter similar to cake) cookie may spread on sheet and cannot retain the shape. This type of cookie are again divided into three types:

- DROP/SHORT COOKIES : It has maximum moisture content among batter type cookies, and because of this, they require more eggs to give structure than the normal range of cookies of this class. The desirable finished product should be soft and moist hence it should be stored or packed under such conditions that will keep them moist, otherwise it becomes crumbly and non-sellable.
- STIFF BATTER COOKIES : It contains less liquid as compared to drop cookies, hence it requires less egg because of the lesser need for hard structure. These cookies also given more drying during baking. Both these conditions help to produce crispness - a desirable characteristic of the finished product. This crispness should be maintained till it is sold. Hence it should be stored and packed in such a condition that would retain the crispness quality
- SHORT BREAD COOKIES: They are similar to stiff batter cookies except that they contain large amount of shortening. It provides them richer texture and high nutritional value. Use of butter (up to 50% of total fat) along with other shortening will impart desirable characteristic flavour to the product.

(ii) *Foam Type:* Foam type cookies are made with large percentage of egg white which provides them structure as well as better leavening action. It can be divided into two varieties:

- MERINGUE: In the preparation of meringue. egg whites are whipped stiff with sugar to entrap air and provide body to hold the remaining ingredients (dried nuts. desiccated coconut. flour etc.). Care should be taken in blending the other ingredients so air should not be forced out of the mixture. e.g. coconut macroons. meringue .
- SPONGE COOKIES : It is made just like the sponge type cake except for large quantity of flour. In this type of cookies. egg white and sugar are beat upto stiff consistency followed by addition of flour.

According to Basic Forming Machine Used for Production This category includes five types:

(i) *Deposit Cookies:* The dough of this type of cookies approaches layer cake batters in fluidity. The dough is mixed by conventional creaming and mixing method. which is placed into the hopper - machine. Where a pair of grooved or fluted rolls forces the dough through a series of nozzles. which deposit the individual dough pieces on the cookies sheets.

(ii) *Wire Cut Cookies:* The consistency of their doughs ranges from soft cake batters to quite stiff doughs. Dough is mixed in a manner similar to the deposit cookies. It is fed to hoppers that are equipped with two grooved feed rolls, which forces the dough through series of die appertures at the bottom. A frame holding a taut wire moves across the ·bottom face of the dies and cuts the emerging dough into cookie shapes.

(iii) *Bar Type Cookies:* Cookies that are processed in a fashion similar to wire cut cookies, except that here rather soft dough is extruded from the hopper through narrow slit dies onto a conveyer belt or an oven band and then cut into desired length by a guillotine cutter either before or after baking.

(iv) *Cutting Machine Cookies* : The dough of such cookies possesses sufficient cohesiveness to produce a uniform thin continuous sheet and yet also exhibit enough shortness to ensure a clean separation of the cut or stamped dough pieces from the remaining scrap dough. The process includes sheeting and / or laminating the dough and then individual cookies are cut or stamped out from the resultant continuous sheet by either reciprocating or rotary cutters.

(v) *Rotary Moulded Cookies:* The dough should be well mixed and with relatively firm consistency. Dough from hopper is forced into dies where a surface of cylinder, which is embossed with variously designed shapes that mould desired cookies.

INGREDIENTS: Only the quality ingredients with correct method of processing will produce products of high standards. Hence. care should be taken in choosing the ingredients for cookies production. The ultimate texture of cookies is established by balance of both toughening and tenderizing ingredients, with flour providing the basic framework.

Flour: To produce premium quality cookies soft wheat flours are ideally suited. These are commonly termed as *paslry flours* and are usually unbleached containing 8 to 10 % protein and less than 0.4 % ash.

Sugar: Wide range of granulated sugar is used for cookie production. Most bakers prefer finely granulated sugar for its rapid solution during dough mixing. Even though coarse granulations yield cookies with a more tender texture and greater spread. Although powdered sugar dissolves still more rapidly, it tends to decrease cookie spread and tenderness. Bold crystal sugar may remain undissolved and hence produces dark brown spots while baking. Large amounts of sugar in a cookie recipe will produce shortness mainly due to its action in dispersing the flour gluten.

Many cookies may be produced by replacing HFCS to sugar. Malt syrup or any other type of malt may also be used as flavour enhancing ingredient and as a humectant in cookies production. Invert syrup can also be used for soft cookies.

Shortening: All types of shortenings available in market are suitable for cookie production. However. the point of principal concern is the proper balance of shortening with other ingredients in the formula rather than specific kind of shortening. Butter, mainly due to its characteristic flavour. should be used in equal palts with the shortening. Shortening mellows gluten and thereby helps to spread cookie. Use of lecithin at 0.25 to 0.3 % of shortening is recommended for richer type cookies.

Egg: Any type of egg (fresh liquid or dried) can be used for making cookies. Egg yolk alone will produce a tender cookie rather than the whole egg. but care should be taken to supplement them with a little extra moisture from either water or milk or both. Egg yolk also contributes to colour.

Milk Solid: Milk solid (particularly non fat dry milk) contributes mainly shortness and controls cookie spread along with the normal functions.

Chemical Leaveners : The sodium & ammonium bicarbonate and other leaveners contribute aerated structure. as well as increase the cookies spread.

MIXING: The particular mixing method employed for cookie doughs depends on the ultimate nature of end product. However. the general procedure for mixing cookie dough, is to first cream the shortening with the sugar. salt and flavour. Then add the eggs and moisture and finally the flour. Fruits or nuts are added at the last stage of mixing. The leavening is added at different stages depending upon the types of leavening used.

Cookie dough should be mixed just enough to blend the ingredients homogeneously. If the dough is slightly over mixed it tends to develop gluten. which will retard the spread of the cookie.

Single Stage Method: All the ingredients are mixed together in a bowl. Once the ingredients are mixed thoroughly it should be mixed on slow speed for 2 to 3 minutes. In this method. the mixing time is long and cookies spread less. To overcome this problem, sugar should be added at a later stage of mixing. because in this condition, sugar granules remain big at the time of baking which spread cookie much.

Creaming Method : Mix the sugar, fat salt etc, in a bowl. Add liquid egg and finally flour and the leavening agent. In this method, sugar granules become smaller. so the cookie spread less.

Blending Method : This method is used for preparation of short bread cookies. The product becomes very shorten and so tender. The flour is sieved with other dry ingredients and creamed with fat. Finally mix sugar and remaining ingredients.

Useful Suggestions in Processing:

- Cookies should be placed enough apart on the pans to avoid sticking during baking. This sticking produces ragged edges (that spoiles the appearance) and excess breakage.
- Most cookies improve in flavour due to the caramelization of the sugar during baking, only if they are baked thin. If the cookie dough is cut too thick it loses such flavour as well as appearance.
- If the lumps of sugar are let in the dough during mixing the cookies will stick to the pan due to the syrup, which is formed during baking. and will become hard & solidify on the pans.
- When the pans are greased (with shortening or margarine). the cookies will spread more. To retard this. dust the pans with flour after they are greased.
- Pan used for cookie should be cool because warm pans will melt the fat in the cookie resulting in inferior products .
- If cookie dough is made up ahead of time and stored in a cool place, then the dough should be made a little softer as this will tighten up during storage. It has been experienced that such doughs can be handled more easily giving the finished products more

tenderness. It is important to note that cookie dough can be refrigerated up to 2 weeks and frozen up to 4 months.

- Make cookie of even size and shape. which will promote even baking and browning.
- If raisins and currents are used for toppings, they should be soaked in a malt solution before they are used. This will help to prevent them from getting burnt. Malt solution is prepared by dissolving I part of malt with 10 parts of water. Soak the fruit until they swell somewhat and then drain thoroughly.
- Egg wash. which is high in egg. will retard the spread of cookie due to the coagulation of these eggs. Hence it is a general rule to prepare egg wash by using 1 part of eggs and 2 parts of milk.

BAKING : Baking temperature depends upon the type of cookie, which may lie between 150° to 190°C (300° to 375°F). The actual temperature varies with dough composition and the weight & shape of the dough pieces. Baking time also varies within the range of 8 to 12 minutes for average weight cookies. If the oven is too hot. cookie will set immediately before it has an opportunity to spread. On the contrary if the oven is too cool, the cookie will have too much spread, too much moisture loss due to longer baking period and also the lose of flavour. In order to obtain best baking results. cookies should be removed from the oven while they are still a little soft. as they will continue to bake on the hot pans. However. if cookies are thoroughly baked in the oven itself. remove the cookie quickly from baking sheet to prevent continued cooking. Cool the cookie on rack to prevent soggy bottom.

COOKIE SPREAD: Uniformity in cookie size has major significance for packing. Excessively spread cookies will present problems while filling in standard packages. Moreover restricted spread cookie normally increased heights and will yield slack package. Hence. a spread is a subject of investigation. It is found that respective ratios of free moisture and sugar in the dough constitute the principal factors that control the spread. Hence. any ingredient or processing condition that reduces the dough moisture that would otherwise be available for dissolving the sugar will restrict the spread. Moreover, it can be said that. ingredients that function as structure builders will usually act to reduce cookie spread. whereas tenderizing ingredients tend to have the opposite effect. There is also a positive correlation between cookie spread and high altitude.

FAULTS AND CAUSES : They are discussed below :

Faults	Causes
• **Lack of Spread**	• Too fine granulation of sugar • Adding all sugar at one time • Excessive mixing • Acidic dough • Too hot oven
• **Excessive Spread**	• Excessive sugar • Too stiff batter • Excessive pan grease • Too cool oven • Improper or excessive fat • Alkaline batter
• **Fall During Baking :**	• Excessive leavening • Too soft batter • Weak Dour • Improper size
• **Tough Cookie**	• Insufficient shortening • Over creamed batter • Too strong flour
• **Sticking out Pans:**	• Too soft flour • Excessive egg content • Too slack a batter • Unclean pans • Sugar spots in dough • Improper metal used for pan construction
• **Colour Fat It**	• Excessive sodium bicarbonate (Produces dark or green colour) • Excessive Ammonium bicarbonate (Produces black spots in crumb)
• **Lose of Flavour**	• Over baking • Fast baking • Lack of moisture • Improper storage

STORAGE: Follow the instructions given below for successful storage of cookie:

- Make sure cookies are completely cool before storing.
- Store cookie in airtight containers such as screw top jars or sealed plastic bags. This will prevent humidity from softening crisp cookie and air from drying soft cookie.
- Never store crisp and soft cookie in the same container otherwise the crisp ones will become soft.
- If cookies require refrigeration, cover them tightly to prevent absorption of other odours.
- Crisp cookies that have softened. can be recrisped by heating in oven at 149°C (300°F) for 3 to 5 minutes. Cool on rack before serving.
- Do not store cookie where air can circulate as air will dry it out.

17

Crackers Manufacture

Introduction : Generally the term crackers covers wide range of products similar to semi-sweet machine cut cookies to fermented, crisp, non-sweet, laminated items. The crackers are similar to the chemically leavened products, include the categories of the semi-sweet grahma crackers and the highly flavoured snack crackers with predominant onion, garlic, caraway, smoked yeast, cheese etc. flavours. Among the fermented types crackers, the soda or salty crackers are the most common. The famous crackers are discussed here :

Graham Crackers : It is produced from whole wheat flour, molasses, malt, honey etc. possesses sweet, nutty, caramel like flavour.

Mix → sweetners with water

↓

Heat → at 74° to 77°C (165° to 170°F) to prepare syrup

↓

Add → flour, shortening, whey and lecithin

↓

Mix → for 5 minutes in a three spindle mixer

↓

Add → the remaining ingredients

↓

Mix	→ for 25 minutes to 1 hour at 48°C
↓	(118°F) temperature
Sheeting & Folding	→ several foldings results into thin shed
↓	which is ready for cutting
Cutting	
↓	
Baking	
↓	
Product	

Cream Crackers : They are produced from flourm, water yeast and salt, as below :

Fermentation	→ with yeast for 4 to 24 hours
↓	
Sheeting	→ in a dual hopper, which sheets the dough
↓	into two sheets of required thickness
Filling	→ between two-sheet layers. Filling is
↓	prepared by mixing :
	• 33 parts plastic shortening
	• 100 parts of flour
	• 1 part of salt
	to a uniform powdery mixer. Keep
	mixture in frizz until use
Reduce thickness	→ through a series of gauging rolls to a
↓	thickness suitable for cutting
Cutting	
↓	
Baking	
↓	
Product	

Soda Crackers : It is produced by sponge and dough process with fermentation time upto 32 hours.

Preparation of Sponge → 60 to 70% of flour, yeast, small amount of old dough and water mixed 1 to 4 minutes

↓

Fermentation → for 16 to 18 hours at 25.5° to 29°C (78° to 84°F) & 78°rh

↓

Remixing → for 3 to 7 minutes with remaining ingredients [i.e. remaining flour, shortening, salt, sodium and ammonium bicarbonate)

↓

Fermentation → for 4 to 6 hours

↓

Sheeting → through laminating machine

↓

Folding → 5 to 7 layer

↓

Sheeting → 3 to 4 mm gap

↓

Baking

↓

Product

18

Manufacturing of Pastry

INTRODUCTION: The products. in which there is a absence of hardness or toughness are known as *pastry.* It is made from *paste.* which is a combination of flour, fat, salt, sugar and water. The quantity of fat is too high as compared to other products. Pastry is a base for making different kinds of products such as puffs. vaul-au-vent. pie crust. tarts. turnovers. cream rolls etc.

Pastry may be considered under two main heads: short crust pastry and puff or flaky pastry.

SHORT CRUST PASTRY: The pastry. in which there is a (complete absence of toughness or hardness. is known as *short crust pastry.* The details on the ingredients. mixing, baking are given below:

Ingredients: Flour. fat. sugar, salt and water are the principai ingredients used in the production of short paste.

(i) ***Fat:*** Tenderness characteristic in any kind of short paste depends on fat, because it prevents the gluten formation.

Normally the fat content varies between 40 to 80 % (on f.b.) in this type of pastry but good quality pastry can be made with 50 % fat (on f.b.). Lard is the best shortening to be used for short pastry because apart from possessing the best shortening properties among all fats. it also confers a good flavour on the pastry. If the fat quantity is low. small quantity of leavening agent (baking powder) could be used. however in such conditions quantity of water should be kept low to prevent gluten formation.

(ii) ***Flour:*** Soft flour is useful for the short crust pastry because it contains soft and short gluten and hence it can make a softer product as compared to hard flour. Flour can be made soft by addition of corn flour or rice flour. Sometimes. when the flour is too soft. the quantity of fat may be reduced to 35 to 40%. depending upon the softness of the flour used.

(iii) ***Sugar:*** If the short pastes are used for sweet lines. it is usual to add sugar at the rate of 10 to 25% (on f.b.). It improves the bloom and shortness of the paste and also enhances the flavour and eating qualities. When short pastes are to be used in the production of non-sweet products like savoury lines (such as meat pies and pastries of all types) then no sugar should be added but more salt is used to give flavour.

(iv) ***Water:*** Water quantity is quiet important in short pastry because too much water would make pastry hard to eat while too less water may make pastry fragile.

Formula : The following table (next page) gives a list of formulas, which may be used to cover a range of short pastes from the richest to the leanest.

Mixing : Mixing operation of short crust pastry is very important. It should be carried out in a manner that gluten development does not take place. otherwise pastry will become hard and not tender, as it should be. Small doughs could be mixed with a pallet knife (by what is known as cutting and folding movements of pallet knife). It should be mixed just sufficiently that water is evenly distributed and taken up by the dough mass till the product is placed in the oven for baking. After sheeting and cutting. the scrap should be neatly placed one over the other and pressed for second sheeting. In this manner gluten development will be minimal and resultant product will remain tender for eating flour and the whole mass joins together. Any undue mixing operation will toughen the pastry. Water content should also be just sufficient so the dough mass neither remains crumbly nor does it become sticky. Larger doughs can be mixed in a vertical mixer at slow and medium speed.

There are three method of mixing for short pastry:

(i) ***Rubbing:*** Chilled fat is cut into small pieces and mixed with the flour. Then flour and fat are rubbed gently till the whole mass resembles bread crumbs. Then water is added and the dough is mixed until it is cleared. Mixing must not be overdone. otherwise the paste will be toughened and it ingredients will be hard and flinty instead of short. In case of machine mixing. there are greater chances of toughening than in the case of hand mixing. Eventhough by correct timing more consistent results can be obtained with machine mixing.

(ii) ***Creaming:*** In this method. the fat with an equal weight of flour is creamed light as in the flour-batter method of cake making. Then the remainder of the flour and water is added and mixed until a clear paste is obtained, This method ensures a complete dispersion of the fat in the flour. hence it produces maximum sholtening effect so this method is particularly useful when less fats or poorer shortenings are to be used.

(iii) ***Boiling:*** This method is mainly used for meat pie pastes. In which the water, fat and salt together are boiled and stirring in the flour so that the starch gelatinizes. With the development of pie making machines. the emphasis is given on making a paste which suits the machines. But still the craftsman can produce paste which is good to eat as well as attractive in appearance. For certain lines of confectionery. a rich. sweet paste may be used containing eggs as part of the liquor.

Sheeting: After mixing. the dough should be rested in cool place (refrigerator) for ½ to 1 hour and then only it should be sheeted for make up. While sheeting short crust pastry. it should be remembered that the pastry is subjected to as little frictional heat (generated by rolling pin) as possible. otherwise fat will melt and get separated from the dough mass making the pastry tough for eating. During the entire operation of making short crust pastry the aim should be to keep the fat evenly distributed in the dough

Ingredients	Quantity (%)				
	No.1	No.2	No.3	No.4	No.5
Flour	100	100	100	100	100
Margarine	62.5	50	-	25	25
Fat	-	-	112.5	12.5	25
Salt	-	-	0.78	-	0.78
Sugar	25	12.5to 25	3 to 12.5	3 to 12.5	9.3 to 25
Water/Milk	7.5	-	25	22.5	7.5
Egg	12.5	12.5	-	-	7.5
Baking Powder	-	-	-	1.5	-

mass till the product is placed in the oven for baking. After sheeting and cutting, the scrap should be nearly placed one over theo ther and pressed for second sheeting. In this manner gluten development will be minimal and resultant product will remain tender for eating.

Baking: Baking temperature and baking time depend on the type of product being baked and the filling employed. The sweet paste goods are baked al 182°C (360°F) temperature. While notched jam, lemon tarts, fruit tarts, custard tarts, small meat pies and patties, madeira & rice tart etc. are baked at 215°C (420°F). The large size of any product requires less temperature. If pastry is to be baked without any filling, it is advisable to prick the pastry with a fork in order to avoid any bubble formation, which may spoil its appearance.

PUFF PASTRY: The paste (dough) from which very light & flaky, crisp and shorten goods are produced is termed as *puff paste* and such goods are known as *puff pastry*.

Ingredients: Flour and fat are two important ingredients for puff pastry:

(i) ***Flour:*** The flour selected must possess a sufficient quantity of good quality extensible gluten, so that when the paste is sheeted, it will form continuous strands throughout the whole mass. It must not be excessively short, otherwise the strands will break when folded over as the layers are built up.

Very often flours possessing too strong gluten are used for this type of paste in an attempt to produce excessive volume, but the finished products are tough to eat and devoid of any shortness. In such case the bread flour can be used for puff pastry production. No doubt some bakers prefer combination of bread and cake flour.

(ii) ***Fat:*** The fat for puff pastry should possess shortness. It should not contain hardness but should be tough enough. Moreover fat used for making puff pastry should have high melting point in order to withstand the frictional heat to which it is subjected during sheeting and folding operations. The consistency or shortening should be similar to that of the dough. Hence. now-a-days special puff pastry margarines available in the market are used for production.

(iii) ***Salt:*** Salt has toughening effect upon the gluten in the dough. Too much salt will deteriorate the strength of the gluten, which will lower the product volume.

(iv) ***Acids***: Addition of edible acids such as vinegar, lemon juice etc. during mixing help in mellowing of the gluten which facilitates the dough to roll out without difficulties and also make the dough shorten.

Richness: Richness of the pastry depends on the quantity of fat used. That are:

Paste Type	Fat (% on f.b.)
• Full paste (richest)	100
• Three quarter paste	75
• Half paste (leaner type)	50

Leavening/Lifting: There are many factors, which lift and expand the puff pastry. The two important are :

- Continuous sheeting and folding of the dough during mechanical manipulation, built up a laminated structure, which consists of at least 729 layers of fat in the dough. With this continuous folding, a small amount of air is included which will expand in the oven while baking.

- The steam produced during baking traped within layers and lift the pastry (within the continuous and extensible gluten films). The care must be taken that the layers of gluten should not be broken by unduly harsh treatment (such as might result from overworking where mechanical rollers are used for pinning out the dough or where the dough is toughened during working and not given adequate time to relax and recover from the toughening action) then the steam may escape and so fail to produce any lift or produce uneven lift and the melted fat may either escape from the layers or partly be absorbed by the paste.

Mixing and Sheeting: There are several methods for preparing puff pastry. However, the important ones are discussed here:

(i) *French Method :*

- FORMULA:

Ingredients	Quantity (%)
Flour (Patent white)	100
Cake Margarine	12.5
Pastry Margarine	87.5
Water (cold)	2.00
Cream of tarter / Lemonjuice	0.75

- **METHOD**

- *MIXING:* The cake margarine is rubbed in the flour as finely as possible as similar to short paste however some baker add it at the last stage of mixing. Add water and prepare dough in order to impart extensibility to the dough. (fat is added before. the·flour has a chance to take up and absorb water. water absorption will be reduced and gluten may not develop sufficient strength to tolerate so many sheeting and folding operations. Dough for puff pastry is made by mixing first chilled water (with salt & diluted lemon juice). Consistcncy of the dough should be such that it could be sheeted easily without being too hard or sticky. Too tight or too loose dough will be difficult to process.

- *RELAXING:* After mixing, the dough should be relaxed in a cool place, covered with moist cloth, which willprevent it from crusting. During that period, puff margarine (or whatever fat being used) is made into a square or rectangular block of 2.5 cm (1") thickness and chilled in refrigerator.

- *SHEETING WITH FAT :* After ½ an hour of relaxation period, dough is sheeted into a square or rectangular shapes, somewhat larger than the margarine blocks. Rolling should be carried out in such a way that the center of the dough is about 3.8 cm (1½") thick and the edges are thinner [about 2.5 cm (1")]. All surplus flour must be removed by brushing. Then the chilled margarine block is placed at the center of the dough so that the sides of the margarine block face the corners of the sheeted dough. At this stage one end of the dough is folded over the margarine block so as to cover it completely. Then the opposite end is brought over and folded. Similarly, the remaining two ends are folded. So that the margarine block is covered by four folds the dough on the top side.

- *RELAXING:* The whole block should be relaxed in a cool place (refrigerator) for about ½ hour. This relaxation period will release the stress of the dough to which it is subjected during sheeting & raiding and also keep the fat in solid state.

- *SHEETING:* After proper relaxation of the dough, it is turned upside down (so that the top side having four folds is down in contact with the table top) and sheeted into a 0.91 m x 0.91 m (3' x 3') square shape. Now they are folded again in book fold, that is both the ends are brought at the center and again folded over so that the entire sheet forms four layers. Finally the dough will be of about 0.93 sq m(1 sq ft) piece. It should be of about 2.54 cm (1") thick. At this stage there wil! be 12 layers of fat.

- *RELAXATION & RE-SHEETING (TWO TIMES) :* The dough should be covered with a damp cloth to prevent skinning and rested for ½ hour. It is then rolled into a 0.84 sq m (3 sq ft) again and folded as earlier. Then again rested for ½ hour before the operation is completed a third time. The paste is then said to have 6 single or 3 double turns. in which very fine layers of dough are interspersed with very thin layers of fat. This mass is known as *Puff Pastry* from which various products are made such as jam puffs. cream horns. palmiers. pinwheels etc. After final sheeting and folding the pastry should be relaxed in cool place for a minimum of I hour before make up. If the pastry becomes too hard. it should be allowed to that at room temperature until it acquires sheetable consistency.

(ii) Scotch Method

- **Formula**

Ingredient	Quantity (%)
• Flour (White)	100
• Pastry Margarine or Fat	100
• Water	2.00
• Lemon Juice	0.75

- **METHOD**: In this method fat is chopped into lumps to the size of walnuts in the flour and with the water. it is made into a dough and left to rest. When it has relaxed. it is rolled out and folded in layers in the same ways as in the French method.

(iii) Three Quarter Method :

- FORMULA :

Ingredient	Quantity (%)
• Flour (White)	100
• Cake Margarine	12.5
• Pastry Margarine	62.5
• Water	2.00

- **METHOD**: This is usually made on the Scotch method but as the fat content is less it is normal procedure to give only two double turns instead of three. This produces a very satisfactory paste. which appeals to many people as it is less rich fat.

(iv) ***English Method:*** This method resembles the French method. In which dough is made up by rubbing cake margarine or fat into the flour and left to rest for 30 minutes before being pinned out into a piece [0.84 sq m (36 sq in)]. The only difference is that the pastry margarine is spread over 2/3 of the surface areas in loafs instead of being placed as a solid block at the center. Then the third portion (on which no pastry fat has been spread) is folded over the fat - spread dough. And then again folded on remaining fat - laminated dough. Thus producing a long piece 0.91 m x 0.35 m (3' x 1'). This paste is then treated in the same way as the other pastes so that three double turns are given when it is ready for cutting out. While much skill and care is required in the makingofthe paste, equal skill must be displayed in the utilization of it.

(v) ***Improved English Method:*** This is quite popular now-a-days among all these method. This method is used to make pie crust. vegetable puffs. khari etc. They all are so called in one term as *flaky pastly* also.

- **FORMULA**

Ingredient	Quantity (%)
• Flour	100
• Fat/Pastry Margarine	50 to 70 (5 to 10 used for rubbing)
• Salt	3
• Water	60

- **METHOD**: Dough is made with flour. salt. food acid, water and fat. It is relaxed for about 1/2 hour. Then the dough is sheeted into a rectangular shape and marked into three equal parts lengthwise.

Fat is divided into three portion. 1 portion of fat is evenly spread onto 2/3 portion of the sheeted dough leaving out 1.27 cm (½") space on the edges. Now1/3 part of the dough (on which fat is not being spread) is folded over the middle part (on which fat is being spread). The remaining 1/3 portion (with fat) is folded over it. We have now alternate layers of dough and fat. relax the dough for 20 to 30 minutes in cool place covered with moist cloth in order to prevent it from crusting.

The dough is again sheeted into rectangular shape. The process is repeated twice more to use up the remaining 2 portions of fat with adequate relaxation time in between the sheetings.

Similarly two foldings are given without fat. Now we have very thin layers of fat interspersed with very thin layers of dough, which will rise during baking to form a light and crisp product. After final sheeting and folding the pastry should be relaxed for about I hour before sheeting for make up.

(vi) ***Precautions Observed while Sheeting:***

- Margarine should not become too hard while the dough is relaxed in the refrigerator. Because very hard margarine will break into small pieces while sheeting hence the desired continuous layering effect may not be achieved.
- Margarine should not be too soft, otherwise during sheeting, operation it will squeeze out at one end. This will also prevent formation of desired layers.
- Relaxation of dough in between two sheeting operations is very important. During sheeting operation, gluten of the dough is subjected to stress and strain hence its extensibility is reduced. During relaxation period extensibility is regained and further processing becomes easier.
- Under no circumstances the pastry should be subjected to undue pressure while sheeting. This may break the continuity of gluten strands and also break the fat into small pieces. Both these actions will disturb the pattern of layers. It will also compress the layers too much. which will adversely affects its rise during baking.
- The entire operation of making puff pastry should be carried out at cool temperature. Frictional heat from sheeting action or the atmospheric temperature (warm table top warm rolling pins) should not make the margarine loose as it (as explained earlier) may be squeezed out and proper layers will not be formed. Air conditioner can be used for this purpose.
- While relaxing the pastry, it should be covered with moist cloth in order to prevent it from crusting. If pastry is crusted during processing, it will loose its stretchability and its rise in the oven will be poor.

Cutting: It is a great mistake to take puff pastry out until it has rested at least 1 hour from its last folding operation. It is desirable to allow it rest longer (preferably overnight in refrigerators).

Once the paste has been taken out. it should be reduced to the correct thickness for cutting into shapes. it should again be left to rest. and after the final cutting out and placing on trays it should be left for some time before taking off. Generally speaking. the longer the rest period. the better the result. The cutting size is generally 1.9 to 3.8 cm (0.75" to 1.5") width & 5 to 10 cm (2 to 4") length for Khari and 60 to 160 sq cm (3 to 5 sq in) square for Puff.

It is important to point out that all goods. which should have a vertical lift or a horizontal one be made from virgin paste. Owing to the delicate nature of the paste it must be handled carefully and rolled out to an even thickness for each particular article. To ensure regular shapes and thickness, suitable templates and guides should be made for only in this way can consistency of size and quality be maintained.

Trimmings from the virgin paste can be used for many lines where accurate lift is not necessary but where flakiness is required. It is quite a good practice to prepare the cut out pastries and leave them overnight in the cold chamber where refrigerators or cooling chambers. That will be ready for baking on the following day.

When good eating qualities are required, it is a good idea to use a proportion of cake margarine with the pastry margarine (say. 1/3: 2/3 ratio) in the machine before using to make puff pastry.

Baking: After cutting the pastry and before baking. it should be relaxed for 20 to 30 minutes. This will stabilize the position of layers and rise in the oven will be even. It is generally baked at 215°C (420"F) for about 20 minutes.

CHOUX PASTRY: Chaux pastry has altogether different kinds of characteristics. This is almost a hollow shell, which is crisp in eating. Shells can be filled with fresh or butter cream and coated with fondant icing. Pastry can be made in the shape of eclairs, swans, cream puffs etc.

- **FORMULA**

Ingredient	Quantity (%)
• Flour	100
• Margarine	50
• Water	4
• Egg	5

Process : Water, fat and salt are boiled together. Then flour is added all together and mixed to form a partially gelatinized paste. Eggs are whisked separately and then added to the paste gradually, with continuing beating.

A very small quantity of sugar is added if desired. Adequate whisking of the paste will ensure desirable rise of the pastry during baking.

Baking: Baking operation of choux pastry is very important. Initially it should be baked at high temperature [232°C (450°F)] so that it achieves optimum rise. Then the temperature is reduced to about 149°to 163°C (300° to 325°F) and it is baked at lower temperature until the structure is stabilized and shells become crisp. Such pastry should not be subjected to unnecessary movements or sudden temperature variations until its structure is stabilized otherwise it will collapse easily. Shells can be stored for short periods and used as required.

FAULTS AND CAUSES: Some common problems of pastry and how to avoid them is illustrated below:

Fault	Causes
• **Lack of volume**	• No plasticity in shortening • Soft shortening • Uneven layering • Too strong or too weak tlour • Low baking temperature
• **Shrinkage of crust**	• Too tight dough (difficult to roll etfortlessly) • Insufficient rest after every turn (sheeting and folding) • Uneven layering • Too strong flour (with higher protein content)
• **Topping over**	• Insufficient • Insufficient rest after every turn • Too thick layers • Thick cutting
• **Irregular shape** (after baking)	• Improper lamination • Insufficient rest after every turn • Excess dusting flour • Hard shortening (which lump while layering)
• **Fat Seepage** (after baking)	• Too soft shortening • Insufficient turn • No pre-heated oven

19

Manufacturing of Icing & Decoration

INTRODUCTION: Icings are sweet covering, plain or with vivid patterns in which sugar is the main ingredient. They are used to make certain products more attractive and appetizing. The icing should:

- Easily be spread and its handling should be possible at normal working temperature.
- Possess good adherence to the baked product without thinning and running off.
- Set firmly within the desired time limit.
- Retain uniform moisture content without either drying out too rapidly or absorbing extraneous moisture to cause melting or stickiness.
- Maintain glossy appearance and true colour during the anticipated shelf life.
- Not develop grittiness during storage.

TYPES: Type of an icing depends upon the materials used (particularly fat) in the preparation as well as the method or mixing. Accordingly it can be divided into two categories:

Flat Icing: It is also referred to as *water icing* because it consists primari ly of water & sugar. usually in the ratio of 12 to 15% : 85 to 88% and generally stabilized with agar. It normally does not contain fat hence it is also non-aerated. Mono and diglycerides are also added to increase opaqueness and improve the gloss. Sugar & water is heated and when they get cool, that sets to the firm coating.

Aerated Icing: It is the creamed mixture of shortening, pulverized sugar, water, salt, flavour, egg and milk powder. Aeration makes it stiff (non fllowing consistency) hence can easily be spread on the product, so it is used for spreading and piping. On the basis of fat content and use this icing can be devided into two types:

(i) *Cupcake Icing:* It contains emulsified shortening which causes aeration during preparation and acquire fudge like consistency.

(ii) *Cake Icing* : It contains relatively high levels of fat, which is useful to provide light, aerated structure to icing. The degree of aeration increased by addition of whipping aids like soy protein, egg white and gelatine etc. The grain, texture & shelf life of icing can be improved by inclusion of surfactants like mono & diglycerides, sorbitan monostearate. polyoxyethelene sorbitan monostearate.

INGREDIENTS: Information on quality of ingredients used for icing preparation is discussed below:

Sugar: The principal sweetener for icing is sugar but specific type of sugar is also preferred for different types or icing. They are:

Sugar	Icing
• Granulated	Flat icing (boiled process)
• **4X** Powder sugar	Flat icing (cold process)
• **6X** pulverize sugar	Smoother icing of any kind
• **10X** pulverize sugar	Much smother icing of any kind

Note : Pulverized sugar is commercially known as *icing sugar* or *confectionery sugar.*

In addition to the sugar, dextrose, corn syrup, invert sugar are also used at low levels mainly to impart gloss to the final product.

Shortening: Emulsified or hydrogenated shortening, having no taste and smell is generally used in icing. Butter may be mixed (about 50% of total shortening) for its specific flavour. Never use butter alone, as it can not aerate sufficiently. Moreover, it should possess mild. clear flavour and its salt content must be included in calculating the total salt in the icing formulation. *Plastic shortening* is used when soft icing is desired or when iced product is to be frozen. For cream-type icings, *special shortening* containing an appropriate- blend of surfactants are used. When chocolate is used, it is to be considered that, it contributes to the fat quantity of icing due to its high fat content. Sometimes *milk cream* is also used as shortening but product containing such icing should be kept under freezing conditions.

Milk Product: Among the milk products. milk powder is commonly recommended because it provides structure, taste and flavour to the icing. It does not require any additional water and on the contrary, it absorbs moisture. Milk powder should always be sieved along with sugar to avoid the lumps because it may make difficult to pipe icing with a fine nozzle. If icing can carry the extra water, sweetened condensed milk may be used as it enhances the product's richness and flavour. Fresh milk has tendency to become sour hence not recommend to use in icing.

Water: Water is used to dissolve sugar to prepare syrup. It further acts to establish the desired spreadability of the icing. In general, it is considered a good practice to use minimum amount of water.

Egg: Egg in the form of whole egg. youlk or white finds use in the preparation of some icing. They contribute the volume and flavour to the icing. Fresh whites intended for icing use should be rather firm so they will whip into a foam with good volume and strength. This will reduce the tendency of the icings to bleed or melt out.

Flavours and Colours: Correct flavour balance and eve appealing colours are of great practical importance in icings for assuring their consumer appeal hence they must be used wisely and carefully. Now-a-days. butter, citrus, vanilla, chocolate and some fruit based flavours are most popular for bakery products.

Salt: Salt. when used in small quantity. supplements and enhances the taste and flavour of the other ingredients.

Stabilizers and Whiteners: Use of low level whiteners like titanium oxide. calcium carbonate and calcium sulphate are useful eye appealing part of consumer preferences.

Stabilizers are used to maintain icing aeration, texture and consistency throughout the shelf life. That includes agar, algin, gum arabic, locust bean gum, guar gum, carrageenan and pectin, gelatine, plant starches, carboxymethylcellulose (C MC) etc.

PREPARATIONS: Different methods are employed to prepare different icings. However, it is good practice to prepare icings just before their intended use because extensive holding period may evaporate moisture and cause changes in the icing character. Maintain a constant temperature during the holding period is also important to maintain the quality.

Flat Icing: It may be prepared either by the cold process, in which all ingredients are worked in special mixers at room temperature or by boiling process. in which sugar syrup is brought to a boiling temperature prior to the incorporation of the powdered sugar. Many a times starch is added to boiling syrup to increase opaqueness and moisture retention capacity of icing. Sometimes egg white or gelatine is also added to impart more body and improve setting properties of the icings. Low level of invert sugar tend to reduce their brittleness and enhance gloss of icing hence it is also added occasionally.

The boiling method is popular, in which all ingredients are to be mixed to a thick paste consistency and warmed to about 43°C (11°F). To avoid direct or over heating of icing. a double boiler method of heating should be used. Many a times. due to over heating, icing loses its gloss after cooling. Whenever flat icing gets thickened after its makeup it should be re-warmed to bring to the correct consistency required. Do not soften the icings with water before they are reheated otherwise it will cause stickiness in icings and also cause difficulties in setting. When through with immediate use of a flat icing. it should be covered with a thin film of water to prevent crust formation.

Among the flat icings type, the water icing is widely used, hence its production deta i1s are given below:

Water Icing: It is easily prepared for covering the cakes. It is prepared by mixing sufficient quantity of granulated or pulverized sugar with boiling water, and make it to the same consistency of fondant. A little glucose and a pinch of citric acid may also be added. The whole mix should be well beaten together before using.

In other method, 3 kg pulverized sugar is mixed with about 600 ml water to bring about appropriate solution thickness. It is heated in a bainmariee and beaten well together. Add about 125 gm glucose and pinch of lemon juice or citric acid. This makes excellent water icing for spreading. It can also easily be coloured to add variety.

Creamed Icing : Creamed icings are prepared with fat, confectioners sugar, water, salt, flavour, egg and milk powder. The general procedure is to cream fat such as butter or shortening with pulverized sugar. Beaten egg is added gradually. Water and flavouring agents are added at the end. Finally all ingredients blend well together. Creamed icing should be stored in a cool place and should be kept covered to avoid crust formation. Creamed icings have tendency to loose their smoothness after long duration storage. In such cases, icing will not have the ability to spread smoothly and evenly. In order to restore their smoothness, they should be placed in warm water bath and creamed well until they become smooth. Do not overheat to avoid fat from melting away.

Methods of preparation of different aerated icings are mentioned below:

(i) ***Butter Icing*** : Butter icing may sometimes be termed as *butter creams.* It is used for decorative and sandwiching purpose. However, the sandwich ing butter cream should be much lighter than those of decorative purpose. Moreover. the decorative icing must be firm enough to keep any desired shape that is given to it on the tops of cakes.

- Formula

Ingredients	Quantity
Butter	250 gm
Icing sugar	300 to 500 gm
Vanilla and / or butter essence	1 to 2 tsp
Colour	as desired

- METHOD: Cream, butter to a smooth consistency in a bowl with a wooden spoon until it gets fluffy. Add sieved icing sugar a little at a time and cream. Finally add essence and colour as desired. Some confectioners add a little condensed milk or egg white to make it lighter.

- **MERINGUE BUTTER CREAM**: Various light butter creams are used as fillings known as *meringue buller cream.* It can be prepared in the following way:

- Formula

Ingredients	Quantity
Butter	750 gm
Lump sugar	500 gm
Water	As required
Egg white	300 gm
Icing suar	300 gm
Essence	As required

- METHOD : Whisk the egg white and icing sugar in a bowl. On the other hand. boil lump sugar and water at 118° C (745° F). Pour this syrup over the whites and whisk continuously until light and cold. The butter is then creamed and blended into the meringue and then flavour is added .

- MARSHMALLOW BUTTER CREAM: A very light cream filling can be made with marshmallow, egg white, butter and milk, that can be called *marshmallow butter cream*
- Formula

Ingredients	Quantity
Marshmallow	1350 gm
Egg white	450 ml
Butter	1350 gm
Condensed milk	450 ml

- *METHOD:* Beat the egg white and marshmallow in machine until a light but stiff foam is formed. On the other hand, cream up butter with condensed milk and blend into the marshmallow - egg white cream. Add flavour as desired .

- **FONDANT BUTTER CREAM**: A light cream which can be used for either filling or decorative work is made with fondant and butter is called *fondant hutler cream.*

Ingredients	Quantity
Marshmallow	1350 gm
Egg white	450 ml
Butter	1350 gm
Condensed milk	450 ml

- *METHOD:* Heat the fondant over warm water to 37°C (100°F). Remove from fire and ·add stock syrup if required to gain sufficient liquidity. Cream the butter and gradually cream up in fondant. This gives a very smooth product, which can be coloured and flavoured as desired.

(ii) *Royal Icing:* Royal icing is also termed as *glaze royal.* It is prepared from egg white, icing sugar, acetic acid / cream of tarter, essence and colour, Dried egg white reconstitutes is preferred as it gives more satisfactory result compared to fresh white. If fresh white is used. it should be separated neatly because minute presence of yolk may spoil the icing. Sometimes egg white are rested for 3 to 4 hours before being used. Utensils used for beating should be absolutely grease free and should not be dirty. The sugar should be carefully sifted through a fine sieve to take out all the hard lumps.

- Formula

Ingredients	Quantity
Icing sugar	3.150 kg
Egg white	600 ml
Acetic acid	As required
Whitening agent	As required
Glycerine	150 ml

- METHOD: Add 2/3 of sugar to the egg white. mix it, and add a pinch of whitening agent and few drops of acetic acid. Beat it to a stiff consistency. Stir the remainder sugar, scrape down the sides of the bowl, covers with damp cloth or plaster of paris covering (preferable) otherwise the icing will soon go hard and gritty on the top. The add ition of acid helps to toughen the albumen. but too much of it should not be used. as it makes the icing very hard and brittle when dry. Icing for covering a cake is best made without acid, as it will not set too hard and will get mellowed. The icing for a coating purpose is reduced with a little white to a thinner consistency than that required for piping. The addition of little glycerin will help to make it softer or mellower. It is added when the icing is ready for application on the cakes.

  Fondant and royal icings are sometimes mixed in equal proportions for coating christmas and birthday cakes. The fondant is heated in the usual way. Then the properly prepared icing is added to it. This will give a nice mellow eating quality to icing which set firmly and yet has a satisfactory gloss.

(iii) ***American Icing:*** A very bright, pure white or coloured icing is sometimes used to cover the cake. It is called *american icing.*

- Formula

Ingredients	Quantity
Egg white	300 ml
Salt	3.5 gm
Vanilla essence	As desired
Lump sugar	1800 gm
Water	600 gm
Cream of tarter	3.5 gm

- METHOD: Beat egg white. cream of tarter. salt and essence to a stiff batter. On the other hand, add water into lump sugar and boil to 115° C (240° F) temperature. Now, add syrup over the white and whisk the the mixture until light. Pour it over cake base just before it grains.

Other Decorative Products: This includes gum paste. meringue, fondant etc. that are used for decoration purpose.

(i) ***Gum Paste:*** For modelling (preparing house, hut etc.) purposes, a paste made of icing sugar and gum is required. Gum tragacanth is generally employed for this purpose. It is used in preparation of plaques and moulded decoration of cakes, and is useful for the reproduction of models for window attraction .

- Formula

Ingredients	Quantity
Gum tragacanth	40 gm
Icing Sugar	2.825 kg
Corn flour	800 gm
Cold water	600 ml

- METHOD: Gum tragacanth flakes are soaked in cold water for about 24 hours. The jelly formed is passed through a muslin cloth to remove impurities and hard pieces of gum, Icing sugar and corn flour are then worked into it until a firm pliable paste is made. Whitening agent is also added during the doughing stage and sometimes some royal icing is also added to make it smoother and produce a better colour. Other colours can be added as required.

(ii) *Gelatine Paste:* A modelling paste. which does not set so hard, can also be made with gelatine.

- Formula

Ingredients	Quantity
Gelatine	56 gm
Water	150 ml
Glucose	225 gm
Icing sugar	3.150 kg
Royal icing	450 gm

- METHOD: Soak gelatine in cold water for 1 hour. On the other hand, boil water, sugar and glucose. Remove from the fire and add the gelatine. Dough up with icing sugar and add royal icing during doughing.

  Marshmallow creams, stiffened with icing sugar can also be used as modelling pastes.

  All of these gum pastes should not be too stiff. otherwise they become shorr & break easily and would be difficult to handle or rollout. The pastes dry readily on exposure to the air and therefore should be kept moist, under cover. The paste should be dusted with corn flour when used for modeling to prevent it sticking to moulds ..

(iii) *Meringues:* Meringues are made from egg white and sugar. They vary according to the proportion of each ingredient used, from the heavy type to the light type. i.e. on the one hand, 16 egg whites and 450 gm sugar will make a souffle suitable for puddings, and, on the other, 6 egg whites and 450 gm sugar will make heavy nougat type of meringue. The point to bear in mind is that as the proportion of egg whites is increases, the meringue becomes lighter, and also it is more difficult to dry out.

In order to assure perfect results, all utensils must be free from grease, that can be ensured by rubbing them with salt and then rinsing in hot water. The egg whites must be strong. The sugar should be free from foreign matter and its grain must suitable for the purpose of the meringue. It may be used as a filling or covering or. when dried out, as a shell or case for fillings. That are prepared by :

Type	Ingredients
• **Shells & Cases**	• 600 ml egg white • 1400 gm castor sugar • As desired flavour • As desired colour
• **Set ornament**	• 600 ml egg white • 1800 gm castor sugar • As desired flavour • As desired colour
• **Coconut**	• 600 ml shells & cases • 1350 gm coconut threads
• **Almond**	• 600 ml shells & cases • 900 gm nakes almonds

- METHOD: Many methods of preparations are:
  - *COLD:* Whisk whites to stiff foam, gradually add of sugar, add flavour and colour. and then mix in remaining sugar.
  - *WARM:* Same as above but warm sugar to 49°C (120°F) before adding to whites.
  - *HOT:* Add sugar to whites and whisk over water [(not below 71°C (160°F)] until a stiff meringue is obtained.
  - *BOILED:* Whisk egg white to stifffoam. While this is being done. boil sugar to 115°C (240°F). Then pour sugar on to white and whisk until stiff.

  Meringue made by any of the above mentioned methods would dry out at 121°C (250°F) temperature in the oven; i.e. below the sugar caramelization temperature.

(iv) ***Fondant:*** Fondant is employed as a covering for small and large cakes and also in making creams for chocolate centers. It is used on cakes because it can be easily applied and sets quickly.

20

Machinery Used in Bakery Unit

INTRODUCTION: Successful bakery production is connected with efficient use of bakery machinery. Machine can work more efficiently. speedy and at a cheaper rate (depending on the labour cost) hence in large scale bakery unit machines are preferred for most of the work. Therefore, mechanical as well as technical knowledge is essential for the baker.

The machines used in bakery units can be divided into four parts:

INGREDIENT HANDLING EQUIPMENTS : It includes storage bins, weighing balance, sifter, conveyer system etc.

Storage Bin: These are used to store flour, sugar etc. dry bulk raw material. They are available in various sizes and shape (mostly cylindrical or square). They are generally underground. Its bottom is slanted at one end, which helps to remove flour other material. They are generally made-up from stainless steel or mild steel covered with corrosion resistant and weatherproof external coating. The interior surface may be either polished steel or a synthetic coating that is smooth, nontoxic, nonabrasive and free of odour and taste.

Ingredient Conveying System: Ingredient transfer from storage bin to production area or at any other place by conveyer belt. The belt moves continuously with constant speed hence when material is placed on the belt, it automatically get transferred.

Unloading System: To unload the truck trolley, the material is transferred directly to storage bin through tube, operated by electric motor. In this device, arrangement is made to switch the machine off automatically, as soon as the truck gets emptied or the bin gets filled.

Dump Bin and Blender : Bakeries that receive flour in bags are generally equipped with dump bin/blender where bags are emptied. From there, it is transferred to production area by conveyer belt.

Dump bin is rectangular metal cabinets whose bottom slopes toward conveyer belt.

Cabinet containing two or more compartments are known as *blender.* Hence, two or more different types of flour can be mixed. Normally, blender can blend 50:50. 25:75, 33:67 and 40:60 flours. However, it can be made according to specific need.

Flour Sifter: Flour sifter sieves are made up of metal. which vibrates mechanically. So the flour is divided into different categories according to particle size. It is generally placed at the end of conveyer belt where flour is transferred from dump bin. Sifters are of various types like cone sifter, vibrating screens type etc.

Centrifugal Machine: In most of the flour mills and in few large-scale bakeries specialized centrifugal machine is used to destroy the insects (particularly in egg form) are known as *rotors.* In this machine, the flour is forcefully thrown to the walls of machine by central shaft. hence flour collides with wall forcefully. So. the eggs of flies, insects or any other unsound material are broken down without affecting flour quality.

Weighing Machine: The accurate quantity of ingredients according to the product formula is essential for the desired quality of finished products. Hence. various types of automatic / semi-automatic weighing machines are developed. Out of them, electronic weighing system is the most effective means. at present.

DOUGH PROCESSING MACHINES: It includes mixer, divider, rounder, moulder, prover etc. All these are covered in bread processing chapter. Some remaining information is covered here.

Mixer: It is advisable to use mixer when at least 90 kg flour is used everyday in the bakery. A unit producing bread, cake, biscuits i.e. assorted bakery products on small scale should install *heavy duty type multipurpose cake mixer* because it would be useful for bread dough kneading and cake mixing as well as egg beating and sugar-fat creaming. Generally, high speed, low speed, variable speed vertical/horizontal mixers are marketed.

(i) ***Horizontal Mixer:*** This is normally high speed heavy duty type mixer machine. It may be of two categories namely. *stationery* *bowl machine* and *tilting bowl machine.* In the former case. dough is removed by hand while in later case the bowl separated from machine. Mixers are generally madeup of sturdy frame of cast iron, tabular steel or channel steel welded construction, whose upper portion houses the mixing bowl. Normally, the bowl fabricated of stainless steel is transverses by a single agitator shaft that is provided with one or more mixer bars either straight or of various configurations. Some mixers, intended for processing exceptionally stiff dough, are equipped with dual agitator shafts. Power is provided by an electric motor located at the base of the mixer frame. The bowls are trough-like shape with a curved bottom and flat ends & sides.

High speed mixer machine produces a lot of heat through friction hence they are provided with jacket, which keeps the dough cool, which is essential for uniform dough development. Modern high speed mixers are provided with the facility for self lubrication. As a precautionary measure, push button switch should be provided to the operator.

(ii) ***Double Arm / Resiprocating Arm Mixer:*** In this machine, mixing action akin to the hand mixing. Where two agitator arms are mounted vertically on circular plones. As these arms rotate at moderate speed, the agitators traverse intersecting elliptical paths in a shallow and slowly revolving bowl. As they do so, they impart a gentle kneading, stretching, lifting and folding action to the dough. Due to slow speed, the dough temperature increases very little, hence there is no need of refrigeration cold jacketing. Because of this, these machines are suitable for temperature sensitive dough, such as for pies and pastries in which the preservation of discrete shortening particles is important. It is also useful for doughs containing nuts and fruits which may breakdown in high speed mixing.

(iii) ***Verticle Mixer:*** It may be used for multipurpose function (beating egg, aerating batter, kneading etc.) hence it is useful to small bakeries preparing different products. They consist of essentially a vertical frame of variable height with a horizontally -extended head which houses the drive mechanism that actuates the vertical shaft with the beater attachments. The mixer head may be either horizontally stationery (in which case bowl is elevated into mixing position), or it may be equipped with a motor drive (for raising and lowering as required), or to spiral mixers (which may be tilt able so the beater can be moved free of the bowl). The motor itself, which may be either of the geared transmission or variable-speed type is enclosed in a base of frame. The arm may be attached with different attachments, meant for beating, . aerating purpose.

The frame of any mixer is made up of mild steel/cast iron. Which is mounted with electric motor of 0.33 to 10 hp (mainly 0.5 to 1.5 hp for small bakeries) as per requirement. They usually possess a gear system hence the speed can be changed. The capacity of bowls may vary from 10 to 200 kg and are made up of stainless steel. The speed of arms varies from 70 to 370 rpm (Revolutions Per Minute) for slow speed and high speed, respectively. The arm shape is made in such a way that it can carry out folding, kneading and stretching action (in case of bread dough) and aerating (in case of creaming purpose) or just simple mixing (in case of cookies and biscuits dough preparation).

Liquid Ferment Equipment: The large scale bakery industry should possess equipments necessary to prepare and keep yeast slurry or flying ferment. It is generally equipped with temperature control, agitator, sanitary pump, valve etc. A tank made up of stainless steel having capacity of 200 to 250 liters is used for this purpose.

Dough Divider: This machine divides the bulk dough volumetrically into individual dough pieces, that confirms as closely as possible to a preset weight. Hence, the dough density (which is highly affected by the extent of fermentation) should be even otherwise the weight might change. Now-a-days, such dough dividers are available which can make 1 to 8 pieces at a time and also make 20 to 30 strokes / minutes (however, it is considered the best practice to run machine have 15 to 18 strokes/ minutes). It is advisable to purchase dough divider when 40 to 50 flour bags are used weekly. Normally, a labour can cut 500 to 600 pieces in an hour, hence it is also again advisable to purchase a divider on comparative economic calculations.

Rounder: Rounding machines basically consist of an external or internal revolving surface against which the freshly scaled dough piece is held by a spiral track or trough. As the surface revolves, it carries the irregularly-shaped dough piece upward in the spiral rounding trough, imparting to the dough a rolling motion. This motion results in uniform rounded dough ball with a thin, smooth and dense skin that not only eliminates the stickiness of the cut dough surface. but also serves as a carbon dioxide gas-retaining membrane. The revolving surface may have the form of a conical bowl, an umbrella or a drum.

Intermediate Proover : Intermediate proover generally consists of overhead enclosures that house an endless, tiered conveyer that supports dough carriers in the form of either trays or canvas loops. In these enclosures dough pieces are rested for 10 to 15 minutes. They are equipped with temperature and humidity controller.

Moulder: It is economically viable for a baker to purchase a moulder when he is using 25 to 30 bags of flour per week.

Final Proover : After moulding and panning the dough loaves are carried to a steam box. which is just like a steam-room. The accurate control system for temperature and rh is established as it may change the quality of products. The final proover are made up of stainless steel.

The proover can be of two type:

(i) *Manual:* Proof box, intended for manual loading, with castered racks moving on floor tracks should be limited to a depth of four racks to facilitate their movement through the box. Where greater capacity is involved, suspending the racks from monorails for easier handling generally provides a satisfactory solution. In the instances, where box depth exceeding seven racks is required, motorized monorails will be found to be most effective in facilitating rack movement.

(ii) *Automatic:* They are of several kinds:

- TUNNEL PROOVER : This is the simplest type of automatic proover. It requires a long floor due to its length [i.e.27.S/m (90') to 91.5 m (300')] that may be costlier particularly in case of high land cost. The problem of length can be alleviated by designing the proover in two adjoining parallel sections with a cross-conveyer at one end. The pan-carrying conveyer in this type of proover is generally the grid design. Where the unprooved dough enters from one end and exists from the other end within a specific time limit.
- TRAY PROOVER: In this type of proover stabilized trays are conveyed by continuous drive chains that travels through the length of proofing chamber in a series of three or six laps or passes. In this type of proover. the trays, on being loaded, are elevated to the top tier and proceeded horizontally back and forth in descending stages

until they reach the discharge level. One of their major advantage is the relatively small floor space required .

- RACK PRQOFER : It is just similar to rack oven. where hot air is replaced by the steam.

OVEN: Oven is sometime referred to as the heart of the bakery. The construction and design of modern ovens depend on types of products to be baked. nature of the fuel to be used. system of heat application & mode of its transmission, flexibility for 3 controlling the amount & intensity of heat and the cost of oven construction, operation & maintenance. Looking to all the above factors most of the small and medium scale bakeries in India use fire-wood oven. But the main drawback of this type of oven is no facility of controlling the temperature hence it requires long experience to maintain and handle such ovens. The large scale baking units may use the electric oven but the operating cost (i .e. cost of electric fuel) is too high. hence it is not preferred much. However, it will be much popular in high class small scale bakeries like bakery division of five star hotels. Diesel fired ovens are preferred as they are cheaper than electric fuel for large scale operations. However, wherever gas (LPG) supply is easily available. gas-oven can also be used. Recently. microwave ovens are introduced for baking purpose. But their use is still limited to the household baking as it is quite costly and requires lots of research. It is important to note that, in the case of microwave oven, the caramelization of sugar does not take place hence there is no browning of the products, therefore it is not accepted because of colour consciousness of the consumers. Some of the modern ovens are:

Reel Oven : They consist of a reel structure that revolves vertically around a horizontal axis within the baking chamber and supports the baking trays in fly-wheel fashion. They require large baking chamber (to accommodate big reel) and more heat consumption hence not accepted by bakers. Moreover, the heat distribution is not proper and moisture may condensed on top portion of the oven hence baking of product is not proper. Reel ovens are normally heated by direct firing with electricity or gas.

Travelling Tray Oven: In this type of oven, two parallel endless chains are replaced to reel of oven, which carry trays through the baking chamber, the third chain acting to stabilize the trays horizontal position during baking cycle. These ovens may be single-lap or double-lap.

Tunnel Oven: It features a long, low baking chamber through which a motor-driven conveyer, carrying the baking hearth, passes in straight line. The length of the chamber may be of 30 to 12.0 m (100 to 400 ft) that is divided into I to 8 heat zones. each zone with 9 to 18 m (30 to 60 ft) length. Each zone has a specific control on temperature and rho The product is loaded from one end and is unloaded from the opposite end.

This kind of oven has several advantages:

- It posses flat and continuous hearth hence any size and shape of pan can be used.
- Zone temperature control is facilitated by providing separate control for both top and bottom heat and for balancing the heat across the oven width.
- Optimum steam conditions are established easily and effectively.

These features render the oven particularly effective for cookie and cracker baking.

Conveyerized Oven: This is developed when integrated approach for continuous proofing and baking is adopted. The oven consists of an enclosure formed by insulated panels, supported by a steel frame. It houses an endless conveyer, which is arranged either in ascending or descending spirals or tiers about the periphery. Depending the particular design, the panned product enters the oven through a small opening either at the top or the bottom of the unit. It travels the total length of the interior conveyer as it bakes and then exits again at either a high or low level. Because every pan passes through the sarne path, a high degree of uniformity of bake is achieved.

Rack Oven: It consists basically of a. vertical baking chamber into which a special rack carrying as many as 100 trays of product is wheeled. The rack rests on a turn table that rotates during the baking phase and thereby exposes the product to uniform convection heating. They may be heated by electricity, gas or fuel oil, and may feature computerized programmable controls for regulating temperature, steam condition and baking cycle.

PRODUCT HANDLING MACHINE: After baking the bakery products are depanned, cooled. sliced (if necessary) and packed. The equipments required for all these processing are:

Bread Cooler: At present. room of suitable conditions is used for cooling the bakery products so that atmospheric conditions does not affect on cooling. The different types of coolers are:

(i) *Continuous Belt Cooler:* This cooler, consists of endless, multiple-tier overhead conveyers that travel in straight flights with 1800 turns at the end of each flight which transport the bread through a 60 to

90 minutes cooling cycle. The flights are generally open on all sides. with an overhead fan exhausting the heat radiating from the loaves to the exterior or they may be enclosed with panels to form a tunnel like structure.

(ii) *Tray Cooler:* In this cooler. trays replace the conveyer belt. It usually consists of stain less steel grills mounted on steel frames that are attached to parallel standard roller chains with the drive sprockets located at the conveyer loops. In loading this type of bread cooler. the loaves being fill continuously from the depanner must be grouped and material for transfer onto the trays or pallets.

(iii) *Rack Cooler:* This is similar to rack oven of bread processing. It is generally air conditioned and hence enclosed and frequently the exterior panels of rack coolers are omitted which facilitates the flow of natural convection air currents through the racks. However, the usually dense concentration of loaves that is found in rack coolers during operation may require forced air circulation to improve the cooling rate.

(iv) *Vacuum Cooler:* This is relatively a new cooling system. Here cooling is carried out by modulated vacuum which brings about very rapid reduction in product temperature. The system consists of a conveyer within a tunnel that serves as the vacuum chamber and whose ends are provided with vertical doors that form an airtight seal when closed. A pivoting bridge conveyer at each end of the tunnel effects the transfer of the product onto the interior conveyer and to the discharge conveyer.

Slicer: Despite many a precautions, the bread loaf cannot be sliced properly by hand. hence every bread producer must purchase bread slicer. Generally reciprocating slicers are used for slicing purpose. In which, straight blades are mounted (at intervals that yield the desired slice thickness) on two frames which move up and down in opposite directions at a high speed. This reciprocating motion is imparted to the frames by a small electric motor through a crank-shaft and levers. Slicing is performed by gently pushing the loaf through the oscillating blades. The frames may be mounted either vertically. in which case the bread conveyer feeding the cutting zone is slanted at a downward angle or they may be tilted toward the feed side, in which case the conveyer is then on a level plane. The purpose is to obtain angle cutting and to have the top crust of the loaf contact the cutting blades first.

The other types of slicers are continuous band slicer. disc slicer etc.

Packing Machine: Normally. the bakery products packed in a polyethylene bags at present. The cottage scale baker seals the bag with candle but it does not look attractive. Instead of that a plate type electric heater is attached to a table. which seals the bag when touches is recommended. The machines are developed on the same basis which can either be foot or hand operated. It seals the bag in between two arm of the machine.

21

Oven

INTRODUCTION: It is advisable to get constructed the firewood oven by specialist (skilled mason) because they make a perfect oven, it would bake the product properly with minimum wastage of heat. However, if the specialists are not available, it can be constructed by ordinary mason. For that, the following information would be useful.

SIZE OF THE OVEN: The size of the oven is to be decided on the quantity of product to be baked at a time. Normally, oven having hearth area of 2.44 m x 1.83 m (8' x 6') [i.e. about 4.65 sq mt (50 sq ft)] is sufficient to bake 100 bread loaves of 400 gm each. But some ordinary baker/oven specialist decides the size of oven on the number of trays that could be arranged at a time in the oven for baking (for example 25 trays, 30 trays etc.) space and it is estimated that generally one tray is equivalent to about 0.09 sq m (1 sq ft). While calculating the space for so man) trays, the space of first row should not be included as it is used to collect the coal hence can not be utilized for baking purpose. So area of 25 trays means hearth area of 2.79 sq m (30 sq ft) [i.e. 2.33 sq m (25 sq ft) for baking + 0.46 sq m (5 sq ft) as non baking area)].

CONSTRUCTION OF OVEN: Following are some of the -points which may be useful while constructing brick oven:

- Construct four walls [45 cm (18'" thick)] as boundary with clear hearth area according to requirement. Height of the walls (i.e. height from floor to hearth) should be about 100cm (40"), so that oven-man need not have to bend while operating the oven. Presently the oven is constructed in such a way that oven-man can operate it while sitting.

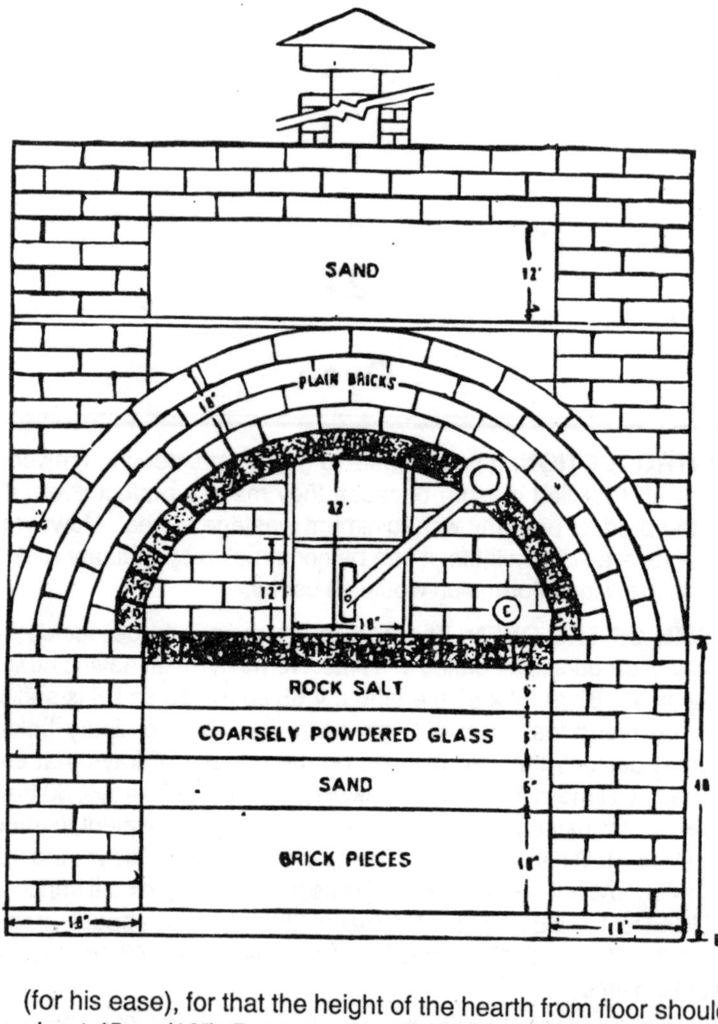

(for his ease), for that the height of the hearth from floor should be about 45cm (18"). But the total height of the hearth should be 100 cm (40"), hence there is need to make pit similar to that of the oven size (including walls). A pit [60 to 90 cm (2 'to 3 ')] also made just outside the oven below the door of oven, so oven-man can also operate oven by standing as well as by sitting. The foundation of the oven is allowed to set for 2 days with sprinkling water 3 to 4 times in a day.

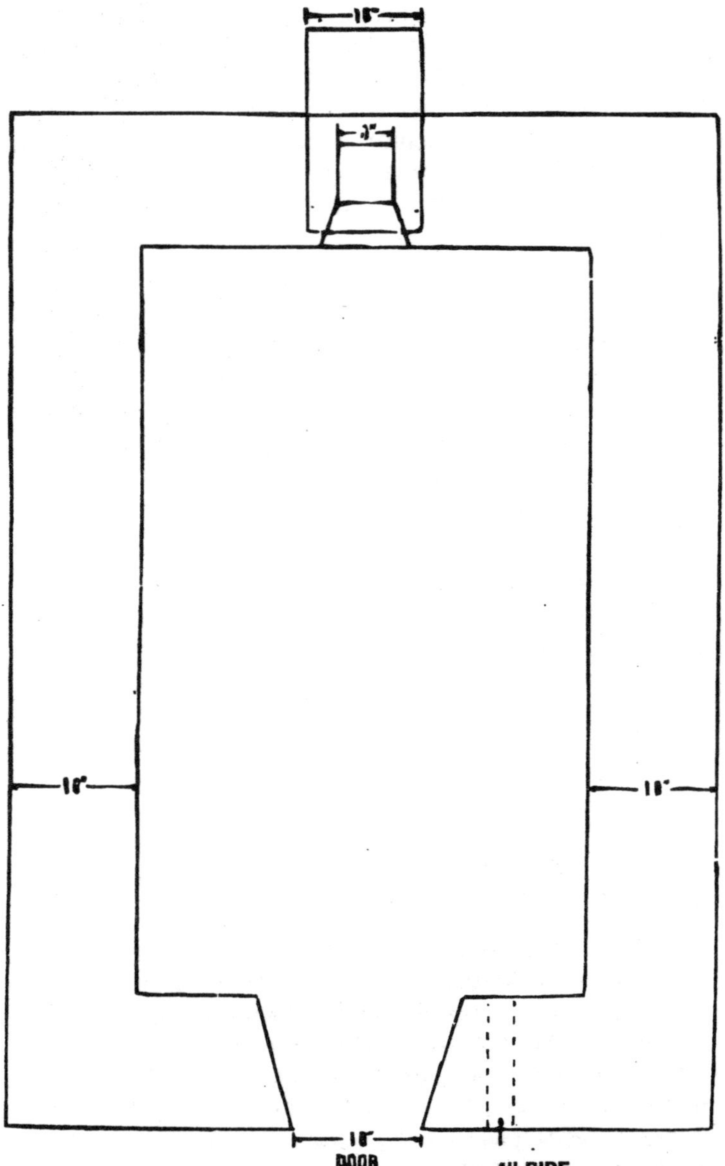

4" PIPE
FOR PLACING
LIGHT ARRANGEMENTS
HORIZONTAL CROSS-SECTION

- Fill-in the brick pieces to a height of 45 cm (18") and pound it lightly in order to set them properly. Fill-in sand on top of the brick pieces to a height of 15 cm (6'") and pound it well so that the gap between brick pieces are filled. On the top of sand, fill broken glass pieces (preferably thick and coloured) and pound. Fill in coarsely powdered rock salt / common salt to a height of 15 cm (6") on top of glass layer. Pound it thoroughly so as to fill any empty pockets down below, which may cause sinking at a later stage. Allow it to settle for overn ight.

- On the top of salt layer, spread thin layer of fire-cement and on that layer arrange firebricks on sides (i.e. breadth of brick should be vertical) close to each other, so as not to have any gap between two bricks. When whole of the surface is covered with bricks, spread a very thin paste of fire -cement on bricks, so that any gap inadvertently left between the bricks will be filled. Allow it to settle for overnight. This part of the oven is known as hearth.

- Using the inner side of the foundation wall as the starting point of the curve, erect at false-dome with loosely knitted bricks and mud plaster. Spread about 1.25 cm (1/2") thick mud plaster on this dome and spread another layer of sand about 0.65 cm (1/4") thick. Over that layer spread another layer of thick plaster made from the fire-cement (one can spread 2.5 cm (1 ")thick layer of sand directly on false dome instead of mud, sand and fire-cement layers). The bricks should be so loosely placed that they could be pulled out easily after real-dome is set. Secondly these bricks should be placed in such a way that the height of the center part of the real-dome from hearth should be 56 to 61 cm (22" to 24"). However, for a big oven this height should be 75 to 90 cm (2½' to 3').

- On the top of that, arrange firebricks on the side (same as above) so as to leave minimum gap between two bricks in the inner side. Special fire bricks are also available for this purpose which have one side thinner than the other so as to arrange conveniently in a dome shape that are termed as tapperedfire bricks. Fill the gaps between the bricks with plaster of fire-cement and sand. Allow it to set atleast for 3 days sprinkling water 2 to 3 times a day. Now pullout the loosely knitted bricks of the false dome and clean the hearth as well as dome of the oven.

- In order to prevent heat loss, as it always goes upside, 2 to 3 layers of plain bricks are placed over the firebricks in curve with cement and sand, so that the thickness of the dome would be 40 to 50 cm (16" to 20"). It is better to spread a layer of insulation-bricks (it is costly, light in weight) on the firebricks for this purpose.
- Before constructing dome, decide the place of chimney. It is desired to construct chimney at the back-end of the oven. Because wood is to be fired at that end, so that the smoke directly escapes from the chimney and does not enter in the working place. However, it can also be constructed in the front wall of the oven. Chimney should be placed exactly at the center of the dome and one end of the chimney should be open in the hollow part of the oven. If chimney is placed at the back-end of the oven, damper should be provided in the chimney, so that chimney could be opened while firing the oven and then can be closed while baking operation is carried on. The size of chimney should be 20 cm (8") in diameter, no doubt two chimneys are more useful instead of one [in that case diameter of chimney should be atleast 15cm (6")]. Chimney should be atleast a couple offeet taller than the tallest building in the immediate neighbourhood for efficient functioning and neighbour does not have smoke problems. Place a hood at the top of chimney twice the area of chimney.
- Construct back-wall with plain bricks. Then eonstruct front wall with a space in the center for oven-door [45 cm x 30 cm (18" x 12")] made up of iron. Insert a china clay or asbestos pipe of 10 cm (4") diameter near the door. approximately 15cm (6") above the hearth level (measured from the lower side of the pipe) across the wall, so that bulb can be placed for lighting inside the oven. A pirexy dish can be placed at the end of the pipe flushed with the inside wall of the oven. Keep lid at the outer side of the pipe to prevent escaping of heat. Instead of pipe place an iron-rod on the top most part of the out side the door and hanging down a bulb. Allow to set these both the walls, sprinkling water 2 to 3 times a day .
- A dial thermometer with rod can be placed in the front-wall to a height of 15cm (6") from the hearth to know the temperature.
- Now construct all the four walls 30 cm (12") taller than dome. Fill the top of dome with sand and place a layer of bricks on the sand to prevent dispersal of sand.

- Rest the oven for 15 days after construction before firing. Firing of the oven should be increased gradually in order to prevent any damage due to fierce heat.

Notes:

- Fire-cement can be replaced by the fireclay or mud and jaggery Uaggery is diluted in water and mixed with mud).
- The simple construction is to be made with cement and sand at the ratio of 1 :4 while fire-cement plaster is to be made with fire-cement and sand at the ratio of 1:6.
- Construction of walls can also be made with mud + sand

MATERIAL REQUIREMENT: Before starting any construction, it is necessary to have an idea about the material requirement. Following is the rough estimation for the oven of 183 cm x 152 cm (6' x 5') i.e 2.79 sq m (30 sq ft) size.

Material	Quantity
Fire bricks	400 nos
Plain bricks	3000 nos
Glass pieces	45 kg
Rock salt	450 kg
Brick pieces	1 no tractor
Sand	½ no tractor
Cement	15 bags (50 kg each)
Fire cement / Fireclay	7 bags (50 kg each
Grog (to be mixed with fireclay)	2 bags (50 kg each
Iron door with frame [45 cm x 30 cm (18" x 12")] (Heavy gauge)	1 no
Damper (if chimney placed at the back-end)	1 or 2 no
Chimney [20 cm (8") diameter if one] [15 cm (6") diameter if two]	1 or 2 no
Top of chimney	1 or 2 no
Dial thermometer with rod	1 no

Notes:

- Discarded firebricks from glass factory may be used for oven, which will help to reduce cost.
- Hood of the chimney could be made from Dabba, which reduces price.

HANDLING OF OVEN:

- Wood is to be fired at the back-end of the oven, which ensures proper distribution of heat, necessary for proper baking. A damper, which is simply a flat piece of steel sheet [atleast 0.42 cm (1/16") thick] is kept out from chimney after the oven has been fired. If the chimney is at the front wall, the door should be opened only enough to allow the proper amount of air to enter the oven for good combustion.
- Once the fire has died down. spread burning coal evenly on hearth and close the damper and the door tightly and allow to rest for 30 minutes. which is known as rest period. This is very important to allow the accumulated heat in the dome to come down and heat the hearth. Then the ash can be pushed to one corner and start the baking.
- During loading of the oven keep the door open only enough to let the pans and trays pass through and as soon as the oven is loaded (in the shortest time possible) close the door tightly. This prevents loss of heat and maintains or replenishes the heat of the hearth.
- Once the oven does not have enough heat for thorough baking of bread, stop the baking and refire the oven. Follow the same procedure again for firing as per the original firing. but the rest period can be cut down for 20 minutes while firing for the second time. Baking should not be done in any circumstances while there is fire in the oven because sometimes it results in the proper colour on top but the sides and bottom remain white and raw. Bread must receive a minimum of 75% heat from the hearth.
- Wood should be dried enough before it is fired. After finishing the baking process for a day, the wood for the next days firing should be put in the warm oven and the door should be closed tightly. This will dry out the wood. Be careful that wood should be placed away from coal otherwise it may get fired during night. Before firing take out the wood that is to be used for the second and third firings.

22

Packaging of Bakery

INTRODUCTION: In the early days packaging considered a merely mean of container for food and therefore, a rough paper, paper-bag or jute bag are used as a packing material. It has several disadvantages like no protection against environmental influences, insect infestation. breakage etc. impairing the safety of the product. In addition to that, the market demand and consumer preference leads to gradual improvement in this trade. As a result now-a-days the bulk to single service packets are marketed in wrapped form and ultimmely packaging becomes whole host of the company.

FUNCTION: Packaging must meet the following requirements:

- It provides mechanical protection to the product, which permit the safer transfer of bakery products from processor through market channel to the consumer. It is possible in case of neat portion packs in the classical enfold style or. by an air (gas) cushion in case of pillow pack.
- It eliminates the hygiene factor risks and thereby protect bakery products from spoilage due to microbial action, damage by insects, rodents and other pests, deterioration by environmental agents like oxygen, moisture, light etc. and thereby preserve the freshness. taste etc. quality of food. The ready-to-sell individual wrapped units are best suited for this purpose.
- It promotes convenience in the use of product and thereby satisfies consumer's demand. i.e. the packet opening facilities (like tear taps. zigzag or incision cut on pillow packs or tin-tie reclosing facilities), ease in eating (like chocolate).

- It maintains the quality characteristics of the product by preventing the transmission of foreign odours to food or the lose of aroma from the food and like wise for other characteristics.
- It serves as a vehicle for providing regulatory information like price, material used. allowed additives. nutritional value etc., as it can be clearly printed on the wrappers. The detail information demanded by consumer can also be displayed in the same fashion .
- It also serves a very good medium for advertising the company. because besides brand name the packets display the manufacturer's name and logo in attractive manner which appeal to the potential customers and stand out against a host of competing products on the retail shelves.

PACKAGING MEDIUM: The polyethylene bags are the most widely used packing material for the bakery products. However, the wax coated papers were used previously by big companies. sometimes for high cost product aluminium foil is used for packing.

Paper: Paper are matted cellulose fiber which have been treated with various chemicals and coated or filled with minerals. plastics etc. When paper used alone, it has in adequate resistance to moisture vapour transfer and grease spotting hence wax coated papers were used for packing bakery products. Previously paraffin wax was used as a coating material to bleached paper, later on it was blended with microcrystalline wax and polyethethylene resin to improve gloss, flexibility and sealing. The paper lost its identity as soon the flexible films or foils are introduced.

Cellophane: The oldest flexible film known is cellophane introduced in 1930 in bakery. It being transparent material gained widespread acceptance in baking industry. It is coated with nitrocellulose or polyvinylidene chloride to improve oil resistance, gas and moisture permeability, heat seal ability etc. Though cellophane was excellent packing material it becomes less popular when polyethylene films were introduced in 1960 due to comparatively high cost.

Polyethylene and Polypropylene: The cellulose films were replaced by plastic polyolefin films in the form of polyethylene and polypropylene. That is made into different strength, stiffness, temperature sensitivity and permeability etc. High. medium and low densities polyethylene film, possessing 1.0. 1.25 and 1.5 mm thickness is widely used for bakery products in performed bags. The film greater than 0.935 mm thickness contributes good stiffness. low moisture vapour transfer rate (MVTR) and fairly good grease resistance. Lower density versions permit good sealing but are relatively low in oil and grease resistance. Polypropylene also possesses all these properties but it is stiffer and tougher at equivalent thickness. The detail is summarized in the below table:

Type	Product
• Low density polyethylene (LOPE)	• All fermented products like bread, bun etc.
• High density polyethylene (HOPE)	• Cakes and cookies
• Bi-oriented polypropylene (BOPP)	• Biscuits

Special printing inks and methods make possible to produce printed films having wide range of designs and colours for merchandising needs. Medium density polyethylene film is normally used for this purposes. However. if the firm is intended for use as a heated - sealed wrapper, a special heat - sealing coating is applied to one side to ensure a secure seal.

Aluminium Foil: The main advantage of aluminium foil is its moisture transmission rate. which is approximates zero when the material is properly used. There is also decorative potential, which can be utilized in many container designs. Because of its opacity, foil affords complete protection against acceleration of fat oxidation by light. Hence, it will be quite useful for fried products like doughnut.

PACKAGING STYLE: There are several popular wrapping style, out of that two important are:

Endfold Wrapping: This is classic. traditional packing style, where the product standing on edge is roll-wrapped or foldwrapped into heat sealable film. The longitudinal packet seal is sealed tightly in a fine seal style. Then the packets ends are folded neatly and heat sealed. This packet gives very good mechanical protection to biscuit type products. Secondly, it gives clear idea of product shape hence better for market presentation compare to pillow type packing.

Pillow Pack Wrapping: The air (gas) is filled in the packing bag, gives pillow like shapes. The gas introduced has ability to preserve the product for longer time. The packing also useful for odd size product. But it has poor mechanical strength. i.e. a small pin-hole make possible to lose the gas and finally no mechanical strength is saved. Hence, such packs must be repacked in secondary containers like boxes for ease in transportation and presentation.

23

Formulae of Fermented Products

General Procedure:

The dough for the fermented products like bun, bread, toast, doughnut, pitza etc. are made by the following procedure:

1. Sieve the flour. If the formula contains bread improvers and preservatives or any other ingredients into powder form, mix into flour before sieving.
2. Take part (about 1/10th of total requirement) of luke warm [i.e. body temperature (37°C - 98.6°F)] water. Add a part (about 1/5th of total requirement) of sugar in it.
3. Add the crumbled yeast and allow to rest aside (for about 5 to 10 min) till it disintegrates and starts to float on the water. If yeast does not disintegrate, it is understood that the yeast is of poor quality. Hence, throw it away and follow the same procedure with fresh yeast.
4. Add sufficient flour to make thin paste and whisk it to incorporate some air. Leave it for 10 to 15 min. during which the paste will arise. That helps in vigorous yeast action.
5. Dissolve salt and left over sugar in remaining water and strain to remove extraneous matter. If formula contains milk powder, add it at this stage in such a way that, it does not make lumps. Add acetic acid at this stage, if formula contains.
6. Add this water in to flour, roughly mix, add the yeast-paste and knead well to prepare a smooth dough. Add shortening (and GMS, ifformula contains) at the last stage of mixing and made a clear dough.

7. Cover the dough with wet cloth and keep it aside for a stipulated time at 26.6 °C (80°F) and 75 rh for *bulkfermentation.*

8. Press out the gas produced after 2/3 of bulk fermentation time. That is known as *knock back.*

9. Divide the dough into the desired size pieces. (The weight of pieces must be 12% extra than the desirable bread weight). That is termed as *dividing / scaling.*

10. Round each dough pieces and allow to rest for 10 min. Technically it is termed as *rounding* & *intermediate proofing.* Use sharp cutter for dividing, do not stretch with hand.

11. Mould the dough pieces. Place it in a greased bread tin, cover the lid and rest for about I hr for *proofing* at 35 to 36°C (95 to 98°P) & 80 to 85 rho

12. Bake and remove from the pan immediately after baking and place on cooling rack. Apply fat on crust.

13. Cool the bread completely for 2 to 3 hr and slice & pack.

Tips:

1. Now-a-days, specialised bread-fats containing improvers, emulsifiers etc. are marketed, which make the bread softer and smoother and keep it fresh for long time.

2. The quantity of water absorbed by flour varies with so many factors. Hence, it should be added in sufficient quantity to obtain desired dough consistency.

3. Commercially, yeast is available in three forms *wet* (compressed / flesh), *dry* and *instant.* They are available in rectangular blocks, granulated & powder form respectively. The average indian baker prefers wet yeast due to its less price & better result of reliability. If a baker uses dry or instant yeast, its quantity should be cut down to half than the wet yeast.

4. Some bakers use oil instead of fat / shortening. In such cases, care must be taken that the smoking point of the oil is high otherwise it may produces smoke - flavour in products.

5. Pan release oil is available commercially, which can replace the fat / oil used for pan greasing. The pan - release - oil may be cheaper than fat / oil.

SIMPLE BREAD

Formula

No	Ingredient	Per cent	Weight		
			White Bread	Whole Meal Bread	Brown Bread
1	Flour	100	10 kg	-	500 gm
2	Shortening	1 to 10	200 gm	20 gm	20gm
3	Sugar	2 to 10	500 gm	50 gm	50 gm
4	Yeast	1 to 2	100 gm	20 gm	20 gm
5	Water	55 to 65	6 lt	600 ml	600 ml
6	Salt	1.5 to 2.5	200 gm	4 tsp	4tsp
7	Bread improvers	0.05	1 tsp	1/8 tsp	1/8 tsp
8	G.M.S.	0.2	4 tsp	1/2 tsp	1/2 tsp
9	Acetic acid	0.1 to 0.2	4 tsp	1/2 tsp	1/2 tsp
10	Calcium propionate	0.35	35 gm	3/4 tsp	3/4 tsp
11	Whole meal flour (Wheat flour)	100/50	—	l kg	500 gm

Baking Temperature	Time	Production
230°C (450°F)	25 to 30 min	**White Bread:** 35 to 40 No (400 gm) **Whole Meal & Brown Bread:** 3 No (400 gm)+ 1 No (200 gm)

Method :

1. Prepare the bread as per the procedure given. The bulk fermentation time will be 3 hr and 1/2 hr in case of white/plain bread & other breads respectively.

(Round Bread)

Method:

1. Prepare bread dough, ferment for 40 min, knock-back.
2. Divide into about 500 gm, round it & allow to rest for 30 min.
3. Mould into round shape, put on greased tray, flatten after 5 min and final proof for 45 min.
4. Follow rest of all the process.

(Tiger Skin Bread)

Method:

1. Prepare the dough as per the procedure.
2. Allow to ferment for 40 min, knock-back & weighed into desired size & mould.
3. Deep the top portion of moulded dough into a smooth tiger skin paste, place on tray and proof 50 to 60 min.
4. Follow the other procedure.

Tiger Skin Paste: (for 10 kg flour)

No.	Ingredient	Weight
1.	Rice Flour	750 gm
2.	White bread crumb	750 gm
3.	Water (luke warm)	1.5 lt
4.	Sugar (Best Quality)	90 gm
5.	Oil	75 gm
6.	Salt	30 gm
7.	Yeast	50 gm

(Seasoned Bread)

Method:

I. Any of the above bread can be made into seasoned bread. For that, apply water or milk wash on the top of moulded/panned dough. Then deep dough top/sprinkle the tops with sesame seed / poppy seed or desired material [about 2 to 10% (i.e. 500 gm for 10 kg flour)] and follow the rest of the procedure.

(Malteser Bread)

Method:

1. Prepare a bread dough. Ferment for 1 hr at 28°C (82°F).
2. Divide into 100 gm pieces, mould into round shape & proof for 45 to 60 min.
3. Make about 1 to 2 cm (½ to 1") deep cut in the middle : with sharp edges before baking. Care must be taken that dough gas does not come out in large quantity.
4. Bake at 230°C (440 - 450°F) for 30 to 40 min.

(French Bread)

Method:

1. Prepare dough as per the procedure. till panning process.
2. After ½ hr proofing, make about 2.5 cm (1") deep cut at 5 cm (2") distance with sharp edges.
3. Apply egg / milk - sugar - solution wash and seasoned with sesame seed at about 5% rate(i.e. 500 gm for 10 kg flour).
4. Allow to proof for some more time, if desired.
5. Bake at 190°C (395°F) for 20 min, take it out of oven, apply egg / milk-sugar-solution wash and rebake for 20 min.

Tips:

1. In case of brown bread, the proportion of whole meal flour and white flour can be changed to individual preference.
2. When proportion of sugar & shortening is increased, the quantity of yeast should also to be increased.
3. If salt of good quality is used, the proportion is to be reduced.
4. There are some other methods of bread preparation like sponge & dough method, salt delay method, no dough time method.
5. Some bakers also add custard powder/vanilla powder at the rate of 0.5 to 2.0 %(i.e. 260 gm for 10 kg flour) which provides specific taste & smell to the bread. However, it is not acceptable to all customers.
6. The volume of whole meal bread & brown bread will be smaller compared to white bread & simultaneously its colour is also dark brown & brown respectively. However, its nutritional value (minerals & vitamins) will be higher & will digest better due to presence of fibre.

(RICH BREAD)

Milk Bread, Fruit Bread, Sweet Bread, Sultana Bread

No	Ingredient	Per cent	Weight			
			Milk Bread	Sweet Bread	Fruit Bread	Sultana Bread
1	Flour	100	10 kg	10 kg	10 kg	10 kg
2	Shortening	5 to 15	800gm	1.5 kg	l kg	750 gm
3	Sugar	5 to 25	1.5 kg	2.5 kg	2.5 kg	500 gm
4	Yeast	2 to 5	200gm	200gm	200 gm	400 gm
5	Milk powder	1 to 10	600gm	100 gm	150gm	350 gm
6	Salt	1 to 3	200gm	250 gm	250 gm	160gm
7	Water	55 to 65	6.2 lt	5.5 lt	5.5 lt	61t
8	Tutee fruity	5 to 10	-	-	500 gm	-
9	Mix dry fruit	5 to 10	-	-	500 gm	-
10	Sultana	50	-	-	-	5 kg
11	Custard powder	2 to 4	-	-	400 gm	-
12	Vanilla powder	2 to 4	-	-	400 gm	-
13	Colour (yellow)	0.25 to 0.5	-	-	as des	-
14	Bread improvers	0.05 to 0.1	1 tsp	1 tsp	1 tsp	1 tsp
15	Acetic acid	0.1 to 0.2	4 tsp	4 tsp	4 tsp	4 tsp
16	Calcium propionate	0.35 to 0.5	35 gm	35 gm	35gm	35gm

Baking Temperature	Time	Production
205°C (400°F)	20 to 30 min	38 to 40 No (400 gm)

Method:

1. Follow the procedure for bread preparation. The bulk fermentation time will be 1.1/2 hr.
2. The custard powder and vanilla powder are sieved with flour, if added.
3. Tutee fruity / dry fruit / sultana are cleaned, washed thoroughly & chopped (if required) and add after bulk fermentation. The care must be taken for thorough dispersion through out the dough. However, for the same reason it may be added at the last stage of mixing operation.

(Cinnamon Sugar Bread)

No	Ingredient	Per cent	Weight
1.	Flour	100	10 kg
2.	Shortening	10	1 kg
3.	Sugar	2 to 5	200 gm
4.	Yeast	3 to 5	300 gm
5.	Water	45 to 50	4.5 lt.
6.	Salt	1.5 to 2.5	200 gm
7.	Milk powder	3 to 5	300 gm
8.	Egg	5	12 no
9.	Sugar(granules)	5 to 8	500 gm
10.	Cinnamon (powder)	0.3 to 0.5	30 gm

Baking Temperature	Time	Production
200°C (400°F)	40 to 45 min	36 to 40 No (400 gm)

Method:

1. Prepare a dough as per the procedure mentioned. Ferment for 1.½ hr with knock - back.
2. Add the filling and mix slowly until the filling is evenly distributed throughout the dough.
3. Scale into 400 to 500 gm weight, mould and proof into greased baking tin / tray for about 20 -30 min. Follow the rest of the procedure.

(OTHER BREAD)
(Masala Bread)

No	Ingredient	Per cent	Weight
1	Flour	100	10 kg
2	Shortening	20	2 kg
3	Sugar	8 to 10	1 kg
4	Yeast	1 to 2	200 gm
5	Salt	2.5 to 3.0	250 gm
6	Water	55 to 65	6 lt
7	Onion	10	1 kg
8	Green chilly	2 to 3	250 gm
9	Coriender leaves	2 to 3	Small bunch
10	Oil	0.5 to 1.0	to saute

Baking Temperature	Time	Production
200°C (400°F)	20 min	38 to 40 No. (400 gm)

Method:

1. Make a dough with first six ingredients as mentioned in procedure.
2. Allow to rest for 10 min.
3. Meanwhile chop the onion, green chillies, coriender leaves. Heat the oil, saute and cool.
4. Add to the dough and mix.
5. Allow to ferment for 1.1/2 hr. and follow the remaining procedure.

(Potato Barm Bread)

Formula :

No	Ingredients	Per cent	Weight
	Part-I :		
1	Potato	3	300 gm
2	Flour	7	700 gm
3	Yeast	0.5	50 gm
4	Sugar	0.2	4 tsp
5	Water	10	1 lt
	Part-2 :		
6	Flour	93	9.300 kg
7	Sugar	4.8	480 gm
8	Salt	2	200 gm
9	Shortening	2	200 gm
10	Water	50	51t
	Baking Temperature 230°C (450°F)	**Time** 25 to 30 min	**Production** 36 to 38 No (400 gm)

Method:

Part - 1 (Prepare before 24 hr of dough preparation) :

1. Boil the potato, peel off and mesh.
2. Add yeast and sugar into water. Rest for 10 min.
3. Add it into flour.
4. Mix the meshed potato and rest for 25 hours.

Part - 2 :

5. Add salt and sugar into water.
6. Add this sugar - salt solution into flour and mix roughly.

7. Add the slurry of part - 1 and prepare a dough.
8. Mix the shortening and knead thoroughly to obtain smooth dough.
9. Now follow the bread making process as shown. However, it requires about 2 hr proofing period.

Bread (Sponge & Dough Method)

Formula :

No	Ingredient	Per cent	Weight
	Part - 1 :		
1	Flour	60	6 kg
2	Yeast	0.5	50 gm
3	Sugar	3	300 gm
4	Water	45	4.5 lt
	Part -2 :		
5	Flour	40	4 kg
6	Shortening	2	200 gm
7	Sugar	2	200 gm
8	Salt	2 to 3	200 gm
9	Water	15	1.5 lt

Baking Temperature	Time	Production
230°C (450°F)	25 to 30 min	37 to 39 No. (400 gm)

Method:

Part - 1 (Prepare before 8 to 12 hr) :

1. Sieve the flour.
2. Dilute sugar and yeast into water. Mix the flour when yeast start to float on water.
3. Rest it for 8 to 12 hr that is known as *sponge.*

Part - 2 :

1. Sieve the flour.
2. Dilute sugar and salt into water.
3. Add the sugar - salt solution into flour and mix roughly.
4. Mix sponge and prepare a dough.
5. Add shortening and knead well to obtain smooth dough.
6. Now follow the procedure given.

(TOAST / RUSK)

No	Ingredient	Per cent	Weight			
			Sweet Toast	Ajmeri Toast	Jeera Toast	Rusk
1	Flour	100	10 kg	10 kg	10 kg	10kg
2	Vanaspati	8 to 12	800 kg	1 kg	1 kg	1.2 kg
3	Oil	5	-	500 gm	500 gm	-
4	Sugar	15 to 25	1.5 kg	2.0 kg	500 gm	2.5 kg
5	Yeast	1.5 to 2.5	200gm	250 gm	250 gm	250 gm
7	Milk powder	2 to 6	600gm	200gm	200 gm	300 gm
8	Salt	1 to 3	200gm	150gm	250 gm	100gm
9	Water	55 to 65	6 lt	6 lt	6 lt	6 lt
10	Tutti fruity	5 to 10	500gm	-	-	-
11	Mix dry fruit	5 to 10	500gm	-	-	-
12	Colour (yellow)	0.1 to 0.25	as des	-	-	-
13	Cardamom & nutmeg (powder)	0.5 to 1.0	-	100 gm	-	
14	Vanilla powder	0.5 to 1.0	-	50gm	-	-
15	Cumin seed	2 to 3	-	-	250 gm	-
16	Sesame seed	5 to 7	-	500gm	-	
17	Bread improvers	0.05 to 0.1	1 tsp	1 tsp	1 tsp	1 tsp
18	Acetic acid	0.1 to 0.2	4tsp	4 tsp	4 tsp	4 tsp
19	Calcium propionate	0.35 to 0.5	35 gm	35 gm	35 gm	35 gm

Baking Temperature	Time	Production
205°C (400°F)	20 to 25 min	10 to 12 kg

Method:

1. Prepare a dough as per the procedure given on earlier pages. However, mix the powdered ingredients with flour before sieving and colour with sugar - salt solution, if desired.
2. Add tutti fruity / dry fruit or other ingredients (whichever applicable) after proper treatment (i.e. chopping etc.) at the last stage of mixing.
3. Divide into 400 gm (or desired size) pieces. Mould longer then bread [i.e. about 35 to 40 cm (15")]. Apply egg / milk / water wash and seasoned with sesame, if applicable.
4. Place it on greased try / special moulds (which are longer then bread

mould and shorter in width & height). Proof till the desired volume achieved (i.e. about 30 to 45 min).

5. Follow the rest of the procedure.
6. The baked toast - loaf is allowed to cool until it acquires room temperature (3 to 4 hr). Slice it. Arrange each slice on baking sheet separately and dry in oven at 80 to 90°C 175 to 190°F) temperature for about 2 hr.

Rusk

Method:

1. Cut the fermented dough into 40 to 50 gm pieces into finger - shape. (Use refined oil to prevent skinning while moulding each pieces).
2. Place the dough pieces into greased tray closely in a line (pressed together lengthwise). Fill the whole tray leaving about 2.5 cm (1") space between the lines. Proof for 30 to 45 min & bake.
3. Allow to cool. While the rusk are still warm, separate each piece and arrange on baking sheet closely together and dry.

Note: This kind of rusk has finger texture and enhanced crispness. That are very popular in rural areas (for single - piece - selling) among children.

Tip:

1. Some bakers only use flour, yeast, salt and sugar as ingredients for rusk dough.

(BUN / ROLL)

No	Ingredient	Per cent	Weight
1	Flour	100	10 kg
2	Shortening	8 to 12	800 gm
3	Sugar	15 to 25	1.5 kg
4	Yeast	1.5 to 2.5	200 gm
5	Milk powder	3 to 6	600 gm
6	Salt	1 to 2	200 gm
7	Water	60 to 65	6.5 lt
8	Tutee fruity	5 to 10	500 gm
9	Mix dry fruit	5 to 10	500 gm
10	Colour (yellow)	0.1 to 0.25	ad des

11 Bread improvers	0.05 to 0.1	1 tsp
12 Acetic acid	0.1 to 0.2	4 tsp
13 Calcium propionate	0.35 to 0.5	35 gm
Baking Temperature	**Time**	**Production**
205°C (400°F)	20 to 25 min	**Bun** 350 to 370 No (50 gm) **Soup stick**: 700 to 750 No.

Method:

1. Prepare dough as per the procedure given. Allow to ferment for 1.1/2 hr along with knock- back.
2. Now shape it differently as below:
- Made into 30 gm pieces and prepare different shaped **dinner - rolls.**
- Add tutee fruity and / or dry fruit (which are chopped to desired size), weigh into 50 to 100 gm pieces and round it to prepare fruit bun.
- For **simple bun**, don't add dry fruit /tutee fruity.
3. Place all these on a greased tray mould and proof till the desired volume achieved (about 30 min). However, the buns are pressed after 15 to 20 min with fat - hand). Follow the rest of the procedure.

Soup Stick

Method:

1. Prepare a dough similar to dinner - roll and ferment.
2. Weigh into 25 gm pieces. Roll with the help of fingers to a pencil thickness. Place in a tray and proof for 30 - 40 min & bake.

Plaited Bun

Formula :

No	Ingredient	Per cent	Weight
1	Flour	100	10 kg
2	Shortening	4 to 6	400 gm
3	Sugar	3 to 6	300 gm
4	Yeast	1.5 to 2.0	160 gm
5	Milk powder	4 to 6	400 gm
6	Salt	1 to 2	150 gm
7	Water	50 to 60	5 lt
Baking Temperature		**Time**	**Production**
240° to 250°C (465 to 485°F)		25 to 35 min	***

Method:

1. Make a normal bread dough according to procedure with bulk fermentation period of 1.1/2 hr.
2. Weigh 450 gm dough, round and allow to intermediate proof about 10 min. Pin them out into 3 to 6 no (as required) with an equal length [approximately 30 cm (12")] and thickness string. This is done by giving the dough pieces a pointed shape as a start and from their on start a gradual pinning out. Do not force the dough pieces otherwise they may tear or break.

Finally it will have:

2 - strings of 225 gm
3 - strings of 150 gm
5 - strings of 90 gm
4 - strings of 112.5 gm
6 - strings of 75 gm

3. Start the plaiting with different strings as below:

- **Plaiting with 2 - strings:**

- Attach the strings at the top and keep them in a place with a weight or heavy utensils.
- Now place lover 2 then 2 over 1 and continue the procedure till the strings have been completely plaited.

- **Plaiting with 3 - strings:**

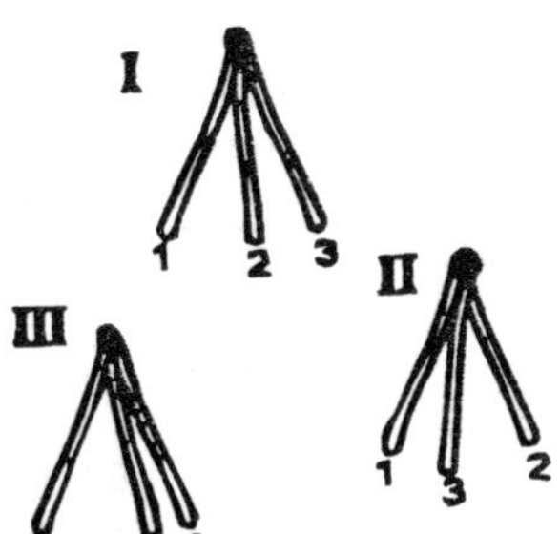

- Keep the strings as shown in figure and attach the strings and place a weight over it.
- The strings are numbered from left to right 1 - 2 - 3.
- Now cross string 3 over and then 1 over 2 as shown in figure II & III.
- Repeat the process till the strings have been completely plaited as shown.

- **Plaiting with 4 - strings:**

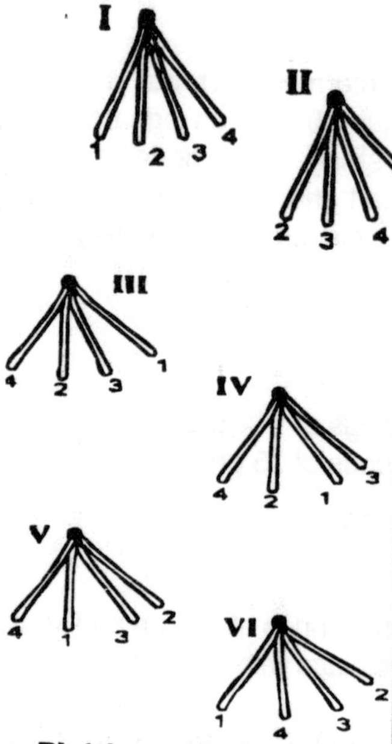

- Keep the strings as shown in figure and numbered from left to right 1 - 2 - 3 - 4.
- Attach the strings at top and keep them in a place with a weight or other heavy utensils.
- Now string are crossed as shown in chart :

Figure	Cross		Position
	String no	Over to string no	
II	1	2-3-4	2-3-4-1
III	4	3-2	4-2-3-1
(This is done only at thebegining and repeat only the following process till strings completely plaitede			
IV	1	3	4-2-1-3
V	2	1-3	4-1-3-2
VI	4	1	1-4-3-2
VII (Not Drown)	3	4-1	3-1-4-2
VIII (Not Drown)	2	4	3-1-2-4

❖ Plaiting with 5-strings :

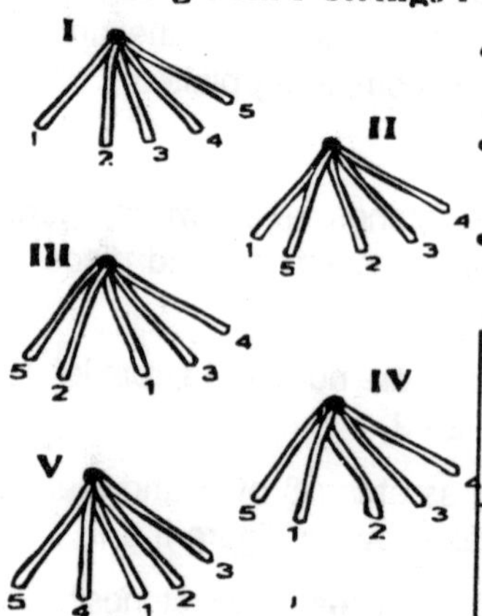

- Arrange the strings as shown in figure I and no them 1-2-3-4-5 from let to right
- Attach the strings at top and keep them in place with a weight or heavy utensils
- Repeat the following procedure till the strings completely plaited.

Figure	Cross		Position
	String no	Over to string no	
II	5	4-3-2	1-5-2-3-4
III	1	5-2	5-2-1-3-4
IV	bring string	i under 2	5-1-2-3-4
V	4	3-2-1	5-4-1-2-3

❖ Plaited with 6-strings :

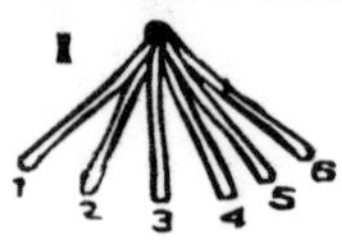

- Place the string as shown in figure-I and numbered them from left to right 1-2-3-4-5-

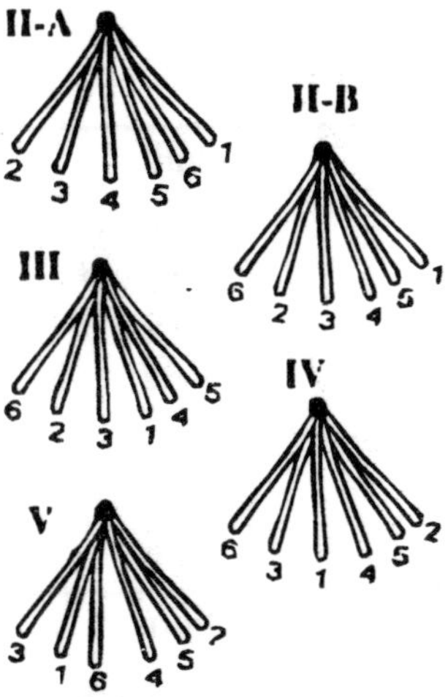

6-. Attach the strings at top.

- Plait the string as shown below :

Figure	Cross: String no	Cross: Over to string no	Position
II-A	1	2-3-4-5-6	2-3-4-5-6-1
& II-B	6	5-4-3-2	6-2-3-4-5-1
(This is done only at the begining of plaiting. Now repeat the following plaiting)			
III	1	5-4	6-2-3-1-4-5
IV	2	3-1-4-5	6-3-1-4-5-2
V	6	3-1	3-1-6-4-5-2
VI (Not drown)	5	4-6-1-3	5-3-1-6-4-2
VII (Not drown)		4-6	5-3-1-2-6-4
& (Not drown)	3	1-2-6-4-	5-1-2-6-4-3

❖ **Winstone :**

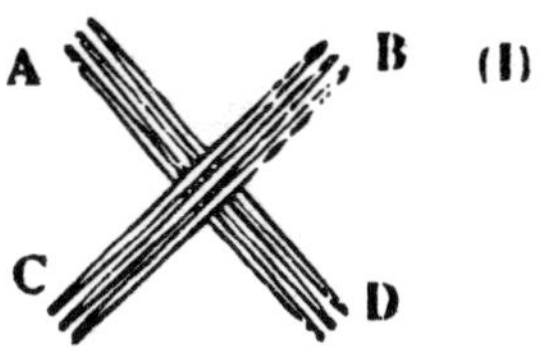

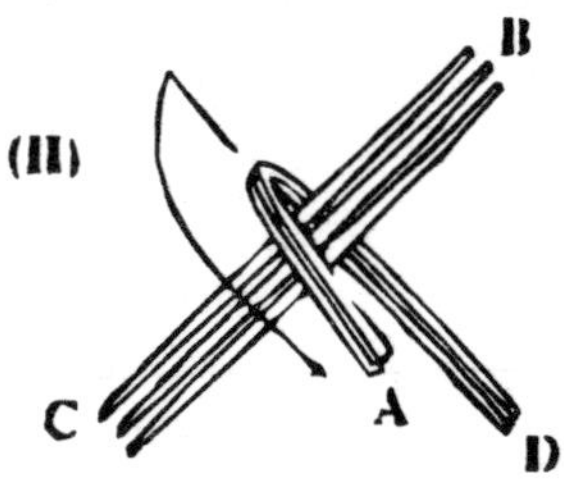

- **Winstone**

Prepare 6 strings as similar to plaited bun. However, the length of strings should be 22.5 cm (9")

- Put one set (i.e. made up of 3 string each) over the other to form an 'X' and mark them 1-2-3-4 as shown in figure-I, And plait the strings as below :

Figure	Fold	Over to	Along side
II	1	3	4
III (Not drown)	4	1	3
IV (Not drown)	3	4	1
V (Not drown)	2	under 1 and over 3	4

4. Put the plaited bun/winston on a baking sheet with sufficient space, brush with egg wash / milk-sugar solution.
5. Proof for 45 to 60 min & bake.

Tip :

1. It has festive look hence extra attention is given during holiday/festival season.

Seli Bun

Formula :

No	Ingredient	Per cent	Weight
1	Flour	100	10 kg
2	Shortening	12 to 15	1.2 kg
3	Sugar	12 to 15	1.5 kg
4	Egg	8 to 10	20 no
5	Yeast	4 to 5	400 gm
6	Milk powder	2 to 3	300 gm
7	Salt	2 to 3	200 gm
8	Water	50 to 60	5 lt
Baking Temperature		**Time**	**Production**
205°C (400°F)		25 to 40 min	39 to 40 No (400 gm)

Method:

1. Prepare a dough as the procedure given. However, a little egg is saved and the remaining is added while preparing a dough.
2. Allow to ferment a dough for 45 min.
3. Divide into 450 gm pieces and place in a suitable cake tin [about 18 cm (7") diameter], cover with damp cloth and proof till double (about 1 hr).
4. Egg wash and bake.

BASIC SWEET DOUGH

Formula :

No	Ingredient	Per cent	Weight
1	Flour	100	10 kg
2	Sugar	15 to 20	2 kg
3	Shortening	12	1.2 kg
4	Yeast	3 to 5	500 gm
5	Water	50	5 lt
6	Egg / Egg yolk	8 to 12	25 no
7	Milk powder	4	400 gm
8	Salt	1.0 to 1.5	100 gm
9	Malt/Liquid glucose	1 to 3	100 gm
10	Mace (powder)	0.5 to l	50 gm
11	Lemon peel (grind)	0.5	50 gm

	To prepare different	products:	
12	Cinnamon (powder)	2 to 3	200 gm
13	Kismis	3 to 5	300 gm
14	Shortening	15 to 20	2 kg
15	Cashewnut	3 to 5	300 gm
16	Jam	2 to 3	200 gm
17	Sugar (granules)	2 to 3	250 gm
18	Mix fruit	20 to 25	2 kg
19	Egg	2 to 3	5 no
20	Cake crumb	3 to 5	300 gm

Baking Temperature	Time	Production
205°C (400°F)	15 to 25 min	—

Method:

1. Prepare a dough as per the procedure mentioned. However, the dry materials like malt, mace powder, lemon peel powder etc. are mixed with flour and egg is added after beating.
2. Allow to ferment for 1 to 1.1/2 hr, knock-back and again relax for 45 min.
3. Now prepare the different items as mentioned below:

Butterfly Bun

Method:

1. Roll out the dough. Brush with egg on all the side to about 1.25 cm (112") width. While the remaining part is brush with shortening (preferably melted butter). Sprinkle with cinnamon powder, sugar (granules), cashewnut, resins, cake crumbs etc. Roll it into a long roll.
2. Cut into desired weight pieces.
3. Press each roll through the centre (with a knife handle) and again press out the folds on the side to make an attractive roll.
4. Allow to proof. When about half proofed, brush with egg wash, finish proofing and bake.
5. After baking finish with glace icing.

Nutty Rolls

Method:

1. Roll out the dough into 5 mm (1/4") thick sheet.
2. Brush lower edge [about 1.25 cm (1/2") width] with egg wash and the remainder with melted butter.
3. Sprinkle. with cinnamon, sugar (granules), cake crumbs and roasted-chopped nuts.
4. Roll up like a jam roll and cut into desired weight pieces.
5. Set upright in pans or in individual Cllp cake moulds.
6. Allow to proof. When half proofed, brush with egg wash and finish proofing & bake.
7. Finish with water icing and chopped nuts.

Jam Filled Buns

Method:

1. Scale the dough into 30 gm pieces.
2. Round up pieces, dip in coarse sugar (granules).
3. Place on bun tray about 5 cm (2") apart.
4. Give half proof. Then make an indentation in the centre of each bun and fill it with jam.
5. Complete proofing and bake.
6. Brush with melted butter/jam immediately after baking.

Cheese Cake

Method:

1. Sheet out the dough [5mm (1/4") thick] and die with a large biscuit-cutter [i.e. about 7.5 cm (3") diameter].
2. Place each piece in the greased mould.
3. Dock with a fork, pour the cheese filling in each mould.
4. Sprinkle cinnamon-sugar mixture on top.
5. Proof slightly and bake.

Hot Cross Bun

Method:

1. Make up sweet dough adding 20 to 25% (i.e 2 to 2.5 kg for 10 kg flour) fruits (raisins, currants, orange peel, tutee fruity, cherry) and spice powder

(cinnamon, nutmeg, clove). Fruits should be added just before mixing is completed. Fruits should be soaked in warm water and drained thoroughly before being used.

2. After proper fermentation (about 1.1/2 hr), scale the dough into pieces of desired weight (approximately 80 gm).
3. Round up and set on bun trays so as to make individual bun or set together to make one whole sheet.
4. When half proofed (30 min), make a cross with sharp blade on each bun. Finish by making a cross with short dough topping. Brush with egg wash.
5. Complete proofing and bake.

Dutch Bread

Method:

1. Prepare the dough similar to hot cross bun (as above). Scale into 250 to 300 gm pieces.
2. Round up and place on baking tray.
3. When half proofed, cut across several times with a sharp blade, brush with egg wash.
4. Complete proofing and baking.
5. Finish with gelatin wash and vanilla icing.

German Coffee Cake

Method:

1. Fill the pan with basic sweet dough.
2. Dock with a fork. Wash with water. Spread butter topping.
3. Proof and bake.

German Coffee Cake (Coconut)

1. After docking, spread over topping made by mixing 500 gm coconut, 150 gm egg and 11.50 gm sugar.

YEAST RAISED FRUIT CAKE

No	Ingredient		Per cent	Weight
1	Basic sweet dough		100	10 kg
2	Sugar (brown)		20 to 25	2 kg
3	Butter		20 to 25	2 kg
4	Egg		14 to 20	40 no
5	Mixed hot spices		0.5 to 1.0	50 gm
6	Molasses		14 to 20	1.5 kg
7	Baking soda		0.25 to 0.4	2 Tsp
8	Fresh liquid milk		10 to 12	1 kg
9	Flour		30 to 40	3.5 kg
10	Fruit mixture (as below) :		80 to 90	8.5 kg
	• Lemon peel	400 gm		
	• Currants	2.3 kg		
	• Figs	1.5 kg		
	• Orange peel	400 gm		
	• Raisins	2.4 kg		
	• Pineapple pieces	1.5 kg		

Baking Temperature	Time	Production
175°C (350°F)	26 Min.	30+ kg

Method:

1. Soak fruits in fruit juice thickened with starch.
2. Cream butter and sugar (brown) and add egg while creaming.
3. Add basic sweet dough and spices.
4. Add molasses and soda dissolved in milk.
5. Add flour & soaked fruits and mix to a homogeneous mass.
6. Put the mixture in paper lined moulds.
7. Proof slightly (about 17 to 22 min) and bake.

DOUGHNUT

Raised Doughnut

No	Ingredients	Per cent	Weight
1	Flour	100	1 kg
2	Sugar	10 to 15	150 gm
3	Shortening	12 to 15	150gm
4	Yeast	3 to 5	40gm
5	Milk powder OR	5 to 10	100gm
	Egg	15 to 20	5 no
6	Salt	1.0 to 1.5	2 tsp
7	Cinnamon (powder)	1.0 to 1.5	2 tsp
8	Nutmeg (powder)	1.0 to 1.5	2 tsp
9	Cardamom (powder)	0.5 to 0.75	1 tsp
10	Essence (vanilla/lemon)	0.5 to 1.0	2 tsp
11	Water	20 to 25	as req
12	Vanspati/Oil (for frying)	45	450 gm
13	Sugar (for decoration)	35	350 gm

Frying Temperature	Time	Production
120°C (250°F)	6 min	41 to 51 No

Method:

1. Add cinnamon powder, nutmeg powder, cardamom powder, milk powder (if added) into flour and sieve twice.
2. Prepare a dough similar to bread preparation. If eggs are used, add (after beating) along with yeast paste.
3. Allow to rest (about 40min). If required knock-back and referment for 30 min.
4. Sheet the dough to desired thickness [0.5 to 1 cm (114 to 1/2")] and cut with doughnut cutter.
5. Proof about 30 min.
6. Fry in a boiled oil/ vanaspati.
7. Allow to cool till becomes slightly warm, roll in a sugar or deep in a sugar syrup or fondant. The syrup or fondant may be made along with coffee, chocolate, strawberry etc.
8. The doughnut can be sliced horizontally into two halves and sandwiched with butter cream and sprinkled with nuts to give special crunch.

Cake Doughnut

Method:

1. Prepare doughnut as the above method. But replace yeast with baking powder at a rate of 2.5% (i.e.25 gm for I kg flour).
2. Mix baking powder into flour along with cinnamon and nutmeg powder and sieve twice.
3. Rub the flour into shortening.
4. Beat egg with essence and add to above mixture.
5. Acid milk / water as required.
6. Prepare smooth dough ball and rest for 15 min.
7. Now follow the procedure from step no 4.

Combination Doughnut

Method:

1. Prepare similar to raised doughnut. But the quantity of yeast should be reduced to 3% (30 gm per I kg flour). And the baking powder should be added at 0.5% (1 tsp for 1 kg flour) . Add baking powder into flour and sieve.

Variation :

Fruit Finger Doughnut

4. Scale 45 gm dough after step no 3 and roll up into finger shape. Proof it and fry.
5. When cool, split horizontally into two exact part. Fill it with chopped seasonal fruits or custard cream and butter cream. May or may not be roll in sugar.

Jam Ball Doughnut

4. Scale 50 gm dough after step no 3 and round, proof and fry.
5. On cooling stuff it with jam alone or jam and butter cream and roll in castor sugar.

Masala Doughnut

1. It can be prepared similar to raised doughnut. Except, add the chopped green masala (below mentioned) before dough preparation. However, the quantity of sugar should be reduced to 50% (50 gm for 1 kg flour) and it is not rolled in sugar/ syrup.

Masala (for 1 kg flour) :

No.	Ingredient	Per cent	Weight
1	Onion	15 to 20	150 gm
2	Green chillies	5 to 10	q.s.
3	Coriander leaves	10 to 15	100 gm
4	Curry leaves	5 to 10	50 gm
5	Garlic, Cumin seed, Salt Cinnamon, Clove, Pepper (Powder) (Each)	2 to 3	as req.

PIZZA

Pizza Base

Formula :

No	Ingredient	Per cent	Weight	
			Simple	Rich Quality
1	Flour	100	1 kg	1 kg
2	Sugar	1 to 3	2 tsp	1 Tsp
3	Shortening	15/50	150 gm	500 gill
4	Yeast	2 to 5	30 gm	50 gm
5	Salt	1.5 to 2.5	3 tsp	3 tsp
6	Water	60 to 65	600 ml	600 ml
7	Milk powder	5 to 6	50 gm	60 grn
8	Egg (yolk) (optional)	6 to 8	60 gm	60 gm
9	Corn grits (optional)	2	20 gm	20 gm

Baking Temperature	Time	Production
205°C (400°F)	9 to 9 min	12 to 14 No.

Method:

1. Rub the shortening into flour and follow bread dough preparation procedure (page no 283).
2. Rest the dough for 20 to 30 min.
3. Knock-back and rest for 15 min (optional).
4. Sheet the dough to 0.5 to 1.0 cm (1/4 to 1/2") thickness and cut into round shape of about 15 to 18 cm (6 to 7") diameter (use of pitza cutter will be beneficial). The scrap dough is mixed and proofed for 5 to 10 min and resheeted.

OR

Divide the dough into 100 to 150 gm pieces. Round and relax for10 to 15 min. Sheet each pieces into round shape like a chapati of above mentioned thickness and size.

5. Place on a baking sheet and dock with a fork.
6. Allow to proof for 15 to 20 min and bake in such a way that bottom gets light brown colour and top surface remains almost white or slightly brownish.

Vegetable Pizza

Formula (for filling) :

No	Ingredients	Per cent (on f. b)	Weight (for 1 kg flour)
1	Tomato sauce	25 to 30	300 gm
2	White/Green chilly sauce	10 to 20	100 gm
3	Cabbage	50	500 gm
4	Onion	25	250 gm
5	Capsicum	5 to 10	50 gm
6	Cheese	25 to 50	250 gm
7	Corn flour	5	50 gm
8	Salt	2 to 3	to taste
9	Black pepper (Powder) Cumin seed, Ajama, Mixed hot spices	2 to 3 (each)	to taste
10	Green chillies	5 to 10	50gm
11	Green masala (Ginger, Coriander leaves etc.)	5 to 10 (each)	to taste
12	Oil/Fat (for frying)	15 to 20	as req
13	Water	5	50 ml

Method:

1. Chop onion, cabbage, green chillies finely.
2. Boil the fat / oil. Saute it with cumin seed.
3. Add green chillies followed by onion and saute till onion gets golden brown.

4. Add green masala followed by cabbage and cover lid and allow to cook (half) for about 15 to 20 min.
5. Meanwhile, mix corn flour into a little water to prepare thick shake.
6. Add corn flour solution into vegetables. Follow by salt and mixed hot spices.

Gravy Pizza

No	Ingredient (on f.b)	Per cent (for 1 kg flour)	Weight
1	Tomato puree OR	200	2 kg
	Tomato	300	3 kg
2	Tomato ketch up (optional)	15 to 25	200 gm
3	Chilly sauce	5 to 10	100 gm
4	Onion	50	500 gm
5	Garlic	5 to 10	100 gm
6	Ginger	5 to 10	50 gm
7	Salt	2 to 3	to taste
8	Black pepper (powder)	2 to 3	to taste
9	Acetic acid (10% strength)	0.5 to 1.0	10 ml
10	Corn flour	3 to 5	30 gm
11	Water	50	as req

Method:

1. Heat the puree/Make puree by boiling, crushing and straining tomato (juice).
2. Meanwhile, chop onion & garlic and grate ginger finely.
3. Add them to boiled tomato puree and continue to boil till it becomes thick.
4. Meanwhile prepare thick paste by mixing corn flour and water.
5. Add tomato ketchup, chilly sauce, salt, pepper and acetic acid into puree.
6. Add corn flour-water paste and boil the gravy until. it acquires spreading consistency.

Variations:

1. Different kinds of fillings can be prepared with the help of mushroom, mince meat, chicken, fish, cheese etc. However, it can be prepared

either as per the vegetable pizza or gravy pizza, with slight alteration required.

2. The pizza may also be variated with flavours by using garlic and such other ingredients.

Formula for Filling

Chanou Pitza

No	Ingredients	Per cent (on f.b)	Weight (for 1 kg flour)
1	Tomato sauce	30 to 50	500 gm
2	White / Green chilly sauce	10 to 20	200 gm
3	Capsicum	5 to 10	100 gm
4	Cheese	25 to 50	500 gm
5	Corn flour	5	50 gm
6	Tomato	200	2 kg
7	Green chilly	20 to 25	200 gm
8	Coriander leaves	50 to 60	500 gm
9	Spring onion	20 to 25	200 gm
10	Noodles	100	1 kg
11	Sesame seed	2 to 5	as req
12	Aji-no-moto	0.25	as req
13	Water	100 to 125	as req

Method:

1. Add noodles into water and boil for about 5 to 10 min.
2. Chop green chilly, coriander leaves (after trimming) and onion leaves finely.
3. Dice the tomato, capsicum and onion.

Assembling (Base and Filling) :

1. Assembling can be done either before or after baking of pizza base:

(i) *Before Baking Base:*

5. After step no 4 for pizza base preparation, spread base with tomato sauce and green chilly / white sauce followed by filling (any type) to about 1.25 to 2.5 cm (1/2 to 1") thickness.

6. Garnish with grated cheese, black pepper powder, ajama and tomato & green chilly sauce. However, garnishing may be carried out after baking which will be more attractive.

7. Rest it for 15 to 20 min and bake at 205°C (400°F) for about 25 to 30 min.

(ii) *After Baking Base:*

1. Turn the pizza base up side down, i.e. the light brown colour should be on top. Brush the surface very lightly with butter/oil.
2. Spread the sauce followed by filling and garnishing as mentioned above.
3. Warm at 205°C (400°F) for 5 to 10 min.

(ii) *Without Baking Base:*

1 Decorate pizza base (as mentioned above) and serve directly.

SURTI BUTTER

No	Ingredient	Per cent	Weight
1	Flour	100	1 kg
2	Shortening	60	600 gm
3	Sugar	2	4 tsp
4	Yeast	2 to 3	20 gm
5	Salt	2 to 3	2 Tsp
6	Water	40 to 45	400 ml
7	Ajwain	1 to 2	4 tsp
8	Cumin seed	1 to 2	4 tsp
Baking Temperature		**Time**	**Production**
205°C (400°F)		16 to 21 min	1.55 kg

Method:

1. Rub 3/4 part of shortening into flour and mix ajma-cumin seed thoroughly.
2. Prepare dough ball as per the bread preparation.
3. Allow to ferment for about 1 hr.
4. Divide dough into pieces of walnut size and made into smooth ball.
5. Place on baking tray to about 2.5 cm (1") distance. Proof for 30 to 45 min and bake it.
6. Allow to cool on cooling rack and dry in oven at 80° to 90°C (175° to 190°F) temperature.The temperature will be obtained in firewood-oven after overnight rest or on the second floor, in case of two-tier-oven along with continuous firing in the first-floor.

STUFFED PRODUCTS

Burger

Formula:

No Ingredient	Per cent	Weight		
		Vegetable	Paneer	Chicken/ Mutton
Fillings (for 400 no) :				
1. Potato/Paneer/ Chicken/Mutton	100	10 kg	10 kg	10 kg
2 Onion	25 to 50	5 kg	5 kg	5 kg
3 Green masala (Coriander leaves, Lemon,Green chilly)	5 to 10 (each)	800 gm	500 gm	500 gm
4 Ginger	2.5 to 3.0	250 gm	250 gm	250 gm
5 Mixed hot spices (powder) (Cinnamon, Pepper,Mixed hot spices)	2 to 3 (each)	as req	as req	as req
6 Miscellaneous masala (Turmeric, Chilly powder, Cumin seed, Mustard seed, Garlic)	2 to 3 (each)	to taste	to taste	to taste
7 Salt	1.5 to 3	to taste	to taste	to taste
8 Vanspati/Oil/Butter (to saute)	5 to 10	500 gm	500 gm	500 gm
9 Acetic acid	1 to 2	100 ml	100ml	100ml
10 Com flour (optional)	5 to 6	-	600 gm	-
11 Egg white (optional)	5 to 6	-	500 gm	-
For stuffing:				
12 Cheese	10 to 30	1.5 kg	1.5 kg	1.5 kg
13 Tomato sauce	20 to 30	2.5 kg	2.5 kg	2.5 kg
14 Soya/White/ Green chilly sauce	10 to 15	1.0 kg	1.0 kg	1.0 kg
15 Butter/Mayonnaise	3 to 5	500 gm	500 gm	500 gm
16 Vanaspati/Butter/Oil	5 to 10	to saute	to saute	to saute

(i) *Filling Preparation Method :*

- VEGETABLE FILLING:

1. Boil potato in salty water, remove skin and mesh them (leaving no lumps).

2. Chop onion, green masala and garlic (optional). Grate ginger finely after washing and trimming.
3. Heat vanspati/butter/oil to saute. Add cumin seed/mustard seed. As soon as it starts cracking add chopped onion, green chilly, garlic and ginger. Fry till the onion turns golden brown ..
4. Add meshed potato and mixed hot spices, cinnamon, clove, pepper, turmeric (optional), chilly powder, lemon/acetic acid, salt, coriander leaves etc.
5. Allow to fry till whole mass becomes somewhat dry.
6. Take off from fire.Allow it to cool and use.

Tip:

1. One may add meshed potato,mixed hot spices, lemon juice/acetic acid once the mass take off from fire. And their after mix thoroughly.

- ***PANEER FILLING:***

1. Grate paneer.
2. Follow the procedure similar to vegetable filling.However,add the corn flour (diluted in little water) and egg white at the last stage in filling .

- ***CHICKEN FILLING:***

1. Mince the chicken/mutton and follow the procedure similar to vegetable filling.

Variation:

1. Round any of the filling mixture,deep it in a beaten egg/milk and coat it with bread crumb. Fry it in hot oil till the crust turns golden brown. And use as filling.
2. Chicken salad,sliced vegetable,green peas may be used as filling (as such) .

(ii) *Assembling/Stuffing:*

1. Slice the bun in half, horizontally.
2. Apply butter/mayonnaise on the cut surface of both the halves and grill it.
3. Now apply white / soya and green chilly sauce.Ommit white/soya/ green sauce, if mayonnaise is applied.
4. Place filling, spread grated cheese and finally tomato and chilly sauce on cut surface of anyone half.
5. Saute in vanaspati/butter/oil and serve hot.

Tips:

1. Filling may be replaced by salad like letuce, cucumber, tomatoes etc.
2. It can be accompanied by wafer, french fries & other snack etc.
3. Burger can be kept in hot-case (after frying) until served.
4. Bun can be replaced by thick sandwich bread slice.

Sandwich

Formula :

No	Ingredients	Per cent	Weight	
			Vegetable	Chicken
1	Sandwich bread slice (25gm)	100	100 no	100 no
2	Butter/Mayonnaise	10 to 15	250 gm	250 gm
3	Letuce leaf	5 to 10	125 gm	125 gm
4	Cucumber	10 to 15	250 gm	250 gm
5	Tomato	10 to 15	250 gm	250 gm
6	Tomato sauce	5 to 10	200 gm	200 gm
7	Soya/White sauce	2 to 5	100 gm	100 gm
8	Main filling (Cheese/Chicken/Croissant)	20 to 25	500 gm	500 gm
9	Salt	2 to 3	75 gm	75 gm
10	Pepper(powder)	2 to 3	75 gm	75 gm

Method:

1. Select two thin even slice [about 6 mm (114")] and keep under damp handtowel or moistened parchment paper to keep them from drying out.
2. Apply a thin coating of soften butter/mayonnaise on anyone side of both the slices.
3. Place letuce leaf, thin dices of cucumber and tomato or any other filling on the butter / mayonnaise applied side of anyone slice.
4. Sprinkle salt and pepper.
5. Spread tomato and / or white sauce.
6. Cover with the second layer of bread (the butter applied side touch to filling) and press gently to set.
7. Trim the sides and cut into half (triangles) or several small pieces (squares).

Tips:

1. Be careful that butter/mayonnaise or fillings not get out side the slice as this ruins the appearance.
2. The filling must be enough so the sandwich remains delicious and moist. However, too much filling spoils their appearance and makes them hard to handle.

Variations:

1. CHEESE SANDWICH : This sandwich is similar to vegetable sandwich, except the vegetable is replaced by a layer of soft grated / sliced cheese. For variation, it may be prepared by applying layer of cheese on vegetable filling.
2. MINT SANDWICH : Sandwich the slices of bread with mint chutney along with vegetable.
3. CHICKEN SANDWICH : Sandwich the slices with chicken salad, letuce leaf.
4. CROISSANT SANDWICH: Replace the vegetable filling with croissants.
5. PLAIN SANDWICH : Omit out the filling is nothing but plain sandwich.
6. CLUB SANDWICH : Any kind of sandwich can be made into club sandwich. It is a three tire sandwich. Made in similar way to vegetable sandwich. But the only difference is prepare three slices instead of two. Fill both layer with same or separate filling.

Tips:

1. The butter or mayonnaise can be accepted with herbs or other flavouring to differentiate the taste.
2. For quick preparation, apply the filling to a whole band of bread at once. Then cover with second layer. Followed by stacking of filled sandwiches and shaping at the same time.
3. The sandwich can be served with sauce/ mayonnaise and wafers.

Stuffed Rolls

Formula :

No	Ingredients	Per cent	Weight
1	Roll	100	10 kg
2	Filling	100	10 kg
3	Butter / Mayonnaise	2 to 5	250 gm
4	Vanaspati/Butter/Oil	5 to 10	500 gm
5	Tomato sauce	2 to 5	500gm

Method:

(i) *Filling:* Stuffing for the rolls can be prepared as similar to burger stuffing. The following stuffing can be prepared:

1. POTATO FILLING: Use steam cooked meshed potatoes.
2. CHEESE FILLING: Use plain grated cheese.
3. PANEER FILLING: Use very finely cut paneer.
4. MUSHROOM FILLING: Use sliced mushroom.
5. EGG FILLING: Use scrambled egg into salted onion with masala.
6. CHICKEN FILLING: Use chopped boneless chicken.
7. MUTTON FILLING: Use minced meat of lamb.

(ii) *Assembling/Stuffing:* Rolls are stuffed similar to burger, as below:

1. Slice the rolls in half, horizontally.
2. Apply butter/mayonnaise on the cut surface of both the halves and grill it.
3. Apply sauce on butter/mayonnaise.
4. Place filling (it may be grated with cheese).
5. Saute in vanaspati / butter oil.

DANISH PASTRY

Formula :

No	Ingredients	Per cent	Weight
Part-I: Base			
1	Flour	100	1 kg
2	Shortening (for rubbing)	5 to 10	50 gm
3	Sugar	15	150 gm
4	Yeast	3 to 5	30 gm
5	Egg (yolk)	12 to 15	8 no
6	Milk powder	4 to 6	50 gm
7	Salt	1 to 2	2 tsp
8	Shortening (for folding)	45 to 70	600 gm
9	Egg (for glazing)	3 to 5	as req
10	Essence (vanilla)	0.5 to 1	as req

11	Water	45 to 50	500 ml
	Part- II : Filling		
	Variety -1 :		
12	Icing sugar	60	600 gm
13	Shortening/Butter	40 to 50	400 gm
14	Cardamom & Nutmeg (powder)	1.5 to 2.5	4 tsp
15	Tutee fruity, Sultan & Cashewnut	40	400 gm
	Variety· 2 :		
12	Milk	50	500 ml
13	Egg (yolk)	8 to 10.	5 no
14	Sugar	10 to 15	125 gm
15	Flour	5	50 gm
16	Shortening/Butter·	5	50 gm
17	Essence (vanilla)	0.5 to 1.0	as des
	Part- II: Decoration		
18	Sugar (granules)	40	400 gm
19	Water	20	200 gm
	Baking Temperature	**Time**	**Production**
	205°C (400°F)	17 to 21 min	2.80 kg

Method: .

1. Prepare dough similar to bread. However, the egg is added along with salt and beat nicely. Mix the dough with minimum kneading because over mixing may toughen pastry. Fat (rubbing) is rubbed with flour prior to mixing.
2. Allow it to ferment for 15 to 20 min.
3. Fold the dough with fat layering as similar to Khari dough.
4. Rest the dough in cool place (refrigerator) for about 30 min.
5. Meanwhile, get ready the filling (as shown below). And chop fruits & nuts finely.
6. Roll the dough into a rectangle to a desired thickness [about 0.5 cm 0/ 4")].
7. Spread the anyone filling leaving apart about 0.5 cm (114") space. uncovered towards end. Sprinkle dry fruit mixture followed by cardamom-nutmeg mixture.

8. Brush the ends with egg/milk wash.
9. Roll the dough into stick form.Be careful that, the ends get stick properly. If required chill the dough.
10. Cut the roll to about 1.25cm(1/2") thickness with the help of thread.
11. Glaze with the egg wash,arrange in a tray and allow to ferment until double in size (approximately 30 to 45 min) and bake.
12. Brush with sugar syrup immediately upon drawing from the oven and place on the cooling rack.(Sugar syrup is prepared by mixing the sugar with water. and boil until thick).

Filling preparation:

Variety -1 :

1. Cream shortening with icing sugar.

Variety - 2 :

1. Beat egg (yolk) and sugar until light and fluffy. Add essence.
2. Add flour and mix thoroughly.
3. Add boiled milk slowly while string vigorously.
4. Boil the whole mass until thick consistency and finally add butter.

Danish Comb

Method : Cut the rolled dough (after step no 9) into about 10 cm (4") long pieces.Then make 3-4 cuts as shown in figure and arrange on the tray by curving slightly. Follow the rest of the process.

Cinnamon Roll

Method:

7. After step no 6 brush half the portion with egg / milk wash.
8. Sprinkle sugar (granules) [at a rate of 6 to 10% (i.e.60 gm for 1 kg flour)] and cinnamon powder [at a rate of 1 to 2% (i.e. 20 gm for 1 kg flour)].
9. Fold the remaining half over it.
10. Cut into strips of about 1.5 cm (112") width.
11. Twist both the ends of strip in opposite direction so as to give a rope like appearance.
12. That can leave as such or shaped into snail or '8' as similar to dinner roll .

13. Follow the remaining process from step no. 11 (of original process).

OR

7. After step no. 6 spread the icing and sprinkle sugar (granules) cinnamon (powder) mixture and follow similar process from step no 8.

Croissant

Method:

7. After step no 6 cut the dough into triangles having base of about 13 cm (5") and the temaining two sides of 15 cm (6") each.
8. Give a vertical cut of about 2 cm (3/4") in the middle of the base.
9. Starting from the base, roll the croissant and place on the baking sheet in a crescent form. Follow the procedure from step no 11 (of original process).

24

Production of Puff Pastry

(KHARI)
(Simple Khari)

No	Ingredients	Per cent	Weight
1	Flour	100	10 kg
2	Shortening (for mixing)	5 to 8	500 gm
3	Shortening (for folding)	50 to 60	5 kg
4	Water (chilled)	60	6 lt
5	Salt	2 to 3	300 gm

Baking Temperature	Time	Production
230°C (450°F)	22 to 31 min	14.8 kg

Method:

1. Sieve the flour twice.
2. Dissolve salt into water and strain.
3. Add salt solution into the flour and knead into a dough.
4. Add the mixing shortening and knead into a smooth clear dough.
5. Cover the dough with wet cloth and relax in cool place (refrigerators) for 20 to 30 min.
6. Sheet the dough into rectangular shape having even thickness of about 0.5 cm (1/4") with free hand rolling. Use plenty of dusting flour to avoid sticking.
7. Mark them vertically into 4 equal parts and call them A,B,C,D.
8. Fold (horizontally) left to centre (i.epart-A on part-B) then right to centre

(i.e part-D on part-C) and again fold to look like a book, (i.e part A-B on part C-D). This is known as book fold. Allow to rest for 15 to 20 min.

9. Divide the shortening (for folding) into 2 equal parts.Cream 1 part slightly and divide into 3 parts.
10. Sheet and mark the dough as earlier.Apply 1 part of creamed fat on (each) part Band C and spread leaving I cm (1/2") end uncovered. Now fold part-A on B and D on C as earlier. Apply 1 part of remaining creamed fat on A-B part and spread it leaving 1 cm (1/2") end uncovered and fold C-D part on A-B.Rest for 15 to 20 min.
11. Repeat the process once as it is and once without applying fat, with 15 to 20 min rest period.
12. Allow to relax for 1 hr in a cool place (refrigerator).
13. Sheet the dough into even thickness of 0.5 to 0.6 cm (1/4"). Cut with dough or khari cutter to desired strips [2 to 3 cm (1 ") width and 5 to 6 cm (2.1/4") length].
14. Place the strips on water wetted baking sheet. Either sprinkle / fill water to wash excess flour, drain off excess water or clean flour with the wet cloth on the strips. Bake it.
15. Allow to cool and arrange vertically and dry in cool oven [i.e. 80 to 90°C (175 to 190°F)] for about I to 1.1/2 hr. The fire-wood-oven will be sufficiently cool on the next day morning.

Variation (in folding) : The folding of the khari dough (after step no 6) may be carried out by any of the following method:

(i) 3-Fold Method:

7. Mark the sheeted dough vertically into 3 equal parts and call them A,B, C.
8. Now turn part - C on B followed by part -A on B. Relax for 15 to 20 min.
9. Meanwhile, cream the shortening (for folding) slightly and divide into 3 equal parts.
10. Sheet and mark the dough-sheet as earlier. Apply 1 part of creamed shortening on part A and B. Fold part C on B followed by A on B. Rest for 15 to 20 min.
11. Repeat the process twice) as it is followed by (twice) without applying fat. Follow all the similar process from step no 10 of the original process.

(ii) Roll-in-Method :

7. Start folding sheeted dough from one end maintaining the same width [about 10 to 13 cm (4 to 5")] of the fold till the end.Relax for 15 to 20 min.
8. Meanwhile,cream shortening (for folding) slightly and divide into 2 equal parts.
9. Sheet the dough,apply & spread 1 part of fat and fold as earlier. Allow to rest for 16 to 20 min.
10. Repeat the process once as it is,followed by once without applying fat.
11. Now follow the original process from step no 10 onwards.

(iii) Strip and Cut Method:

7. Apply and spread all the folding fat (after light creaming) on thin sheeted dough.
8. Cut into even size [2 to 3 cm (1")] strip lengthwise.
9. Stack them one over other.
10. Now cut them into 5 to 6 cm (2.1/4) pieces.
11. Now follow all the original procedure from step no 12.

Tips:

1. The shortening used for khari preparation should be smooth.That types of specialised fats are available in the market. **OR** It can be prepared by melting fat,cool it.Now take big bowl than fat-pot,fill with chilled water or ice and keep the fat-pot on that. Now stir the fat constantly.Mesh the set fat.Use that when all the fat sets.This type of fat can be used for biscuit / cake preparation for better quality.
2. Some bakers add custard at a rate of 0.5 to 1.0 % (i.e 100 gm for 1 kg flour) which develop cream colour and specific smell.
3. Always cover the dough with slightly wet cloth and keep the dough in cool place (preferably in refrigerator) during relaxation period.
4. Remove excess dusting flour before folding.
5. Roll the dough with smooth hand without pressing much at particular place.

Variation:

(Masala Khari)

Method:

1. Add turmeric powder or yellow colour at the rate of 0.25 to 0.5% (i.e. 50 gm for 10 kg flour) in water before mixing the dough.
2. Sprinkle equal quantity of black pepper powder from total 2 to 3 % (250 gm for 10 kg flour) on every layer of fat and follow rest of the procedure.
3. After cutting strips i.e. step no 13 of original procedure) turn like rope by twisting both the ends in opposite direction or the strip may be twist to make open knot and follow the rest of the procedure.

(Cheese Khari)

Method:

1. Spread equal quantity of grated cheese from total 15 to 25 % (i.e. 2.5 kg for 10 kg flour) on every layer of fat and follow rest of all the process. One may mix cheese spread with shortening.

OR

1. Divide cheese [total amount 15 to 25 % (i.e. 2.5 kg for 10 kg flour)] and black pepper powder [total amount 2 to 3% (i.e. 250 gm for 10 kg flour)] into two equal parts.
2. After completion of folding (i .e.after step no 11) roll out the dough into rectangle. Place 1 part of cheese block on 1/3 part (on middle portion) of dough. Sprinkle 1 part of black pepper powder over it. Fold the 1/3 part of dough in such a way that it covers the cheese portion. Place the remaining 1 part of cheese block followed by black pepper & cover with remaining 1/3 part of the dough. Follow the same procedure from step no 11.

(Fenugreek Khari Garlic Khari)

Method:

1. Add finely chopped fenugreek leaves (dried kasuri methi leaves is desired) or minced garlic into dough before mixing and follow the rest of the procedure.

Tip:

1. One may develop such types of khari using locally available food material looking to the taste of people.

(PUFF PASTRY)

Method:

1. Make a dough as per the formula and procedure mentioned for khari. After sheeting the dough (i. e. step no 13), shape into various products, as below:

(Vegetable Pastry)

1. Cut dough into squares of 10 cm (4") and fold into triangle. Follow rest of the procedure.

(Pinwheel)

2. Cut dough into squares of 10 cm (4"). Cut the edges leaving the centre intact, brush with water. Fold the alternate corners towards the centre to form a pinwheel. Follow rest of the procedure.

(Feuillette)

Cut the dough into 4 rectangles of 10 cm x 7.5 cm (4" x 3") each. Cut 2 rectangles again leaving 2.5 cm (I") periphery around. Brush the uncut rectangles with water. Place the inner rectangle caps and follow the same procedure. **OR** Place the outer edges of cut rectangle over water-brushed-rectangles and place vegetable filling and follow the rest of the procedure.

(Palmiers)

Apply egg/milk on sheeted dough and sprinkle with sugar (granules) [5 to 10% (i.e. 500 gm for 10 kg flour) & cinnamon and/or cardamom-nutmeg (powder) [2 to 3% (i.e. 200 gm for 10 kg flour)]. Press gently by rolling it out, if required. Mark them horizontally into 6 equal parts [about 3 to 4 cm (1.½") width]. Fold from both the sides lengthwise (i.e. A on Band F on E). Repeat the fold again. Complete to form the book fold. Wrap with wet cloth or butter paper and freeze until hard (about 1 hr). Cut with sharp knife into thick slice [about 1.25 to 2.5 cm (1/2 to 1")]. Place on baking tray (cut surface up) and sprinkle with sugar (granules). Relax for about 20 min & bake.

(Exotic Varieties)

After step no 12 roll the dough and cut into various geometric shape like round, triangle, square, hexagonal, pentagonal, star etc. with specific dye-cutter. Follow the rest of the process. Allow to coo!' Grate each piece with filling of your choice i.e. Jam & raisins, cream & almonds, coconut, sesame etc.

(Vanilla Slice)

Cut sheeted dough (after step no 12) into rectangular shape [about 15 x 7 cm (6" x 3")]. Prick with a fork, rest for 20 min. Place in tray & bake as similar to khari. Cool to room temperature. Cut each pieces into 3 equal parts with pointed sharp knife. Join all pieces with custard cream. Cover the top with custard or vanilla icing.

(Mille Feuillies)

After step no 12 sheet the dough thinner than khari. Cut into round shape [about 10 cm (4") diameter], prick with fork and bake. Join three baked piece by filling fresh cream & sugar, icing or custard. Cover the top with the same filling and place acherry/tutee fruity in the centre.

(Cheese Straw)

Method:

1. Mix grated cheese [about 15 to 25% (i.e. 2 kg for 10 kg flour)] into flour before preparing dough. **OR** Sprinkle it on sheeted dough with chilly powder [3 to 5% (i.e.300 gm for 10 kg flour)].
2. Fold the dough by 3 - fold methods. Roll out again to required thickness.
3. Cut into strips having about 4 to 6 cm (1.½ to 2. 1/2") length and 1 to 2 cm (1/2 to 314") width.
4. Twist both the end in opposite direction to have 5-6 rope like turn & bake.

Alteration:

1. After sprinkling cheese-chilly powder mixture on sheeted dough, cut _ into finger size strips directly and bake.

(PUFF)

(Masala Puff)

Formula: [filling (for 10 kg flour)] :

No	Ingredient	Per cent	Weight				
			Potato	Mixed Veg.	Paneer	Mush room	Non veg.
1.	Potato	100	10 kg	1.5 kg. (Optional)	-	-	-
2.	Onion (chopped)	50 to 100	5 kg.	-	10 kg.	600 gm	-
3.	Carrot (diced)	25	-	2.5 kg	-	-	-
4.	Beans (boiled)	15	-	1.5	-	-	-
5	Green peas (boiled)	10 to 15	-	1.0 kg	-	-	-
6	Cauliflower (chopped)	10	-	1.0 kg	-	1.5 kg	-
7	Tomato (chopped)	5 to 15	-	1.5 kg	-	600 gm	500 g
8	Paneer (pieces)	25	-	-	2.5 kg	-	-
9	Mushroom(diced)	20	-	-	-	2kg	-
10	Chicken (chopped)	40 to 50	-	-	-	-	4.5 kg
11	Salt	2 to 3	to taste	to taste	to taste	to taste	to taste
12	Green masala • Coriender leaves • Green ginger • Green chillies • Lemon	5 to 10 (each)	to taste	to taste	to taste	to taste	to taste
13	Mixed hot spices • Clove (powder) • Cinammon (powder) • Green mango(powder)	2 to 3 (each)	to taste	to taste	to taste	to taste	to taste
14	Other masala • Turmeric powder • Red chilly powder • Cumin seed • Garlic	2 to 3 (each)	to taste	to taste	to taste	to taste	to taste
15	Vanaspati / Oil	5 to 10	to saute	to saute	to saute	to saute	to soute

Method:

1. Prepare a dough similar to khari using 40 to 50% (i.e. 4 kg for 10 kg flour) shortening (for folding), upto step no 12.
2. Prepare filling as per the raw material used by different methods mentioned below:
   - Potato : Boil potato in salt water. Allow to cool till become warm. Remove skin & mesh.
   - Paneer : Fry the paneer pieces in the vanspati till it become golden brown.
   - Vegetable : Boil the diced vegetables. Beans are to be soaked overnight in water before boiling.
   - Mushroom : Soak the mushroom in water and boil.
   - Chicken : Take boneless chicken, add 2 tsp of oil, salt to taste, 1 tsp of ginger-garlic paste and 1/2 tsp of chilly powder. Mix together and marinate for 30 min. Bake in oven for 15 min until almost done. Cool and dice.
3. Clean & chop or grate the green masala & garlic.
4. Heat oil in a pan.
5. Add cumin seed and allow to crackle.
6. Add onion and saute until golden brown.
7. Add green masala (except coriander leaves), garlic & saute.
8. Add chopped tomato (if used), turmeric powder, chilly powder, mango powder and saute little and mix thoroughly.
9. Add prepared raw material filling i.e. meshed potato / fried paneer / boiled vegetables / baked - diced chicken etc. Mix thoroughly.
10. Add salt, mixed hot spices, coriender leaves, lemon juice etc. Mix thoroughly, cook if required (for about 15 to 20 min), remove from fire and allow to cool.

Alteration:

1. Mixed hot spices can be mixed once the filling is cool. Which will provide better taste when preheating the puff before selling.

2. All the filling ingredients can be mixed and used.
3. The ginger & garlic may be mixed and made into paste and used.

Filling: [(Cauliflower Manchurian) for 10 kg flour] :

No	Ingredients	Per cent	Weight
1	Cauliflower (Gobhi)	50 to 60	5.0 kg
2	Corn flour or Maida	3 to 5	300 gm
3	Egg	40	10 no
4	Iodized Salt	2 to 3	to taste
5	Pepper (powder)	2 to 3	to taste
6	Ajinomotto	2 to 3	as desired
7	Ginger & Garlic paste	5	as desired
8	Onion	5 to 10	500 gm
9	Spring onion	5 to 10	500 gm
10	Coriander leaves	5 to 10	500 gm
11	Oil	10 to 20	to fry

Method:

1. Cut cauliflower into small pieces and boil with little Iodized salt. Mixed with chopped onion, spring onion, coriander leaves etc. Made into (ball desired) form.
2. Prepare paste by mixing maida / corn flour, egg, pepper (powder), salt, Ajinomotto and ginger-garlic paste.
3. Dip cauliflower ball into paste and deep fry in sufficient oil. That is used as filling.

Stuffing:

1. Prepare a dough similar to khari using 40 to 50% (i.e. 4 kg for 10 kg flour) shortening, upto step no 12.
2. Roll out the dough into even thickness of 0.3 to 0.4 cm (1/8 to 1/6").
3. Cut into rectangular [7.5x12.5 cm (3x5")] or square [12.5x12.5 cm (5x5")] shape.
4. Divide the filling into equal parts (similar to oblong or square pieces) and made oblong (if pieces are oblong) or round (if pieces are square) ball.
5. Place one oblong ball in the centre of each rectangular dough piece.Egg/

milk wash the 0.5 cm (1/4") horizontal ends and turn both together and press gently.

OR

Place one round ball in the centre of each square dough piece. Egg\milk wash the periphery [0.5 cm (1/4")] make it triangle shape and press gently.

7. Arrange on the baking tray. Apply egg/milk wash on top and bake.
8. Serve it hot or allow to cool and send to retailer.It may be sold by retailer on rewarming into domestic oven.

(Sweet Puff)

No	Ingredients	Per cent	Weight		
			Turn Over	Oil Pasand	Apple Strudel
	Part I: Base				
1	Flour	100	1 kg	1 kg	1 kg
2	Shortening	40 to 50	500 gm	500 gm	500 gm
3	Sugar (optional)	20 to 30	250 gm	250 gm	250 gm
4	Baking powder	0.5 to 1	2 tsp	2 tsp	2 tsp
5	Salt	0.25	pinch	pinch	pinch
6	Water (chilled)	20	200ml	200 ml	200ml
Part	**II : Filling**				
7	Sugar (granules)	10/25	250 gm	100 gm	100 gm
8	Lemon juice	3	2 tsp	-	-
9	Date	80	800 gm	-	-
10	Cashewnut	2 to 5/25	250 gm	50 gm	25 gm
11	Vanaspati (for frying)	25	250 gm	-	-
12	Mixed hot spices (Ginger, Nutmeg Cardamom, Mace-all powder)	2 to 3 (each)	2 Tsp	-	-
13	Lemon rind powder	2	20 gm	-	-
14	Sugar (granules)	20	200 gm	-	-
15	Egg/Milk/Water	2 to 5	as req	as req	as req

16	Apple	50	-	-	500 gm
17	Raisins	2 to 3	-	-	25 gm
18	Dried bread crumb	10	-	-	100gm
19	Cinnamon powder	0.5 to 1	-	-	1 tsp
20	Fresh coconut (slightly dried in oven)	-	-	1/2 no	-
21	Tuti fruity	5 to 10	-	-	50 gm
22	Cardamom powder	0.5 to 1	-	1 tsp	-

Baking Temperature	Time	Production
190°C (375°F)	12 to 14 min	50 no

Method:

1. Prepare dough similar to Khari upto step no 12. Do not add baking powder. Sugar is mixed with flour, if used.

(i) Tartlets :

2. Roll the dough into 0.4 to 0.5 cm (1/6 to 1/4") thickness & cut with big biscuit cutter [5 to 7 cm (2 to 2.½") diameter].
3. Keep it in greased-dusted (flour) petty-tin and glace with jam.
4. Make dough strip [0.5 cm (1/4") width] cross on that & bake.

(ii) Turnover:

2. Saute date (deseeded & sliced) & cashewnut (pieces) in vanaspati.
3. Add mixed hot spices, lemon juice, lemon rind powder, mix thoroughly and stop heating.
4. Add sugar (for filling) immediately.
5. Prepare ball bigger.
6. Roll the dough into 0.3 to 0.4 cm (1/8 to 1/6") thickness and cut into square [10 x 10 cm (4 x 4")].
7. Place one ball in each piece and fold into triangle shape.
8. Wash with egg / milk, sprinkle sugar (granules) and bake.

(iii) Apple Strudel:

2. Mix cinnamon powder and sugar (for filling).
3. Peel-off, de-seed and dice the apple. Mix with cinnamon-sugar mixer.
4. Add dry fruit (pieces) & bread crumb (pieces) and mix thoroughly.
5. Roll out the dough [0.5 cm (1/4") thickness] into rectangle shape having 20 to 25 cm (8 to 10") width. Prick with fork.

6. Cut lengthwise into 2 strips of about 10 to 13 cm (4 to 5") width.
7. Arrange the apple mix on one strip leaving about 0.5 cm (1/2") edges. Apply egg/milk wash on the edges.
8. Cover with second strip of the dough and seal the edges.
9. Make little cuts on the top with sharp knife. Apply egg/milk wash.
10. Bake and cut horizontally.

(iv) Dil Pasand :

2. Dice coconut and break cashewnut into pieces.
3. Mix all filling ingredients together.
4. Roll the dough into 0.5 cm (1/4") thickness.
5. Cut into 2 round shape having about 25 cm (10") diameter and 23 cm (9") diameter.
6. Place filling on bigger piece leaving about 2.5 cm (1 ") peripheri.Apply egg/ milk wash on the edges.
7. Cover the mixer with smaller piece and fold the bottom dough edges on the top dough and press to seal the border.
8. Glace with milk / egg wash and bake.

(Vol-au-Vent)

Formula [for filling (for 10 kg flour) 1 :

No	Ingredient	Percent	Weight
1	Garlic	5	500 gm
2	Onion	16 to 21	1.5 kg
3	Mushroom	26 to 31	2.5 kg
4	Green peas	25 to 30	2.5 kg
5	Spinach	10 to 15	1.0 kg
6	Flour	2 to 3	300 gm
7	Butter	5	500 gm
8	Milk	25 to 30	3 lt
9	Water	5 to 10	as req
10	Pepper (powder)	2 to 3	200 gm
11	Salt	2 to 3	250 gm
12	Oil	10	1 lt

Method:

Filling:

1. Dice green mushroom, boil green peas, blanch & chop spinach.
2. Heat oil in a pan and saute garlic (pieces) until light brown.
3. Add chopped onion and saute till brown.
4. Add mashroom, green peas & spinach and saute.
5. Sprinkle flour, salt, pepper and stir to mix.
6. Pour milk slowly and stir briskly. Add water if required.
7. Add butter to finish.

Stuffing:

1. Prepare a dough similar to khari upto step no 12.
2. Roll the dough into 0.5 cm (1/4") thickness.
3. Cut even number rounds of about 8 cm (3") diameter.
4. In half number of the pieces, cut a round hole in centre of about 5 cm (2") diameter, so as to prepare a ring shape.
5. Brush the intact round pieces with water and place ring on that.
6. Glace with egg wash and bake [at 200°C(390°F) for 15 to 20 min]. The small round pieces are baked as such.
7. Fill the cases with filling and serve with small-round piece topping.

25

Manufacturing Methods of Cookies

Cookies can be manufactured by the following methods : -

(i) *Creaming Method:*

1. Add all the ingredients like baking powder, baking soda, ammonia, custard powder, corn flour, milk powder, iodized salt etc. (as per formula) into flour and sieve twice to mix thoroughly and remove forign materials.

2. Cream the vanaspati / shortening till light and fluffy.

3. Add sugar slowly, continuing the creaming process, till the mixture become light, bright and fluffy.

4. If formula contains egg, whip it with beater in a clean, greaseless vessel to a stiff consistency. Then, gradually add to sugar-shortening mixture. Mix egg with straight finger. Then again whip the egg, add & mix. Follow the procedure until all egg is mixed. Mix any essence or colour, if formula contains. Add little flour to overcome that effect.

5. Add milk, water or curd in sufficient quantity and mix lightly. Add essence & colour. Add any fruits or dry fruits if eggs are not added, after proper treatment (i.e. chopping, dicing, soaking in water). However, for cake preparation it should be added at last stage of mixing.

6. Now, add flour (already mixed with dry ingredients). Mix lightly and made into smooth dough. It is advisable to divide flour into 2 to 3 parts and add one after another.

Tip:

1. The batter for cake have dropping consistency.

(ii) *Rubbing Method*:

1. Mix all the dry ingredients into flour and sieve twice.
2. Add shortening and rub thoroughly.
3. Add sugar and mix lightly.
4. Add dry fruits, fruits, colour, essence etc., as per formula.
5. Now add egg gradually as similar to creaming method, if formula requires.
6. Finally mix water/milk/curd and made into smooth dough.

Tips:

1. To improve the quality of any kind of biscuits/cookies:
   - Add 10 to 20% (i.e. 100 to 200 gm for I kg flour) extra shortening and roll the dough into 0.5 cm (1/4") thickness instead of 0.3 cm (1/8") & bake at lower temperature.
   - Presently, specialised shortenings are available in market which again improves the product quality.

(NANKHATAI)

No	Ingredient	Per cent	Weight
1	Flour	100	1 kg
2	Shortening	50. to 70	600 gm
3	Sugar	50 to 60	500 gm
4	Amm bi carb/ Baking soda! Both (equal quantity)	0.5 to 1.0	1 tsp
5	Milk / Water / Curd	5 to 7	as req
6	Cardamom (powder)	0.75 to 1.5	1 Tsp
7	Nutmeg (powder)	0.5 to 1.0	2 tsp

Baking Temperature	Time	Production
160°C (320°F)	17 to 22 min	1.8 kg

Method:

1. Prepare dough by creaming process.
2. Break the dough into required size (i.e. about bundi laddu), round each piece.
3. Place in baking tray 1cm (1/2") apart, press gently and bake.

Tips:

1. If desired, granish the nankhatai ball-top with pista flakes, cashewnut piece, almond or *charoli* etc.
2. Nankhatai is renowned throughout the country. Hence, possesses very wide range of structure i.e. smooth/ cracked / flat and rough/hard or porous etc. That can be achieved by varying the quantity of ammonium bi-carbonate/ baking soda or sugar / shortening.
3. Some manufacturers use 10 to 20 % (100 to 200 gm for 1 kg flour) suji / rawa, which makes nankhatai more crispy and tasty.
4. Whole wheat flour can be used partially to flour. In that case shortening per cent should be increased to about 75%.

Variation:

Chocolate Nankhatai

1. Prepare a dough similar to above mentioned recipe and method. Divide into two parts.
2. Add cocoa powder / chocolate powder to taste [i.e. about 5 to 10% (i.e. 50 to 100 gm for 1 kg flour)] in one part and mix homogenously.
3. Take equal quantity of dough from both the part and prepare ball, place on baking tray and bake.

(Crunchy Nankhatai)

Method:

1. Prepare nankhatai similar to above mentioned formula and method. However, add 5 to 10 % (i.e. 50 to 100 gm for 1 kg flour) bournvita or butter scotch powder into flour before the dough preparation.

(Surti Nankhatai)

Method:

1. Surti nankhatai possess light brown colour, which can be obtained by addition of 5% (i.e. 50 ml for 1 kg flour) caramel. Moreover the shortening quantity increased to about 70% (i.e. about 700 gm for 1 kg flour). Due to high shortening, milk / water is added, only if they required to maintain dough consistency. Rest of the formula and procedure are similar to nankhatai. Suji / rawa can be added at 10 to 20% (i.e. 100 to 200 gm for 1 kg flour).

   Caramel Preparation : Add 250 ml water into 500 gm sugar and heat until sugar gets dissolved with constant stirring. Now stop stirring and add few drops of lemon juice, which makes the impurities floating over, remove it. When mixture gets dark brown colour, stop heating. Then add 160 to 260 ml water.

   OR

   Heat 475 gm sugar until dark brown and add (slowly) 260 ml water. Continue to heat for few minutes. Fire it off and allow to cool.

(BESAN NANKHATAI)

No	Ingredient	Per cent	Weight
1	Besan (Gram Flour)	100	1 kg
2	Sugar	190 to 295	2 kg
3	Ammonium Bi-carbonate/ Baking soda	3 to 5	30 gm
4	Water	18 to 30	as req

Baking Temperature	Time	Production
150°C (3000P)	12 to 15 min	2.5 to 3 kg

Method:

1. Mix sugar and besan.
2. Dilute Ammonium Bi-carbonate or baking soda in little water, and add the besan.
3. Add remaining water and prepare smooth dough.
4. Cut & make very small ball.
5. Place in a baking tray about 5 cm (2") apart and bake immediately.

Tip:

1. This nankhatai contains pulse, which possesses high quantity of protein, that is useful for growth and development of children.

(FALAHARI NANKHATAI)

No	Ingredient	per cent	Weight
I	Poppy seed flour	40	400 gm
2	Coconut (dessicated)	30 100	300 gm
3	Groundnut	30	300 gm
4	Shortening	40 to 60	500 gm
5	Sugar	40 to 60	500 gm
6	Amm bi carb / Baking powder	0.25 to 0.5	1 tsp
7	Milk/Water	2 to 5	as req
8	Cardamom -nutmeg (powder)	3 to 5	1 Tsp

Baking Temperature	Time	Production
150 ° C (300°P)	10 to 12 min	1.750 kg

Method:

1. Replace flour with poppy seed flour, dessicated coconut & roasted dehulled-finely crushed groundnut mixture and prepare dough by creaming method.
2. Made into small ball of walnut size, place in a baking tray & bake.

MELTING MOMENTS ALMOND COOKIE GROUNDNUT COOKIE

No	Ingredient	Per cent	weight		
			Melting Moments	Almond Cookie	Groundnut Cookie
1	Flour	100	1 kg	1 kg	1 kg
2	Shortening	70 to 80	750 gm	700gm	750 gm
3	Sugar	60 to 75	600 gm	700 gm	750 gm
4	Baking powder	0.5 to 1	1 tsp	-	1 tsp
5	Baking soda	1	-	1 tsp	-
6	Egg	15 to 25	4 no	6 no	5 no
7	Coconut (dessicated) /Corn flakes	20 to 30	300	-	-

8	Almond / Kaju	10 to 20	-	200 gm	-
9	Groundnut	100	-	-	1 kg
10	Essence (vanilla/ almond/groundnut)	0.5 to 1.0	2 tsp	2 tsp	2 tsp
11	Cream of tarter	0.25 to 0.5	-	1 tsp	-
12	Colour (yellow)	0.25 to 0.5	as req	-	-
13	Iodized salt	0.5	1 tsp	1 tsp	1 tsp

Baking Temperature	Time	Capacity
190°C (375°F)	15 to 18 min	2.5 kg

Method:

1. Soak cashewnut *1* almond in water about 1/2 hr. Roast and dehull the peanut. 3/4 part peanut are crushed finely.
2. Prepare the dough by creaming method. However, to prepare peanut cookie add finely crushed peanut along with flour. Allow to relax about 1/2 hr in refrigerators, if required.
3. Divide dough into small pieces similar to walnut and made into ball. Use wet hand for this purpose;
4. Apply Water/Milk wash on all the side (either by rolling in water or dipping in water) and roll in coconut or crushed corn flakes, (which are already thoroughly mixed with yellow colour). That is *melting moments.*
5. Place on baking tray and bake.

CRUNCHY COOKIE

CORN FLAKE COOKIE & HONEY COOKIE

No	Ingredient	Per cent	Weight		
			Crunchy Cookie	Corn Flake Cookie	Honey Cookie
1	Flour	100	1 kg	1 kg	1 kg
2	Shortening Butter	100/50	1 kg	1 kg	500 gm
3	Sugar of Best Quality	100/65	1 kg	650 gm	650 gm
4	Egg	40	10 no	10 no	-
5	Egg (yolk)	20	-	-	12 no
6	Baking powder	0.5 to 1.5	2.1/4tsp	2.1/4tsp	Itsp

7	Baking soda	0.5 to 1.0	-	2 tsp	1 tsp
8	Main filling (bournvita)	30 to 50	500 gm	500 gm (cornflake)	400 gm (honey)
9	Dry fruit'(optional)	30 to 50	500 gm	500 gm	500 gm
10	Iodized Salt	0.25 to 0.5	pinch	pinch	pinch
11	Caramel	5 to 10	-	75 gm	-
12	Essence(vanilla)	1 to 2	2 tsp	2 tsp	2 tsp
13	Milk chocolate bar	150	-	1.5 kg	-
14	Mixed hot spices (powder)	2 to 3	-	-	2 Tsp

Baking Temperature	Time	Capacity
150°C (300°F)	17 to 22 min	3 to 4.7 kg

Method:

1. Soak dry fruit [Kaju / almond / pistachionut (either mixture or anyone)] in water for about 1/2 hr and chopped finely. Crush the corn flakes. Chop the chocolate bar.
2. Prepare the dough by creaming method. However, add the dry fruit / corn flakes / chocolate bar into flour before mixing. Add honey / caramel into creamed mixture before flour addition.
3. Keep the dough in refrigerator till become hard (about 30 to 45 min).
4. Break the dough and made into smooth ball of small size, place in baking tray & bake.

(COFFEE BUNS JAM BUNS)

No	Ingredient	Per cent	Weight	
			Coffee Buns	Jam Buns
1	Flour	100	1 kg	1 kg
2	Shortening	50 to 60	500 gm	500 gm
3	Sugar	50	500 gm	500 gm
4	Egg	20 to 25	6 no	5 no
5	Baking powder	4/1 to 2	2.1/2 Tsp	1 Tsp
6	Coffee/Cocoa	8	80gm	-
7	Sultan/ Tutee fruity	100	1 kg	-
8	Essence (vanilla)	1 to 2	2 tsp	2 tsp
9	Sugar (granules)	50	500 gm	-

10	Iodized Salt	0.25 to 0.5	pinch	pinch
11	Milk	20	as req	as req
12	Jam	10	-	100 gm

(COFFEE BUNS)

Baking Temperature	Time	Production
205°C (400°F)	20 min	100 no.

Method:

1. Prepare dough by rubbing method.
2. Divide into 50 gm pieces and round it.
3. Egg wash, roll into sugar (granules), place on baking tray and bake.

(JAM BUNS)

Baking Temperature	Time	Production
190°C (375°F)	15 to 20 min	2 kg.

Method :

1. Prepare dough by rubbing method.
2. Break the dough & made into small balls of walnut size.
3. Make a small depression and fill with jam. Place in a baking tray & bake.

COCONUT MACROON
CHERRY COCONUT MACROON
PEANUT MACROON
CASHEWNUT MACRON

No.	Ingredient	Per cent	Weight			
			Coconut Macroon	Cherry Macroon	Peanut Macroon	Cashewnut Macroon
1.	Coconut (dessicated)	100	1 kg.	1kg.	-	-
2.	Peanut	100	-	-	1 kg	-
3.	Cashewnut	100	-	-	-	1 kg.
4.	Sugar	80 to 100	1 kg	800 gm	800 gm	800 gm
5.	Egg (white)	30 to 40	10 no	10 no.	10 no.	10 no
6.	Lemon Juice OR Cream of tarter	0.1 to 0.25	1/4 tsp	1/2 tsp	1/4 tsp	1/4 tsp
7.	Essence (vanilla)	0.5 to 1	1 tsp	1tsp	1tsp	1tsp
8.	Essence (as per ingrdient)	0.5 to 1	1 tsp	1 tsp	1 tsp	1tsp

9. Salt	0.25	pinch	pinch	pinch	pinch
10. Colour (yellow)	0.25	as req.	as req.	-	-
11. Water	30 to 40	-	as req	-	-
12. Liquid glucose	4 to 5	40 gm	40 gm	40 gm	40 gm
13. Cherry	10 to 15	-	150 gm	-	-

Baking Temperature	Time	Production
100°C (210°F)	2 hr	2kg

COCONUT MACROON

Method :

1. Separate the egg white and place in a deep, dry, ceramic dish. The egg white can easily be separated by making a small whole in the egg-top
2. Add cream of tarter or lemon juice and allow to wet at peak stage (about 10 to 15 min).
3. Whisk it thoroughly with fork.
4. Add sugar gradually and keep on whisking, until the mixture becomes stable enough to stand upright without spreading.
5. Ada essence, colour, liquid glucose and salt just before the whisking is about to finish.
6. Fold in the coconut very gently so that aertion is not lost and mixture remain stable.
7. Made into rock shape, place on baking tray and bake.

Tips:

1. Be careful that, even the small portion of egg (yolk) not get mixed with white, as it makes whisking difficult.
2. The ceramic dish should be completely dry and free from greasy material i.e. fat /oil /shortening for proper whisking.

(CHERRY COCONUT MACROON)

Method:

1. Dissolve sugar in water on gentle heat in a brass bottom pan with continuous stirring. Do not allow the solution to boil until all the sugar gets dissolved.

2. Increase the heat and let it boil to 240°C (465°F) temperature. Add lemon juice or cream of tartar once the mixture start to boil. Do not stir the mixture while boiling.
3. Continue to boil to soft ball consistency (i.e. syrup should form a soft ball when poured in cold water).
4. Add cream of tartar, vanilla & coconut essence, iodized Salt and colour to egg white.
5. When the syrup is just about to reach soft ball consistency, take boiled water in a bowl, place vessel containing egg white on that (the vessel should not touch to water) and start whisking until egg white reaches to wet peak stage.
6. Now, start pouring the syrup in a slow stream whisking all the while.
7. Fold in the dessicated coconut gently by hand.
8. Place star nozzle in a icing bag and pipe out the mixture into star shape on the greased & dusted baking sheet to about 1.25 cm *(1/2")* distance.
9. Put 1/2 cherry or dot of jam in the centre of each macroon and bake.

[PEANUT MACROON]

Method:

1. Follow the above mentioned process with following changes:
   - Add roasted, dehulled, crushed peanut instead of coconut.
   - Replace peanut essence to coconut essence.

(CASHEWNUT MACROON)

Method:

1. Replace roasted, crushed cashewnut to peanut and follow the rest of the procedure.

CHOCOWAL COOKIE AND CHOCOCHIP COOKIE

Formula :

No	Ingredients	Per cent	Weight	
			Chocowal Cookie	Chocochip Cookie
1	Flour	100	1 kg	1 kg
2	Shortening	50 to 80	500 gm	800 gm
3	Sugar	50 to 60	550 gm	-
4	Sugar (granules)	10	100 gm	-
5	Sugar (brown)	10/65	100	650 gm
6	*Egg*	16 to 35	4 no	9 no
7	Baking soda	0.5 to 1.0	1 tsp	2 tsp
8	Baking powder	1.5	-	1 tsp
9	Ammonium bi-carbonate	0.25 to 0.5	1/2 tsp	-
10	Essence (vanilla)	0.5 to 1.5	1 tsp	1 tsp
11	Essence (chocolate)	0.5 to 1.0	1 tsp	1 tsp
12	Salt	0.5 to 1.0	1.1/2 tsp	1.1/2 tsp
13	Liquid glucose	2	4 tsp	-
14	Milk powder	2	4 tsp	-
15	Cocoa	5	50gm	-
16	Caramel	1	2 tsp	-
17	Corn flour	2	4 tsp	-
18	Walnut	15	150 gm	-
19	Covering chocolate	25/100	250 gm	1 kg
20	Milk chocolate bar	90	-	900 gm
21	Corn flakes	50	-	500 gm

Baking Temperature	Time	Production
193°C (380°F)	20 to 25 min	**Chocowal :** 1.80 kg **Chocochip :** 2.90 kg

Method:

1. Prepare a dough by creaming method.
2. However, mix milk powder, cocoa, corn flour etc. dry powdered with flour before being sieved.
3. Mix liquid glucose, caramal, sugar (granules), sugar (brown), chopped walnut, chopped covering chocolate, chopped milk chocolate bar, corn flakes etc. (whichever given in formula) into creamed fat- sugar mixer before flour is being mixed.
4. Break the dough into pieces of walnut size and place on baking tray and bake.

26

Manufacture of Biscuits (Assorted)

(PLAIN BISCUIT)

Formula :

No	Ingredients	Per cent	Weight
1	Flour	100	1 kg
2	Shortening	50 to 80	600 gm
3	Sugar	50 to 60	500 gm
4	Essence (vanilla/orange)	0.25 to 0.5	1/2 tsp
5	Baking powder/ Baking soda Ammonium Bi-carbonate/Mix all together	0.5 to 1	1 tsp
6	Custard powder/ Corn flour	5	50 gm
7	Milk powder	3 to 5	50 gm
8	Milk/Water	15 to 20	as req

Baking Temperature	Time	Production
175°C (350°F)	12 to 14 min	1.75 kg

Method:

1. Prepare the dough.
2. Rollout it to about 4 to 5 mm (1/6") thickness.
3. Prick with fork or design with grooved rolling pin.
4. Cut with desired shaped biscuit cutter.
5. Place on a baking tray 1 cm (½") apart from each other and bake.

(VARIETY BISCUIT)

Method:

1. Prepare dough as per the given recipe & process given & sheet to biscuit thickness.
2. Apply milk / egg wash on sheeted dough.
3. Sprinkle liberally with roasted/chopped/sliced dry fruit (i.e.kaju, walnut, pistachionut, almond etc.), cherry / tutee fruity at a rate of 10 to 15% (i.e. 100 gm for 1 kg flour) or cumin seed at a rate of 3 to 5% (48 gm for 1 kg flour).
4. Roll the dough just to fix dry fruit, rest 10 to 15 min and follow rest of all the process.

These biscuits can be termed as *Dry fruit Biscuit, Cashewnut Biscuit, Walnut Biscuit, Pistachionut Biscuit, Almond Biscuit, Cherry Biscuit, Tuti fruity Biscuit, Cumin Biscuit* etc.

Tips:

1. The quantity of shortening can be increased upto 80% (i.e.800 gm for 1 kg flour) depending on richness of the product.
2. Essence (similar to main ingredient) is to be replaced the vanilla (i.e. for cashew nut biscuit use cashewnut essence).

ORANGE BISCUIT, PINEAPPLE BISCUIT

MANGO BISCUIT, LEMON BISCUIT

Formula :

No	Ingredients	Per cent	Weight
1	Flour	100	1 kg
2	Shortening	50 to 70	600 gm
3	Sugar	50 to 70	500 gm
4	Liquid glucose	2	4 tsp
5	Egg	16 to 25	4 no
6	Baking powder	0.25 to 0.5	1/2 tsp
7	Baking soda	0.25 to 0.5	1/2 tsp
8	Ammonium Bi-carbonate	0.25 to 0.5	1/2 tsp
9	Milk powder	2 to 5	2 tsp
10	Corn flour	2 to 5	2 tsp

11	Water	2 to 5	as req
12	Iodized Salt	0.25	pinch
13	Essence (vanilla)	0.5 to I	1 tsp
Following Ingredients are chosen as per desired flavour:			
14	Essence	0.5 to 1	1 tsp
15	Essential oil/ Emulsion	0.5 to 1	2 tsp
16	Fruit juice	5 to 10	60ml
17	Colour	0.1 to 0.2	as des

Baking Temperature	Time	Production
150°C (300°F)	18 to 23 min	1.75 kg

Method:

1. Prepare the dough. However, save little egg before beating and add little bit of colour.
2. Sheet it into about 5 mm (1/6") thickness and apply egg wash.
3. Shaped with desired biscuit cutter, place on baking tray & bake.

Alteration:

1. Add about 10% (100 gm per 1kg flour) mix dry fruit (chopped/sliced), on sheeted-egg washed dough. Gentle press by rolling.

BALANCED BISCUIT

BAJARA BISCUIT AND ATTA BISCUIT

Formula :

No	Ingredients	Per cent	Weight		
			Balanced Biscuit	Bajara Biscuit	Atta Biscuit
1	Flour (Atta)	100	500 gm	500 gm	500 gm
2	Besan (Gram flour)	100	500 gm	-	-
3	Bajara flour	100	-	500 gm	-
4	Wheat flour	100	-	-	500 gm
5	Shortening	100	500 gm	500 gm	500 gm
6	Sugar	100	500 gm	500 gm	500 gm
7	Baking soda	1	1 tsp	1 tsp	1 tsp
8	Ammonium Bi-carbonate	1	I tsp	I tsp	1 tsp
9	Milk	40	as req	as req	as req

10	Essence (vanilla) (optional)	1	1 tsp	1 tsp	1 tsp

Baking Temperature	Time	Production
175°C (350°F)	12 to 14 min	1.75 kg

Method:

1. Mix the besan/ bajara flour/wheat flour with flour and prepare biscuit similar to plain biscuit.

Variation:

1. Replace the besan/ bajara flour / wheat flour with any other locally available cereal/pulse flour (i.e. jowar, rice, maize, mung etc.) and prepare sweet or masala biscuit.

Alteration:

1. Apply egg/ milk wash to sheeted dough, sprinkle with sesame seed / poppy seed or such other material, re-roll lightly to fix seeds, and follow the rest of the procedure.

MASALA BISCUIT, SWEET & SALTY BISCUITS

Recipe :

No	Ingredients	Per cent	Weight	
			Masala Biscuit	Sweet & Salty Biscuit
1	Flour	100	1 kg	1 kg
2	Shortening	40 to 50	500 gm	500 gm
3	Sugar	7/12	70 gm	120 gm
4	Baking powder	2.5	2 Tsp	-
5	Ammonium Bi-carbonate	3 to 5	-	2 Tsp
6	Salt	2 to 3	2 Tsp	2 Tsp
7	Curd / Milk	15 to 20	as req	as req
8	Green chillies	15 to 20	200 gm	-
9	Coriander leaves	15 to 20	200 gm	-
10	Green ginger	5 to 10	100gm	-
11	Curry leaves	10	100 gm	-
12	Ajwain	1 to 3	-	2 Tsp
13	Mint leaves	2 to 3	20 gm	-
14	Garam masala	2 to 3	4 tsp	-

Baking Temperature	Time	Production
175°C (350°F)	14 to 17 min	1.6 kg

Method:

1. Chop green chillies, curry leaves, mint leaves, coriander leaves, ginger etc. very fine and made into paste in a mixer jar.
2. Prepare a smooth dough as per the rubbing method. However, mix the green masala paste or ajwain into fat rubbed flour for masala biscuit and sweet & salty biscuit respectively.
3. Sheet the dough to about 5 mm (1/6") thickness. Prick with fork, die with biscuit cutter, place on tray & bake.

Variation:

1. Replace flour with bajara flour [50 to 100% (i. e. 500 gm for I kg flour)] and prepare bajara-masala-biscuit

CHERRY SHORT BISCUIT
CINNAMON CRESCENT BISCUIT

Formula :

No	Ingredients	Per cent	Weight	
			Cherry Short Biscuit	Cinnamon Biscuit
1	Flour	100	1 kg	1 kg
2	Shortening	60 to 70	700 gm	600 gm
3	Sugar	50	500 gm	500 gm
4	Egg	30	-	8 no
5	Baking powder	0.5 to 1	-	1 tsp
6	Essence (vanilla)	0.5 to 1	1 tsp	1 tsp
7	Essence	0.5 to 1	1 tsp (cherry)	I tsp (cinnamon)
8	Milk	5 to 10	as req	as req
9	Cherry/Tutee fruity	15 to 20	150 gm	-
10	Sugar (granules)	5 to 10	-	60gm
11	Cinnamon (powder)	1 to 2	-	4 tsp
12	Bread crumb/ Rice flour (optional)	10 to 15	150 gm	-

Baking Temperature	Time	Production
175°C (350°F)	12 to 15 min	2.0 kg

Process :

1. Prepare the dough by creaming method. However, mix the finely chopped tutee fruity and bread crumb into fat-sugar creamed mixture before addition of flour.
2. Sheet it in as mm (1/4") thickness, die with biscuit cutter, place in a tray and bake.

CINNAMON CRESCENT BISCUIT

Process :

1. Mix sugar (granules) and cinnamon (powder).
2. Prepare dough by rubbing method. However, save little egg for washing.
3. Place it on butter paper/simple paper and sheet the dough into rectangular shape to 3 mm (1/8") thickness.
4. Apply egg wash on half portion of the dough, sprinkle sugar -cinnamon mixture.
5. Fold the remaining half portion of dough over it and roll to biscuit thickness, if required. It will also help to fix the sugar.
6. Die with small-round biscuit cutter and again into the crescent and leaf shape.
7. Place on tray & bake.

COCONUT BISCUIT
COCONUT BURFI BISCUIT

Formula :

No	Ingredients	Per cent	Weight	
			Coconut Biscuit	Coconut Burfi Biscuit
1	Flour	100	1 kg	1 kg
2	Shortening	50 to 70	600 gm	700 gm
3	Sugar	50 to 70	500 gm	700 gm
4	Egg	12 to 16	4 no	-
5	Baking powder	0.5 to 1	1.1/2 tsp	1 tsp

7	Essence (coconut)	0.5 to 1	1/2 tsp	1/2 tsp
8	Coconut (dessicated)	20 to 25	200 gm	-
9	Coconut (fresh)	20 to 25	-	2 no
10	Cardamom powder	0.5 to 1	-	1 tsp
11	Milk powder	10	-	100 gm

Baking Temperature	Time	Production
150°C(300°F)	16 to 21 min	2.0 to 2.6 kg

Method:

1. Mix the dough by creaming method. However, mix all the grated fresh coconut for *burfi biscuit* and half of dessicated coconut for *Coconut biscuit* along with flour. Also save little egg before beating. .
2. Roll out the dough into 5 mm (1/6") thickness. Apply egg/ milk wash and sprinkle dessicated coconut liberally and sheet it again to fix the coconut.
3. Die with desired cutter, place in a tray & bake.

OR

2. Break the dough into small size, make into smooth ball. Only in case of coconut biscuit, roll out the ball in egg/milk liquid followed by dessicated coconut & re-press to fix the coconut. However, in case of burfi biscuit, ball is directly placed on tray.
3. Place on baking sheet [2.5 cm (1 ") apart], press with fork to biscuit thickness & bake.

FALAHARI BISCUIT, GAURI VRAT BISCUIT, EKADASHI BISCUIT

Formula :

No	Ingredients	Per cent	Weight		
			Falahari Biscuit	Gauri Vrat Biscuit	Ekadashi Biscuit
1	Poppy seed flour	40	400 gm	-	-
2	Dessicated coconut	30	300 gm	300 gm	-
3	Groundnut	30/70/100	300 gm	700 gm	1 kg
4	Shortening	30 to 50	500 gm	400 gm	300 gm
5	Sugar	40 to 60	500 gm	500 gm	500 gm
6	Baking powder	0.25 to 0.5	1/2 tsp	1 tsp	1/2 tsp
7	Milk/Water	2 to 5	as req	as req	as req
8	Cardamom-Nutmeg (powder)	3 to 5	1 Tsp	1 Tsp	1 Tsp

Baking Temperature	Time	Production
125°C (225°F)	22 to 27 min	1.5 to 1.8 kg

Procedure :

1. Rcast, dehulled and crush the groundnut finely.
2. Prepare dough by creaming method. Replacing flour by dessicated coconut, groundnut and/or poppy seed flour (as per formula).
3. Place the dough inbetween two plastic layer and sheet to 5 mm (1/6") thickness. Place cn tray & bake.

HEALTH BISCUIT

No	Ingredients	Per cent	Weight
1	Wheat flour	100	1 kg
2	Jaggery	100	1 kg
3	Butter	20	200 gm
4	Baking soda	2 to 3	2 Tsp
5	Ginger (dry-powder)	5 to 6	60gm
6	Water	25	as req
7	Sugar (granules)	10 to 15	as req

Baking Temperature	Time	Production
150°C (300°F)	13 to 15 min	1.750 kg

Method:

1. Mix ginger and baking soda with wheat flour.
2. Place jaggery, water and butter in a thick copper bottom steel *kadai.* Heat to melt & mix evenly.
3. Mix wheat flour properly and allow to cool.
4. Sheet into 5 mm (1/6") thickness, sprinkle with little sugar (granules), press to stick sugar.
5. Die with cutter, place on tray & bake.

TRI COLOUR BISCUIT
LEMON CREAM BISCUIT
CHOCO - MINT BISCUIT

Formula :

No	Ingredients	Per cent	Weight		
			Tri Colour Biscuit	Lemon Cream	Choco- mint Biscuit
1	Flour	100	1 kg	1 kg	1 kg
2	Shortening	50 to 60	600 gm	600 gm	500 gm
3	Sugar	45 to 65	500 gm	450 gm	650 gm
4	Castor sugar	5 to 10	-	75 gm	-
5	Egg	12	-	5 no	5 no (white)
6	Baking powder	0.5 to 1	2 tsp	3/4 tsp	3/4 tsp
7	Essence	0.5 to 1	2 tsp	2 tsp	2 tsp
8	Milk/Water	5 to 10	as req	as req	as req
9	Colour (red/yellow/green)	0.25	as req	as req	as req
10	Jam/Icing	30	300 gm (butler icing)	300 gm (lemon cream)	300 gm (mintneam)
11	Mixed spices (powder) (cinnamon, nutmeg, clove)	2 to 3	-	5 tsp	-
12	Ginger (powder)	0.5 to 1	-	1 tsp	-
13	Salt	0.25	pinch	pinch	pinch
14	Lemon juice	2 to 3	-	2 Tsp	-
15	Lemon rind	0.5 to 1	-	1 tsp	-
16	Chocolate	20 to 25	-	-	225 gm
17	Sugar (granules)	5 to 10	-	50gm	-
18	Chocolate (for glaze)	50	-	-	500 gm

Baking Temperature	Time	Production
180°C (355°F)	13 to 16 min	2.500 kg

(TRI COLOUR BISCUIT)

Method:

1. Prepare dough.
2. Roll it into 3 mm (1/8") thickness.
3. Cut even number of biscuit with cutter of about 7 cm (2.½") diameter.
4. Prick half the biscuit with fork and make three holes (similar to shirt

button size) in the remaining biscuit in such a way that it forms triangle. Place it on baking tray & bake.

5. Allow to cool completely. Sandwich one plain biscuit each white biscuit having holes with jam/butter icing.
6. Divide Jam/icing into three parts. Colour them differently (yellow Ired/ green). Fill each one into three holes. Jam may be replace with thick syrup.

Lemon Cream Biscuit

Method:

1. Prepare dough by creaming method.
2. Roll it into 3 mm (1/8") thickness. Die even number of biscuit with a round cutter having 5 cm (2") diameter. Place it on baking tray.
3. Apply egg/milk wash. Sprinkle liberally with sugar (granules) on the top & bake it.
4. Allow to cool. Sandwich two biscuits with lemon cream icing.

Tip:

1. The flavour can be changed to Chocolate, Orange or pineapple etc.

CHOCO - MINT BISCUIT

Method:

1. Prepare dough by creaming method. However, mix melted chocolate before addition of flour.
2. Roll it into 3 mm (1/8") thickness. And cut even number of biscuit with a round cutter having 5 cm (2") diameter.
3. Place on baking tray & bake. Then the same may allow to cool.
4. Sandwich two biscuit with mint cream icing.
5. Prepare glaze. For that, place chocolate in a bowl and place it in big bowl containing hot water. Stir till the chocolate melt. If required, hit the water again. Never melt chocolate on direct heat as it will burn out.
6. Dip the creamed biscuit in chocolate glaze upto half level.
7. Allow it to set. See that the glazed portion does not disturbed.

VANILLA CREAM FINGER
VIENNESE FINGER
CHOCOLATE ECLAIRS

Recipe :

No	Ingredient	Per cent	Weight		
			Vanilla Cream	Viennese Finger	Chocolate Eclairs
1	Flour	100	1 kg	1 kg	1 kg
2	Shortening	50/100	500 gm	1 kg	1 kg
3	Sugar	40 to 50	50 gm	400 gm	pinch
4	Egg	25/15/110	6 no	4 no	28 no
5	Baking powder	1	2 tsp	-	-
6	Lemon rind powder	1.5	1 Tsp	1 tsp	-
7	Essence(vanilla)	0.5 to 1	2 tsp	2 tsp	2 tsp
8	Essence (chocolate)	0.5 to 1	-	-	1 tsp
9	Milk/Water	5 to 10	as req	as req	as req
	For filling				
10	Butter icing	25 to 30	300 gm	300 gm	300 gm
	For glazing				
11	Chocolate	30	-	300 gm	
12	Couverture chocolate	45	-	-	450 gm
13	Milk	100	-	-	1 lt
14	Shortening	5	-	-	50 gm
15	Dessicated coconut	10 to 20	-	-	150 gm

Baking Temperature	Time	Production
180°C (355°F)	16 min	2.300 kg

Method:

1. Prepare dough by creaming method. The dough should be of piping consistency (i.e. it can be pass through the icing nozzle). Mix lemon rind powder into flour (as per formula).
2. Place star nozzle in a icing bag & fill the dough.
3. Pipe out 5 cm (2") long strips on baking tray & bake. Dry at lower temperature just like toast, if required .
4. Allow to cool. Sandwich two strips with butter icing.

Glazing: except vanilla cream finger.

Viennese Finger:

1. Melt the chocolate by double boiler method (i.e. as per the method given. Deep both the edges [about 5 mm (1/4")] of each sandwich biscuit in a melted chocolate.

Chocolate Eclairs:

1. Melt the chocolate with the help of hot water i.e. double boiler method. Add milk & shortening. Keep stirring to the smooth pest and cool. Coat it to the top of sandwich biscuit and granish with silver almond slices or dessicated coconut.

VANILLA BUTTON

Recipe:

No	Ingredients	Per cent	Weight
1	Flour	100	1 kg
2	Shortening	70	700 gm
3	Sugar	40	400gm
4	Egg	30	8 no
5	Baking powder	0.5 to 1	1 tsp
6	Essence (vanilla)	1	2 tsp
7	Milk/Water	5 to 10	as req
8	Jam	10 to 15	150 gm
9	Iodized Salt	0.25 to 0.5	pinch

Baking Temperature	Time	Production
190°C (375°F)	17 min	2.05 kg

Procedure :

1. Prepare the pipeable dough.
2. Place a big star nozzle in a icing bag. Fill with dough and pipe out to button shape directly on baking tray.
3. Decorate with small drop of jam in the centre of the biscuit & bake.

Tip:

1. Wet the icing bag with water before filling dough so that shortening does not leak out from bag.

COLOUR PASTRY
CHECK BISCUIT

Recipe :

No	Ingredients	Per cent	Weight Colour Pastry Check Biscuit
1	Flour	100	1 kg
2	Shortening	60	600 gm
3	Sugar	40 to 50	500 gm
4	Egg	16	4 no
5	Baking soda	0.5 to 1	-
6	Baking powder	0.5 to 1	1 tsp
7	Milk powder	5 to 10	-
8	Essence (vanilla)	0.5 to 1	1 tsp
9	Essence (orange)	0.5	-
10	Essence(almond)	0.5	1 tsp
11	Essence(rasburry)	0.5	1 tsp
12	Colour (red/yellow/green)	0.25 to 0.5	as req
13	Cherry/tutee fruity	10 to 25	-
14	Groundnut	20 to 25	-
15	Iodized Salt	0.25 to 0.5	pinch

Baking Temperature	Time	Production
190°C (375° F)	13 to 16 min	1.8 kg

COLOUR PASTRY

Procedure :

1. Prepare a dough by creaming procedure.
2. Divide into 2 portion. And again divide only 1 portion into 2 parts.
3. Add pink & green colour in each quarter portion and roll out into pencil shape.
4. Roll out the half portion into 7 to 8 cm (2.1/2 to 3 ") wide strip of 3 mm (118") thickness. Apply egg wash.
5. Place both the pencil (joint together) in the middle of the strip and apply egg wash.

6. Now fold the dough strip on pencil so as make a diagonal shape.
7. Allow to cool in refrigerator until it sets properly (about 1 hr).
8. Cut dough into 5 mm (1/6") thickness slices. Place in tray & bake.

CHECK BISCUIT

Procedure :

1. Prepare the dough by creaming process.
2. Divide it into 2 portions and again divide only 1 halves into 2 parts (i.e. quarter part).
3. Mix yellow colour and vanilla essence into a half part.
4. Mix green colour and almond essence into quarter portion.
5. Mix red colour and raspberry essence into other quarter portion.
6. Roll out the yellow colour part into 9 to 10 cm (3.1/2 to 4") wide strips of 3 mm (1/8") thickness. Apply egg/ milk wash.
7. Roll out the green and pink doughs into pencil shape and divide exactly into two part.
8. Place 1 pink and 1 green pencil & join together in the middle of yellow strip.
9. Now place the pink & green pencil alternatively on the previously arranged pencils.
10. Now fold the dough strip on pencil so as to make a diagonal.
11. Allow to cool in refrigerator until sets properly (about 1 hr).
12. Slice the dough into biscuit thickness [i.e. about 5 mm (1/6")]. Place on tray & bake.

Alteration:

1. Divide dough into 2 parts. Add green colour & almond essence in 1 part and pink colour & raspberry essence in another part. Made into pencil shape having about 2.5 cm (1 ") diameter. Apply egg/milk wash. Place both the pencil joint together on wax or butter paper as indicated earlier and follow rest of the process.

NUT SQUARE

Process :

1. Prepare the dough by creaming method. However, mix the roasted, dehulled, finely crushed ground nut with flour.
2. Made the dough into diagonal. Place in refrigerator till sets properly (about 1 hr).

3. Slice with sharp knife into biscuit thickness [i.e. about 5 mm (1/6")].
4. Apply egg/ milk wash, place on tray & bake.

CHERRY IBC

Process :

1. Prepare the dough. However, add finely chopped tutee fruity / cherry into flour before mixing.
2. Made into triangle shape and allow to cool in refrigerator for about 1 hr.
3. Slice with sharp knife into biscuit thickness [i.e. about 5 mm (1/6")].
4. If desired, apply milk/egg wash and place on tray & bake.

Re-Check :

1. If desired, divide the dough into 3 or more parts, colour them differently as per choice and made into desired shape (i.e. round, oblong, pentagonal etc.).
2. Orange pill powder can also be mixed at the rate of 2 to 3% (i.e. 20 gm for 1 kg flour).
3. Replace dry fruit [i.e. 10% cashewnut (100 gm for I kg flour), 4% pistachionut (40 gm for 1 kg flour) & 1 % cardamom-nutmeg powder (2 tsp for 1 kg flour)] to cherry/tutee fruity. The cashewnut & pistachionut should be soaked in water for 2 hr before mixing and chopped/sliced finely.

FANCY CHOCOLATE BISCUIT

Recipe :

No	Ingredient	Per cent	Weight
1	Flour	100	1 kg
2	Shortening	60 to 70	650 gm
3	Sugar	50 to 60	600 gm
4	Baking powder	0.5 to 0.75	1 Tsp
5	Milk powder	2 to 5	2 Tsp
6	Cocoa powder	5 to 7	50 gm
7	Essence (chocolate)	0.5 to 1	1 tsp
8	Milk / Water	2 to 5	as req
9	Iodized Salt	0.25 to 0.5	1/2 tsp

Baking Temperature	Time	Production
150°C (300°F)	16 to 21 min	1.95 kg

Procedure :

1. Prepare dough by desired method. However, do not mix cocoa powder. Now shape differently as mentioned.

CHOCO STRIP

2. Divide dough into 2 portions. Add cocoa powder in 1 half and mix thoroughly. If required, add about 2% (20 gm for I kg flour) shortening to mix cocoa powder thoroughly.
3. Place this half on plain halve and roll out into oblong shape to 5 mm (1/6") thickness.
4. Divide it lengthwise into 3 to 4 strip and apply milk wash. Arrange the strip on one another and press gently to stick.
5. Made in into diagonal shape and place in refrigerator till sets (about 1 hr).
6. Slice into biscuit thickness [5 mm (1/6")], arrange in tray & bake.

CHOCO HALF

2. Divide the dough into two parts and mix cocoa in 1 portion as mentioned above.
3. Sheet both (the plain & cocoa dough) half to 3 to 4 mm (1/8 to 1/6") thickness separately (the size of both portion should be similar). Apply milk wash on plain portion and place cocoa portions on that & sheet gently just to stick.
4. Die with desired shape biscuit cutter. Place on tray & bake.

CHOCO ROUND

2. Divide the dough into two equal portions & mix cocoa powder in 1 portion as earlier.
3. Take equal parts of both the portions and made into smooth ball of walnut size.
4. Place on baking sheet about 2.5 cm (1") distance. Press with fork to biscuit thickness [i.e. 5 mm (1/6")] and bake.

CHOCO CHECK

2. Divide dough into two equal parts and mix cocoa powder into one part.
3. Now prepare a check board replacing white & brown colour dough to red & green colour dough as shown in alteration of check biscuit.

OR

2. Divide dough into 2 halves and again divide 1 halve into 2 parts i.e. quarter part.
3. Mix cocoa powder into 1 quarter (if required decrease the quantity of cocoa powder to half) and yellow colour in halve portion.
4. Prepare checks similar to check biscuit. Replacing white & brown dough to red & green dough respectively.

CHOCO SPRING

2. Separate 1/4 or 1/5 dough and mix with cocoa powder (decrease the quantity of cocoa powder proportionately).
3. Sheet the plain dough to about 3 mm (1/6") thickness into oblong shape and apply milk wash.
4. Roll out the brown dough into very thin [about 1 mm(1/25")] oblong sheet (similar to brown dough size).
5. Place it on white sheet.
6. Roll it just like swees-roll so as to form distinct spiral spring. Place in refrigerator to set (about I hr).
7. Slice to biscuit thickness [5 mm (1/6")] with sharp knife.

CHOCO RING

2. Divide dough into 2 equal parts and mix cocoa powder in 1 part.
3. Roll out the plain dough into oblong shape of 3 mm (1/8") thickness, apply milk wash, cut (lengthwise) into 6 to 7 cm (2.1/2") wide strips.
4. Roll out the brown dough into pencil shape (to the thumb size thickness) Divide into similar number of strip. Place one brown strip over plain strip each and fold from all the side to cover brown dough completely, so as to have a brown ring inside and white covering outside.
5. Place it in a refrigerator to set (about I hr).
6. Slice into biscuit thickness [5mm (1/6")]. place on tray and bake.

CHERRY KNOB
NUTTY PRETZELS
NUT RING

Recipe:

No	Ingredients	Per cent	Weight		
			Cherry Nut	Nutty Pretzels	Nut Ring
1	Flour	100	1 kg	1 kg	I kg
2	Shortening	100/50	1 kg	500 gm	500 gm
3	Sugar	40 to 50	400 gm	500 gm	500 gm
4	Egg	15 to 30	4 no	5 no	8 no
5	Baking powder	0.5 to 1.5	1 Tsp	-	1 tsp
6	Groundnut	100/20/30	1 kg	200 gm	300 gm
7	Milk	5 to 10	as req	as req	as req
8	Cherry/Tutee fruity	15	150 gm	-	-
9	Essence (vanilla)	0.5 to 1	1 tsp	1 tsp	1 tsp
10	Essence (lemon /orange/pineapple)	0.5 to 1	1 tsp	1 tsp	1 tsp
11	Essence (groundnut/almond)	0.25 to 0.5	1/2 tsp	1/2 tsp	1/2 tsp
12	Salt	0.25 to 0.5	pinch	pinch	pinch
13	Lemon/orange rind (powder)	0.5	1 tsp	1 tsp	1 tsp

Baking Temperature	Time	Production
175°C (350°F)	14 to 16 min	2 to 2.4 kg

CHERRY KNOB

Process :

1. Prepare the dough. However, separate half of egg white before beating. Add half portion of roasted, dehulled, braked groundnut pieces to the flour.
2. Break the dough to the walnut size and roll into smooth ball.
3. Wash with egg white/milk. And roll into remaining groundnut pieces.
4. Place it on baking tray and press half cherry on top and bake.

NUTTY PRETZELS

Process :

1. Prepare the dough by rubbing method. However, save half of the white before beating.
2. Sheet the dough into about 3 mm *(1/8")* thickness and cut into strips of about 20 to 25 cm (9 to 10") length and 5 to 6 mm (1/4") width.
3. Made into pencil shape and knot into fancy tie.
4. Wash with egg white on top and sprinkle freely with braked pieces (medium size) of roasted, dehulled groundnut. Press gently to stick properly. If desired, press half cherry/tutee fruity on one or two places.
5. Place on tray & bake.

NUT RING

Process :

1. Prepare the dough by rubbing recipe. However, separate half of the egg white before beating.
2. Sheet the dough into 5 mm(1/6") thickness and made into ring shape with doughnut cutter or die with big round biscuit cutter and make hole in the centre with a smaller cutter. Doughnut cutter may be much useful for this purpose.
3. Brush the biscuit with egg white (separated previously) and sprinkle freely with roasted, dehulled, crushed ground nut pieces and press gently to stick.
4. Place on tray & bake.

FRUIT ROCK BISCUIT
COCONUT ROCK BISCUIT
ROCK BUNS

Recipe :

No	Ingredients	Per cent	Weight		
			Cherry Nut	Nutty Pretzels	Nut Ring
1	Flour	100	1 kg	1 kg	I kg
2	Shortening	30/60	300 gm	300 gm	600 gm
3	Sugar	30/60	300 gm	300 gm	600 gm
4	Egg	20 to 30	5 no	5 no	8 no
5	Baking powder	2 to 3	2 Tsp	2 Tsp	4 tsp
6	Milk powder	8	80 gm	-	-
7	Sultana/Tutee fruity	20 to 25	250 gm	-	200 gm
8	Desicated coconut	20 to 25	-	250 gm	-
9	Orange rind powder	2 to 3	20gm	20 gm	20gm
10	Salt	0.25 to 1.0	1.1/2 tsp	1.1/2 tsp	1/2 tsp
11	Essence (vanilla)	0.5 to 1.0	1.1/2 tsp	1.1/2 tsp	-
12	Essence (lemon)	0.5 to 1	1/2 tsp	1/2 tsp	-
13	Essence (orange)	1	1/2 tsp	1/2 tsp	-
14	Colour(yellow)	0.25 to 0.5	as req	as req	-
15	Colour(orange)	0.25 to 0.5	-	-	as rcq
16	Sugar(brown)	8 to 10	80gm	80gm	-
17	Water	40 to 60	500 ml	600ml	400ml

Baking Temperature	Time	Production
175°C (350°F)	16 to 20 min	2.100 kg

Process :

1. Prepare the dough by rubbing method. However, mix the sultana/tutee fruity or dessicated coconut and orange rind powder (whatever added) into flour. For fruit rock & coconut rock biscuit save little egg before beating.
2. Break into walnut size pieces and made into rock shape. Do not press much.
3. Brush with egg and sprinkle with sugar (granules) (except rock buns). Place half cherry on each piece.
4. Arrange in tray and bake.

27

Manufacturing of Cakes

(CUP CAKE)

Formula :

No	Ingredients	Per cent	Weight
1	Flour	100	1 kg
2	Shortening	70 to 90	750 gm
3	Sugar	80 to 100	1 kg
4	Egg	80 to 100	20 no
5	Baking powder	1.5 to 2	1 Tsp
6	Essence (vanilla and/or desired)	1.5 to 2	1 Tsp
7	Milk/Water	15 to 20	as req

Baking Temperature	Time	Production
175°C (350°F)	20 min	100 to 108 Nos.

Process :

1. Prepare cake batter by creaming method.
2. Place paper-cup in cup-cake-tin and fill the batter upto 3/4 part, place on baking tray & bake.

Variation:

CHOCOLATE BUNS

Process :

1. Mix 15% (150 gm for 1 kg flour) cocoa powder into flour and follow rest of the formula & procedure mentioned above.

CHERRY BUNS

Process :

1. Chop the glazed cherry finely and mix into flour at the rate of 25% (i.e. 250 gm for 1 kg flour). Follow rest of formula & method mentioned above.
2. Allow to cool the cup cakes. Roll the top of cake in icing sugar/ powder sugar and decorate with half cherry. It will require about 15 to 20% (200 gm for 1 kg flour) sugar and cherry.

ALMOND / CASHEWNUT CUP CAKE

Process :

1. Add roasted, crushed almond or cashewnut to flour at the rate of 10 to 20% (i.e. 200 gm for 1 kg flour) and follow rest of formula & procedure of cup cake. Save little nuts & sprinkle on top before baking.

CHOCO-CHIP CUP CAKE

Process :

1. Grate chocolate bar into chips and add to batter at the rate of 10 to 20% (i.e. 200 gm for 1 kg flour) and follow rest of the formula & procedure of cup cake. The top may be decorate by sprinkling little choco chips before baking.

BUTTER CUP CAKE

Process :

1. Mix butter and fat in equal quantity and use as shortening. Follow rest of the formula & procedure of cup cake given on earlier page.

MAWA CUP CAKE / MAWA CAKE

Recipe :

No	Ingredients	Per cent	Weight
1	Flour	100	1 kg
2	Shortening	140 to 150	1.4 kg
3	Sugar	100	1 kg
4	Egg	80	20 no
5	Essence(vanilla)	0.5 to 1	1 tsp
6	Cardamom-Nutmeg (powder)	2 to 4	2 Tsp
7	Khoa (mawa)	40 to 50	400 gm

Baking Temperature	Time	Capacity
150°C (300°F)	18 to 23 min	3 to 4 kg

Process :

1. Prepare batter as per creaming method. However, mix broken pieces of khoa with creamed shortening before adding sugar. The cardamom-nutmeg (powder) is to be mixed with flour.
2. Place paper-cup in cup-cake-tin and pour batter upto 3/4 part into it, arrange in a baking tray and bake.

MUFFINS

Recipe :

No	Ingredients	Per cent	Weight
1	Flour	100	1 kg
2	Shortening	50 to 60	500 gm
3	Sugar	80 to 100	1 kg
4	Egg	50	12 no
5	Baking powder	2 to 3	25 gm
6	Essence (vanilla and/or desired)	0.5 to 1	2 tsp
7	Milk/Water	10 to 30	as req
8	Liquid glucose	2 to 5	50 gm
9	Milk powder	5 to 10	50 gm
10	Corn flour	5 to 10	50 gm
11	Iodized Salt	0.25 to 0.5	1/2 tsp
12	Essential oil (as per flavour i.e. Orange, Vanilla, Chocolate)	0.5 to 1	1 tsp
13	Emulsion(optional) (as per flavour i.e. Vanilla/Orange)	0.5 to 1	1 tsp
14	Colour (if required) (as per flavour)	0.1 to 0.2	as req
15	Icing	25 to 30	300 gm
16	Jam/Cherry/Gem ball etc. (optional)	10 to 20	as req

Baking Temperature	Time	Production
175°C (350°F)	18 min	100 to 123 no

Process :

1. Prepare cup-cakes as mentioned above and allow to cool.
2. Cover with butter icing. Garnish top with drop of jam, half cherry, jams ball or chopped dry fruits.

ORANGE MUFFINS

Method:

1. Prepare the cup cake as mentioned. However, use about 30% (300 ml for I kg flour) fresh orange juice instead of water/ milk for good quality.
2. Cover with orange butter cream. The top may be decorated.

(MANGO MUFFINS)

Method:

1. Prepare cup cake as described earlier, except mix fresh mango pulp at the rate of 20 to 25% (i.e. 200 gm for I kg flour) into batter. As a result the quantity of water / milk is reduced.
2. Decorate with mango flavoured butter cream. Followed by topping with cherry, choco-chips, gems and/or dry fruits etc.

(BANANA MUFFINS)

Method :

1. Prepare the cup cake as earlier described. However, mix about 80 to 90% (i.e. 800 gm for 1 kg flour) ripe banana into batter instead of milk/ water.
2. Let it be cooled. Cover with banana or coconut flavoured butter cream and decorate with chopped almond and /or cherry etc.

(COCONUT MUFFINS)

Process :

1. Prepare cup cake as described earlier.
2. Allow to cool & cover with coconut flavoured butter cream. Roll out into dessicated coconut 10% (i.e. 100 gm for 1 kg flour). Place half cherry on top centre.

Tips:

1. Any other type of cup cake can be transferred into muffins by coating it with same type of butter cream & decorate with same kind of ingredient i.e. choco chip cup cake can be coated with choco butter cream & decorated with choco chips.
2. The muffins without covering & decoration can be sold out as a cup cake of a particular flavour i.e. orange muffins as *orange cup cake.*

WELSE CHEESE CAKE

Manufacturing Recipe :

No	Ingredients	Per cent	Weight
	Part-I:		
1	Flour	100	1 kg
2	Shortening	50	500 gm
3	Sugar	15	150 gm
4	Baking powder	1	2 tsp
5	Cold water	10 to 20	as req
6	Jam	50	500 gm
	Part-2 :		
7	Flour	100	1 kg
8	Shortening	100	1 kg
9	Sugar	100	1 kg
10	Egg	65	16 no
11	Baking powder	1 to 2	4 tsp
12	Essence(vanilla)	1 to 2	4 tsp
13	Milk/Water	10 to 20	as req

Baking Temperature	Time	Production
175°C (350°F)	18 to 23 min	145-150 Nos.

Process :

Part-1:

1. Prepare biscuit dough by rubbing method or desired procedure.
2. Roll it out into 3 mm (l/8") thickness & round cut with biscuit cutter of about 7 cm (3 ") round.
3. Place it on greased dusted petty cake tin (individually in one compartment) and spread a little jam.

Part-2 :

1. Prepare cake batter as described earlier.
2. Add tea spoonful of batter on each biscuit dough piece & bake.

QUEEN CAKE
MEDELINS
COCONUT CASTLE

No	Ingredients	Per cent	Weight		
			Queen Cake	Medelins	Coconut Castle
1	Flour	100	1 kg	1 kg	1 kg
2	Shortening	80 to 100	1 kg	1 kg	800 gm
3	Sugar	80 to 120	1.2 kg	1 kg	800 gm
4	Egg	40/120/60	10 no	30 no	15no
5	Baking powder	1.5 to 2	4 tsp	4 tsp	3 tsp
6	Essence (vanilla)	1 to 2	4 tsp	2 tsp	2 tsp
7	Essence(coconut)	0.5 to 1	-	2 tsp	2 tsp
8	Mix dry fruit (cashewnut, sultana, tutee fruity-optional)	25 to 50	500 gm	250 gm	250 gm
9	Dessicated coconut	25 to 30	-	-	250 gm
10	Milk	10 to 20	as req	as req	as req
	For Decoration:				
11	Jam and/or sugar syrup	50	500 gm	500 gm	500 gm
12	Dessicated coconut	30 to 50	-	300 gm	300 gm
13	Cherry/Tutee fruity	20 to 40	-	200 gm	-
14	Colour (red/yellow)	0.1 to 0.2	-	as req	as req

QUEEN CAKE

Baking Temperature	Time	Production
170°C (350°F)	13 to 16 min	145 to 150 Nos.

Process :

1. Prepare the cake by creaming method.
2. Grease the fat into patty cake tin, dust with flour, turn up side down to remove excess dusting.
3. Place spoonful batter on each compartment and bake.

(MEDELINS)

Baking Temperature	Time	Production
205°C (400°F)	11 to 14 min	57 to 62 no.

Process :

1. Add baking powder into flour and sieve twice.
2. Cream shortening & flour till light and fluffy as similar to sugar & fat.
3. Break egg in a bowl having smaller bottom than top and add essence. Place it on pot (*tapeli*) containing hot water- Be careful that the water does not touch to pot. Beat until stiff.
4. Add sugar gradually with continuous beating.
5. Remove from hot water as soon as all the sugar added.
6. Add flour-shortening mixture and blend thoroughly.
7. Grease and dust the medelins tin and fill batter upto 3/4 portion.
8. Place on tray & bake.
9. Remove immediately from tin and allow to cool.
10. Roll it out into jam-sugar syrup mixture. Followed by rolling in dessicated coconut.
11. Place upside down & gently press half cherry/tutee fruity on top.

Tips:

1. Use of red colour jam is preferable. However, other colours can also be used, if desired. Add more colour, if required.
2. If the medilins top is round in shape, flatten it with knife.

(COCONUT CASTLE)

Baking Temperature	Time	Production
190°C (375°F)	16 to 21 min	54 no

Method:

1. Prepare the batter by creaming method. However, mix the dessicated coconut into batter before filling into tin.
2. Fill the batter into greased dusted medelins tin upto 3/4 portion, place on baking tray, bake, cool, roll into jam-syrup mixture & dessicated coconut similar to medelins.

SPONGE & POUND CAKE

Recipe :

No	Ingredients	Per cent	Weight	
			Sponge Cake	Pound Cake
1	Flour	100	1 kg	1 kg
2	Shortening	80 to 100	800 gm	1 kg
3	Sugar	80 to 120	1.200 kg	1 kg
4	Egg	80 to 100	20 no	25 no
5	Baking powder	2 to 3	5 tsp	2 tsp (optional)
6	Essence (vanilla)	1 to 2	2 tsp	2 tsp
7	Salt	0.25 to 0.5	1/2 tsp	1/2 tsp
8	Milk powder	5 to 10	100 gm	-
9	Corn flour	5 to 10	100 gm	-
10	Milk/Water	10 to 20	as req	as req

Baking Temperature	Time	Production
170°C (3500F)	16 to 21 min	3 to 3.75 kg

Process :

1. Prepare cake batter by creaming method.
2. Pour in greased & dusted cake-tin & bake.

ORANGE CAKE, MANGO CAKE AND BANANA CAKE

Recipe :

No	Ingredients	Percent	Weight		
			Orange Cake	Mango Cake	Banana Cake
1	Flour	100	1 kg	1 kg	1 kg
2	Shortening	72 to 80	800 gin	700 gin	700 gin
3	Sugar	63 to 90	650 gin	900 gin	800 gm
4	Egg	60 to 80	15 no	20 no	20 no
5	Baking powder	1.5 to 5	3 Tsp	1 Tsp	2 Tsp
6	Essence (vanilla)	0.5 to 1	1 tsp	1 tsp	1 tsp

7	Essence (as per flavour)	0.5 to1	1 tsp	1 tsp	1 tsp
8	Essential oil (as per flavour)	0.5 to 1	1 tsp	1 tsp	1 tsp
9	Emulsion (as per flavour)	0.5 to 1	1 tsp	1 tsp	1 tsp
10	Milk powder	4 to 5	50 gm	50 gm	50 gm
11	Corn flour	5 to 10	50 gm	50 gm	50 gill
12	Iodized Salt	0.25 to 0.5	1/2 tsp	1/2 tsp	1/2 tsp
13	Orange rind powder	1 to 2	2 tsp	-	-
14	Orange juice	30 to 40	400 ml	-	-
15	Banana pulp	40 to 50	-		400 gm
16	Cinnamon powder	2 to 3	-	2 tsp	-
17	Mango pulp	15 to 25	-	150 gm	-
18	Water	2 to 5	as req	as req	as req
Baking Temperature 175°C (350°F)		**Time** 16 to 21 min		**Production** 3.0 to 3.5 kg	

Method:

1. Prepare batter by creaming method. Mix mango pulp/ orange juice/ banana pulp into batter before pouring into cake tin.
2. Pour the batter into greased dusted cake tin. Place on tray & bake.

ORANGE MARMALADE CAKE

Process :

1. Replace orange juice with orange marmalade jam in the same quantity and follow rest of all the process of orange cake.

BANANA WALNUT CAKE

No	Ingredients	Per cent	Weight
1	Flour	100	1 kg
2	Shortening	100	1 kg
3	Sugar	100	I kg
4	Egg	125	30 no
5	Baking powder	1 to 2	1 Tsp
6	Banana pulp	40 to 50	400 gm
7	Walnut	75 to 80	750 gm

Baking Temperature	Time	Production
180°C (355°F)	30 min	4.0 kg

Process :

1. Crush the walnut & cut the banana into small pieces.
2. Prepare batter as per the creaming method.
3. Mix banana & walnut. Pour batter in greased-dusted cake-tin. Place in tray & bake.

DRY FRUIT CAKE, DESSERT CAKE, CHRISTMAS CAKE / RICH PLUM CAKE

Recipe:

No	Ingredients	Per cent	Weight		
			Dry Fruit Cake	Dessert Cake	Christmas Cake/ PlumCake
1	Flour	100	1 kg	1 kg	1 kg
2	Shortening	60 to 80	800 gm	600 gm	800 gm
3	Sugar	80 to 100	1 kg	800 gm	1 kg
4	Corn flour	10	100 gm	100 gm	100 gm
5	Egg	80 to 100	20 no	24 no	24 no
6	Baking powder	1 to 2	2 tsp	2 tsp	2 tsp
7	Essence (vanilla lemon, almond, mix fruit, rum)	0.25 to 0.5 (each)	1/2 tsp	1/2 tsp	1/2 tsp
8	Glycerin	5 to 10	50 gm	50gm	50gm
9	Sultan	80 to 100	800 gm	800 gm	1 kg
10	Currants	80/200	-	800 gm	2 kg
11	Almond	10 to 25	100gm	250 gm	100 gm
12	Cashewnut	20 to 50	500 gm	-	250 gm
13	Cherry	20 to 50	500 gm	400 gm	250 gm
14	Tuity fruity	50	500 gm	-	-
15	Lemon & Orange rind powder	0.5 to 1	2 tsp	2 tsp	2 tsp
16	Lemon & Orange juice	5 to 10	50 ml	50 ml	50ml
17	Cardamom-Nutmeg powder	2 to 3	2 Tsp	2 Tsp	2 Tsp
18	Mixed spices	3 to 5	-	-	40 gm
19	Caramel	10 to 25	100 ml	-	250 ml
20	Iodized Salt	0.25 to 0.5	1 tsp	1 tsp	1 tsp
21	Rum	10	-	-	100 ml
22	Liquid glucose	10	100 ml	100 ml	100 ml
23	Water	5 to 10	as req	as req	as req

Baking Temperature	Time	Production
150°C (300°F)	38 to 49 min	6 to 6.75 kg

Process :

1. Wash the fruit and whip with dry cloth. Mix with lemon and orange juice, lemon & orange rind powder, cardamom-nutmeg/mix spice powder, rum (whichever formula contains), and rest about 2 hr.
2. Prepare batter by creaming method. Add caramel, liquid glucose, glycerine etc. and fruit at the last stage of mixing.
3. Place in suitable size cake tin and bake.

BOILED FRUIT CAKE

Process :

1. Prepare cake similar to dry fruit cake (as described earlier), Except the fruits are boiled as below:

For boiling fruit:

Recipe :

No	Ingredients	Per cent	Weight
1	Cashewnut	10 to 15	125 gm
2	Tuity fruity	25 to 30	250 gm
3	Raisins (Kishmish)	10 to 15	125 gm
4	Water	125 to 150	1.5 lt
5	Sugar (granules)	50	500 gm
6	Lime juice	2 to 3	2 Tsp

Method:

1. Boil sugar & water together, add tuty fruity and heat. Add lime juice.
2. Add raisins & cashewnut (if desired chopped) and allow to cook for 18 to 20 min. Cool & use to mix with batter.

SULTAN CAKE, MEXICAN CAKE, LUXURY CAKE

Recipe :

No	Ingredients	Per cent Cake	Weight: Sultan Cake	Weight: Mexican Cake	Weight: Luxury
1	Flour	100	1 kg	1 kg	1 kg
2	Shortening	100/45/30	1 kg	450 gm	300 gm
3	Sugar	75 to 100	1 kg	850 gm	750 gm
4	Egg	60 to 100	15 no	16 no	25 no
5	Baking powder	1 to 2	2 tsp	1 Tsp	1 Tsp
6	Essence(vanilia)	0.5 to 1	1 tsp	2 tsp	2 tsp
7	Essence(lemon)	0.5 to 1	1 tsp	-	-
8	Raisins	80	800 gm	-	-
9	Walnut	25 to 30	-	300 gm	-
10	Iodized Salt	0.25 to 0.5	pinch	pinch	-
11	Milk/Water	50 to 60	-	550 ml	-
12	Lemon rind powder	2 to 5	-	2 tsp	2 tsp
13	Orange juice	25	-	-	250 ml
14	Nutmeg(powder)	0.75	-	-	1.1/2 tsp
15	Chocolate	40	-	-	400 gm
16	Cashewnut	15	-	-	150 gm

Baking Temperature	Time	Production
150°C (300°F)	27 to 32 min	2 to 2.65 kg

Method:

1. Prepare batter by creaming procedure. However, add presoaked fruits as described above.
2. Pour it into cake-tin and bake.

CHERRY CAKE
PINEAPPLE, CHERRY UPSIDE DOWN CAKE

Recipe:

No	Ingredients	Per cent	Weight	
			Cherry Cake	Pineapple Cherry Upside Down Cake
1	Flour	100	1 kg	1 kg
2	Shortening	60 to 70	700 gm	600 gm
3	Sugar	70 to 75	700 gm	750 gm
4	Egg	40 to 50	10 no	10 no
5	Baking powder	2 to 2.5	4 tsp	5 tsp
6	Essence (vanilla)	1	2 tsp	2 tsp
7	Cherry/Tutee fruity	50/10	500 gm	100 gm
8	Walnut	5	-	50 gm
9	Pineapple slices	500	-	as req
10	Cinnamon powder	1	-	2 tsp
11	Mixed spice powder	1	-	2 tsp
12	Water/Milk	10 to 20	as req	as req
13	Iodized Salt	0.25 to 0.5	pinch	pinch
14	Fat	25	-	250 gm
15	Sugar (brown)	25	-	250 gm

(CHERRY CAKE)

Baking Temperature	Time	Production
175°C (300°F)	24 to 29 min	2 to 2.45 kg

Method:

1. Chop & clean cherry & mix into flour and follow rest of all the creaming process to prepare cake.

PINEAPPLE CHERRY UPSIDE DOWN CAKE

Baking Temperature	Time	Production
205°C (400°F)	35 min	3.5 to 4.0 kg

Process :

1. Cream fat & sugar (brown) and apply it on the bottom of cake tin.
2. Place pineapple slices on that and keep half cherry at the centre of each slice and fill the remaining part with walnut.
3. Prepare the batter by creaming Process. Pour it on pineapple slices & bake.
4. Allow to cool for 5 to 10 min after baking and then transfer from tin to cooling rack in such a way that it turns upside down.

DATE CAKE, DATE & WALNUT CAKE, DATE & GINGER CAKE

No	Ingredients	Percent	Weight		
			Date Cake	Date & Walnut Cake	Date & Ginger Cake
1	Flour	100	1 kg	1 kg	1 kg
2	Shortening	75/90/35	750 gm	900 gm	350 gm
3	Sugar	100/45	1 kg	1 kg	450 gm
4	Egg	65/16	16 no	16 no	4 no
5	Baking powder	1.5 to 2.5	1.1/4 tsp	3 tsp	5 tsp
6	Baking soda	0.1 to 2	4 tsp	2 tsp	2 tsp
7	Essence(vanilla)	0.5 to 1	1 tsp	1 tsp	1 tsp
8	Essence (date/almond)	0.25 to 0.5	1/2 tsp	1/2 tsp	1/2 tsp
9	Essence(rose)	0.25 to 0.5	1/2 tsp	-	-
10	Date	250/75	2.5 kg	750 gm	-
11	Walnut/Cashewnut	50	500 gm	500 gm	-
12	Ginger powder	3 to 3.5	-	-	2 Tsp
14	Molasses/ Tea Decoction	40/60	600ml	600ml	400ml
15	Iodized Salt	0.25 to 0.5	pinch	pinch	pinch
16	Milk/Water	10 to 20	as req	as req	as req

Baking Temperature	Time	Production
175°C (355°F)	52 min	5.0 to 6.0 kg

Process :

1. Clean the date with water. Cut vertically into fine slices and soak into warm tea decoction I molasses & baking soda. Keep it aside till it becomes soft (about 2 to 4 hr).
2. Prepare cake batter by creaming method. However, mix ginger powder / cinnamon powder into flour before sieving.
3. Finally mix soaked date slice, chopped walnut, cashewnut (whatever formula contains). Pour into cake tin & bake.

CHOCOLATE CAKE, MOCHA CAKE

Recipe :

No	Ingerdient	Per cent	Weight	
			Chocolate Cake	Mocha Cake
1	Flour	100	1 kg	1 kg
2	Shortening	80/50	800 gm	500 gm
3	Sugar	120	1.2 kg	1.2 kg
4	Egg	60 to 80	20 no	16 no
5	Baking powder	2.5 to 0.5	5 tsp	5 tsp
6	Baking soda	0.5 to 1	1 tsp	2 tsp
7	Essence(vanilla)	0.5 to 1	1 tsp	1 tsp
8	Essence(choco late)	0.5 to 1	1 tsp	-
9	Milk powder	10 to 12	100 gm	120 gm
10	Cocoa powder	5 to 15	150 gm	50 gm
11	Instant coffee	3	-	2 Tsp
12	Molasses	10	-	100 ml
13	Water	10 to 20	as req	as req
14	Iodized Salt	0.25 to 0.5	1/2 tsp	1/2 tsp
Baking Temperature 175°C (350°F)		**Time** 16 to 21 min	**Production** 3.0 to 3.5 kg	

Process :

1. Prepare the batter as per the creaming method. However, mix the cocoa powder, coffee etc. with flour.

CHOCO FRUIT CAKE, SACHER CAKE

No	Ingredients	Per cent	Weight	
			Choco Fruit Cake	Sacher Cake
1	Flour	100	1 kg	I kg
2	Shortening	100	1 kg	1 kg
3	Sugar	100/175	1 kg	1.750 kg
4	Egg	120/360	30 no	90 no
5	Baking powder	1.5 to 2.5	4 tsp	1 Tsp
6	Essence(vanilla)	1 to 3	2 tsp	2 Tsp
7	Essence(chocolate)	0.5 to 1	1 tsp	2 tsp
8	Cocoa powder	15 to 25	150 gm	250 gm
9	Cashewnut	40	400 gm	-
10	Sultan	30	300 gm	-
11	Icing sugar	100	-	1 kg
12	Biscuit	50	-	500 gm
13	Corn flour	25	-	250 gm
14	Iodized Salt	0.25 to 0.5	pinch	pinch
15	Milk/Water	10 to 20	as req	as req

Baking Temperature	Time	Production
180°C (355°F)	25 to 30 min	3.5 to 4.0 kg

CHOCO FRUIT CAKE

Process :

1. Mix baking powder & salt into flour and sieve twice.
2. Add warm water into cocoa powder and make into paste.
3. Melt shortening by double boiler method. Add cocoa paste and mix thoroughly. Add sugar and mix.
4. Add essence into egg and mix to paste.
5. Add chopped (previously soaked) dry fruit.
6. Finally add flour & mix and pour into greased dusted swiss roll tray & bake.

SACHER CAKE

Process :

1. Separate yolk & white. Add half of essence to each one.
2. Cream shortening and sugar well.

3. Add cocoa powder and continue to cream.
4. Gradually add egg yolk and cream till light & fluffy.
5. Whip egg white & icing sugar to a light meringue separately and gently fold into above mixture.
6. Sieve baking powder & salt with flour, add crushed biscuit & corn flour into it and mix thoroughly.
7. Fold it into previously made mixture. Pour in suitable cake tin and bake.

MADERIA CAKE BROWN CAKE

Formula:

No	Ingredients	Percent	Weight	
			Maderia Cake	Brown Cake
1	Flour	100	1 kg	1 kg
2	Shortening	70 to 80	700 gm	800 gm
3	Sugar	70/100	700 gm	! kg
4	Egg	50 to 65	16 no	12 no
5	Baking powder	1.5 to 2	4 tsp	4 tsp
6	Baking soda	0.5 to 1	-	1 tsp
7	Cocoa powder	15	-	150 gm
8	Milk powder	5 to 10	50gm	100 gm
9	Liquid glucose	12	-	120 gm
10	Walnut/Groundnut	30	-	300 gm
11	Lemon/Orange rind	25	250 gm	-
12	Sugar (granules)	5	50 gm	-
13	Salt	0.25 to 0.5	pinch	pinch
14	Water	10 to 20	as req	as req
15	Glycerine	1.5	1 Tsp	1 Tsp
	Baking Temperature 175°C (350°F)	**Time** 40 to 45 min	**Production** 3.0 to 4.0 kg	

MADERIA CAKE

Process :

1. Prepare batter by creaming method.
2. Chop about 200 gm peel and add to batter. Remaining peel should be cut into long and thin slice.

3. Pour batter in paper lined moulds and bake.
4. When cake is half baked, it will develop a break on top surface. Put thin slices of peel on the break and complete baking.

Brown Cake

Procedure :

1. Prepare the batter by creaming procedure.
2. Mix liquid glucose and walnut / groundnut. Keep in tin & bake.

CHECK CAKE , RIBBON CAKE, MARBLE CAKE

No	Ingredients	Percent	Weight		
			Check Cake	Ribbon Cake	Marble Cake
1	Flour	100	1 kg	1 kg	I kg
2	Shortening	75/100	750 gm	1 kg	1 kg
3	Sugar	100	1 kg	1 kg	1 kg
4	Egg	65/100	16 no	25 no	25 no
5	Baking powder	1.5 to 2.5	4 tsp	5 tsp	4 tsp
6	Essence(vanilla)	0.5 to 1	1 tsp	1 tsp	I tsp
7	Essence (strawberry, lemon,pista)	0.1 to 0.25 (each)	1/4 tsp	1/4 tsp	-
8	Essence (chocolate)	0.1 to 0.25	-	-	1/4 tsp
9	Colour (red/yellowl green)	0.1 to 0.2	as req	as req	as req
10	Chocolate	10 to 15	-	-	100 gm
11	lodized Salt	0.25 to 0.5	1/2 tsp	1/2 tsp	1/2 tsp
12	Com flour	5 to 10	50gm	50gm	50gm
13	Milk/Water	10 to 20	as req	as req	as req

Baking Temperature	Time	Production
170°C (340°F)	35 to 45 min	3 to 3.75 kg

CHECK CAKE
RIBBON CAKE

Process :

1. Prepare batter by creaming method.
2. Divide batter into 3 parts. Add red colour & strawberry essence, yellow colour & lemon essence. and green colour & pista essence in 1 part each.
3. **For check cake:** Place a small and a big ring in greased cake tin, so as to make 3 part in cake tin. Pour 1 part batter in each compartment. Now remove both the rings & bake.
4. **For ribbon cake:** Pour 1 part of batter, followed by second and finally third, so as to prepare 3 different coloured layers.

MARBLE CAKE

Process :

1. Prepare batter by creaming method.
2. Separate about 1/4 part of the batter, add melted (by double boiler method) chocolate & chocolate essence and mix thoroughly.
3. Pour plain batter in a greased cake tin and pour brown batter in the middle portion of the plain batter & bake.

BLACK FOREST CAKE

No	Ingredients	Percent	Weight
1	Flour	100	1 kg
2	Shortening	200	2 kg
3	Sugar (Fine)	200	2kg
4	Egg	240	60 no
5	Essence(vanilla)	2 to 4	2 Tsp
6	Water/Milk	5 to 10	as req
7	Baking soda	0.5 to 1	1 tsp
8	Drinking chocolate/ Chocolate	100	1 kg
	For filling :		
9	Fresh cream	150	1.5 kg
10	Icing sugar (optional)	150	1.5 kg
	Baking Temperature	**Time**	**Production**
	205°C (400°F)	22 min	5.4 to 6.1 kg

Method:

1. Sieve drinking chocolate, baking soda & flour together. If using chocolate, it should by melted by double boiler process and added at the last stage of mixing (i.e. after addition of flour & butter).
2. Break egg into a bowl, and place it on the hot water bowl. Be careful that it does not touch the water.
3. Add essence and beat egg to thick consistency.
4. Add sugar gradually along with beating.
5. Add flour and melted shortening.
6. If required,add water/milk and prepare batter having dropping consistency.
7. Pour in the greased-dusted cake tin & bake.
8. Remove from tin & allow to cool. Cut from the middle in the form of sandwich. Place cream/cream icing inbetween two parts.

POUND CAKE, SPONGE CAKE, SWISS-ROLL YULE-LOG CAKE

No	Ingredients	Percent	Weight		
			Pound Cake	Sponge Cake	Swees-roll Yule-log Cake
1	Flour	100	1 kg	1 kg	1 kg
2	Sugar	100/110/65	1 kg	1.1 kg	650 gm
3	Egg	90 to 140	22 no	35 no	25 no
4	Baking powder	1.5 to 2	1 tsp	4 tsp	-
5	Essence (vanilla)	0.5 to 2	1 tsp	2 tsp	4 tsp
6	Essence (lemon)	0.5 to 2	1 tsp	-	-
7	Essence (butter)	0.5 to 1	1 tsp	-	-
8	Essence (almond)	0.25 to 0.5	1/2 tsp	-	-
9	Milk powder	5 to 10	50 gm	-	100 gm
10	Corn flour (optional)	5 to 10	50 gm.	-	100 gm
11	Liquid glucose	2 to 5	-	3 Tsp	-
12	Water	30 to 35	300 ml	350 ml	-
13	Iodized Salt	0.25 to 0.5	pinch	pinch	-
14	Emulsifier **OR**	0.02	0.2 gm	0.2 gm	0.2gm
	Gel (or as specified)	2 to 5	40 gm	40 gm	40 gm
15.	Melted shortening	2 to 10	-	100 gm	30 gm
	Or Glycerine	1.5 to 2	1 Tsp	1 Tsp	1 Tsp
	for Filling :				
16.	Jam Or Butter scotch cream	20 to 25	-	-	200 gm

Baking Temperature	Time	Production
230°C (450°F)	9 to 11 min	2 to 2.65 kg

Process :

1. Sieve the baking powder & flour twice. Add any other dry Ingredient like corn flour etc.
2. Break egg into bowl. Keep it on hot water bowl in such a way that water does not touch the bowl.
3. Whisk egg, essence(s) and emulsifier/gel, till thick.
4. Add sugar gradually and continue whisking till sponge acquires thick consistency.
5. Dissolve salt and liquid glucose in water and add to the sponge gradually, if the formula contains.
6. Fold in flour carefully, so as to not loose the aeration.
7. Fold in fat/glycerine carefully. Add hot water, if required for dropping consistency.
8. For pound cake & sponge cake: Pour the batter into cake tin and bake.
9. For swiss roll: Place a butter paper on swiss-roll tray [i.e. baking tray having 1 cm (1/2") height] and grease. Pour the batter on it & bake.
10. Sprinkle sugar (granules) on butter paper.
11. Baked cake is separated from swiss-roll tray with the help of knife politely. Be careful that the cake does not crack. And place it on butter paper in such a way that the sugar stick on the top ..
12. Cut the edges and spread jam or butter scotch cream followed by butter scotch liquid and roll it. If required, place in refrigerator to set. Decorate with butter scotch/ chocolate just like yule-log.

EGG LESS CUP CAKE
EGG LESS CAKE
CONDENSED MILK CAKE

No	Ingredients	Percent	Weight		
			Egg Less Cup Cake	Egg Less Cake	Condensed Milk Cake
1	Flour	100	1 kg	1 kg	1 kg
2	Shortening	65/50	650 gm	650 gm	500 gm (butter)

3	Sugar	85/20	850 gm	850 gm	200gm
4	Baking powder	1.5 to 2	4 tsp	1 Tsp	4 tsp
5	Baking soda	0.5 to 2	-	-	2 tsp
6	Essence(vanilla)	0.5 to 1	I tsp	1 tsp	1 tsp
7	Essence(milk)	0.5 to 1	1 tsp	1 tsp	1 tsp
8	MilkfWater	10 to 20	as req	as req	as reg
9	Corn flour	5 to 10	50gm	50gm	50gm
10	Milk powder	25	250 gm	250 gm	-
11	Condensed milk (sweetened)	160	-	-	1.6 kg
12	Soda bottle (limca/orange)	70 to 80	-	-	4 no
13	Cardamom-Nutmeg (powder) (optional)	2 to 3	2 Tsp	2 Tsp	-

EGG LESS CUP CAKE

Baking Temperature	Time	Production
190°C (375°F)	20 to 25min	90 no.

Process :

1. Prepare batter as per the creaming method.
2. Place paper-cup into cup-cake-mould and pour batter upto 3/4 part. Keep on tray & bake.

EGG LESS CAKE

Baking Temperature	Time	Production
175°C (350°F)	15 to 20 min	3 to 3.5 kg

Process :

1. Prepare cake batter by creaming method.
2. Grease with fat and dust with flour the cake tin. Then made upside down to remove excess flour.
3. Pour the batter in the cake tin and make pit at the centre, place on baking tray & bake.

CONDENSED MILK CAKE

Baking Temperature	Time	Production
150°C (300°F)	15 to 10 min	3 to 3.5 kg

Process :

1. Mix corn flour, baking powder, baking soda into flour.
2. Place butter in bowl and cream lightly with wooden spoon, add sugar slowly.
3. Add condensed milk gradually with continuous creaming.
4. Now add flour & soda bottle gradually alternatively and mix thoroughly after each addition.
5. Pour batter in greased dusted cake tin and bake.

EGG LESS CAKE II
EGG LESS CHOCO CAKE

No	Ingredients	Percent	Weight	
			Egg Less Cake	Egg Less Choco Cake
1	Flour	100	1 kg	1 kg
2	Butter(melted)	30 to 40	325 gm	325 gm
3	Oil	30 to 40	325 gm	325 gm
4	Sugar (granules)	80 to 90	850 gm	850 gm
5	Baking soda	2 to 3	4 tsp	4 tsp
6	Essence(vanilla)	2 to 3	4 tsp	4 tsp
7	Milk powder	5 to 10	65 gm	65 gm
8	Corn flour	5 to 10	85 gm	85 gm
9	Cake gel	3 to 5	30 gm	30 gm
10	Curd	40.to 50	400 gm	400 gm
11	Milk	40 to 50	400ml	400ml
12	Cocoa powder	5 to 10		65 gm

Baking Temperature	Time	Production
80°C (355°F)	35 to 45 min	3.0 to 3.85 kg

Process :

1. Mix flour, baking soda, cocoa powder/corn flour and milk powder together & sleve twice.
2. Take sugar (granules). Add cake gel and cream. Add milk gradually with creaming and add curd similarly. Mix essence.
3. Add flour, mix.
4. Finally pour butter (melted) & oil and mix thoroughly.
5. Pour in cake tin & bake.

CAKE PASTRY

No	Ingredients	Percent	Weight
1	Flour	100	1 kg
2	Sugar	100	1 kg
3	Egg	120	30 no
4	Baking powder	2 to 5	2 Tsp
5	Baking soda	0.5 to 1	1 tsp
6	Essence(vanilla and/or as per flavour (Optional)	1 to 2	4 tsp
7	Oil emulsion (as per flavour) (optional)	0.5 to 1	1 tsp
8	Fruit peel rind powder (as per flavour) (optional)	0.5 to 1	2 tsp
9	Colour(as per flavour) (optional)	0.1 to 0.2	as req
10	Glycerine OR	1 to 2	1 Tsp
	Fat OR	8 to 10	100 gm
	Gel (or as desired)	4 to 5	40gm
11	Liquid glucose (optional)	2 to 10	50gm
12	Emulsifier (optional)	0.02 to 0.03	0.3 gm
13	Acetic acid(10%)	0.5 to 1	1 tsp
14	Water/Milk	30 to 40	as req
	For filling:		
15	Icing	20 to 30	200 gm
	For Decoration:		
16	Icing	200	2 kg

Baking Temperature	Time	Production
220°C (400°F)	8 to to min	2 to 2.5 kg

Process :

1. Prepare cake as per fat less cake.
2. Cut like slice into 2 or 3 part. Place butter (if desired) icing/liquid glucose/ sugar syrup/jam etc. in between two layers and made into sandwich form. Cover the top by icing. Cut into suitable pieces [i.e. 2.5 x 5 cm (1 "x 2") oblong / 5 x 5 cm (2"x2") square/5 x7.5 cm (2" x 3") strip or into triangle or desired shape] and decorate individually.

No	Ingredients	Percent	Weight
1	Flour	100	1 kg
2	Shortening	60	600 gm
3	Sugar	100	1 kg
4	Liquid glucose	4	40 gm
5	Egg	65	650 gm
6	Baking powder	1 to 2	2 tsp
7	Baking soda(optional)	0.25 to 0.5	1 tsp
8	Essence (vanilla)	1 to 2	2 tsp
9	Essence (lemon, almond)	0.5 to 1	1 tsp
10	Essential oil (as per flavour)	0.5 to 1	1 tsp
11	Fruit peel rind powder (as per flavour)(optional)	0.5 to 1	2 tsp
12	Colour (preferably yellow) or any other	1 to 0.2	as req
13	Miik powder	5 to 10	50gm
15	Emulsifier	0.02 to 0.03	0.3gm
16	Glycerine	1 to 2	1 Ts'p
17	Iodized Salt	0.25 to 0.5	1/2 tsp
18	Acetic acid(10%)	0.5 to 1	1 tsp
19	Milk / Water	5 to 10	as req
20	Mix dry fruit/cherry/ tutee fruity	5 to 10	100 gm

Baking Temperature	Time	Production
180°C (355°F)	20 to 25 min	3.10 kg (Approx.)

Process :

1. Prepare batter by desired method. Add chopped dry fruit/cherry/tutee fruity.
2. Pour it in a cake tin (similar to bread toast tin), cover it with lid and bake.
3. For slice cake: Allow to cool and slice (similar to bread).

   For cake rusk : Arrange each slice on baking sheet and dry it at 100°C (232°F) (just like bread toast).

28

Fermented Cereal Products

INTRODUCTION

Legumes and cereal meet a considerable part of protein and carbohydrate needs of the world population. These are consumed as such or after being acted upon by natural micro-organisms or those inoculated and thus, are known as *fermented foods.* Microbial activity in foods makes them more attractive in terms of appearance and flavours. Such foods are more appetizing, easily digestible and form an important sector of food industry. Fermentation improves the digestibility of the ingredients for human consumption and enhances the keeping quality and shelf-life. Fermented foods add to the variety of foods available and protect against the food poisoning and transmission of pathogenic micro-organisms.In many cases they serve as important source of protein calories and contain vitamins.The biological agents involved in food fermentations include filamentous fungi, bacteria and yeasts occurring in succession or in combination. In general, filamentous fungi bring about the saccharification and proteolysis of the starting materials, bacteria cause acidification and leavening while yeasts ferment the sugars to produce alcohol and esters which impart desirable flavours to the products. The reports about the origin of fermented foods are lacking but it is believed that the discovery of fermentation was purely by chance.

Some of the common indigenous fermented foods consumed in various parts of the world are listed in Table 28.1 which indicates the geography, substrates employed, the nature and uses of various products. Indigenous fermented products constitute an important part of human diet in South-East Asia including India (Plate 1), the middle East and Africa. They are also becoming popular in the developed world due to their high nutritional value and organoleptic characteristics. People of Asia are the pioneers in the development of means of fermenting vegetable proteins to produce meat-like flavours. Indonesians developed the fermentation methods for introducing meat-like texture into the vegetable products. Koreans are credited for the production of acid fermented vegetables. People of Egypt developed wheat breads leavened with yeasts while Indians discovered methods for souring and leavening cereal-legume batters.

Generally, the traditional methods of preparing indigenous fermented foods are simple and inexpensive. However the ancient methods of making such foods are changing rapidly through modern microbial technology. Some of the fermented products including dairy products, coffee, cocoa and bread have been studied extensively for many decades and their production methods have been modernised keeping pace with the advancement in modern science. During the last few years, much interest has been generated in the fermented foods of Asian and African countries including India where such foods are still being manufactured according to the traditional but technologically less advanced methods using simple equipments and are produced at cottage industry scale by means of natural microflora from the staples and the surroundings.

Table 28.1. Some important indigenous fermented foods of the world

S.No.	Fermented food	Country/place	Ingredient(s)	Nature of product	Product use
Legume products					
1.	*Bhallae*	India	Black gram	Deep fried patties	Snack after soaking in curd, water
2.	*Chee-fan*	China	Soybean, whey curd	Solid	Eaten fresh, cheese like
3.	*Dawadawa*	West Africa, Nigeria	African locust bean	Solid	Eaten fresh, supplement to soups, stews
4.	*Khaman*	Western India	Bengal gram	Spongy cake	Breakfast food
5.	*Kenima*	Nepal, Sikkim, Darjeeling district of West Bengal in India	Soybeans	Solid	Snack
6.	*Keljap*	Indonesia	Black soybeans	Syrup	Seasoning agent
7.	*Meitauza*	China,Taiwan	Soybean cake	Solid	Fried in oil or cooked with vegetables
8.	*Meju*	Kortrea	Soybeans	Paste	Seasoning agent
9.	*Miso*	Japan, China	Soybeans/ Soybeans and rice	Paste	Soup base, seasoning agent

10.	*Natto*	Northern Japan	Soybeans	Solid	Roasted or fried in oil used as a meat substitute
11.	*Oncom*	Indonesia	Peanut press cake	Solid	Roasted or fried in oil used as a meat substitute
12.	*Papadam*	India	Black gram and spices	Circular tortilla like wafers	Condiment
13.	*Soybean* milk	China, Japan	Soybeans	Liquid	Drink
14.	*Sufu*	China, Taiwan	Soybean, whey curd	Solid	Soybean cheese, condiment
15.	*Soy sauce*	Japan, China, Philippines wheat	Soybeans! Soybeans and vegetables	Liquid fish, cereals and	Seasoning agent for meat
16.	*Tempeh*	Indonesia and its vicinity	Soybeans	Solid	Fried in oil, roasted or used as meat substitute in soup
17.	*Vadai*	India	Black gram	Deep fried patties	Snack
18.	*Warries_*	Northern India	Black gram and spices	Ball like hollow, brittle	Spicy condiment, eaten with vegetables, legumes, rice
Legume-cereal products					
19.	*Dhokla*	Western India	Rice, Bengal gram	Spongy cake	Condirnent
20	*Dosa*	Southern India	Rice, black gram	Spongy, pan cake	Staple food
21.	*Hama natto*	Japan	Wheat flour, whole soybeans	Raisin like, soft	Flavouring agent for meat and fish, eaten as snack
22.	*Idli*	Southern India	Rice, Black gram	Spongy	Breakfast food
23.	*Kecap*	Indonesia and vicinity	Wheat, soybeans	Liquid	Condiment,seasoning agent
24.	*Tao-si*	Philippines	Wheat flour, Soybeans	Semi-solid	Seasoning agent
25.	*Taoljo*	East Indies	Roasted wheat meal or glutinous rice, soybeans	Semi-solid	Condiment
Cereal products					
26.	*Ang-Kak* (Chinese red rice)	China, Taiwan, Philippines, Thailand	Rice	Solid	Colouring other foods
27.	*Ambali*	India	Millet Flour	Semi-solid	All time food
28.	*Bhatura*	India (North)	White wheat flour	Deep fried Bread	Breakfast
29.	*Fermented rice*	India	Rice	Semi solid	Breakfast
30.	*Hopper (Appa)*	Sri Lanka	Rice or white wheat flour and cocco nut water	Semi solid	Breakfast

31.	*Jalebie*	India and Pakistan	White wheat flour	Deep fried crispy pretzel	Confection food
32.	*Kenkey*	Ghana	Maize	Semi-solid	Breakfast, lunch and supplement to fish stews
33.	*Kisra*	Sudan	Sorghum flour	Spongy Bread	Staple food
34.	*Kulcha*	India (North) and Pakistan	White wheat flour	Flat bread	Staple food
35.	*Mahewu*	South Africa	Maize meal	Liquid	Beverage food
36.	*Nan*	India (North) Pakistan, Iran and Afganistan	White wheat flour	Flat bread	Staple food
37.	*Ogi*	Nigeria	Maize, Millet or Sorghum	Semi-solid	Breakfast and Infant food
38.	*Pozol*	Mexico	White maize	Liquid	Beverage or Porridge
39.	*Puto*	Philippines	Rice	Semi solid	Breakfast and snack food
40.	*Shamsy* bread	Egypt Wheat	flour	Spongy bread	Staple food Breakfast and lunch
41.	*Uji*	Kenya, Uganda and Tanzania	Maize, Sorghum or Millet flour	Semi-solid	

MAJOR TYPES OF CEREAL FERMENTED PRODUCTS

Soybeans, black grams, mung beans and Bengal grams are the principal legumes used in the preparation of a variety of fermented foods in different parts of the world. These are fermented separately or in combination with cereals. Lists of fermented foods with short descriptions of the nature of products, raw materials and micro-organisms involved have been compiled by several workers. Saybeans are fermented as such, as a paste or as a

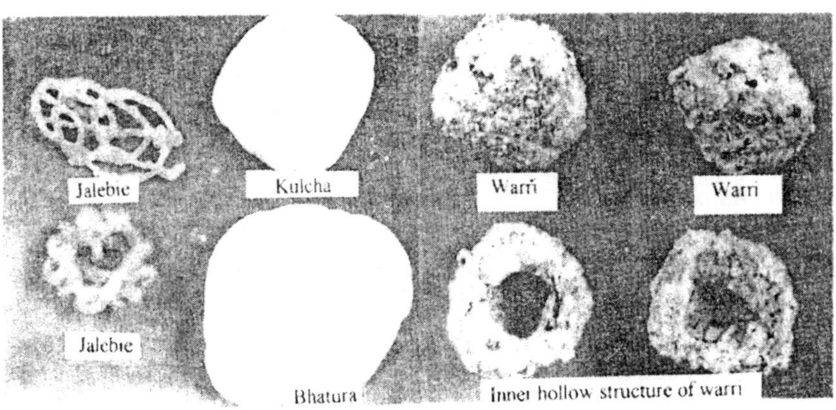

Plate 1 Some of the cereal based fermented foods.

liquid to produce *tempe, natto, miso, soy sauce* and *sufu.* Peanuts and locust bean are also fermented in some parts of the world to prepare *oncom* and *dawadawa.* Oriental fermented foods have been described in depth in a separate chapter and would not be discussed in detail here.

Tempe kedele, a fermented product of Indonesia, is prepared by incubating the soaked soybeans at a warm place, which are knitted into compact cake by a fibrous mould mycelium for 1-3 days.The cake is then sliced thin and deep fried or used as a meat substitute in soups. Fermented whole soybeans are known as *natto* in Japan, *tu-si* in China, *tao-si* in Philippines and *tnua-nao* in Thailand. These are consumed with boiled rice or used as a seasoning agent with cooked meat, sea foods and vegetables. Fermented soybean pastes are known as *miso* in Japan, *chiang* in China, *tauco* in Indonesia, *doenjang* in Korea and believed to have been originated in China in 600 AD. In addition to soybeans and salts, most of these products also contain cereals. *Miso* has been manufactured in Japan for atleast 1000 years and used as a base for soups, sauce served with meat, poultry, sea foods and vegetable dishes. Fermented soybean liquids, light brown to black in colour with meat-like salty flavours, commonly known as *soy sauces,* are prepared by hydrolyzing soybeans (in China and Korea) and mixture of soybeans and wheat (in Japan) using enzymes produced by *Aspergillus oryzae,* in a strong salt solution. These are known as *shoyu* . in Japan, *chiang-yu* in China, *kecap* in Indonesia and *kanjang* in Korea. Chinese have been using *soy sauce* for over 3000 years. Production of *soy sauce* in Japan was probably a result of introduction of Buddhism from China and consequent changes in vegetarian diet in 552 AD.29 *Sufu,* a mold fermented soybean curd, which is highly creamy bean paste made by overgrowing soybean curd with mold, is popular among Chinese as *fu-zu.* It is known as *chao* in Vietnam, whereas in the West, *sufu* has been referred to as *Chinese cheese. Oncom* is a fermented peanut presscake product consumed largely in Indonesia[9-11] as a roasted snack, covered with water and seasoned with salt or sugar. *Dawadawa,* a fermented locust bean product, consumed largely in West Africa, is also known as *daddowa* in Nigeria. The seeds after removing the powdery pulp are boiled in water and stored overnight. The swollen cotyledons are then boiled for 30 min, put into a hole in ground and left to ferment for 2-3 days.

Warries, somewhat like Japanese *miso*[6] are spicy, hollow, brittle, friable balls 5-8 cm in diameter, very popular in Northern India, especially in Amritsar city and are used as condiment in cooking with vegetables, legumes or rice (Plate 1) The black gram paste after being spiced with asafoetida, caraway, cardamom, cloves, fenugreek, ginger and red pepper[7] is moulded into small balls and fermented in open air for 2-8 days. *Papadam,* another condiment is similarly prepared from black gram paste but without fenugreek and ginger. It is allowed to ferment for 4-6 hours and rolled into tortilla like wafers which are served roasted or deep fried. *Bhallae* are prepared from unspiced black gram paste fermented for 6-24 hours. The paste is pan or deep fried and consumed as a snack as such or after briefly soaking in water or curd.

Foods of acidified and leavened type like Indian *idli,* constitute a very interesting group of cereal-pulse based foods of considerable importance in the developing and under-developed world. *Idli* is closely related to sour dough bread of western world but does not depend upon wheat or rye as a source of protein to retain CO_2 during leavening which is produced by bacterial rather than yeast activity. *Idlis* are spongy pancakes, steamed in a special container and consumed as a staple food primarily in South India. They have been in use since 1100 AD. Proportion of rice and black gram ranges from 1:4 to 4:1.65 *Dosa,* a thin, fairly crisp, fried pancake-like food of South India is prepared by spreading the fermented batter on hot greasy griddle. The batter is prepared in a similar way as that of *idli* but the proportion of rice and black gram is 1:1 kept instead of 4:1.

Several attempts have been made in the past to prepare new indigenous products by replacing the conventional ingredients containing great Northern beans in place of black gram was evaluated and found that *idli* prepared from the former had somewhat different flavour and a sticky top surface. Incorporation of great Northern beans into *idli* was suggested which would offer the advantage of increased roughage. *Idlis* made by replacing either rice or black gram were found compatibility in physicochemical characteristics like viscosity, titrable acidity, in different test and conventional preparations. Two new *idli* types prepared by replacing black gram with mung beans and soybean, as compared with the conventional rice-black gram *idli* and the organoleptic evaluation of these revealed wide acceptance of the conventional product due to its aroma, taste and consistency followed by the mungbean product. Some attempts have also been made to prepare new *dosa-like* products by replacing the conventional black gram component with other legumes which were evaluated for nutritional value and acceptability in comparison to the conventional product. Batter types containing soybeans were most nutritious in terms of total nitrogen, protein, amylase, proteinase and vitamin B contents followed by mungbean batters while the conventional black gram product was organoleptically most preferred.

MICROBIOLOGY OF CEREAL, FERMENTATIONS

A large number of bacteria, yeasts and yeast-like fungi have been isolated from various cereal fermented foods (Table 28.2). A reyiew of published reports shows that filamentous fungi belonging to *Aspergillus, Mucor, Neurospora* arid *Rhizopus,* bacteria belonging to *Leuconostoc mesenteroides, Lactobacilli, Streptococcus· faecalis, Pediococcus* and yeasts belonging to *Saccharomyces cereuisiae, Candida* spp, *Debaryomyces hansenii* and *Hansenula anomala* are most commonly associated with the traditional fermentations. These organisms are generally contributed by the ingredients, workers and the surroundings. Since the source of inoculum is not apparent, the study of biological agents actually associated with fermentations has attracted considerable attention over the years. Dehulled black gram grains, used for the production of various indigenous Indian products, have been reported to harbour *Leuconostoc mesenteroides* and other lactic acid bacteria in large numbers which play a major role in black gram fermentations. Ordinarily, the microbes developing during the initial soaking of ingredients and later are sufficient to bring about the fermentations.19 Presoaking of the ingredients release the free sugars and non-protein nitrogen which support the growth of lactic acid bacteria. Spices, as added in some ingredients, also enhance the food fermentations by stimulating the development of certain lactic acid bacteria and accelerating lactic acid production. *Lactobacillus plantarum* and *Pediococcus cereuisiae* have shown their ability to grow in the presence of upto 10-12 g/L of the majority of spices including pepper, cardamom, cinnamon, ginger, garlic, turmeric and celery seed with enhanced lactic acid production from carbohydrates.

Stimulation of other microbial species such as micrococci and yeasts was also observed. All the species contain high manganese content which has been identified as a factor responsible for stimulatory effect in the enhancement of acid production. Seasonal variations affect qualitative and quantitative prevalence of bacteria and yeasts in different traditional fermented foods with summers favouring the former and winters the latter.

Table 28.2. : Micro organisms associated with fermented foods

S. No.	Organism	Fermented food	References
1.	*Actinumucor elegans*	*Sufu*	29,27
2.	*Aspergillus niger*	*Soy sauce*	124
		Tempe	23

3.	*Aspergillus oryzae*	*Doenjiang*	15
		Miso	119,31,54
		Natto	65,41
		Soysauce	70
		Tauco	120
4.	*Aspergillus soyae*	*Miso*	54
		Soysauce	126,124,70
5.	*Bacillus amyloliquefaciens*	*Dosa*	88,93,74,90
		idli	88,93,74,91,95
6.	*Bacillus pumilis*	*Doenjang*	15
7.	*Bacillus subtilis*	*Bhallae, warri*	88,93,73
		Dosa	88,93,90
		Doenjang	15
		Kawai	21
		Natto	29
8.	*Candida boidini*	*Dosa*	75
9.	C. *cacaoi*	*Idli*	75
10.	C. *curvata*	*Bhallae, Warri*	74,75
11.	C. *famata*	*Bhallae, Warri*	74,75
12.	C. *fragicola*	*Idli*	75
13.	C. *glabrata*	*Dosa*	75
		Idli	115
14.	C. *kefyr*	*Idli*	75
15.	*C.krusei*	*Punjabi warri*	88,93,6,74,73
16.	C. *membraneafaciens*	*Bhallae*	75
17.	C. *parapsilosis*	*Punjabi warri*	75
18.	C. *pseudotropicalis*	*Idli*	75
19.	C. *sake*	*Dosa*	75
		Idli	115
20.	C. *tropicalis*	*Idli*	115
21.	C. *vartiovaarai*	*Bhallae, Warri*	88,93,74
22.	*Cryptococcus humicolus*	*Bhallae, Warri*	88,93,74
23.	*Debaryomyces hansenii*	*Bhallae, Warri*	88,93,74
		Dosa,Idli	88,93,74,90,95
24.	*Deb. tamarii*	*Idli, Warri*	75
25.	*Geotrichum candidum*	*Bhallae, Warri*	88,93,74
26.	*Hansenula anomala*	*Bhallae*	74
		*Idli_*	115
		Punjabi Warri	88,93,74,73
27.	*H. polymorpha*	*Bhallae, Dosa*	75
28.	*Issatchenkia terricola*	*Dosa,/dli*	75
29.	*Kluyveromyces marxianus*	*Bhallae, Warri*	88,93,74
30.	*Klebsiella pneumoniae*	*Tempeh*	18,46
31.	*Lactobacillus coryniformis*	*Idli*	1

32. *L. delbrueckii*	*Idli*	88,93,6,74,79 51,90,95,61,43,44,78
	Soysauce	70
	Tauco	120
33. *L. fermentum*	*Dosa*	88,93,74,90
	Idli	8,93,6,74,51,95, 61,43,44,78
	Bhallae	88,93
	Punjabi warri	88,93,6
34. *L. lactis*	*Idli*	51,61,44,78
35. *L. plantarum*	*Kawai*	21
36. *Leuconostoc mesenteroides*	*Bhallae*	88,93,74
	Dosa	88,93,74,90
	Idli	88,93,6,74,91,51, 114,61,115,43,44, 78,62,124
	Punjabi warri	88,93,6,73,100
37. *Mucor corticolus*	*Sufu*	29,27
38. *M. javenicus*	*Tempe*	23
39. *M. hiemalis*	*Sufu*	29,27,116
40. *M. praini*	*Sufu*	27
41. *M. racemosus*	*Sufu*	29
42. *M. rouxii*	*Tempe*	23
43. *M. silvaticus*	*Sufu*	29,27
44. *M. subtilissimus*	*Sufu*	29,27
45. *Neurospora crassa*	*Oncom*	22
46. *N. intermedia*	*Oncom*	33
47. *N. sitophila*	*Oncom*	22,77
48. *Pediococcus acidilactis*	*idli*	6
	Soy sauce	70
49. *P cerevisae*	*Idli*	88,93,51 ,61 ,44,78
	Soysauce	70,125
50. *Phalophilus*	*Miso*	118,31
	Soy sauce	127,109
51. *P streptococcus*	*idli*	1
52. *Pichia membranaefaciens*	*Bhal/ae, Warri*	74
53. *Rhizopus achlamydosporus*	*Tempe*	29
54. *R. arrhizus*	*Tempe*	32,33
55. *R. chinensis*	*Sufu*	29,27
56. *R. formosaensis*	*Tempe*	29
57. *R. oligosporus*	*Miso*	83,84,53
	Oncom	122,13,12
	Tauco	120
	Tempe	32,23,105,28

58. *R.oryzae*	*Tauco*	120
	Tempe	32,23
59. *R. stolonifer*	*Tempe*	32,23
60. *R. graminis*	*Dosa,Idli*	75
61. *R.lactosa*	*Punjabi warri*	75
62. *R. marina*	*Bhal/ae*	75
63. *Rhodotorula flava*	*Doenjang*	15
64. *Saccharomyces cerevisiae*	*Bhal/ae*	74
	Dosa	74,90
	Papadam	8,65,7
	idli	88,93,74,91,95
	Punjabi warri	88,93,8,6,65,74,7,73
65. S. *rouxii*	*Miso*	118,119,31
	Punjabi warri	6
	Soy sauce	124,70,127
66. S. *soyae*	*Miso*	120
67. *Staphylococcus sciuri*	*Kawai*	21
68. *Strepcoccus faecalis*	*Bhal/ae*	88,93
	Dosa	88,93,90
	Idli	88,93,6,91,51,95,44,78
	Miso	118,31
	Punjabi warri	88,93,73
69. *Torulopsis candida*	*Idli*	8,7,115
70. *T. dattila*	*Doenjang*	15
71. *T. holmii*	*IdII*	115
72. *Trichosporon beigelii*	*Bhallae*	88,93,74
	Dosa	88,93,74,90
	Punjabi warri	88,93,74,73
73. *Tr. pullulans*	*Bhallae*	88,93,74
	Dosa	75
	Idli	75,115
	Punjabi warri	88,93,74,73
74. *Wingea robertsii*	*Bhallae,*	
	Idli,	75
	Punjabi warri	
75. *Zygosaccharomyces soyae*	*Tauco*	120

Tempeh has been known and produced by Indonesians for centuries, but it was Prinsen Geerligs[57] who first emphasized the identification of *tempeh* mold, which was followed by Boorsma[14] who analysed tempeh and soybeans to determine the changes that were occurring during fermentation. Extensive survey of the tempeh mold indicated *Rhizopus oryzae* to be the principal mold taking part in the fermentation.[47] A variety of molds belonging to *R. oligosporus, R. stolonifer, R. oryzae* and *R. arrhizus* were isolated[23,32] from *tempeh,* while others demonstrated only a single mold species belonging to *R. oligosporus* is essential for the high quality tempeh fermentation.In addition to these species, *R. formosaesis* and *R. achlamydosporus* were isolated.Fungi belonging to *Aspergillus niger, Fusarium* sp., *Mucor javenicus, M. rouxii* and yeast *Trichosporon pullulans* from the samples of *tempeh* were isolated.Stahel was the first to report that the fungal fermentation is preceded by the bacterial fermentation during the soaking of soybeans. *Tempeh* production involves two distinct fermentations. The first occurring during soaking is bacterial fermentation resulting in the acidification of beans while the second fermentation results in the overgrowth of bean cotyledons by mold mycelium. The number of species of bacteria present in the commercial *tempeh* are remarkably few, *Klebsiella pneumoniae* being predominant. While studying *tempeh* samples of Malaysian markets fungi belonging to *Aspergillus, Mucor, Penicillium* and *Rhizopus,* bacteria belonging to *Bacillus* and *Micrococcus* and yeasts belonging to *Trichosporon* were isolated.

The studies on natto indicated the three main types of the soybean products prepared in Japan. *Itohiki natto,* referred to simply as *natto,* is prepared by steaming the beans for about 15 min and inoculating with *Bacillus natto,* a variant strain of *Bacillus subtilis. Yukiwari natto,* a second type of fermented whole soybean product is made by mixing *Itohiki natto* with salt and rice koji, the source of enzymes to hydrolyze the soybean components in fermentation, produced by *A. oryzae.* In case of *Hamma natto,* the third major type of fermented whole soybean product in Japan, the soybeans after soaking in water for about 4 hours are steamed without pressure and are then inoculated after being cooled with koji. Bacteria such as *Micrococcus, Streptococcus* and *Pediococcus* are also reported to be widely distributed on the surface and in the inner part of *Hamma natto.*

The essential micro-organisms involved in fermentation of miso include a mold *Aspergillus oryzae* and a yeast *Saccharomyces rouxii.* These are the only microorganisms required to make a satisfactory misO, but under tradtional conditions lactic acid bacteria such as *Pediococcus halophilus* or *Streptococcus faecalis* were also present and contributing flavour through the production of acids. Koji is prepared from polished rice which are inoculated with *Aspergillus oryzae.* Cooked, cooled beans are mixed with salted koji and fermented. Osmophilic yeast belonging to *Saccharomyces rouxii, Torulopsis* spp. and bacteria *Pediococcus halophil us* and *Streptococcus faecalis* were the most important organisms in *miso* fermentation. Miso production containing low levels of salt was investigated. The use of *R. oligosporus* instead of *Aspergillus oryzae* as a koji mold and peanuts in place of soybeans indicated that the total microbial population of *miso* during the fermentation period was altered by the salt level in *miso* containing *R. oligosporus* koji but not in miso containing *A. oryzae*. Higher population of yeast *Saccharomyces rouxii* in low salt *miso* was reported. A technique for making low salt miso by yeast fermentation was proposed.

The essential micro-organisms taking part in Indonesian *tauco* fermentation were reported to be *Aspergillus oryzae, R. oligosporus, R. oryzae, Lactobacillus delbrueckii, Hansenula* spp. and *Zygosaccharomyces soyae*. However, the occurrence of *Mucor* sp., *Penicillium* sp., *Rhizopus* sp., *Aspergillus ozyzae, Bacillus subtilis, B.* pumilis and *Rhodotorula flava* or *Torulopsis dattila* and many other organisms in the naturally inoculated soybean koji of Korean *Doenjang* has been observed.

Various methods of using soybeans for the preparation of different fermented foods including *soy sauces* were studied. Soy sauce fermentation has been reviewed in detail indicating the involvement of two distinct basic processes. The first one includes the fermentation with micro-organisms and the other chemical process involves the use of acids to promote the hydrolysis of the ingredients. The essential micro-organisms in *soy sauce* fermentation are moulds, *Aspergillus oryzae* or *A. soyae*, homofermentative lactic acid bacteria *Pediococcus cerevisiae* or *Lactobacillus delbrueckii* and yeasts *Saccharomyces rouxii*. Various groups of bacteria and yeasts predominate in sequence during the fermentation producing lactic acid from simple sugars and causing a fall in pH. Later, *Saccharomyces rouxii, Torulopsis* sp., *Zygosaccharomyces* sp. and other yeasts predominate. Molds belonging to *Aspergillus niger, A. soyae, Monilia* sp., *Penicillium* sp. and *Rhizopus* sp. may appear on the surface of the mash but have no relation to proper fermentation. Koji, the source of enzymes used in *soy sauce*, is prepared by culturing a number of mixed strains of *Aspergillus oryzae* or *A. soyae* either on steam polished rice in Japan or a mixture of wheat bran and soybean flour in China. It is then mixed with saline water to form a mash. The mycelium of the koji mold is milled during the very early stages of mash preparation.

Various molds belonging to Mucoraceae have been isolated from *sufu* which includes *Mucor corticolus, M. hiemalis, M. prajni, M. racemosus, M. silvaticus, M. subtilissimus, Actinumucor elegans and Rhizopus chinensis*.

Oncom is fermented with a mixed culture of micro-organisms with *Rhizopus* or *Neurospora* spp. predominating. Depending upon the predominant mold, there are two types of oncoms, viz., *Oncom hitam* (black *oncom)* having *Rhizopus* sp. as principal molds and *Oncom merals* (red *oncom)* in which the principal molds are *Neurospora* spp. Dwidjoseptro identified *Neurospora sitophila* and *N. crassa* as being the typical molds in oncom. *Ne. intermedia* as the essential fungus. Though presence of yeasts and other micro-organisms is reported, but the essential organisms required to form the typical cake belongs to the mold *N. sitophila.* However, an unidentified bacterium to be responsible for the vitamin B_{12} activity in *oncom* has been indicated.

The micro-organisms responsible for *dawadawa* fermentation have not been determined but undoubtedly include spore forming bacilli, lactic acid bacteria and probably yeast.

Microbial populations, whether mixed or pure, vary in their number and types with progress in fermentations. The reports describing microbial population dynamics, their prevalence and succession in Indigenous Indian Food fermentations suggest the involvement of bacteria alone or in combination with lesser proportion of yeasts during fermentations. The occurrence of bacteria in all the commercial and laboratory fermented samples has been observed, while only half of the samples had yeasts. Seasonal variations generally affect the development and prevalence of micro-organisms during fermentations (Table 28.3); summers were found to favour a higher bacterial load ($l0^{10}$—10^{12}/g) than winters (10^9-10^{10}*lg).* It was also found that *Bacillus subtilis* occurred mainly during summers whereas *Leuconostoc mesenteroides, Streptococcus faecalis* and *Lactobacillus fermentum* were the principal bacteria associated during both the seasons (Table 28.4). Yeasts including *Candida uartiouaarai, Kluyueromyces marxianus,* and C. *krusei* were largely encountered during winters while *Saccharornyces cereuisiae, Pichia membranaefaciens, Trichosporon beigelii* and *Hansenula anomala* were commonly involved during both the seasons (Table 28.5). The common occurrence of bacteria belonging to *Leuconostoc mesenteroides, Lactobacillus fermentum, Streptococcus faecalis, Bacillus subtilis* and less prevalence of yeasts in all the Indian fermented foods represents the direct involvement of the former in traditional Indian indigenous fementations. Moreover, since the source of inoculum is not apparent in such products, it is likely that legumes, cereals and spices mixture used in the preparation of dough/batters and the aeriel environment are contributing the initial inoculum for the fermentations. Several reports have indicated that black gram, the basic ingredient of all the Indian products harbours *Leuconostoc mesenteroides* and many other lactic acid bacteria in large numbers which multiply rapidly during the initial soaking of the ingredients

Table 28.3 : Prevalence of bacterial and yeasts in Indian fermented foods during different seasons

Food	Season	Micro-organisms					
		Bacteria			Yeasts		
		Range of total (CFU/g dry matter)	No. of isolates		Range of total (CFU/g dry matter)	No. of isolates	
			Genera	Species		Genera	Species
Warri	Summer	10^{10}-10^{12}	6	6	0-10^{4}	6	6
	Winter	10^{9}-10^{10}	5	5	0-10^{7}	8	8
Papadam	Summer	10^{9}-10^{10}	3	3	0-10^{2}	3	3
	Winter	10^{9}-10^{10}	3	3	0-10^{3}	6	6
Bhallae	Summer	10^{9}-10^{10}	6	6	0-10^{4}	3	3
	Winter	10^{9}-10^{10}	4	4	0-10^{5}	7	8
Vadai	Summer	10^{9}-10^{10}	5	5	0-10^{4}	4	4
	Winter	10^{7}-10^{9}	4	4	0-10^{6}	7	8
Idli	Summer	10^{7}-10^{8}	5	6	0-10^{3}	2	3
	Winter	10^{6}-10^{8}	4	4	0-10^{6}	5	6
Dosa	Summer	10^{7}-10^{9}	6	8	0-10^{4}	4	5
	Winter	10^{4}-10^{8}	4	4	0-10^{7}	7	9

due to the release of free sugars and non- protein nitrogen. The loss frequency of occurrence of yeast in the traditional Indian fermentations is probably due to their less prevalence on the dry grains or ingredients. Since the grains are presoaked in water and ground to pastes, yeasts are likely to develop only after the softening of the ingredients. Successional studies on various Indian fermented foods[88, 93] indicated the rapid multiplication of micro-organisms supported by the solubilization of carbohydrates and proteins during the soaking of the ingredients. The increase in microbial load is accompanied by a decrease in pH and rise in volume in all the foods. Both bacteria and yeasts, whenever present, increase significantly with the progress in fermentation followed by a decrease in pH and rise in volume. The principal bacteria appearing initially in legume based foods are *Leuconostoc mesenteroides* and lactobacilli along with *Bacillus subtilis, Flauobacter* and *Achromobacter* sp., the last two species disappear with the progress in fermentation suggesting that they have no role in fermentations. *Streptococcus faecalis* develops subsequently and persists till the end of fermentations along with *Leuconostoc mesenteroides* and *Lactobacillus fermentum.* The pattern is similar in cereal- legume based *dosa* and *idli* except that *Bacillus amylo- liquefaciens* and *B. polymyxa* are also present in the initial stages. *Trichosporon beigelii, Saccharomyces cereuisiae, Candida krusei, Pichia membranaefaciens* and *Hansenula anomala* are among the yeast appearing first but eventually only *Saccharomyces cereuisiae* and *Trichosporon beigelii* remain.

The biochemical and physiological characterization of predominant microorganisms associated in Indian fermentations (Table 28.6) indicates that both *Leuconostoc* and lactobacilli, the common bacteria associated with staples, presumably produce acid and gas from various carbohydrates thus, making the environment unfit for other contaminants which gradually disappear with the progress in fermentation. *Streptococcus faecalis* perhaps comes from air in later stages and produces more acid, causing further acidification, thus enhancing the shelf-life of the products. *Bacillus amyloliquefaciens* a.nel *B. polymyxa,* which are generally associated with *idli* and *dosa* batter fermentation are likely to be contributed by rice and help in the degradation of starch into maltose and glucose by producing extracellular amylolytic enzymes. Some strains of *Saccharomyces cereuisiae* also produce acid and gas from starch itself and may thus, play a significant role in adding to the acidification and leavening during fermentation.

Table 28.4 Occurrence of various bacteria in Indian fermented foods during different seasons

Bacteria type	Food					
	Warri	Papadam	Bhallae	Vadai	Idli	Dosa
Achromobactor sp.	-	-	S	S	-	-
Bacillus amyloliquefaciens	-	-	-	-	W	S
B. polymyxa-	-	-	-	-	-	S
B. subtilis	S	-	S,W	S,W	-	S
Enterobactor sp.	S	-	-	-	-	W
Flavobactor sp.	S,W	-	S	-	-	-
Lactobacillus delbrueckii	-	-	-	-	S	S
L. fermentusm	S,W	S	S,W	S,W	S,W	S,W
Leuconostoc measenteroides	S,W	S,W	S,W	S,W	S,W	S,W
Micrococcus varians	-	-	-	-	-	W
Pediococcus cerevisiae	-	-	-	S	S	S,W
Steptococccus faecalis	S,W	S,W	S,W	S,W	S,W	S

S : Prevalent during summers, W : Prevalent during winters, S.W. : Prevalent during both the seasons (-) not applicable

TABLE 28.5 : Occurrence of various yeasts in Indian fermented foods during different seasons

Yeast type	Food					
	Warri	Papadam	Bhallae	Vadai	Idli	Dosa
Candida aquuatica	W	-	-	-	-	-
C. curvata	-	-	W	W	-	-
C. famata	-	-	W	-	-	-
C. kefyr	-	-	-	-	-	W
C. krusei	W	W	-	W	-	W
C. robusta	-	-	-	-	-	-
C. vartiovaarai	W	-	-	-	-	-
Cryptococcus humicolus	W	-	-	-	-	S,W
Debaryomyces hansenii	-	W	W	S.W.	W	-
Geotrichum candidum	W	-	-	-	-	S.W
Hansenula anomala	S,W	S,W	S,W	S,W	S,W	S,W
Kluyveromyces marxianus	W	-	-	-	-	W
Oosporidium margaritiferum	-	-	-	-	-	-
Pichia membranaefaciebns	S,W	W	W	W	W	-
Rhodotorula glutinis	-	-	W	-	-	W
R. muciloginosa	-	-	-	-	-	W
Saccharomyces cerevisiae	S,W	S,W	S,W	S,W	S,W	S,W
Torulopsis candida	-	-	-	-	W	W
Trichosporon beigelii	S,W	S,W	S,W	S,W	W	S,W
T. pullulans	-	-	W	W	W	S,W

DIFFERENT FERMENTED CEREAL PRODUCTS

Bread

Baked foods are produced and consumed in most of the countries of the world. Considerable variation exists in the type of baked foods, that are made, from country to country, and often among regions within a given country. Bread is one of the most commonly used baked foods and has traditionally been an important factor in human nutrition. In many countries bread consumption accounts for a large part of the diet. Bread was first baked in Egypt over 6000 years ago 20 and from that time and place, it travelled west varying in ingredients, flavour, texture, and form. European and Middle Eastern immigrants brought recipes for their native breads and these have been handed down to second and third generations.

Classification of Bread Types

There are various types of bread available in the world and these can be classified in different ways, some of which are summarised as follows:

Table 28.6 : Some biochemical and physiological characteristics of predominant micro-organisms isolated from various indian fermented foods.

Organims	Production of acid and gas from			Assimilation of		Vitamin free medium	Growth in/at		
	Glucose	Maltose	Sucrose	Maltose	Starch		37°C	42°C	pH 4.0
Lactobacillus delbrueckii	+a	+,-	+a	-	-	ND	+	+	+
Lactobacillus fermentum	+	+	+a	-	-	ND	+	+	+
Leuconostoc mesenteroides	+	+a	+a	-	+	ND	+	+	+
Streptococcus faecalis	+	+	-	-	+	ND	+	+	+
Candida krusei	+	-	-	-	-	+	+	-	+
Debaryomyces hensenii	+	-	+,-	+	+	-	+,-	-	+
Hansenula anomala	+	+	+	+	+	+	+,-	+,-	+
Kluyveromyces marxinus	+	+	+	+	-	-	+	+,-	+
Pichia membranefaciens	-	-	-	-	-	+,-	+,-	-	+
Saccharomyces cerevisiae	+	+	+	+	+,-	+,-	+,-	+,-	+
Trichosporon beigelii	-	-	-	+	+	-	+,-	+,-	+

a : Poduction of acid butnot gas, +,-: Variable in different isolates, ND: Not detacted

Leavening: Breads may be unleavened such as chappatti, leavened with yeast, such as pan breads, chemically leavened, such as Irish soda bread; or leavened with bacteria, such as salt rising bread.

Formulation: Many breads around the world are made with lean formulas comprising wheat flour, water, yeast and salt, while some breads such as certain premium breads also contain considerable amounts of other ingredients such as fat, eggs and milk.

Shape and size: A virtually endless variety of shapes and sizes have evolved; some breads are baked in pans while ·many are baked in open hearth.

Specific volume: This factor can vary from the low-density, high volume white pan breads in North America to the dense, dark breads of Central Europe.

Crust characteristics: Some breads, such as Vienna loaves, have thin crispy, crust, while others, such as German pumpernickel breads have thick crusts. Colours range from quite light to dark colours.

Crumb characteristics : Continuous mix breads in the United States have a very fine, uniform crumb structure, while other breads such as French baguettes have coarse, Irregular structures. Some Middle East breads have little crumb structure at all, being comprised largely of crust because of the high baking temperatures that are used.

Bread Making

The actual baking process is really the last and most important step in the production of bakery products. Through the agency of heat, an unpalatable dough mass is transformed into a light, porous, easily digestible and most appetizing product.

The biological activities that have been taking place in the dough are stopped by baking, with the destruction of micro-organisms and enzymes present. The unstable colloidal system is stabilized. The basic characteristics of the native starch and proteins are drastically changed. At the same time new flavouring substances are formed including caramelized sugars, pyrodextrins and melanoidins, which give the baked product ita desirable and distinctive organoleptic properties.

All the desirable reactions involved in changing a dough into a bakery product must occur in certain sequences and require controlled conditions. While each of the chemical and physical reactions that occur in a baking dough is still not fully understood, there is an increasing information on the subject and it has expanded our knowledge about the baking process.

(a) *Dough:* The protein of the wheat flour is unique in that when the flour is mixed with water in certain proportions, the protein forms an elastic colloidal mass or dough which can hold gas and which forms a spongy structure when baked. It is this characteristic of wheat flour, not found in other cereal grains, which makes possible the manufacture of soft white bread.

Initially the protein exists in a coiled condition in the dough and gives it its elastic behaviour. The linkages between the chains are not equally strong at all points so that when the dough is mixed some of the linkages break while others remain intact. This slow but constant adjustment that occurs within the dough during mixing takes place in the presence of the starch and other materials present in the dough (Table 28.7). The starch-water paste itself has distinct physical characteristic which also come into play from a physical point of view. Salt also influences the structure as do sugar, shortening, emulsifiers, enzymes etc. The bread dough is usually leavened by bread yeast which ferment the sugars in the dough and :produce mainly carbon dioxide and alcohol. However, other actively gas forming micro-organisms such as wild yeasts, coliform bacteria, saccharolytic *Clostridium* spp., heterofermentative lactic acid bacteria and various naturally occurring mixtures of these organisms have been used instead of bread yeasts for leavening. Leavening may also be accomplished by the direct incorporation of gas (CO_2) in the dough.

Table 28.7 : Typcial White Bread Formula

Ingredient	Per cent on the basis of flour
Flour	100
Water	60-65
Yeast	3
Yeast food	0.3-0.5
Salt	2
Sugar	4
Mould inhibitor	0.125
Non-fat dry milk solids	3
Lard	2
Emulsifier	0.25

(b) *Leavening systems:* The porous structure of the baked foods is due to the leavening action of a gas, carbon dioxide (CO_2), which is evolved either by fermentation or by the reaction of inorganic chemicals. The CO_2

derived from leavening does not generate new gas cells in the dough but diffuses into the cells already already present in the dough system. These primary cells arise from air bubbles occluded during dough mixing or from air adsorbed on flour particles.

Yeast fermentation under the anaerobic conditions of the dough forms 2 moles each of ethanol and CO_2 from 1 mole of glucose. This means that fermentation of 180 mg of glucose (1mMole) results in the formation of 88 mg of CO_2 (2 mMole) which occupies a volume of about 480 ml at atmospheric pressure. The metabolic reactions of yeast are relatively slow in comparison with chemical reactions. One can calculate that a dough containing 3% compressed yeast will produce enough carbon dioxide gas during 1 hr of proofing to yield bread of specific volume of. This assumes that all of the evolved gas is retained in the dough and a good oven spring.

Chemical leavening is carried out with baking powder, a mixture of sodium bicarbonate and acid salts (usually phosphates or pyrophosphates); 336 mg of $NaHC0_3$ (2mMole) produces 88 mg of CO_2 (2mMole) which occupy a volume of 480 ml at atmospheric pressure. The reaction is almost instantaneous and has to be slowed down by coating the inorganic acid salts with fat. The coating coating is chosen in such a manner that a part of the reaction takes place on the bench and most of it in the oven.

Baked. goods produced by fermentation with yeast are usually preferred because of the desirable flavour whlch results from the reaction of fermentation by-products with other dough ingredients. However, the leavening power of the yeasts is very poor in dough systems of hlgh osmotlc pressure, that is with low moisture or with high salt or sugar content. Therefore, breads, rolls and buns are usually leavened with yeast and cakes, cookies and biscuits with chemical leavening. There are some borderline areas in which either of these two leavening systems is used. For instance, doughnuts may be produced as yeast raised doughnuts or as cake doughnuts (leavened by baking powder). This also apples to pizza crusts which may be produced with either of leavening system. Flat dough pieces such as pancakes are leavened with baking powder.

Not all yeast-raised products are baked in ovens. The yeast raised dumplings of central Europe, the steamed yeast raised bread of the Chinese, and English muffins (grilled on a hot surface) are some exceptions.

With very flat doughs, leavening may also be obtained by the steam generated in the doughs during baking. This is true of soda crackers, which are laminated during processing and of some of the flat breads of the Mid-East.

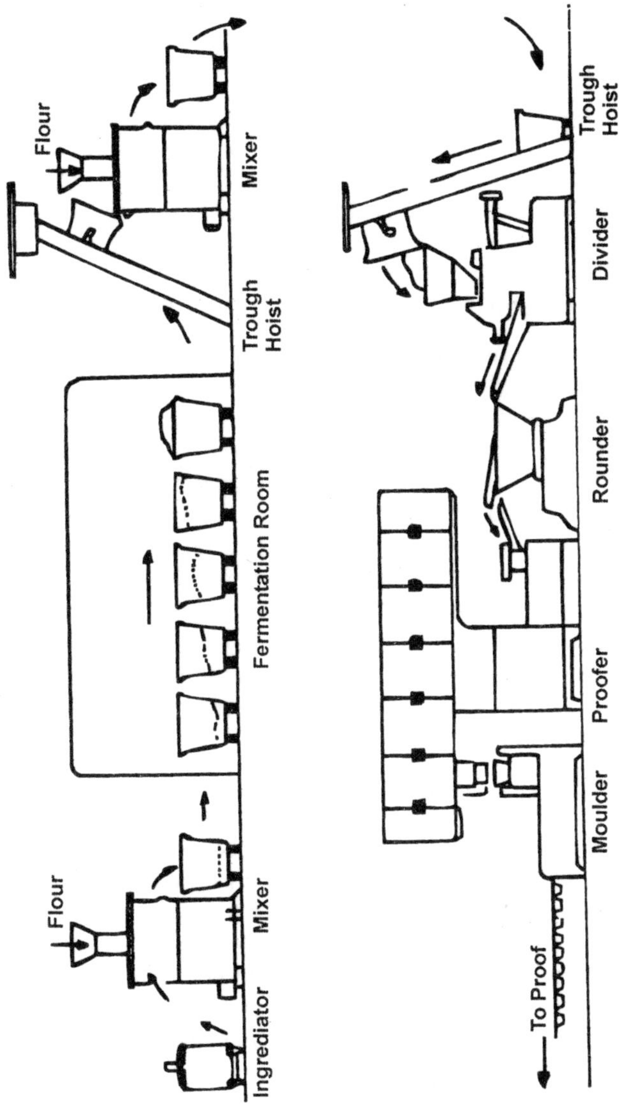

Fig. 28.1 : Schematic diagram of sponge dough process.

Methods of bread production

The type of bread most widely produced and consumed in different parts of the world is white pan bread. This is made by a number of procedures, but the most common methods utilized are: (1) sponge dough (2) straight dough, (3) continuous mix and (4) liquid ferment.

(a) *Sponge dough:* This process was introduced during the 1920s and is today the predominant breadmaking method used by the baking industry. The popularity of the sponge dough method is due to the greater processing tolerance of the procedure and to the flavour of the bread, generally regarded as superior compared to breads made by other methods.[81] A schematic diagram of the sponge dough process is illustrated in Fig. 28.1 and its comparison with straight dough is made in Table 28.8.

The sponge consisting about 65% of the total flour plus a portion of the total dough water, yeast and yeast food, sometimes also called as dough conditioners, including the ammonium salts to stimulate the yeasts and various salts e.g. $KBrO_3$, KIO_3, CaO_2 and $(NH^4)_2S_2O_8$ to improve the dough characteristics are first mixed. The mixing period is relatively brief and merely aims at uniformly combining the sponge ingredients. The sponge is then discharged into a trough where it undergoes a fermentation period of 4.5 hr in a controlled environment. From a starting temperature of about 25°C the final temperature will increase by approximately 6°C due to the exothermic reactions brought about by the yeast activity. Sponge volume will increase by a factor of 4 or 5 as a consequence of carbon dioxide production during fermentation. Complex biochemical and physical changes take place during the fermentation period.

At the end of the sponge fermentation, the sponge is transferred into a dough mixer. The balance of the flour is also placed into the mixer alongwith the water and other ingredients. This is mixed until the dough has been transformed from a sticky, wet-appearing mixture into a smooth, cohesive dough, characterized by a glossy sheen. This change occurs because of the unique properties of wheat flour. Upon the addition of water and the input of energy, wheat proteins and lipids form gluten which has film-forming and gas retaining properties. As *Saccharomyces cerevisiae* evolves carbon dioxide, the gas diffuses into previously-formed gas vesicles and is retained in the dough due to the unique nature of gluten.

The mixed dough is placed in troughs and allowed to rest for 20-30 min during which the dough recovers from mechanical stress, relaxes and is better able to undergo the remaining processing stages.

Table 28.8 : White pan bread formulations—sponge and straight dough

	Sponge dough		Straight dough
	Sponge	Dough	
Flour	65.0	35.0	100
Water (variable)	40.0	25.0	65
Yeast	2.5	—	3.0
Yeast food	0.2-0.5	—	0.2-0.5
Salt	—	2.	2.25
Sweetner (solid basis)	—	8-10	8-10
Fat	—	3.0	3.0
Dairy product		0.5-3.0	0.5-3.0
Crumb softner	—	0.2-0.5	0.2-0.5
Rope and mold inhibitor	—	0.125	0.125
Dough improver	—	0-0.05	0.5
Enrichment	—	As needed	As needed

Ingredient based on 100 parts flour.

Dividing the dough is the next stage. During this stage the dough is cut into pieces of desired weight by machine that volumetrically divides the pieces and discharges them onto a moving belt. The dough pieces are conveyed to a rounder where the rough appearing pieces are forced along a metal sleeve such that the pieces become rounded and have a smooth, dry skin. In this condition the dough pieces retain more carbon dioxide and are less sticky.

The dividing and rounding operations impose a certain amount of stress to the dough pieces, with the result that they are somewhat degassed and unpliable. To compensate for this effect, the dough pieces upon leaving the rounder are accorded rest period of some 8-12 min. This takes place in tray-type conveyors enclosed within cabinets of different configurations.

The dough pieces are then conveyed to moulding machines which transform the more or less round pieces of dough into cylinders which are then fed to bread pans.

Pans containing the dough pieces are placed in fermentation units called proof boxes for the last fermentation period prior to baking. The environment in these units is typically maintained at 35-43°C at a relative humidity of 80-95%. The dough pieces expand in the pans to a desired volume, a process

Table 28.9 : Continuos-mix process formula for flour brew

	Formula	Stage1	Stage2	Stage3
Flour	100.0	30	-	70
Water	67.0	56	0	7.0
Yeast	3.0	3.0	-	-
Yeast food	0.5	0.5	-	-
Salt	2.0	-	2.0	-
Sugar	6.0	-	1.0	5.0
Milk	3.0	-	-	3.0
MCP	0.1	-	-	-
Mold inhibitor	0.1	-	-	0.1
Shortening	3.0	-	-	3.0
Oxidation/variable				

Ingredients based on 100 parts flour.

usually requiring approximately 60 min. The proofed loaves are then placed in an oven for baking. Gas within the dough fabric expands; steam and alcohol vapours also contribute to this expansion. Enzymes remain active until the bread reaches about 75°C. At this temperature the starch gelatinizes and the dough structure is set. With the bread surface temperature reaching 130 to 140°C sugars and soluble proteins react chemically to produce an attractive crust colour. The centre of the loaf does not exceed 100°C.[55]

Remaining stages in the bread making process include cooling of the baked bread, slicing, wrapping and distribution to stores for sale to the consumer.

(b) *Straight dough:* All the ingredients for the straight dough are combined and mixed in one operation (Table 28.8). *After* mixing the straight dough is given a bulk fermentation period of 2-4 hr and is then processed in a manner similar to that described for the doughs in the sponge dough process.

Straight doughs require less labour, time and equipment compared to sponge doughs, but exhibit less tolerance to processing variations. This factor along with the characteristically blander flavour of straight dough bread had led over the years to the commercial preference of sponge doughs over straight doughs. Today straight doughs are used mostly by smaller bakeries or for specialty bread production by larger bakers.

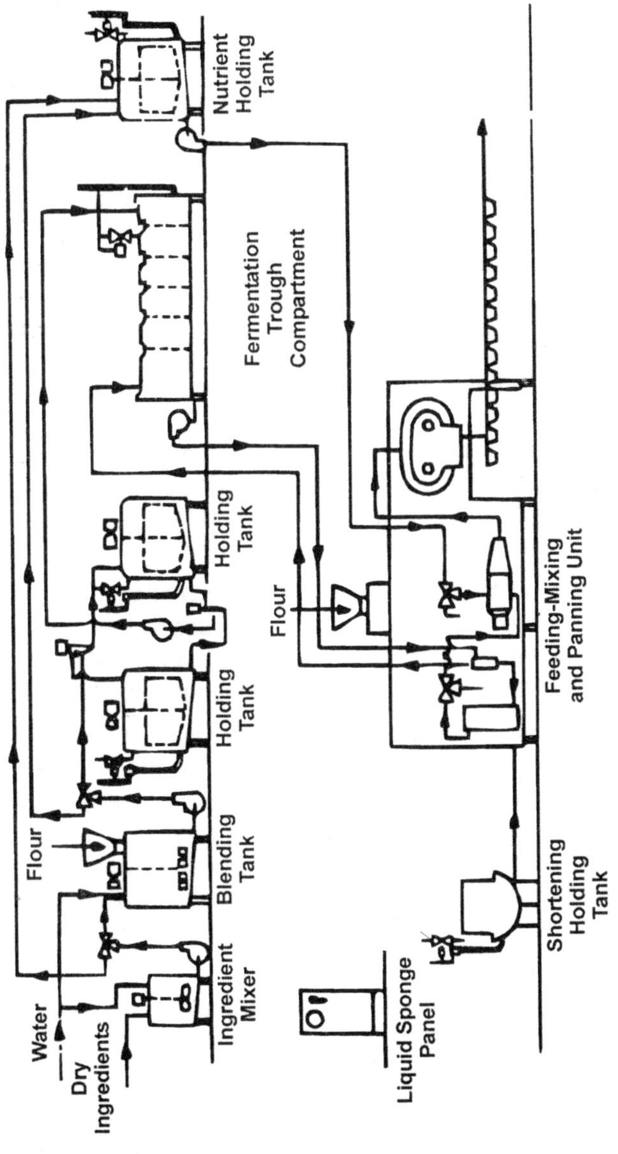

Fig. 28.2 : Schematic diagram of continuous mix breadmaking (Amflow method).

(c) *Continuous mix:* This was introduced in the United States during the 1950s. The Do-Maker process4 and the Aroflow method are the continuous mix processes. Figure 28.2 and Table 28.9 show a flow diagram and a formula for Aroflow procedure. This method and Do-maker method share the essential features of each other.

Initially a ferment or brew (stage 1) is made (with or without some flour in the case ofthe Do-Maker) and this is fermented in a holding tank for about 1 hr. A second stage (water, salt and sugar) is added to the system and the fermentation continues for a total of about 2.5 hr. At the end of fermentation, the brew is pumped into a premixer; cooling of the brew is achieved by means of a heat exchanger. The remaining flour and water, sugar, melted fat, oxidant and other optional ingredients are also fed into the premixer. After the premixer combines all of these ingredients, the loosely mixed mass is pumped into a developing chamber. As the dough passes through the chamber it is under pressure and is subjected to intense mechanical energy. Under these conditions the dough is quickly developed and is then extruded into pans from a slit in the bottom of the chamber by a system of intermittently actuated knives. The dough from the continuous mix developer is much softer and warmer (about 37°C) compared to sponge doughs. The dough pieces are proofed and baked in a manner similar to that of sponge doughs.

Continuous mix breads differ from conventional breads. They have a much finer, more fragile crumb structure. These factors coupled with a flavour that some consumers feel is less desirable than that of sponge dough bread have limited the acceptance of continuous mix breads if. some markets.

(d) *Liquid pre-ferment:* Procedures for making bread employing liquid or semi-liquid ferments have been known for many years. Advances in equipment design stemming from continuous mix technology made the utilization of liquid ferment breadmaking systems more feasible. Such systems combine standard equipment to mix and process doughs with pumps and tanks to handle liquid brews. The advantages of liquid ferment systems include (1) saving in plant space, (2) labour saving, (3) more processing flexibility and (4) improved sanitation.

A flow diagram and representative formula for the liquid ferment process are shown in Fig. 28.3 and Table 28.10 respectively.

In this system a liquid ferment or brew is prepared and allowed to undergo fermentation much as desired for continuous mix operations. After fermentation the brew is pumped to a dough mixer (same as used in conventional sponge dough processing) along with remaining ingredients.

Table 28.10. : Bread formula made with flour containing ferment

Ingredient	Liquid Formula[1]	Sponge Formula[1]	Materials Added at Mix[1]
Flour	100	50.02	49.98
Water	66	55.77	10.23
Yeast	3	3	—
Yeast food	0.625	0.625	—
Salt	2.25	0.5	1.75
Sugar	8	1.5	6.5
Milk	3	—	—
Mold inhibitor	0.125	0.125	—
Fat	3	—	3
Emulsifier	0.5	—	0.5
Total	186.500	111.540	74.960

Ingerdients based on 100 parts flour

The dough is mixed and then subjected to the same processing steps as outlined for the dough in the sponge dough process.

The basic differences between sponge process and liquid ferment process are summarised in Table 28.11.

Flavour development

Fresh bread has a pleasing and appealing flavour that in part is responsible for its universal acceptance as a human food. Bread flavour is derived from two main sources: yeast fermentation and crust browning.

(a) *Yeast fermentation:* Doughs made with high concentrations of yeast yield baked products with yeasty or slightly cooked flavours.[121] Thiamin and thiamin diphosphate were the major flavour compounds in yeast which may contribute to an undesirable flavour of the bread.

The characteristic flavour of yeast raised breads arises from yeast fermentation and subsequent reaction of fermentation products with other dough compounds during baking. The taste and odour of fermenting dough resemble that of fermenting beer wort and fermenting wine and the flavour compounds which have been isolated are qualitatively the same. During the baking some of these compounds escape and others react with amino acids and other compounds of the dough to yield the characteristic flavour of the

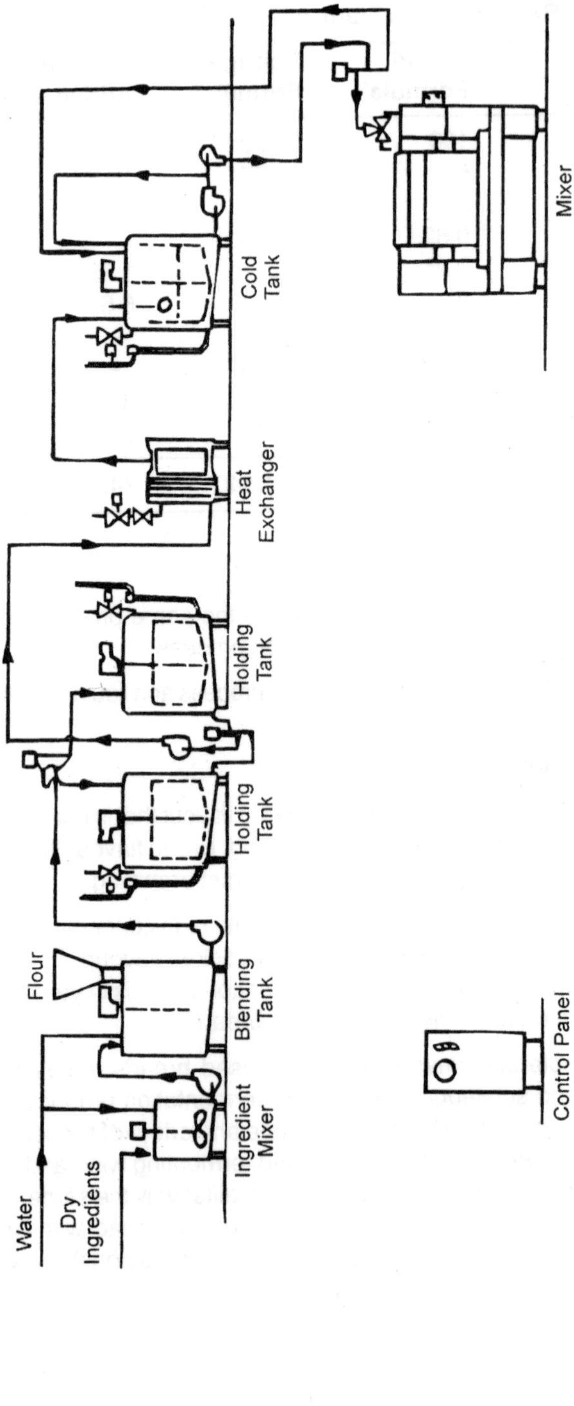

Fig. 28.3 : Schematic diagram of liquid-ferment process

Table 28.11 : Basic difference between sponge dough process and liquid ferment process

	Sponge dough	Liquid Pre-ferment		
Flour levels	50-100%	40-70%	15-40%	0-15%
Sugar in pre-ferment	non required	0.5%	2%	2-3%
Set temperature	23-27°C	24-27°C	27-30°C	28-31°C
Fermentation time	3.5 hr	2-3 hr	2 hr	2 hr
Yeast percentage	2.5%	gradually increases to 3.5%		
Yeast nutrient and oxidation	15 ppm	20-50 ppm	25-60 ppm	35-75 ppm
Buffers, enzymes, acidity additives mix reducing agents	none required	gradual increase to high levels		
Dough mixing time	normal	+10%	+40%	+60%
Dough temperatures	normal-27°C	gradual increase to 35°C		
Dough flour time	normal 20 min	gradual increase in time		

bread. The fermentation by-products formed during yeast fermentation fall largely into the class of organic esters, acids, alcohols and carbonyl compounds.

Traditional methods of bread making involving substantial periods of bulk fermentation yield bread with most desirable flavour. A number of studies have been conducted showing that certain organic compounds increase as a function of fermentation time. On the other hand other investigators have found no flavour differences in bread made with or without bulk fermentation. These findings indicate that flavour compounds formed during baking and during proofing are sufficient to yield satisfactory bread flavour.

Some of the organic compounds formed during fermentation may also arise from bacterial action. Lactic acid bacteria found in the dough presumably are associated with yeast; commercial bakers' yeast normally contains a low number of contaminating micro-organisms. In addition to *S. cerevisiae,* other yeasts may be responsible for characteristic flavour of certain breads.

(b) *Crust browning:* The extent of crust browning is influenced substantially by previous activities of *S. cerevisiae* in the dough. The importance of crust browning in the flavour development can be shown by removing the crust of freshly baked bread and storing the bread until it has cooled or by baking bread in a microwave oven where crust browning does not occur. Under these conditions the product will lack the flavour usually associated with bread. Presumably, therefore, a part of bread flavour is formed in the crust during baking and then diffuses into the crumb where it becomes absorbed. Over 100 flavour compounds have been found in the bread.Table 28.12 lists some of the compounds reportedly produced during fermentation and/or baking.

Dough maturing

Another function of yeast is to cause many changes in the dough that are often summarized as dough maturing or ripening. A properly matured dough is one that exhibits optimum rheological properties (optimum balance of extensibility and elasticity) such that it may be machined well and will lead to bread with desirable volume and crumb characteristics. Some of the reactions leading to dough maturation have also been documented. Alcohol and carbon dioxide, among other products, are derived from yeast fermentation. Alcohol is water miscible and, since appreciable amounts are formed, it therefore influences the colloidal nature of the flour proteins and alters the interfacial tension within the dough. Some of carbon dioxide dissolves in the aqueous phase of the dough and forms weakly ionizable carbonic acid which

Table 28.12 Compounds reportedly produced during fermentation and/or baking

Organic acids	Organic acids	Alcohols	Aldehydes and Ketones	Carbonyl Compounds
Butyric	Acetic	Ethanol	Acetaldehyde	Furfural
Succinic	Lactic	n-Propanol	Formaldehyde	Methional
Propionic	Formic	Isobutanol	Isovaleraldehyde	Glyoxal
n-Butyric	Valeric	Amyl alcohol	n-Valeraldehyde	3-Methyl butanal
Isobutyric	Caproic	Isoamyl alcohol	2-Methyl butanol	2-Methyl butanal
Isovaleric	Caprylic	2,3-Butanediol	n-Hexaldehyde	Hydroxymethyl furfural
Helptanoic	Isocaproic	ß-Phenylethyl alcohol	Acetone	
Pelargonic	Carpic		Propionaldehyde	
Pyruvic	Lauric		Isobutyraldehyde	
Palmitic	Nyristic		Methyl ethyl ketone	
Crotonic	Hydrocinnamic		2-Butanone	
Itaconic	Benzylic		Diacethyl	
Levulinic			Acetoin	

lowers the pH of the system. Carbon dioxide also distends the dough as the gas expands, thereby contributing mechanical work into the dough system. Ammonia, ammonium sulphate and ammonium chloride added to the dough as yeast foods are assimilated by *S. cerevisiae* causing a liberation of sulfuric acid and hydrochloric acids. These acids alongwith carbonic acid further lower the pH which in turn significantly influences gluten hydration and swelling, the reaction rate of enzymes in dough, oxidation-reduction reactions and various chemical reactions. *S. cerevisiae* also produces reductases which affect dough rheological properties by acting through intermediate substrates found in dough.

Bread-like products

A large number of other bread-like, leavened and baked foods are also produced in different parts of the world. Some of them are discussed here:

Sour dough bread

Sour dough bread is usually made from a mixture of rye and wheat flour containing upto 80% of wheat flour. The acid taste may be obtained by adding mixtures of lactic acid and acetic acids. Such breads are usually leavened with yeast a.nd the action of lactic acid bacteria. In Europe and for some American rye sour breads the use of sour dough starters are preferred because these give the full flavour which depends upon the microbial souring action. The use of such rye sour cultures predates recorded history. It is relatively easy to produce such starter by mixing rye flour and water in equal proportions and permitting it to ferment for several days at 30°C. This forms the basis of the culture which can then be maintained by further additions of rye flour and water.

Sour dough starter cultures are also available commercially which can be used to inoculate the doughs. Such cultures usually contain mixtures of lactic acid bacteria. These organisms have been classified as subgroups of the genus Lactobacillus as follows: *Thermobacterium (L. acidophil us), Streptobacterium (L. casei, L. plantarum, L. farciminis, L. ulimentarius)* and *Betabacterium (L. brevis, L. buchneri, L. fermentum, L. fructivorans)*. All the strains ferment maltose, about three-fourths ferment fructose, one-half ferment sucrose and about one-fourth ferment lactose. Ordinary bakers yeast *(S. cerevisiae)* usually contains 10,000 to several million lactic acid bacteria per g and its use will result in souring of the dough if the fermentation is carried out for prolonged periods of time and at relatively elevated temperatures.

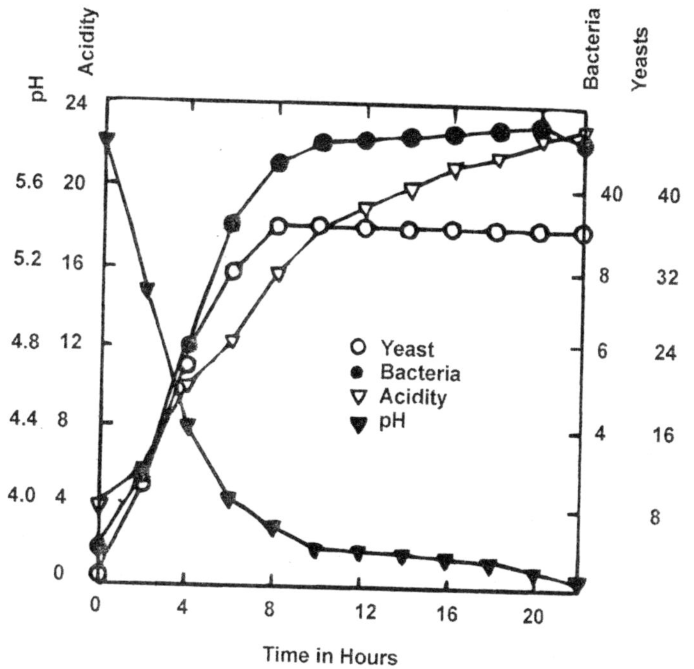

Fig. 28.4 : Multiplication of yeasts and bacteria and pH of rye sourdough

The lactic acid bacteria usually found in sour rye fermentations are *L. plantarum, L. brevis* and *L. fermenti.* Homofermentative bacteria producing only lactic acid are usually thermophiles and donot grow at the relatively low temperatures of dough fermentations. Homofermentative bacteria producing only acetic acid also do not find a favourable climate in the anaerobic doughs. Therefore, lactic and acetic acids are mainly produced by heterofermentative bacteria found in the doughs.

Bakers yeast is frequently added to sour doughs to increase the leavening activity of the system. In spontaneous sour doughs (to which no bakers yeast had been added) yeasts belonging to *S. cerevisiae, Pichia saitoi* and *Trichosporon penicilliatum* respectively were found. The number of yeasts in spontaneous sour doughs was about 1.3 x 109/g and that of bacterial cells varied from 4 to 6 x 109/ g. The growth of yeasts and bacteria in such doughs is illustrated in Fig. 4 together with the concomitant drop in pH and increase in titrable acidity. *Fig. 28.4 Multiplication of yeasts and bacteria and pH of rye sourdough.*

A white sour dough bread produced only in the Western United States is the San Francisco sour dough bread. It is of special interest because It is still produced by propagation with sponges from the previous day's production. The characteristic yeast of this process is *Torulopsis holmii* and the bacterium producing both lactic and acetic acids has been named as *Lactobacillus sanfrancisco.* The sponges contain only water, flour and micro-organisms and require about 8 hr at 25°C for full development. The final pH may be as low as 3.9. About 20% of the starter sponge is used in the dough.

The Italian *Pannetone* is a traditional Christmas fruitcake which is also made from starter sponges. The characteristic yeast is identical with that of San Francisco sour dough. The dominant lactic acid producer was identified as *L. brevis.*

Rye Bread

Rye bread may be made with or without a starter or sour, but only the type made with starter is of interest. The old method of preparing sour depended upon the bacteria naturally present in a mixture of rye flour and water. The mixture was allowed to ferment for 5 to 10 hr; then more flour and water were added and the fermentation was continued for an additional 5 or 6 hr; which was repeated several times. Half of the sour was incorporated in the sponge or dough for the bread and the rest carried over to start a new sour. This sour was modified by some bakers by the addition of yeast and of lactic acid bacteria from cultured buttermilk or Bulgarian buttermilk to a sour that was made anew daily.

Modern methods involve addition of considerable amounts of cultures of acid-forming bacteria to the dough mass to be used as a sour and controlling the time of fermentation (18-24 hr) and the temperature of incubation (about 25°C). An excessively high incubation temperature, for example, 32-35°C, favours the growth of undesirable gas-formers, such as coliform and butyric bacteria. Some bakers prefer to use low-temperature lactic acid bacteria e.g. *Lactobacillus plantarum, L. brevis* and *Leuconostoc mesenteroides* whereas others use high-temperature lactics, such as *Lactobacillus bulgaricus* and *Streptococcus thermophilus* and adjust the incubation temperature, accordingly. The growth of heterofermentative lactic acid bacteria is considered desirable. The starter imparts a desired sour flavour to the rye bread that is not given by the addition of lactic and acetic acids.

Crackers

There is a considerable similarity between the bacteriological events in sour dough sponges and in cracker dough sponges.' Cracker sponges ferment for about 18 hr before the doughs are made up and a portion of the cracker c;ponge is often kept for inoculation of the next sponge. Very small percentages of bakers yeast are used (0.125 to 0.2%). The yeasts multiply rapidly during the first 10 to 15 hr of the sponge fermentation to reach 40 x 106 cells per g. This alcoholic fermentation is followed by a bacterial fermentation which results in the production of lactic acid, a further drop in pH and a growth to about 75 x 106 cells per g.[37,50] When the cracker sponges are mixed with additional flour, soda is added to raise the pH and the dough is sheeted after a 4 hr dough fermentation. The leavening action is largely due to formation of steam during the short baking period in a hot oven.

(a) *Soda cracker:* The soda cracker, often called a saltine, appears to have originated in the 1850s in America. The first cracker bakery in the United States was established at Newburyport, Mass in 1792. However, crackers made before 1850 were unleavened. At present, soda crackers represent about 50% of the total biscuit and cracker production in United States. The evolution from empiricism to a science has not been completed, but the industry has become standardized in the use of spindle mixtures; an 18-20 hr sponge fermentation; a 4-5 hr dough proof; automatic lamination qfthe dough; a short bake (1.5-3.0 min, depending on the thickness of the crackers) and the use of a band oven equipped with a woven wire mesh band.

Important factors in the production of a superior soda cracker are the choice of flours for the sponge and dough, the selection of the fermentation equipment and the baking conditions. For the sponge a standard patent of straight milled flour is commonly employed, usually milled from soft red winter wheat, possibly blended with some hard red winter wheat. A slightly softer flour is used for the dough. A basic formula for the soda crackers is shown in Table 28.13.

The production of superior crackers requires the use of uniform and high quality raw materials, and the adoption of, and adherence to precise production procedures. The setting temperatures of sponge is about 24°C, but varies from 21-26°C, depending upon the several factors, chiefly the flour available. Flour and water are the basic ingredients of a cracker sponge. Yeast and the bacteria are the fermentation agents. Bacteria originate in the yeast, the flour, the surface of the trough, when employed, and inoculum added from the sponge of the previous day. During the proofing period profound chemical and physical changes occur by virtue of the simultaneous fermentation by yeast and bacteria. Amylases convert starch into dextrins and fermentable sugars. Defficiency in the flour amylases may be corrected by adding diastatically active malt flour or a fungal diastase. As the sugars are produced by the amylases the yeast produces carbon dioxide and alcohol. The bacteria convert the sugars to organic acids. The acids increase the activity of the amylases, accelerating the production of sugars, thus speeding up the entire process.

Table 28.13: A basic formula for soda crackers

Sponge		
	Flour	800
	Water (variable)	350
	Shortening	60
	Yeast	2
	Yeast food (optional)	1
	Ferment (optional)	20
Dough		
	Flour	400
	Shortening	60
	Sugar malt (optional)	10
	Salt	18
	Soda (variable)	7
	Diammonium phosphate (optional)	2

Significant physical changes occur in the sponge during fermentation. Immediately after mixing, the flour and water form a very stiff mass. During fermentation, the sponge becomes elastic and pliable. Several factors are responsible for the development of these changes: (1) the hydration of the gluten, which prepares it for the following step; (2) a slight enzymatic hydrolysis of flour proteins; and (3) a mechanical development of the gluten. The carbon dioxide produced during the fermentation forms the cells which expand and contract, stretching the gluten network, producing an effect similar to mechanical mixing. Sponge temperature increases at 5-8°C. There is a marked increase in the acidity: as measured by the pH, a change from near to 6 to about 4.5. Neutralization of the acids is an important element in the preparation of the dough, involving an estimate of the amount of sodium bicarbonate required to produce the desired pH in the baked cracker. The optimum pH lies between 7.2 and 8.0; the addition of diammonium phosphate at the dough-up stage to aid in achieving uniformity of cracker pH.

Sensory properties of a superior crackers are readily defined. Symmetry, with unifirm brown blisters on top and smaller lighter blisters at the bottom provide visual appeal. Crispness gives a cracker snap or crunch. Tenderness provides a pleasant mouth-feel and quick get-away. A superior flavour derives from a blend of yeasty, nutty, buttery, and roasted grainy notes is considered desirable while a raw starchy note is deleterious.

(b) *Chemically leavened crackers:* Many cracker varieties which were formerly yeast-leavened and classified as sponge goods are now chemically-leavened. The most popular crackers in this category are the familiar round crackers, about 2 in. in diameter with 7 docker holes. In the production of these crackers, a medium soft flour is commonly used. On the basis of 100 kg of flour, the average cracker is made with about 10 kg shortening, 5 kg sugar, 2 kg invert syrup, 2 kg nonfat dry milk, malt extract, salt, and leavening. Many varieties of this crackers are being produced by the addition of other materials, some of which are : whole wheat flour, poppy seeds, sesame seeds, soy grits, and meaty flavours plus spices, onion powders, and cheese. Although some advantages accrue from the use of the sponge and dough method, most cheese crackers doughs are chemically leavened.

Many of the numerous varieties of the chemically leavened crackers are sprayed with hot oil as they emerge from the band oven. For many years, coconut oil was used almost exclusively. At present, several lightly hydrogenated domestic vegetable oils are being employed. Graham crackers are a special case of chemically leavened crackers. These, too were originally made by the sponge and dough procedure. They are unique in that they are much sweeter than other crackers and are alkaline in reaction (pH about 8.0). A considerable degree of expertise is required to produce an excellent graham cracker. Usually, the flour consists of 70 to 80 parts of straight milled medium soft flour and 20-30 parts of whole wheat flour. On the basis of 100 kg of flour, the typical dough is composed of 13 kg shortening, 25 kg sugar, 5 kg invert syrup, 5 kg molasses, salt, ammonium bicarbonate, and water. Some bakers may include one or more of the following: brown sugar, dextrose, and dried whey.

In the production of honey graham crackers, honey replaces the molasses usually with the addition of some more sugars.

Dough nuts

The dough nut, or fried cake was known to man apparently as early as the 5th century B.C. There is no great body of literature describing the rise of dough nut's popularity but for occasional references indicating that it was known, made, and eaten in most of countries of Europe from antiquity.

Actually, dough nuts are of two main varieties or families, and many sub-varieties which include crust and crumb, textural differences and shape differences. Dough nuts are made as twists, sticks, rings, balls, half moons, and various other shapes. The two families of products are characterized by the leavening used to make them; thus one type is called yeast-raised dough nuts while the other is known as the cake dough nut, signifying that chemical leavening is used.

Both varieties are deep fat fried and are made with the exception of the leavening from similar ingredients. Yet these products are distinctly different in every thing from the physical characteristics of the crust to shelf-life. These differences are the result of the varying the proportion of the ingredients used, the wheat variety from which the flour used is derived, and the method of preparation. Yeast-raised dough nuts have bread-like crumb appearance and texture while cake dough nuts are more like cake, having the finer cell structure and a more tender crumb.

Essential ingredients for any type of dough nuts include water, flour, sugar, shortening and some form of leavening. All other ingredients used are included to produce a specific quality characteristics such as a specific shape, flavour or shelf-life, or to improve eating quality etc.

In both families of dough nuts a variety builders are used to fortify or modify the base wheat flour to give such things as machine ability, mixing tolerance, or floor time tolerance. Therefore, some dough nuts formulas will be found to contain flours made from soybean, cotton seed, rye, potato, corn and rice, as well as quantities of egg yolk, sodium caseinate, milk solids, guar gum and carboxy methyl cellulose.

A major difference between yeast-raised and chemically leavened dough nut formulation is the reliance on sugar as the primary tenderizer in the case of cake dough nuts while shortening serves this purpose in yeast-raised product. Sugar constitutes less than 3% of yeast-raised dough, while cake dough nut doughs contain upto 15%. On the other hand yeast-raised dough consists of about 5% of shortening while cake dough nut doughs generally have less than 2%.

Before the advent of the automatic machinery, the dough nut baker purchased and scaled each of the ingredients in his formula separately adding them one by one to the bowl during the mixing. Mixing time and speeds varied widely depending upon the quality of the ingredients, the baker was able to get.

By far the largest portion of the *dough nuts* of both varieties are made by automatic machinery. In the case of cake dough nuts, the dough is dumped into hoppers from which it is forced mechanically or by air pressure through extruder nozzles that shape and cut individual rings, balls, sticks etc, directly into the fryer. Cake dough nut machines of this type are available with 1 to 10 extruder nozzles and production capacities ranging from 40 to 2000 doz per hr. Yeast raised dough nuts are similarly extruded from pressurized hoppers after the fermentation stage and are shaped and cut onto screens for transfer to the proofer before frying.

The frying process is similar to both the varieties. Average frying time is about 90 sec, 45 sec on the side at temperatures of 190-198°C. There are a few varieties that are fried submerged and are not turned; but most dough nuts are allowed to float so that one side fries while the other is permitted free expansion; then the doughnut is flipped to fry the other side. Frying fats used are hydrogenated vegetable oils, or hydrogenated lard with good heat stability. Since large amounts of the frying fat becomes part of the dough nuts, it must be bland or have good flavour initially and should not develop off-flavours during heating. Cake dough nuts contain about 18% frying fat while yeast- raised average about 25% for machine made product and 15% for hand cut.

Dough nut must be cooled after frying and before coating or boxing. This is a necessity because the doughnut has a great deal of sensible heat which accounts for the continued loss of moisture almost equal to that lost during frying. In addition, the frying fat in the skin of doughnut must be permitted to cool and at least partially set up or it will be absorbed by the coating or the box. Coatings used on doughnuts include powdered sugars, granulated sugars, glazeicing and chocolate.

Pretzls

Pretzels or Bretzels are a traditional German snack food generally consumed with beer. Today pretzels are eaten by themselves with beer, wine or soft drinks, cheese or other foods. The name pretzel is derived from the diminutive of the Latin "brachium" arm (bracelet).

Pretzels are characterized by a crisp, brittle texture, a pleasant, cracker-like taste which is modified by the glutinous lye-treated crust and by a brown, glossy surface colour. As with soda crackers, salt is sprinkled onto the dough just prior to baking and salt particles protrude from the surface of the pretzels.

Pretzels are produced in a well known shape of a twisted (two looped) ring (Plate 1). The most common dimensions are: overall length, 7 cm; width, 5 em; height, 0.5 cm; diameter, 4 mm. The weight of a pretzel is about 5.4 g for the most common size and 3.3 g for the very thins. Pretzels are also made in the form of rings and in the form of thin or thick rods. The typical pretzel with a moisture content of about 4% is rather hard and a method for the production of such hard pretzels is described here. However, soft pretzels much larger than the hard pretzels and with a higher moisture content are also available. Hard pretzels have a shelf-life as long as that of crackers or cookies, while soft pretzels are as perishable as rolls.

The most important ingredient is flour. A soft wheat flour with a protein content of 8.5-9.5% and an ash content of 0.35- 0.45% is suitable for this purpose.

A basic formula for pretzel doughs is as follows:

	(Kg)
Flour	100
Shortening vegetable	2-3
Corn syrup	3-4
Yeast, compressed	0.5
Water	Variable

Pretzel doughs are usually mixed in horizontal, high speed mixers as they are common in the baking industry. However, the absorption is kept low (40-45%) so that the doughs are quite stiff and they are under-mixed as compared to well developed bread dough. A desirable dough temperature out of the mixer is 26-32°C but temperatures upto 35°C can readily be tolerated because the small size of the pretzels prevents heat retention and heat buildup. The doughs are immediately transferred to the hoppers of the forming or die cutting equipment.

Traditionally, all *pretzels* were made by rolling and trying of the twisted dough piece. But today most pretzels are made by (wire cutting) extrusion machines. From the cutting or forming equipment, the pretzels travel on a wire mesh belt to the cooker. The time spent on the belt may vary considerably. Generally, it is of the order of several minutes. The pretzels pass a hot alkaline bath on the wire mesh belt. The alkaline solution may be prepared with sodium carbonate but sodium hydroxide is commonly used. The hot solution has a concentration of 0.5-1.0% NaOH. The dimensions of the bath are such that a cooking time from 10-20 sec results. Following the cook, the pretzels enter the baking oven, coarse salt is sprinkled over the surface of the pretzels where it adheres to the surface.

The pretzels are baked in gas fired ovens at 178-288°C for 4-8 min to a mositure content of 12-18% and then kiln dried or oven dried for 20-40 min at 93-149°C. Pretzels may be packaged in trays, boxes or bags protected with glassine, cellophane or polyethylene combinatons.

The chemical composition of the pretzels is as folows:

Moisture (%) 3.5-4.8

Nitrogen (dry basis) (%) 1.7-2.1 Salt (dry basis) prepared (%) 2.8-6.7

Warries

Warries, in the form of spicy, hollow, brittle, friable balls 5-8 em in diameter (Plate 1), very popular in Northern India, and are used as condiment in cooking with vegetables, legumes or rice. Dehulled black gram *(Phaseolus mungo)* grains after being washed and soaked overnight in water are ground to a paste. The paste is then spiced with asafoetida *(Ferule- foetida,* 0.5-1.0%), caraway *(Carum carvi, 0.5-1.0%),* cardamom *(Elettaria cardamomum,* 1.0%), cloves *(Syzygium aromaticum, 0.4-0.5%),* fenugreek *(Trigonella foenumgraecum,* 1.0%), ginger *(Zingiber officinale,* 8.0%) and red pepper *(Capsicum annum,* 1.0%) and moulded into small balls7,73,88 which are allowed to undergo fermentation and. drying in open air for 4-8 days.

Microflora associated with warri fermentation

Several bacteria and yeasts constituting the natural flora of black grams, spices added to the dough and the surroundings are associated with *warri* fermentation. Some reports7,8,65,75 suggest the involvement of yeasts especially *Candida* spp., *Saccharomyces cerevisiae, Rhodotorula lactosa, Candida famata, Wingea roberstii, Debaryomyces hansenii, Hansenula anomala* and C. *parapsilosis* in *warri* fermentation. The role of *Candida* spp. was tested[7] by inoculating the autoclaved paste of black grams with these yeasts. The inoculated material was easily friable, had many air pockets in the interior and a characteristic surface crust of commercial *warri.* Later studies[6,73,74,88,93] however, revealed the involvement of both bacteria and yeasts in the fermentations. Bacteria and yeasts generally occur in the unfermented paste of *warri* in the range of 106 and 103 per g which increase to the levels of 107 and 106 per g respectively with the progress in fermentation.[6] The gas producing *Leuconostoc mesenteroides* was found to be the most abundant bacterium involved in fermentation alongwith *Lactobacillus fermentum* and yeasts *Candida krusei, Saccharomyces rouxii, Candida* spp. and

Saccharomyces cerevisiae. The study also revealed that only the mixed inocula of *Leuconostoc mesenteroides* and *Candida krusei* yield a product similar to that available commercially.

More comprehensive reports describing microbial population dynamics, the predominant types,their prevalence and succession suggest the involvement of bacteria alone or in combination with lesser proportion Of yeasts during the *warri* fermentation. The occurrence of bacteria in all the commercial and laboratory fermented samples has been observed, while only half of the samples had yeasts. The commercial samples contained bacteria in the range of 10^9-10^{12} cfu/g belonging to four types. *Leuconostoc mesenteroides* was the most commonly encountered bacterium and was present in all the samples followed by *Streptococcus faecalis, Lactobacillus fermentum* and *Bacillus subtilis.* Yeasts were found to vary from 0-10^7 per g and were present in 55% samples. *Saccharomyces cerevisiae, Pichia membranaefaciens* were the most predominant yeast species isolated from all the positive samples followed by *Candida vartiovaarai, Kluyveromyces marxianus, Trichosporon beigelii, Candida krusei* and *Hansenula.* Laboratory fermented samples were found to contain comparatively higher bacterial load (10^{10}-10^{12} cfu/g) while yeasts were present in the range of 0-10^6 per g in a total of 45% samples yielding eight genera and ten species. The common microflora included *Enterobacter* ap. *Flauobacter* sp., *Candida aquatica, Cryptococcus humicolus* and *Geotrichum candidum* in addition to bacteria and yeasts observed in commercial samples.

Seasonal variations generally affect the development and prevalence of micro-organisms during fermentations (Tables); summers were found to favour a higher bacterial load (10^{10}–10^{12}/g) than winters (10^9-10^{10} /g). It was also found that *Bacillus subtilis* occurred mainly during summers whereas *Leuconostoc mesenteroides, Streptococcus faecalis* and *Lactobacillus fermentum* were the principal bacteria associated during both the seasons. Yeasts including *Candida vartiovaarai, Kluyveromyces marxianus,* and C. *krusei* were largely encountered during winters while *Saccharomyces cerevisiae, Pichi a membranaefaciens, Trichosporon beigelii and Hansenula anomala* were commonly involved during both the seasons.

Both bacteria and yeasts whenever present, increase significantly with the progress in fermentation followed by a decrease in pH and rise in volume of the *warri* dough. The bacteria appearing initially in traditional *warri* fermentation have been found to be *Leuconostoc mesenteroides, Lactobacillus delbrueckii,* L. *fermentum* and *Bacillus subtilis* alongwith *Flavobacter* spp. which mainly

Table 28.14 Successive changes in microflora during *warri* fermentation

Incubation period (days)	pH	Volume (ml)	Bacteria		Yeasts	
			Count (CFU)/g	Predominant types	Count (CFU)	Predominant types
0	5.65	200	$1.3X10^{10}$	*Leuconostoc mesenteroides* *Lactobacillus delbrueckii* *Lactobacillus fermentum* *Bacillus subtills* *Flavobactor sp.*	$0\text{-}8.0x10^{4}$	*Trichosporon beigelii* *Saccharomyces cerevisiae* *Candida krusei* *Pichia membranaefaciens* *Hansenula amomala*
1	4.70	420	$2.1X10^{12}$	*Leuconostoc mesenteroides* *Lactobacillus fermentum* *Streptococcus faecalis* *Bacillus subtills*	$0\text{-}1.7x10^{6}$	*Trichosporon beigelii* *Saccharomyces cerevisiae* *Candida krusei* *Pichia membranaefaciens*
2	3.90	420	$3.0X10^{12}$	*Leuconostoc mesenteroides* *Lactobacillus fermentum* *Streptococcus faecalis*	$0\text{-}2.1x10^{6}$	*Trichosporon beigelii* *Saccharomyces cerevisiae* *Candida kruseil*
3	3.50	420	$4.1X10^{12}$	*Leuconostoc mesenteroides* *Lactobacillus fementum* *Streptococcus faecalis*	$0\text{-}9.1x10^{6}$	*Trichosporon beigelii* *Saccharomyces cerevisiae* *Candida kruseil*
4	3.25	420	$4.7X10^{12}$	*Leuconostoc mesenteroides* *Lactobacillus fermentum*	$0\text{-}6.9x10^{7}$	*Saccharomyces_cerevisiae* *Trichosporon beigelii*
5	3.20	420	$6.5X10^{12}$	*Leuconostoc mesenteroides* *Lactobacillus fermentum*	$0\text{-}6.9x10^{6}$	*Saccharomyces cerevisiae* *Trichosporon beigelii*

produce acid and gas from various carbohydrates thus, making the environment unfit for the contaminants. *Streptococcus faecalis* develops subsequently and produces more acid. The disappearance of most of the bacteria with the progress in fermentation except *Leuconostoc mesenteroid"es* and *Lactobacillus fermentum* was observed. In their study, *Trichosporon beigelii, Saccharomyces cerevisiae, Candida krusei, Pichia membranaefaciens* and *Hanscnula anomala* were predominant among the yeasts appearing first but eventually only *Saccharomyces cerevisiae* and *Trichosporon beigelii* were present (Table 28.14).

Biochemical changes accompanying warri fermentation

Observations on the physicochemical, biochemical and nutritional changes occurring during *warri* fermentation 74,88,94 indicated that the pH of dough generally declined from 5.65 to 3.20 while the total acids incraeased from 0.50 to 1.50. Fermentations brought about an increase in volume and soluble solids whereas reducing sugars decreased significantly following fermentation and drying of *warri* doughs in open air. Total nitrogen and total proteins did not vary significantly although non-protein nitrogen increased from 0.2-0.68%. The soluble nitrogen and free amino acids exhibited a rise from 0.95-1.50% and 9.79 to 45.15 mg/g, respectively whereas the level of soluble proteins generally decreased significantly. Amylase activity increased initially and declined thereafter. On the other hand proteinase activity increased from 4.82 to 6.04 IV/g. *Warri* fermentation also brings about an appreciable rise in water soluble B-vitamins including thiamine, riboflavin and cyanocobalamin (Table 28.15; Figures 28.5a-28.5b). To replace the conventional black gram grains with mung beans as the substrate was also attempted[88,94] and found similar changes during the latter fermentation as observed in the traditional black gram doughs except for amylases which revealed a gradual rise till the end. Data on the biochemical and nutritional constituents mentioned above revealed the levels of soluble solids, reducing sugars and amylases to be higher in the new product than achieved in the conventional product. The remaining biochemical characteristics revealed compatibility with the conventional preparations. The test doughs caused sufficient acidification and leavening and the texture of the mung bean *warri* was quite comparable with that of conventional types, which however, exhibited better organoleptic charcteristics than the former.

Idli

These have been in use in South India since 1100 A.D.63 These are prepared by steaming the fermented batter consisting of rice *(Oryza sativa)*

Table 28.15 Values of microbiological, physico-chemical, biochemical parameters and nutritional constituents in various fermented foods at the start and end of fermentation.

Parameter	Warri (120)*		Idli (30)*		Dosa (30)*	
	Initial	Final	Initial	Final	Initial	Final
Bacteria (cfu/g)	$2\pm2\times10^{10}$	$6\pm5\times10^{10}$	$1.7\pm1\times10^{6}$	$4.7\pm4\times10^{9}$	$2.6\pm2\times10^{6}$	$3.8\pm2.5\times10^{8}$
Yeasts (cfu/g)	$0\text{-}9\pm5\times10^{4}$	$0\text{-}9\pm4\times10^{6}$	$0\text{-}6.7\pm3\times10^{2}$	$0\text{-}8.2\pm4\times10^{5}$	$0\text{-}2.7\pm2\times10^{4}$	$0\text{-}1\pm1\times10^{6}$
pH	6.5±0.52	3.20±0.29	6.58±0.36	4.92±0.21	5.80±0.36	4.0±0.14
Total acids (%)	0.50±0.20	1.50±0.10	0.30±0.05	0.60±0.14	0.40±0.09	0.90±0.11
Volume (ml)	200	420±20	200	390±20	200	400±40
Soluble solids (%)	8±2	15±2.5	1±0.02	6.4±0.08	2±0	6±1.2
Reducing sugars (mg/g)	13.8±0.8	5±0.5	5±0.5	5.8±1.2	2.5±0.5	4±0.8
Non-protein nitrogen (%)	0.20±0.07	0.68±0.21	2±0.15	2.1±0.05	2.8±0.4	2.9±0.4
Total Nitrogen (%)	4.5±0.3	4.9±0.5	0.06±0.02	0.12±0.05	0.07±0.07	0.31±0.07
Total proteins (%)	27±1	27±2	12±1	12±1.5	16.8±0.5	16±0.4
Soluble nitrogen (%)	0.95±0.12	1.50±0.13	0.28±0.09	0.60±0.12	0.50±0.20	1.0±0.07
Soluble progeins (mg/g)	50±8	20±6	19±3	19±6	35±5	38±7
Amylases (IU/g)	3.07±0.52	3.05±0.8	30±5	25±5	31.1±4.2	33.2±2.1
Proteinases (IU/g)	4.82±0.92	6.04±1.12	1.8±0.1	2.1±0.2	2.3±0.4	2.7±0.7
Free amino acids (mg/g)	9.79±4.39	45.15±9.30	8.31±2.10	12.97±1.20	10.23±2.4	17.8±2.0
Vitam B_1 (mg/100 g)	0.4±0.1	0.95±0.60	0±0.05	0.74±0.06	0.1±0.05	0.3±0.06
Vitam B_2 (mg/100 g)	0.3±0.1	1.2±0.2	0.28±0.08	0.78±0.06	0.1±0.01	0.08±0.02
Vitamin B_{12} (ug/100 g)	0.2±0.1	0.8±0.3	0.1±0.02	0.3±0.04	0.15±0.01	0.03±0.015

* Fermentation period is her.

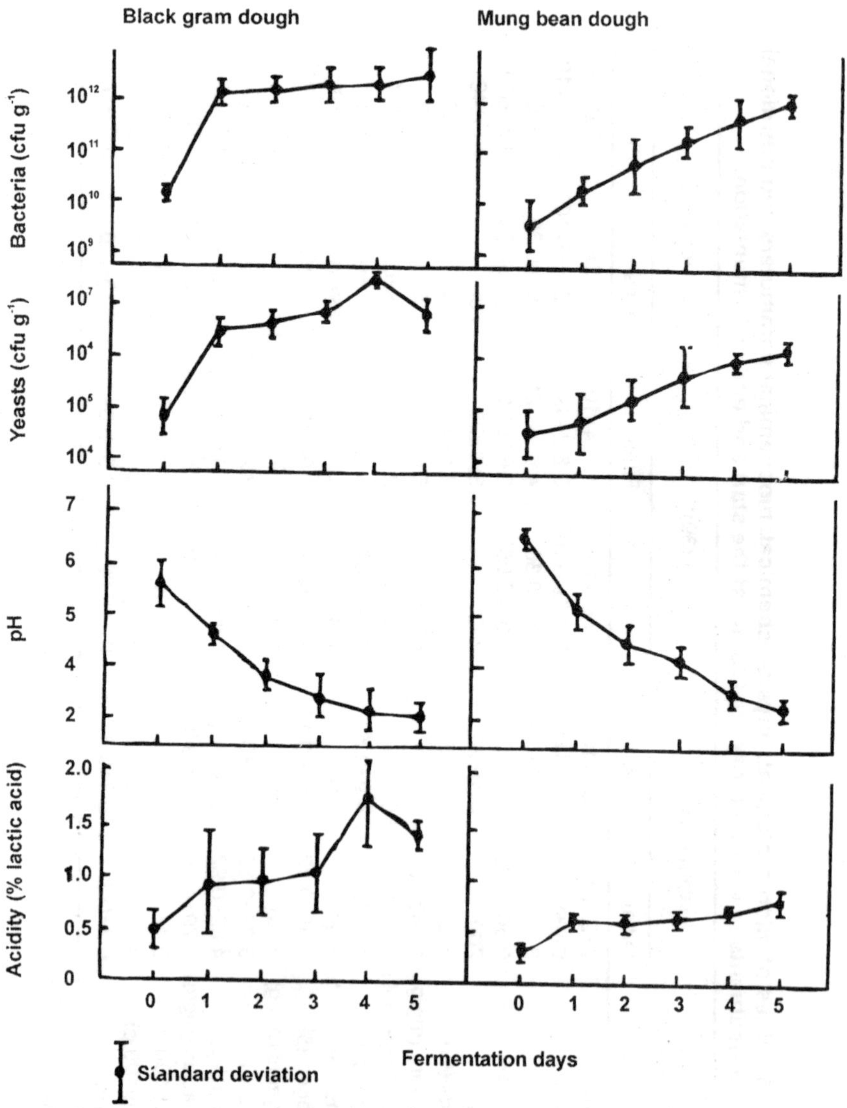

Fig. 28.5a Various changes accompnying warri fermentation (Data represent average values of 20 batches)

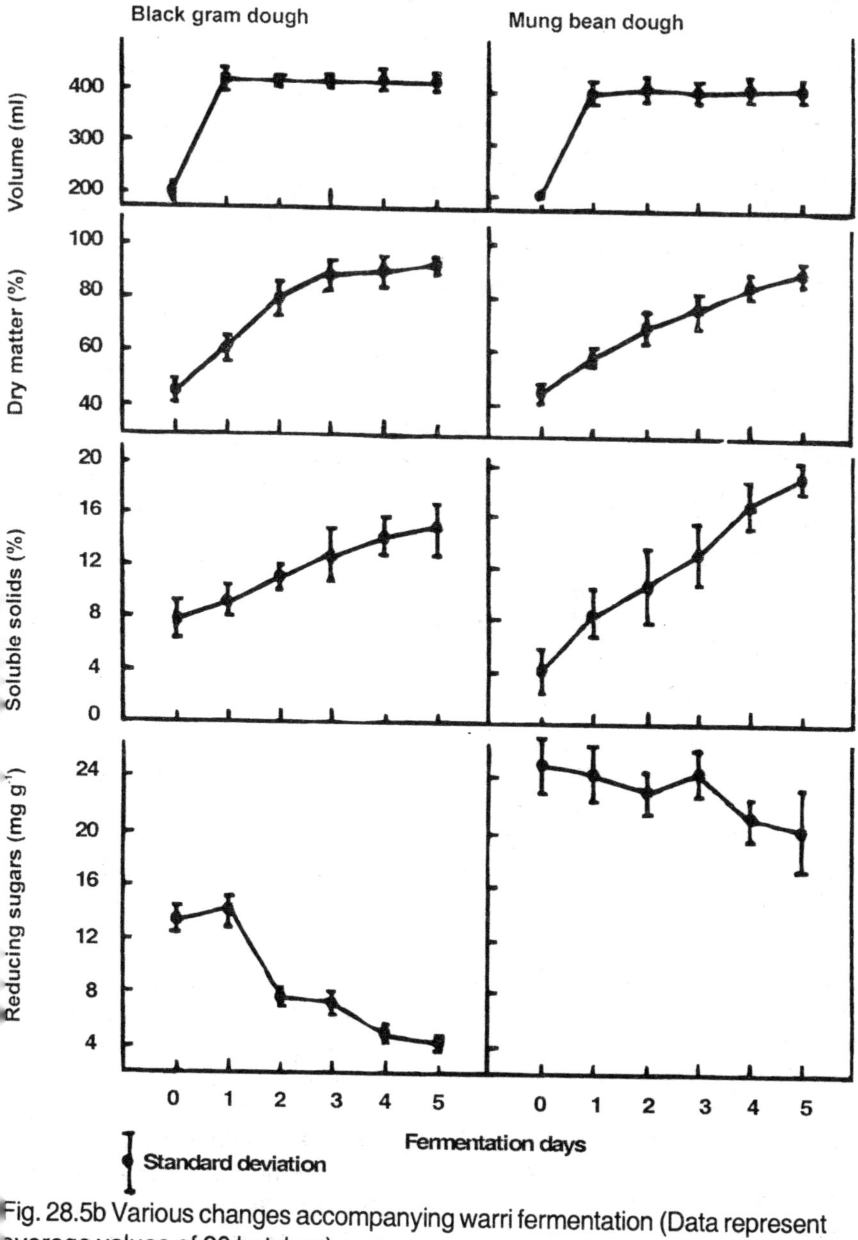

Fig. 28.5b Various changes accompanying warri fermentation (Data represent average values of 20 batches)

and black gram *(Phaseolus mungo)* grains and are served with butter and honey or jams and sauces. The proportion of rice to black gram grains used in *idli* fermentation ranges from 1:4 to 4: 1.65 Rice to black gram ratios of 2:1 to 4:1 were tested and was 2:1 and a ratio of 3:1 over 4:1 where the rice flavour predominates. The amount of water required to prepare the batter of desirable and uniform consistency varies from 1:5 to 2:2 times the dry weight of the ingredients. The traditional method of *idli* preparation consists of washing and soaking rice and black gram in the proportion of 3:1, grinding to a fine paste and mixing the two together. The paste is then allowed to ferment for 18-30 hr by means of natural microflora or by inoculating with fermented batter from a previous batch.

Black gram component of *idli* has also been substituted by several legumes such as common bean, soybean great Northern bean and mung bean but none of these were found to be fully acceptable. Although a variety of legumes can be used with rice to make *idli,* the rice variety chosen can be critical. Attempts to prepare *idli* like products by replacing either *ricve* or black gram *dhal* used in conventional *idli* batter have also been made. *Bhagar* was used in place of rice while *rajmah,* black gram and horse gram were used as legume components. The products obtained from *bhagar* and either black gram or *rajmah* were satisfactory but *bhagar* when combined with horse gram did not yield acceptable taste.

Microflora associated with idli fermentation

Many workers have investigated the methods of preparation, microbiology and nutritional value of *idli.* Ordinarily, the micro-organisms developing during the initial soaking of ingredients and later are sufficient to bring about the fermentation. Both bacteria and yeasts have been reported to participate in *idli* fermentation and are generally introduced by the two main ingredients.

However, acid and gas production has been found to be mostly dependent upon the bacterial growth. Black gram, the leguminous component of *idli* batter serves not only as an effective substrate but also provides the maximum number of micro-organisms for fermentation. Black gram *dhal* soaked in water has a higher concentration of soluble nutrients to support the growth of lactic acid bacteria. Some investigators have added yeasts and buttermilk as the inocula but *idli* prepared with added yeast and/or sour butter milk inoculum was similar to that prepared without inocula. However, no fermentation failures have been experienced with added inocula but occasional failures were encountered without the inoculum. A variation often used in some parts of India is to mix the ingredients with water at 80°C. But normal bacterial flora is

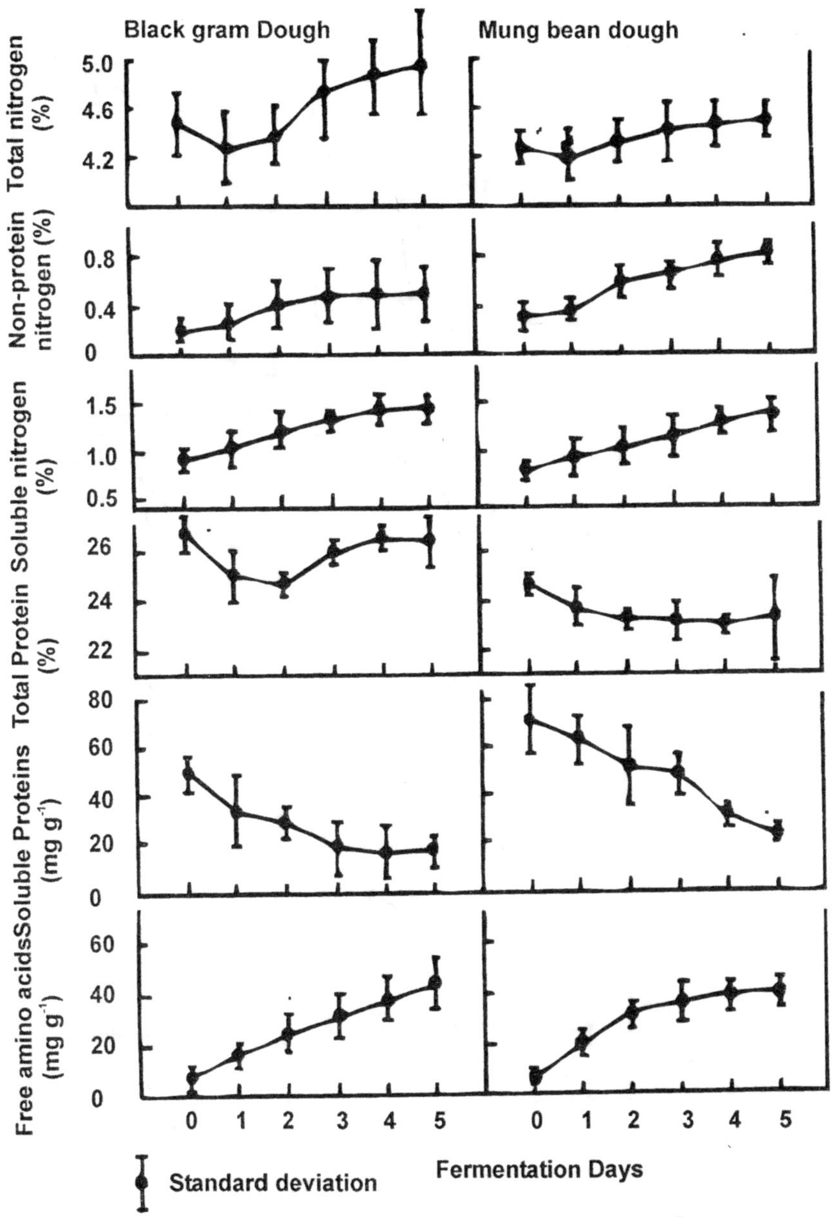

Fig. 28.5c Various changes accompanying warri fermentation (Data represent average values of 20 batches)

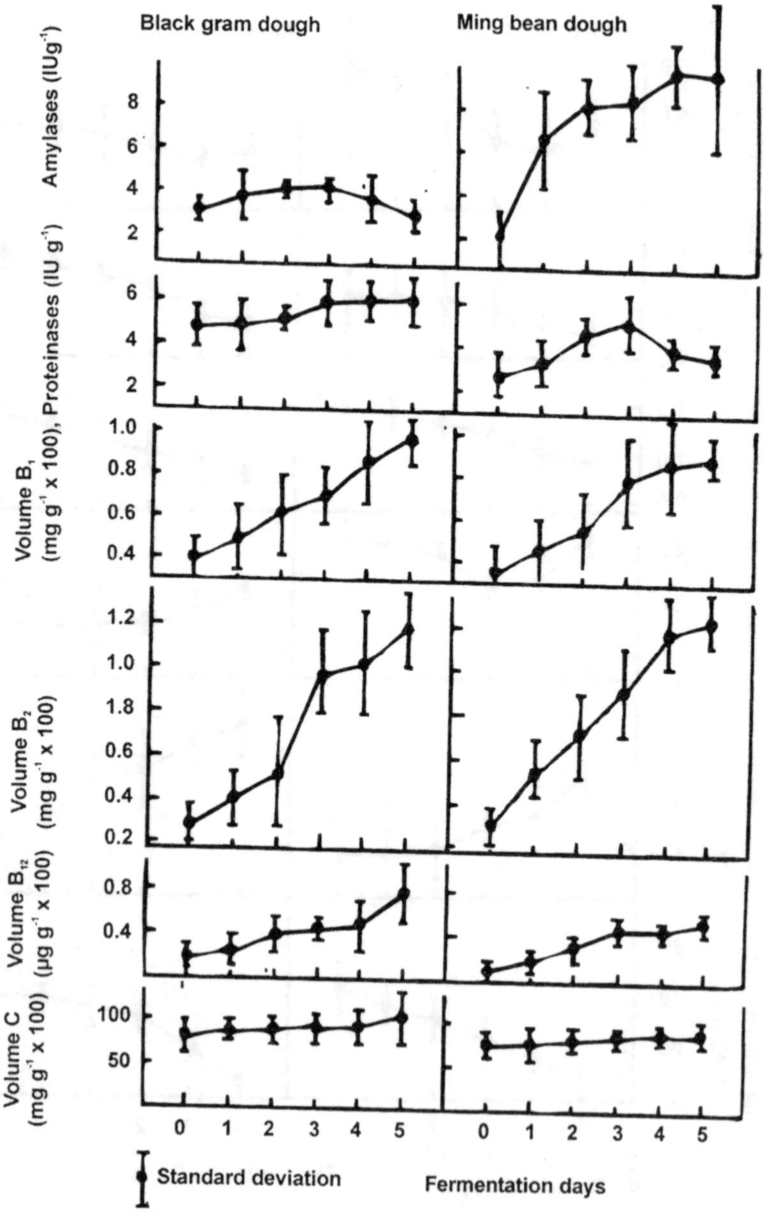

Fig. 28.5d Various changes accompanying warri fermentation (Data represent average values of 20 batches)

markedly decreased from 15,000 to about 600 cfu/g even if the batter is maintained at 80°C for only four min.The practice generally resulted in slower fermėntation and an *idli* with an altered aroma and flavour is produced.

Bacteria identified as part of the microflora responsible for the production of good *idli* include *Leuconostoc mesenteroides, Lactobacillus coryneformis, L. delbrueckii, L. fermentum, L. lactis, Streptococcus faecalis* and *Pediococcus cerevisiae6,* while the yeast flora generally involved in fermentation include *Torulopsis candida, Trichosporon pullulans, Candida cacaoi, Debaryomyces tamarii, Rhodotorula graminis, Candida fragicola,* C. *kefyr, Wingea robertsii, Issatchenkia terricola, Hansenula anomala, Candida glabarata,* C. *troipicalis,* C. *sake,* C. *krusei* and *Torulopsis holmii.*

Rapid disappearance of common aerobic contaminants during the initial soaking of the ingredients have been reported. They indicated that *Leuconostoc mesenteoides* and *Streptococcus faecalis* develop concomitantly during soaking and then continue to multiply following grinding and playa significant role in *idli* fermentation. In the later stages, the number of these two micro-organisms decreases and *Pediococcus cerevisiae* develops. The essential roles played by *Leuconostoc mesenteroides* and lactobacilli in the leavening of *idli* batter and the production of acidity have also been substantiated by several workers. In contrast the yeasts *Torulopsis candida* and *Trichosporon pullulans* were found sufficient for proper fermentation. *Idlis* prepared in the laboratory with the above two yeasts were reported to be superior to the uninoculated tráditionally prepared *idlis.* The involvement of both bacteria and yeasts in gas production during *idli* batter fermentation is also observed and that the total lactic acid producing bacteria are always' higher than the yeast. In their study parboiled rice were used to support the growth of yeasts which was absent in the batter when raw rice was used alone. The role of yeast flora in *idli* fermentation by inoculating the ingredients with individual yeast in combination with *Leuconostoc mesenteroides* revealed that yeasts not only contribute towards gas production resulting in good texture but also towards sensory qualities. The role of lactic acid bacteria to red-uce the pH of the batter to an optimum level (4.4-4.5) for yeast activity. Organoleptic tests indicated that *idlis* prepared from batter fermented by *Torulopsis holmii* to be better in taste, flavour, texture and overall acceptability.

An extensive microbiological evaluation of traditional commercially fermented *idli* batter samples and those experimentally prepared in the laboratory revealed the involvement of several bacteria along with yeasts. It was found that the market batter samples contained bacteria in the range of

106-108 cfu/g belonging to four genera. *Leuconostoc mesenteroides* was the most commonly encountered bacterium followed by *Streptococcus faecalis* and *Pediococcus cerevisiae.* Yeasts varied from 0-10^6 cfu/g. Of these *Saccharomyces cerevisiae* and *Debayomyces hansenii* were the most predominant species isolated from 65 and 60% samples, respectively followed by *Hansenula anomala* (35%) and *Trichosporon beigelii* (10%). The laboratory fermented samples contained comparatively higher microbial load including bacteria (107-109 cfu/g; belonging to five general and six species) and yeasts (0- 10^7/g; present in 60% samples). In addition to the common microbial types found in commercial samples, laboratory fermentations also exhibited the predominance of *Bacillus amyloliquefaciens, Lactobacillus delbrueckii, Torulopsis candida* and *Trichosporon pullulans.* The prevalence of higher bacterial load (10^7-10^8 cfu/g), during the summer than during winter (10^6-10^7 cfu/g) was also observed. *Leuconostoc mesenteroides* and *Lactobacillus fermentum* were found *to* be involved during both the seasons while *Streptococcus faecalis* and *Pediococcus cerevisiae* were observed during summer only (Tables 28.3, 28.4). Yeasts were isolated from 60% of the summer samples (0-10^3/g; two isolates) and 90% winter samples (0-10^6 cfu/g; four isolates). *Saccharomyces cerevisiae* and *Hansenula anomala* were the principal yeasts occurring during both the seasons while *Debaryomyces hansenii* and *Trichosporon beigelii* were encountered during winter only (Table 28.5). Both the bacteria and yeasts whenever present tended to increase significantly with the prograss in fermentation. The bacteria appearing initially were *Leuconostoc mesenteroides, Bacillus subtilis, Lactobacillus del'brueckii* and *L. fermentum. Streptococcus faecalis* and *Pediococcus cerevisiae* developed subsequently and persisted till the end of fermentation along with *Leuconostoc mesenteroides. Debayomyces hansenii, Saccharomyces cerevisiae, Trichosporon beigelii* and *Hansenula anomala* were predominant among the yeasts appearing first while *Trichosporon beigelii* developed subsequently but eventually only *Saccharomyces cerevisiae* was observed (Table 28.16).

Biochemical changes accompanying idli fermentation

Two more significant changes occurring during *idli* fermentation are leavening and acidification of the batter. These have been used as criteria for judging the progress in fermentation. During fermentation, the volume of *idli* batter increases from 1.6-3.1 times its original volume. The pH decreases from 6.0 to 4.3-5.3 and the acidity increases from 3.2 to 19.0 ml of 0.IN lactic acid per 5 g *idli* batter. Soluble solids and non-protein nitrogen generally show a slight increase during fermentation whereas soluble nitrogen and reducing sugars declined. A constant increase in reducing sugars over a 12 hr fermentation, a final volume .level to be nearly twice the original, protease activity and amino nitrogen and subsequently increased slightly soluble protein were recorded.

Idli is generally considered a nourishing and easily digestible food. However, the results obtained from growth and nitrogen balance experiments with rats did not show the nutritional value and digestibility of proteins of rice and black gram mixture to be improved by fermentation process. On the other hand, feeding of fermented *idli* reduced -the live fat content of rats fed with a high fat and low protein diet. The results were further substantiated by the findings that there was an increase in choline, methionine and folic acid content of rice and black gram mixture after the fermentation. *Idli* was found superior to unfermented product. Results on the effects of fermentation on methionine and cystine content of the substrate mixture varied showing an increase in some and a decrease in others. An apparent increase in both methionine and cystine in *idli* prepared from 1: 1 proportion of rice to black gram was obtained. The effects of *Leuconostoc mesenteroides, Lactobacillus fermentum, L. delbrueckii* and *Bacillus* spp. on the increase in amino nitrogen, free sugars, thiamine, riboflavin and inorganic phosphate content as well as sensory qualities of *idli* has also been investigated.

There is some debate regarding the effect of fermentation of *idli* on the protein efficiency ratio (PER). Improvement in PER of *idli* as a result of fermentation is reported, while another report concluded that fermentation apparently does not improve the PER. An improvement in the availability of essential amino acids and a loss of most of the inorganic sulphur during black gram and rice fermentation has however been shown.

In a more comprehensive study on the various changes accompanying *idli* batter fermentation, it was found that besides successive increase in microbial populations, the pH declined from 6.6 to 4.9 while total acids increased from 0.3 to 0.6% following incubation of rice-black gram *idli* batter for 30 hr at room temperature. Fermentation also brought about an increase in batter volume and soluble solid contents (Table 28.15). The reducing sugars were found to increase after a 12 hr lag. Total nitrogen, total protein and soluble proteins did not exhibit any significant change although non-protein nitrogen increased from 0.06 to 0.12%. Soluble nitrogen and free amino acids exhibited an increase from 0.3 to 0.6% and 8 to 13 *mg/g* respectively. Water soluble group- B vitamins including thiamine, riboflavin, cyanocobalamin and ascorbic acid (vitamin C) also increased significantly with the progress in *idli* batter fermentation. Studies on the substitution of other ingredients in place

Table 28.16 Successive changes in microflora during *idli* fermentation

Incubation period (hr)	pH	Volume (ml)	Bacteria		Yeasts	
			count (CFU/g)	Predominant types	count (CFUt/g)	Predominant types
0	6.58	200	1.7×10^6	*Leuconostoc mesenteroids* *Bacillus subtillis* *Lactobacillus delbrueckii* *L. fermentum*	0-6.6×10^2	*Debaryomyces hensenii* *Saccharomyces cerevisiae* *Trichosporon beigelii* *Hansenula anomala*
6	6.05	240	7.3×10^6	*Leuconostoc mesenteroides* *Bacillus sbutillis*	0-9.3×10^2	*Debaryomyces hensenii* *Saccharomyces cerevisiae* *Trichosporon pullulans*
12	5.60	300	3.6×10^7	*Leuconostoc mesenteroides*	0-4.3×10^3	*Debaryomyces hansenii* *Saccharomyces cerevisiae* *Trichosporon pullulans*
18	5.10	340	8.9×10^7	*Leuconostoc mesenteroides* *Streptococcus faecalis* *Lactobacillus fermentum* *Pediococcus cerecisiae*	0-8.8×10^3	*Saccharoymces cerevisiae* *Debaryomyces hansenii* *Trichosporon pullulans*
24	4.95	390	6.3×10^8	*Leuconostoc mesenteroides* *Streptococcus faecalis* *Pediococcus cerevisiae*	0-7.1x104	*Saccharomyces cerevisiae*
30	4.92	410	4.7×10^9	*Streptococcus faecalis* *Pediococcus cerevisiae*	0-8.2x105	*Saccharomyces cerevisiae*

of black gram indicated an increase in amino nitrogen and free sugars in *idli* containing soybean. *Idli* containing great Northern beans in place of black gram was evaluated and found that *idli* prepared from the former had somewhat a different flavour and a sticky top surface. It was suggested that the incorporation of great Northern beans into *idli* would offer the advantage of increased roughage. While studying the *idlis* made by replacing either rice or black gram compatibility in physico-chemical characteristics like viscosity, titrable acidity, batter volume and displaced volume in different tests and conventional preparations were found. Two new *idli* types prepared by replacing black gram with mung bean and soybean, as compared with the conventional rice-black gram *idli* in terms of vanous physico-chemical, biochemical and nutritional constituents and organoleptic characteristics were evaluated. Rice-mung bean and rice-soybean *idli* batter fermentations showed similar changes as observed in rice-black gram batters with differences only in some parameters (Table 28.15; Figures 28.6a-d). Soybean batters contained the highest levels of soluble solids, reducing sugars, total nitrogen, proteins, amylases, proteinases and group-B vitamins. The organoleptic evaluation of different *idlis* prepared from these batters revealed wide acceptance of the conventional product due to its aroma, taste and consistency, followed by mungbean product.

Several attempts to improve the *idli* fermentation by standardization of various physico-chemical factors have been made. An increasing rate of *idli* batter fermentation with a rise in temperature is reported with a decrease in batter ripening time from 16 hr at 31°C to 10hr at 41°C. Organoleptically, *idlis* made from batter fermented at 31°C were soft, retaining full and characteristic aroma while those fermented at 41°C, though soft, lacked the aroma. Fortification of *idli* batters with glucose at 1% level had a beneficial effect on gas production and leavening during fermentation. *Idli* batter under variable sets of physicochemical conditions such as temperature (28°C, 40°C), initial pH (4.5, 7.5) and supplementation with sucrose (1,2%) was fermented keeping in mind the optimum values for bacteria and yeasts which are the main microbial types involved in this fermentation. It was observed that fermentation at 42°C supported a rapid multiplication of bacteria followed by a sharp decline in pH and significant rise in volume, soluble nitrogen, proteinases and vitamins B_{12} and C. On the other hand, fermentation at 28°C supported the rapid multiplication and activity of yeasts. Initial pH around 7.5 encouraged the occurrence and prevalence of a higher bacterial load followed by a sharp decline in pH and increase in volume, total nitrogen and vitamin B_{12}, whereas an initial acidic pH (4.5) favoured the occurrence and

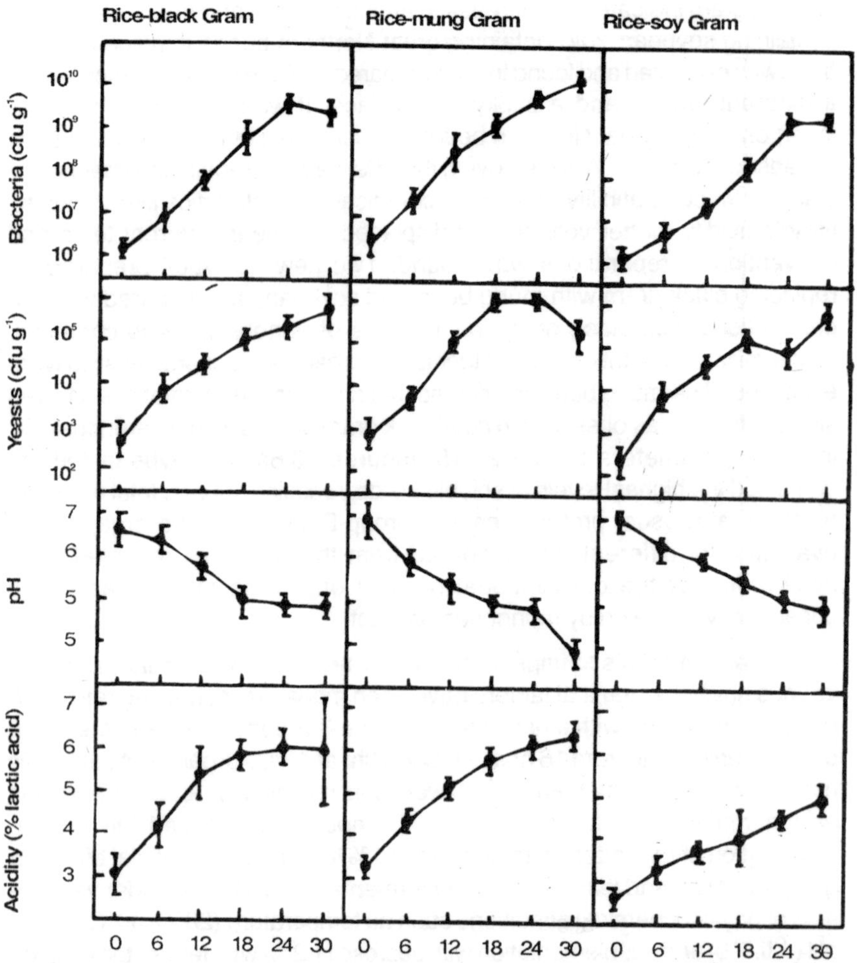

Fig. 28.6a Pattern of microbial load, pH and acidity during fermentation of various idli batters. Bars indicate the standard deviation. Data represent average values of 15 replicate of black gram and five replicates each of mung bean and soybean batters.

prevalence of yeasts and a sharp increase in amylases, proteinases, soluble solids, free amino acids, non-protein nitrogen and vitamins B_1,B_2 and C. Supplementation with sugar was found to support rapid multiplication of the microbial load and favoured a pronounced rise in various nutritional constituents including soluble solids, reducing sugars, free amino acids and vitamins B_1,

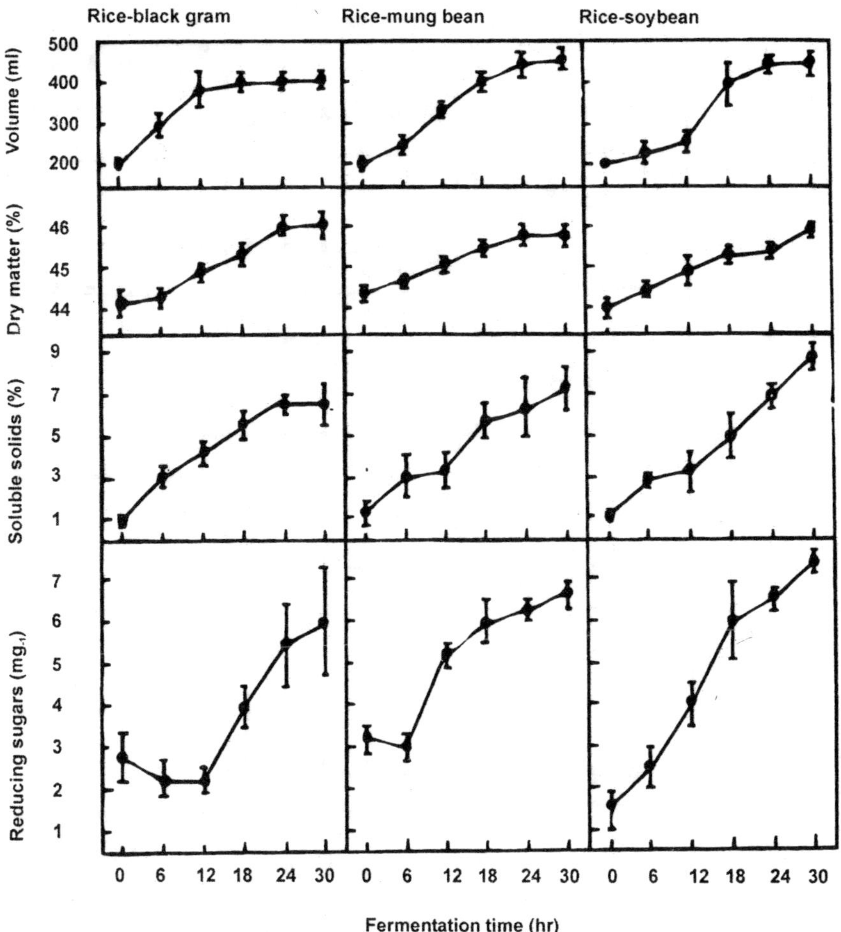

Fig. 28.6b Pattern of volume, dry matter, soluble solids and reducing sugars during fermentation of various idli batter. Bars indicate the standard deviation. Data represent average varlues of 15 replicates of black gram and five replicates each of mung bean and soybean batters.

B_2, B_{12} and C, besides acidification and leavening.

The effect of yeast domination in *idli* batter fermentations revealed that adding *Saccharomyces cereuisiae* alongwith natural bacterial flora of the ingredients is the best method for standardizing *idli* fermentations in terms of improved organoleptic characteristics,leavening and nutritional

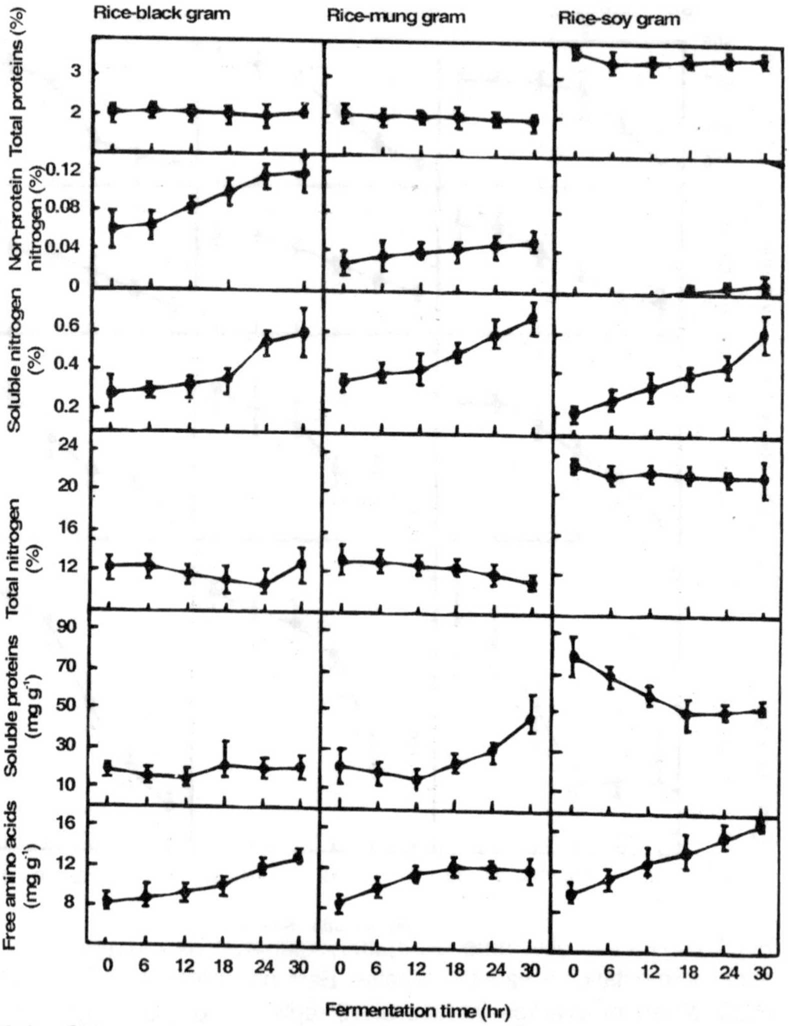

Fig. 28.6c. Changes in various nitrogenous constituents accompanying idli batter fermentations. Bars indicate the standard deviation. Data represent average average values of 15 replicates of black gram and five replicates each of mung bean and soybean batters.

constituents. Different sets of *idli* batters were fermented by inoculating, separately, with either *Sacharomyces cereuisiae, Debaryomyces hansen ii, Torulopsis candida, Hansenula anomala* or *Trichosporon beigelii,* without eliminating the natural bacterial flora of the ingredients. The higher activity of

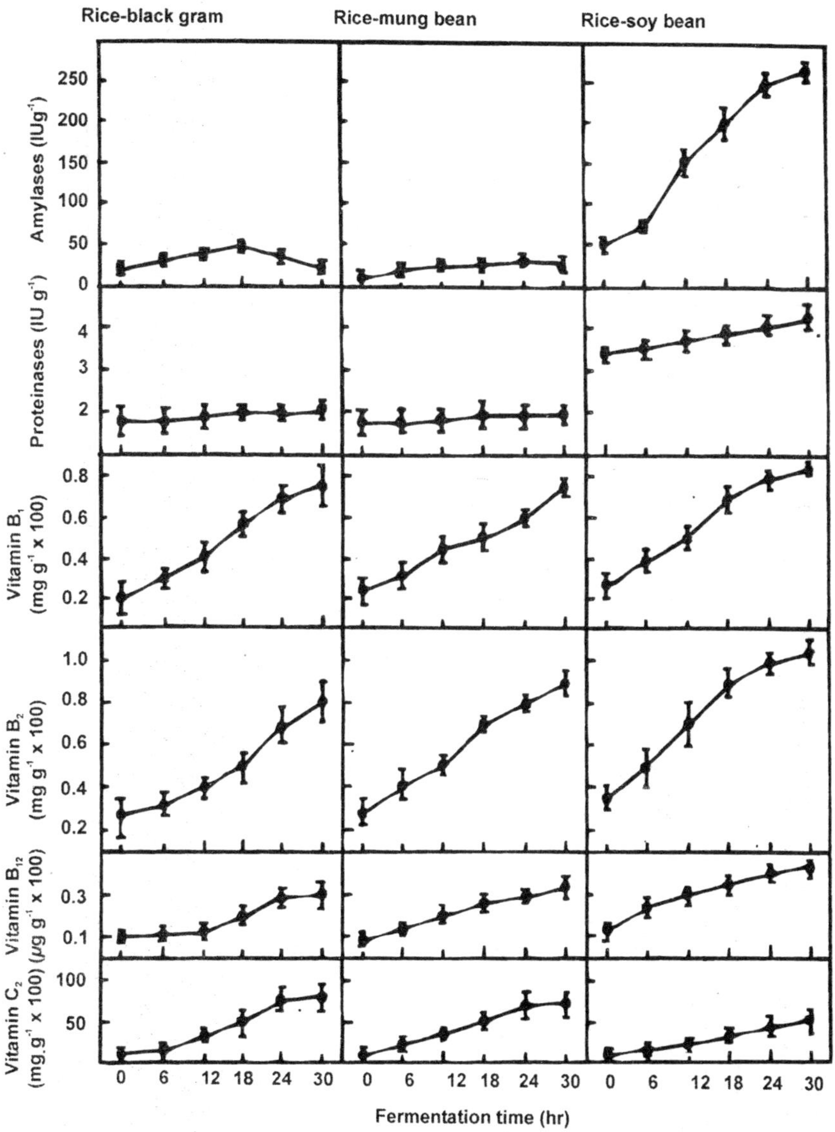

Fig. 28.6d. Changes in amlyases, proteinases and vitamin contents during idli batter fermentations. Bars indicate the standard deviation. Data represent average values of 15 replicates of black gram and five replicates each of mung bean and soybean batters.

Table 28.17 Values of various parameters attained in different *idli* batter fermentation.

Parameter	Added yeasts*											
	Control		E1		E2		E3		E4		E5	
	Initial	Final	Initial	Final	Initial	Final	Initial	Final	Initial	Final	Initial	Final
Bacteria (cfu/g)	$2x10^6$	$8x10^{10}$	$9x10^5$	$1x10^9$	$1x10^5$	$8x10^8$	$2x10^5$	$8x10^8$	$6x10^5$	$2x10^8$	$1x10^5$	$8x10^8$
Yeasts (cfu/g)	$4x10^2$	$8x10^5$	$5x10^6$	$5x10^{10}$	$3x10^6$	$2x10^{10}$	$4x10^6$	$7x10^9$	$4x10^6$	$2x10^{10}$	$4x10^6$	$1x10^{10}$
pH	6.6	4.9	6.9	5.2	6.8	5.3	6.7	5.8	6.5	5.3	6.5	5.4
Volume (ml)	200	410	200	490	200	475	200	470	200	430	200	400
Amylase (IU/g)	18	22	20	30	19.8	29	21	29.6	21.5	29	21	31.2
Reduging sugars (mg/g)	3.6	6	4	10.6	4	9.4	3.6	9.6	3.8	9	4.2	8.2
Free amino acids (mg/g)	8	13	13	26	13	25	14	26	10	17	9	15
Total proteins (% w/w)	12	12.4	14	16	13.6	14.8	13.5	17.7	14	15.9	12	13.6
Vitamin B_1 (mg/100 g)	0.20	0.75	0.70	1.50	0.65	1.45	0.75	1.40	0.25	0.45	0.30	0.65
Vitamin B_2 (mg/100 g)	0.25	0.75	0.70	1.60	0.65	1.50	0.70	1.50	0.25	0.45	0.35	0.75

Control : Uninoculated batter
*E1 : *Saccharomyces cere visiae enrichment*; E2: *Torulopsis candida enrichment*; E3 : *Hansenula anomala enrichment*; E4; *Debarymyces hansenii enrichment*; E5: *Trichosoporon beigelii* enrichment

amylases, amounts of B-vitamins and free amino acids attained in yeast-enriched fermentations (Table 28.17) suggest the positive contribution of yeasts to these constituents.

Dosa is a thin, crisp, fried, pancake-like staple food of South India. It is prepared by soaking overnight, equal quantities of rice and dehulled black gram separately in water, grinding to a fine paste by adding 2.0-2.5 parts (w/w) water and mixing the two together. The batter mixture is then allowed to ferment for another 24 hr by means of the natural microflora or by inoculating with the fermented batter of the previous batch which serves as the starter. The batter is then spread on a hot greasy griddle where it assumes the form of a crisp pancake.

Microflora associated with dosa fermentation

Traditional *dosa* batter fermentation has revealed the occurrence and role of several bacteria alone or in combination with yeasts in bringing about various biochemical changes. The prevalence of bacteria in all the commercial and laboratoryfermented samples examined was observed. The commercial samples contained bacteria in the range of 104-108 cfu/g belonging to six genera and nine species while the laboratory fermented batters had bacteria in the range of 107-109 cfu/g. *Leuconostoc mesenteroides* was the most commonly encountered bacterium followed by *Streptococcus faecalis, Lactobacillus fermentum, Bacillus amyloliquefaciens, Lactobacillus delbrueckii, Bacillus subtilis, Pediococcus cerevisiae, Bacillus polymyxa* and *Enterobacter* sp. On the other hand, yeasts were found to vary from 0-107 cfu/g and were present in 70% commercial and 53% laboratory fermented batters. *Saccharomyces cerevisiae* was the most predominant yeast involved in the fermentation followed by *Debaryomyces hansenii, Hansenula anomala, Trichosporon beigelii, Oosporidium margaritiferum, Trichosporon pullulans, Kluyveromyces marxianus, Candida kefyr* and C. *krusei. Streptococcus faecalis, Bacillus amyloliquefaciens, Lactobacillus delbrueckii, Bacillus subtilis* and *B. polymyxa* were the principal bacteria observed during summer while the remaining species were associated during both the seasons. On the other hand, *Oosporidium margaritiferum,*

Kluyveromyces marxianus, Candida kef yr' and C. *krusei* were among the main yeasts encountered only during the winter while the remaining species were associated during both the seasons (Tables 28.3-28.5). Both bacteria and yeasts, whenever present, increased significantly with the progress in fermentation which was followed by acidification and leavening.

Table 28.18 Successive changes in microflora during *dosa* fermentation

Incubation period (hr)	pH	Volume (ml)	Bacteria		Yeasts	
			Count(CFU/g)	Predominant types	Count(CFU/g)	Predominant types
0	5.20	200	2.6×10^6	*Leuconostoc mesenteroides* *Bacillus polymyxa* *B. amyloliquefaciens* *Micrococcus varians*		*Debaryomyces hansenii* *Saccharomyces cerevisiae* *Trichoposporon beigelii* *Hansenula anomala*
6	4.90	250	3.3×10^6	*Leuconostoc mesenteroides* *Bacillus polymyxa* *B. amyloliquefaciens*		*Debaryomyces hansenii* *Saccharomyces cerevisiae* *Trichoposporon beigelii*
12	4.80	320	1.5×10^7	*Leuconostoc mesenteroides* *Bacillus polymysa*		*Debaryomyces hansenii* *Saccharomyces cerevisiae* *Streptococcus faecalis*
18	4.70	350	2.3×10^8	*Leuconostoc mesenteroides* *Streptococcus faecalis*		*Saccharomyces cerevisiae* *Debaryomyces hansenii_* *Kluyveromyces marxianus*
24	4.55	410	1.0×10^9	*Leuconostoc mesenteroides*		*Saccharomyces cerevisiae* *Streptococcus faecalis*
30	4.20	450	3.0×10^8	*Streptococcus faecalis*		*Saccharomyces cerevisiae* *Lactobacillus fermentum*

Both the ingredients of *dosa* i.e rice and black gram have been found to contribute the microflora responsible for the fermentation· Rice contributed bacteria belonging to five genera namely *Leuconostoc, Streptococcus, Lactobacillus, Micrococcus and Bacillus* and yeasts, belonging to three genera, *Saccharomyces, Debaryomyces* and *Trichosporon.* Black gram contributed bacteria belonging to the genera *Leuconostoc, Enterobacter, Flavobacter, Bacillus, Lactobacillus, Streptococcus* and yeasts *Debaryomyces, Torulopsis, Kluyveromyces* and *Candida.* The bacteria appearing initially during *dosa* batter fermentation generally belonged to *Leuconostoc mesenteroides* along with bacilli and micrococci. Streptococci developed subsequently and persisted till the end of fermentation when the other types usually disappeared. *Debaryomyces hansenii, Saccharomyces cerevisiae* and *Trichosporon beigelii* were found to be predominant among the yeasts appearing first. Later, only *Saccharomyces cerevisiae* persisted (Table 28.18).

Biochemical changes accompanying dosa fermentation

Observations on the changes accompanying *dosa* batter fermentation indicate that the pH declined from 5.0±0.36 to 4.00±O.14 while the total increased from 0.40±0.09 to 0.90±0.11 %. Fermentation also brought_about an increase in volume, soluble solids and reducing sugars. Total nitrogen and total proteins did not vary significantly although non-protein nitrogen increased from 0.70±0.4 to 1.31±0.07%. Soluble nitrogen and free amino acids exhibited a rise from 0.50±20 to 1.00±0.07 % and from 10.23±2.40 to 17.80±3.00 mg/g respectively. Amylase activity showed an early rise (31.1±4.20 to 39.4±4.10 IU/g) and finally declined to 33.2±2.1 IU/g, whereas proteinase activity increased slightly. Water soluble group-B vitamins including thiamine (B_1), riboflavin (B_2) and cyanocobalamin (B_{12}) also increased significantly with the progress in *dosa* batter fermentation (Table 28.15).

Some attempts have also been made to prepare new dosa-like products by replacing the conventional black gram component with other legumes and evaluated for nutritional value and acceptability with comparison to the conventional product Batter types containing soybeans were most nutritious in terms of the total nitrogen, protein, amylase, proteinase and vitamin-B contents followed by mungbean batters, while the conventional black gram product was organoleptically most preferred. For further raising the nutritional levels, *dosa* batter fermentation has also been optimized by standardization of various physico-chemical conditions and microbial combinations. The best combination of physico-chemical parameters was incubation at 28°C with an initial pH 4.5 and supplementation of the batter with sucrose (1-2%). Since the level of yeasts in traditional fermentations is significantly lower than the bacteria the possibility of yeast enrichment has been investigated by experiments in which common yeasts isolated from traditionally fermented *dosa* batters were used. *Saccharomyces cereusiae, Debaryomyces hansenii, Hansenula anomala, Trichosporon beigelii* and *Torulopsis candida* have been used to inoculate the experimental batter without eliminating the natural bacterial flora of the ingredients. In such experiments, *Saccharomyces cerevisiae* enriched fermentations were found to be best in terms of the degree of leavening, final levels of amylases, reducing sugars, free amino acids, total proteins, vitamins B_1 and B_2 and organoleptic characteristics. The batters enriched with *Torulopsis candida* and *Hansenula anomala* also produced good leavening, other nutritional constituents and organoleptic characteristics but *Debaryomyces hansenii* enrichment did not have a significant rise in vitamin levels as obtained in other fermentations although it showed good leavening, amylolytic activity, higher free amino acids and total proteins. *Trichosporon beigelii* dominated experimental fermentations did not produce significant differences in their nutritional constituents except for having good enzyme activities than control which had maximum acidities.

Other Cereal Products

Bhatura

Bhatura is leavened, deep fried bread (Plate 1) made from white wheat flour, *consumed* as a breakfast food and snacks with *masala chana* in Northern India. *amyl* is prepared by mixing white wheat flour with water and kneading for 20 min. at room temperature temperature. The dough is supplemented with 1% common salt and inoculated with a portion of previous batch ripe batter and kept in open to undergo fermentation for 8-14 hr. The dough is then made into balls, which are then flattened by hand using vegetable oil to 12-18 cm in diameter before deep frying in oil.

Jalebie

This is prepared by mixing equal quantities of white wheat flour and water and inoculating with some portion of a previous batch to raise the batter. It is then allowed to ferment at room temperature for 8-12 hrs. The fermented soft and silky batter is squeezed through an embroidered hole, about 4 mm in diameter, deposited as continuous spirals into hot vegetable oil and deep fried. The light brown crispy pretzels of 5-7 cm in diameter are removed from oil with the help of a sieve-like spatula, and immediately immersed in 70% sucrose syrup while hot. Quite oftenly, rose *(Rosa Indica*

L.) or *kewda* water *(Pandanus tectarius)* and orange food colour is added to the syrup. The crispy pretzels are finally removed from the syrup with spatula and served hot as a confection food in India and Pakistan.

Kulcha

It is a popular North Indian bread eaten with vegetables and meat and is generally used as a staple diet. Dough preparation is usually made by the straight dough method. White wheat flour, sugar, portion of the dough from previously fermented batch and water are mixed (100:1:10:50) at room temperature, kneaded by hand and allowed to ferment overnight in earthen pots. Sometimes gram flour (Cicer aerietinum L.) is also added at 20 per cent level. Mter fermentation, the dough is worked into balls, placed on a smooth surface, lightly sprinkled with flour and flattened by hand to 15-20 cm in diameter. Smoothly flattened dough is transferred onto a metallic baking tray or scooped in a special oven, made of clay. The baking is carried out for 30-40 min to get the final product. In some areas of Pakistan, the dough is raised with low level of inoculum but fermentation is prolonged which gives characteristic flavour and taste to the product, whereas in some parts of India commercial baker's yeast and some chemical leaveners are also added to raise the dough.

Nan

Nan is generally consumed as a staple food by the people of India, Pakistan, Afghanistan and Iran. Its dough is raised by using white wheat flour, salt, inoculum from previous fermented batch and water (100:2:10:50) which are then kneaded with hand at room temperature and allowed to ferment in open for 6-8 hrs. Sometimes the dough is prepared by sponge dough method when yoghurt is added as inoculum alongwith baker's yeast alongwith some chemical leaveners. The flattened dough is then transferred onto a circular pad of cotton cloth and plastered onto the inner wall of a clay oven called *tandoor.* Before baking, some spices like caraway seeds *(Carum carvi),* coriander *(Coriandrum sativum)* and *kalaunji (Bochanania lauzan)* are sprinkled on it. The finished product is obtained by baking at 120-150°C for 10-15 mln.

Future Outlook

It is apparent that indigenous fermentations improve the digestibility and nutritional value of various foods and contribute towards the nutritional well-being of the world population. Due to the uncontrolled increase in Indian population and rising cost of milk and other proteins of animal origin, the consumption of fermented foods is expected to increase in future in view of the protein malnutrition particularly among the people belonging to the low income group. Since fermentations also produce meat-like flavour and texture in vegetable foods, the products prepared by controlled fermentations can provide a cheaper alternative to feed the additional segments of low income group in developing countries like India.

As the traditional methods of preparing indigenous foods are simple and the fermentations are brought about by the microflora coming from staples and the environment. Although this microflora brings about several changes leading to improved digestibility and nutritional value, there is a possibility of development of various undesirable micro-organisms and the production of toxic substances by certain species which is a point of serious concern to the food microbiologists. There is much to be learnt about the role of individual micro-organisms, standardization of their levels by artificially inoculating the ingredients with different microbes alongwith the optimization of various physico-chemical factors like temperature of incubation, pH of dough batter and supplementation of some free sugar in the fermenting ingredients which may lead to further improvements in the nutritional and organoleptic quality of the end products.

29

Macaroni Products

Macaroni products are also known as pasta products (alimentary pastes). They include:

1. Macaroni
2. Spaghetti
3. Noodles
4. Vermicelli

Macaroni products originated in the orient many years ago were taken to Italy in Middle ages. Macaroni products are widely consumed and manufactured in Italy and other European countries, USA, Canada and Australia. The common form of macaroni product consumed in India is vermicelli. Other macaroni products are not very popular in India.

The alimentary pastes are made by mixing wheat semolina (preferably derived from 100 per cent Triticum durum wheat) with . the minimum water to form an unleavened dough. In areas where wheat is not available, the local cereal or other starchy foods are used instead. The traditional types of long pastas e.g. spaghetti are made with durum wheat in Italy but with local cereals such as rice in Asia. Alimentary pastes may also contain eggs, salt and other minor ingredients. They differ from bakery dough in that alimentary pastes are not leavened.

Method of Manufacture

Raw material for macaroni products is durum semolina. The grain of durum wheat is physically very hard, much harder than the hard common wheats. This wheat can be milled to give good yields of semolina, which is purified middling from durum wheat. This wheat is so hard that it is difficult to reduce to a flour fineness. The optimum size for the semolina particles for pasta is about 150 microns.

Water is added to semolina to obtain 28 to 30 per cent moisture (w /w). The semolina and water are introduced into the mixing chamber. Other ingredients viz. eggs, spinach powder, tomato powder, groundnut meal, soy flour, cassava flour, vitamins and minerals etc. can also be added. The blend is then mixed together until it forms a stiff dough, which when squeezed by hand, just holds together as a solid lump. Mixing should not develop the gluten. It is better to mix the dough under vacuum to protect the appearance and mechanical strength of the finished pasta. Air is determined for two reasons:

1. If air is trapped as tiny bubbles during mixing, it gives chalky appearance to the pasta.
2. All flour contain some lip oxygenase activity. The grain also contains free fatty acids. In the presence of oxygen, the enzyme bleaches the yellow carotenoid pigment. This oxidative action is limited when the air is removed. Best pastas are known to have yellow colour appearance.

After mixing, the dough is then either rolled into sheets, cut into flat noodles and then dried or extruded at high pressure through appropriate dies to make products of different shapes. An excessive increase in the temperature of pasta during extrusion irreversibly denatures the protein, and the pasta has very poor cooking characteristics. the barrel and die temperature is, therefore, . maintained at around 45°C and extrusion is best carried out at intermediate speeds (25 rpm). Finally, the product is dried (10-12 per cent moisture) at controlled temperature and humidity and cut into desired lengths.

Noodles

Noodles are thought to have origin in China. They are a type of pasta that is generally made from flour rather than semolina and contain salt in addition to flour and water. In USA, noodles must contain less than 13 per cent moisture and more than 5.5 per cent egg solids. But the oriental noodles do not contain egg.

Method of Preparation

Noodles are made from relatively strong flours, so that they can be handled in wet form. This gives the cooked noodles a chewy texture. Noodle making is relatively simple. The dry flour is placed in the mixer and the water and salt are added. The amount of water is usually less than 35 per cent based on the flour weight. Mixing is done for 5-10 minutes basically to uniformly distribute water. After mixing, the dough is allowed to rest for 10-15 minutes, which helps again to distribute water evenly throughout the flour particles. The crumbly dough is then pressed between two large-diameter rolls to produce a dough sheet about 1 cm thick. The dough sheet is rolled thinner by seven to ten successive passes through reduction rolls. After reaching the desired thickness of 1-2 rnm, it is passed through a pair of cutting rolls. Freshly cut noodles are dried over wooden dowels. The purpose is to obtain white, uniformly shaped noodles. Steamed noodles are produced to give instant products.

Different Types of Noodles

Dry noodles are not precooked but are formed at a moisture content of about 35 per cent and then dried to 8-10 per cent moisture. The drying is traditionally done in the sun but can be done under controlled low humidity. Instant noodles or ramen noodles or quick-cooking noodles, are made by steaming the cut and waved noodles dough for precooking and then frying (5-8 per cent moisture). Frying removes moisture and the noodles are not further oven dried. They are usually packaged with seasonings. Steamed noodles are precooked with low pressure steam, shaped and then dried to about 10 per cent moisture in the sun or oven. Such noodles have a good shelf life.

Alternative Raw Materials for Macaroni Products

Alternative Raw Materials for Macaroni Products Cereals other than wheat semolina, legumes or other food crops can be used for pasta making to have products of better nutritional quality than durum wheat pastas. Durum wheat dough has been substituted successfully with, for example, maize flour at 20 per cent, and 40 per cent w /w levels. Products from semolina-maize flour mixtures can successfully be supplemented with either 8 per cent defatted soy flour or 0.3 per cent l-lysine. Amaranth, spinach, eggs, peanut flour, cassava flour, pea flour (33 per cent), pea protein concentrates (20 per cent), rice, tapioca, fish protein concentrate etc. be added to improve the nutritional quality of pasta.

ALL FOLLOWING PROJECT REPORTS ARE READILY AVAILABLE

AUTOMOBILES, MECHANICAL, STEEL & IRON & METALLURGICAL

- Agricultral Equipments
- Aac & Acsr Aluminium Conductors (All Aluminium Conductors)
- Agricultral Equipments Including Threshers
- Air Brake Helical Coil
- Air Cooler
- Air Filters (For Scooter Car & Excavators Etc.)
- Aluminium & Aluminium Alloys From Aluminium Scrap To Make Utensils (Induction Furnace Melted)
- Aluminium Alloy Wheels
- Aluminium Alloys From Aluminium Scrap To Make Utensils (Induction Furnace)
- Aluminium Hot & Cold Rolling Mill
- Aluminium Conductors
- Aluminium Bottle Manufacturing (Cold Extrusion Of Aluminium)
- Aluminium/Copper Cable Lugs
- Aluminium Cans For Beer Pkgs.
- Aluminium Cans For Capacitors
- Aluminium Caps For Injection Vials
- Aluminium Extrusion
- Aluminium Furniture & Hardware
- Aluminium Sheet Rolling Mill
- Alloy Steel Casting (Foundry)
- Aluminium Utensils
- Aluminium Utensils & School Boxes
- Aluminium Wire Drawing And Super Enamelling For Winding
- Anodised Aluminium Utensils
- Anodizing Of Aluminium
- Antimony Oxide From Lead Scrap
- Anti Scale Compound For Adding In Sugar Boilers
- Arc Welding Filter Glass
- Aluminium Foil Cutting & Roll Making
- Auto Flaps For Trucks & Buses
- Automobile Workshop (Garage & Service Centre)
- Auto Bulb
- Auto Electrical Parts (Armature)
- Auto Gears
- Auto Horns
- Auto Leaf Spring
- Auto Tubes
- Auto Piston Ring
- Auto Piston
- Auto Parts (Electricla And Electronic)
- Auto Rubber Parts And Turned Components Silent Block Bush And Ceiling Fan Shaft+
- Auto Wire Outer (Outer For Auto Wire)
- Bakery And Biscuits Equipments Fabrication
- Ball Point Pen Refills
- Ball Roller & Taper Bearing
- Band Saw Blades
- Barbed Wire
- Barrels (Oil)/(Metalliic Barrels)
- Bath Fittings, Turned Components (All Type) Sheet Metal (Job Work) And Hdpe/Pp Moulded Articles
- Battery For Car (Dry)
- Battery Operated Three Wheelers
- Benefication Of Chromite Ore Processing Charge Chrome
- Bicycle Spokes
- Bicycle Assembly
- Brake Lining Asbestoes/Resin Based & Asbestoes Free
- Brass Artware/Hollow Ware Casting (With Thehelp Of Phenolic Resin)
- Brass Casting
- Brass Pipes From Brass Sheet With Longitudinally Welding
- Brass Ware By Casting Method (Brass Articles Viz. Brass Pooja Lamps And Other Casted)
- Bright Bars
- Buffing And Polishing Industry (Job Work)
- Butt Hinge (Brass Sheet)
- Carbon Brush Holder & Slip Ring
- Co Welding Wire Electrodes (Copper/Copper Alloy Coated M.S.Wire)
- Carbon Film Resistors
- Car Dealership (Hyundai)
- Carburettors
- Cast Steel Body Valve
- Cast Steel Panes For Melting Furnace
- Ceramic Coated Steel Pipes
- Chemical Etching Of Stainless Steel
- Chemical Resistant Iron & Steel
- Concast Steel Bars
- Cold Form Section Mill
- Cold Rolled Forming Of Section And Other Sections
- Cold Rolling Of Ms Strip
- Cold Twisted De-Formed Ribbed Steel
- Cold Rolling Mill
- Compressor (Hermetic) For Air Conditioners
- Compressed Natural Gas (Cng Kit) For Autovehicle
- Continuously Cast Steel Wire Rods (5 Mm)
- Continuous Casting Copper Wire Rods
- Conveyor Beltings
- Conveyor Belt, Transmission Belt & V Belts
- Cooking Ranges
- Copper/Brass Sheets,Circle & Utensils
- Copper Foil
- Copper Ingots, Rods Making & Wire Drawing
- Copper Products From Copper Scrap
- Copper Smelting Plant
- Copper Wire Rods From Copper Scrap
- Corrugated Box Making Machinery And Other Their Parts
- Cylinder Liner For Automobiles
- Disposable Plastic Razors
- Door Locks/Pad Locks
- Drill Bits & Tool Bits
- Drum Closures
- Erw Steel Pipes And Tubes
- Erw Steel Conduit Pipe
- Earth Moving Eqpt.
- Engine Valves For Automobiles
- Fabrication Of Heat Exchanger
- Fabrication Of Storage Tanks And M.S. Drum
- Ferrous Alloy Ni-Hardy I.V Casting
- Ferrous Mn Alloy Casting By Alumina Thermic Process
- Ferro Alloys
- Ferro Silicon & Ferro Manganese From Dolomite (Sms Grade)
- Fire Extinguishers
- Fire Fighting Equipments And Appliances
- Flip-Tone Cans
- Forged Conecting Rod
- Forging Unit
- Fountain Pen Nibs
- Foundry Sand
- Free Wheels, Free Wheel Bushes And Free Wheel Plates For Autorickshaws
- Fuel Briquettes From Agro Waste
- Fuel Injection System
- Fused Magnesia
- Generator Canopy
- Galvanized M.S.Strips
- Galvanizing Plant
- Galvanized Iron Wire (G.I. Wire)
- G.I. Pipes
- Gas Welding Torches And Nozzles
- Gasket Sheet
- Gate Grills & Window Frames
- Generating Set (Diesel)
- Hard Anodised Aluminium
- High Pressure Cylinder

Market Survey Cum Detailed Techno Economic Feasibility Report on all Projects are available Contact.
"ENGINEERS INDIA RESEARCH INSTITUTE". 4449, Nai Sarak (D), Main Road, Delhi-110006 (India)
Ph. : 09811437895, 91-11-23918117, 23916431, 45626431, 64727385 Fax : 91-11-23916431
E-mail : eiriprojects@gmail.com, eiribooks@yahoo.com • website: www.eiri.in, www.eiriindia.org

ALL FOLLOWING PROJECT REPORTS ARE READILY AVAILABLE

- Offset Printing Press
- Old Age Home
- P.C.C Electric Poles
- Photographic Developer & Fixer
- Pvc Extrusion Profile (Door & Windows)
- Pop-Corn
- Photo Etching Of S.S.
- Pre Stressed Cement Concrete Pipes
- Pilfer Proof Caps
- Pilfer Proof Caps And Crown Cap
- Pouch Making & Gravure Printing (Roto Printing)
- Poultry & Fish Farming (Integerated Unit)
- Printing Of Tin Sheets
- Radio Station
- Radio Taxi
- Readymade Garments
- Refractories With Ceramics
- Restaurant
- Rose Plantation And Rose Oil Extraction
- Rotogravure Printing
- Safety Belts
- Safety Matches
- School
- School With Hostel
- Shoe Laces
- Silk Cocoon Cultivation (Growing Of Silk Cocoon Warm)
- Silk Screen Printing Formulations For Plastic, Paper & Cloth
- Spikenard (Jatamansi)
- Stencil Coating Solution
- Sugar Candy (Misri)
- Sugar Cane Plantation
- Sugar Cane Juice Preservation
- Super Speciality Diagnosis Centre
- Surat Zari
- Synthetic Shoes & Soles
- T.V. News Channel
- Tea Packaging Industry
- Toughened Glass
- Tennis Balls
- Three Star Hotel
- Travelling Agency
- Trays, Trolleys For Hospital With Scratchless Coating
- Wax Extracts (Tanning Powder)
- Wire Rope Slings
- Wood Wool Slab
- Wooden Cane Furniture With Export Potential
- Wooden Door And Windows
- Wooden Furniture
- Wooden Panel Including Kiln Seasoning
- Wooden Furniture
- Watch Case Buffing
- Watch Dial
- Wrist Watches
- Watches (Electronic)
- Zedoary (Kachur)

Contact **EIRI** for required Project report apart from this list.

EDIBLE OILS, ESSENTIAL OILS LURICATING OILS, GREASES, VEGETABLE OILS, WAXES, CAMPHOR, PERFUMES & PERFUMERY COMPOUNDS AND REFINED OILS ETC.

EDIBLE OILS, ESSENTIAL OILS, LURICATIING OILS, GREASES, VEGETABLE OILS, WAXES, CAMPHOR, PERFUMES & PERFUMERY COMPOUNDS AND REFINED OILS ETC.

- Aromatic Perfumery Compound
- Aerosol
- Agarbatti Perfumery Compound
- Bees Wax Manufacture
- Camphor
- Cardanol From Cashew Nut Shell Liquid
- Castor Oil
- Castor Oil Derivative Oleoresins
- Chilli Oil
- Citronella Oils
- Clove Oil
- Concentrate Of Rose Jasmine & Lily Etc.
- Coloured Flame Candle
- Candles (Semi-Automatic)
- Corn Oil (Maize Oil)
- Dehydrated Castor Oil
- Eugenol From Cinnamon Leaf Oil
- Extraction Of Essential Oil (Cardamon, Jeera, Ajowan, Ginger Oils Etc. & Packaging Of Ground Spices)
- Extraction Of Jasmine Essence
- Extraction Of Essential Oils By Super Critical Fluid Method From Flowers, Herbs & Spices
- Eucalyptus Oil
- Extraction Of Oil From Oil Seed Expander Extrusion Technology)
- Fat Liquor Sulphated Oil
- Flavours For Food
- Fish Oil
- Garlic Oil & Powder
- Ginger Oil, Sandalwood Oil And Nagarmotha Oil
- Ginger Oil
- Ginger Oil & Ginger Dust
- Ground Nut Oil
- Integerated Wax Complex
- Ionone From Lemon Grass Oil
- Jasmine & Lilly Flower Oil
- Lemon Grass Oil
- Liquid Paraffin
- Lube Oil & Grease
- Lubricating Oil
- Menthol Crystals
- Menthol Oil & Crystal
- Micro Crystalline Wax
- Mustard Oil (Edible Oil)
- Oleoresin From Spices
- Oil From Artemisia Herbs
- Palm Oil Crushing Unit
- Pan Masala
- Paraffin Wax
- Paraffin Wax From Slack Wax
- Perfume For Food Industries With Pan Masala Perfume
- Pouch For Oil And Ghee Packaging
- Refined Oil-Sun Flower Oil, Groundnut Oil, Staff Flower Oil & Cotton Seed Oil
- Refined Vegetable Oil
- Reclamation Of Used Engine Oil
- Rice Bran Oil (R.B.O)
- Rose Oil Extraction
- Smoke Less Candle
- Spice Oil & Oleoresins
- Solvent Extraction Plant (Oil Cake Based)
- Synthetic Almond Oil
- Synthetic Wax
- Synthetic Tallow
- Synthetic Ghee
- Synthetic Musk
- Turmeric Oil Oleoresin
- Vanilla Cultivation And Extraction/Processing
- Vegetable Oil Extraction & Refining
- Wadding Oil (100%) For Wadding Of Cotton Hosiery Cloth In Dyeing Process
- Wax Emulsion For Textile
- Wax Floor Polish

ELECTROPLATING, ANODIZING & ALLIED PROJECTS

- Nickel Plating Brightener
- Pcb With Garphite & Silver Coating
- Rainbow Colours On Metal
- Silver Refining By Electrolysis & By Acid
- Silver Extraction
- Silver Extraction From Waste Hypo Solution
- Silver & Gold Plating On Pvc & Nylon-6
- Tin Printing
- Titanium Jewellery Plating
- Vacuum Metallizing
- Zinc Electroplating Brightner
- Zinc Electroplating On Nut, Bolts,

ALL FOLLOWING PROJECT REPORTS ARE READILY AVAILABLE

PAINT, ENAMEL, SOLVENTS, THINNERS, INKS & VARNISH

PAINT, ENAMEL, SOLVENTS, THINNERS, INKS & VARNISH

- Acrylic Emulsion Paints
- Acrylic Cement Paint (Dry Powder)
- Aluminium Paint
- Automobile Paints
- Ball Point Pen Refill Ink
- Bituminious Road Emulsion
- Bitumen
- Bituminious Felts For Water & Damp Proofing
- Bituminious Road Emulsion Rapid Medium & Slow Setting
- Buffing & Polishing
- Cement Paint For White & Grey Cement
- Dispersant
- Dry Distemper
- Dry Distemper & Cement Paint
- Duplicating Ink Black For Gestner Duplicator
- Emulsion Paints (Water Based)
- Hammertone Paint
- Insulating Varnish & Wire Enamel
- Iron Oxide Pigments
- Insulating Varnish (Poly Vinyl Butyral Based, Ffc Grade)
- Lime Colour (Cement Colour)
- Synthetic Red Oxide For Floorings
- Solvent & Thinners
- Marking Inks (Water Proof)
- Metal Naphthanate (As Drier For Paints)
- N.C.Putty
- Offset Printing Ink
- Oil Bound Distemper Paint
- Paint Brushes
- Paint Manufacture For Rolling Coating Of Aluminium And Steel Coil
- Paint Removers
- Paint Industry
- Paint & Varnish
- Picture Varnish
- Powder Coating Paint
- Printing Inks (Offset,Flexo & Roto Gravure)
- Primer Paint & Enamel Paint
- Putty & Water Proofing Paint
- Printing Inks (Flexo-Graphic Ink)
- Putty (Metal Casement)
- Red Oxide Primer (Anti Corrosive)
- Refrectory Paint (Graphite Based)
- Screen Printing Inks
- Silk Screen Printing Ink Formulation For Plastic, Paper, Cloth
- Stamp & Pad Ink
- Stoving Paint
- Spirit Soluble Maleic Resin
- Texture Paint
- Thinners And Its Allied Products
- Toner Ink
- Varnish Thinner (Solvent)
- Vacuum Metallizing Lacquers
- Wood Primer

PHARMACEUTICAL, DRUGS, AYURVEDIC/HERBAL COSMETICS & MEDICINES, HOMOEOPATHIC MEDICINES, HOMOEOPATHIC MEDICINES, DISPOSABLE SYRINGE, DENTAL COLLEGE & FINE CHEMICALS ETC.

MEDICINES, HOMOEOPATHIC MEDICINES, DISPOSABLE SYRINGE, DENTAL COLLEGE & FINE CHEMICALS ETC.

- Aromatic Pills
- Alumina From Bauxite
- Aspirin
- Ayurvedic Pain Balm Ointments
- Ayurvedic Churan And Tablets
- Ayurvedic Tablets (Hajmola Type)
- Ayurvedic/Herbalpharmacy
- Ayurvedic Sherbats
- Ayurvedic Products
- Bulk Drugs (E.O.U)
- Blood Bags
- Calcium Gluconate
- Capsule, Tablet & Injection With Modern Instruments
- Cashew Feni
- Chloroquinone Phosphate (Bulk Drugs)
- Clinical Thermometer
- Dental Clinic
- Dental College
- Dental Grade Eugenol
- Dextrose Monohydrate, Liquid Glucose
- Dehydrated Onion & Onion Powder
- Dextrose Powder (Anhydrous From Starch)
- Dextrose Saline Solution
- Distillery (I.M.F.L)
- Disposable Needles For Syringes
- Disprin
- Distilled Water
- Empty Hard Gelatine Capsules
- Fairness Cream
- Filling & Packing Of Capsules
- Glucose - D - Powder
- Glycerine
- Hair Colour Mate (Formulations And Process Only)
- Herbal Cosmetics
- Herbal Shampoo
- Herbal Shampoo And Cream
- Herbal Hair Oils (Ayurvedic)
- Homoe & Bio-Medicines With Mother Tincture
- Homoepathic Medicines
- Hypodermic Needles
- I.V. Fluids
- Ibuprofen
- Infusion & Transfusion Sets (I.V. Set)
- Injectable For Pharmaceuticals
- Injection Ampoules Packaging Box
- Integerated Surgical Cotton
- Ice Making Plant
- Ice & Cold Storage
- Lactose & By Products Processing From Milk
- Lichen (Jatamansi Charila)
- Liquid Glucose And Its By-Products
- L-Lysine Monohydro Chloride
- Liquid Glucose From Potatoes
- Medical College
- Methanol (Hpcl Grade)
- Nicotine From Tobacco Waste
- Ointment-Ayurvedic (Yellow & White)
- Pharmaceutical And Food Grade Gelatine
- Pharmaceutical Industry (Tablets, Capsules, Liquid, Gel, Ointment Powder Injectable)
- Pharmaceutical Unit (Eou) With Formulations, Injectables, Etc.
- Pyridine & Derivatives
- Salt (Iodized Salt)
- Saline & Injection Water
- Saline Water & Dextrose Solution (I.V.Fluid In Plastic Bottles)
- Sorbitol
- Starch (Maize)
- Surgical Adhesive Plaster
- Surgical Bandages
- Surgical Gloves
- Surgical Cotton
- Surgical Cotton And Bandage
- Synthetic Camphor Powder
- Tablets & Capsules
- Tissue Culture
- Tincture From Rectified Spirit
- Trimethopime
- Veterinary College With Hospital
- Veterenary Medicines (Only Formulations)
- Vitamin 'C', Sorbitol' Anhydrous Dextrose, Starch

Market Survey Cum Detailed Techno Economic Feasibility Report on all Projects are available Contact.
"ENGINEERS INDIA RESEARCH INSTITUTE", 4449, Nai Sarak (D), Main Road, Delhi-110006 (India)
Ph. : 09811437895, 91-11-23918117, 23916431, 45626431, 64727385 Fax : 91-11-23916431
E-mail : eiriprojects@gmail.com, eiribooks@yahoo.com • website: www.eiri.in, www.eiriindia.org